Man and the Landscape in Ireland

(*Frontispiece*) Provinces and Counties of the Irish Republic and Northern Ireland.

Man and the Landscape in Ireland

F. H. A. Aalen

Department of Geography,
Trinity College, Dublin, Ireland

1978

Academic Press
London   New York   San Francisco
A Subsidiary of Harcourt Brace Jovanovich, Publishers

ACADEMIC PRESS INC. (LONDON) LTD
24/28 OVAL ROAD
LONDON NW1

U.S. Edition Published by
ACADEMIC PRESS INC.
111 FIFTH AVENUE
NEW YORK, NEW YORK 10003

Library of Congress Catalog Card Number: 77–76681
ISBN: 0–12–041350–7

Printed in Great Britain by
Willmer Brothers Ltd, Birkenhead

Preface

Numerous individuals have assisted me in the writing of this book. I am indebted in particular to my colleague J. H. Andrews for much valuable discussion and criticism. J. P. Haughton, K. Danaher, P. Harbison, G. L. Davies, G. F. Mitchell, D. A. Gillmor and A. Clarke kindly read portions of the book and suggested improvements. Despite this assistance I have no doubt that errors persist and I must accept responsibility for them. The photographs are from a variety of sources but the majority was supplied by Bord Failte and I am grateful for their assistance.

The bibliography is relatively full. This should enhance the value of the book to readers and scholars outside Ireland: writings on Irish geography, history and archaeology, although plentiful, tend to be little known outside the country. Throughout the text references are made to various authorities, sufficient, I hope, to direct the reader to most of the key pieces of relevant work. Reference to an author does not necessarily mean that his work is the source of my assertions but rather that it can be usefully consulted for further information on a topic. I have also tended to provide references where very specific points are made which could not be elaborated on within the framework of this book but might reasonably prompt the reader to demand supporting evidence.

F. H. A. Aalen   April 1978

Contents

Preface v

List of Illustrations ix

Introduction 1

1
The Natural Habitat 9
  Physiography, glaciation, climate and soils 9
  The evolution of the vegetation pattern 28

2
The Mesolithic and Neolithic Periods 40
  Mesolithic Ireland: the first settlers 40
  The Neolithic period and the spread of farming . . . 47

3
The Bronze Age 60

4
The Iron Age and Early Christian Period . . . 75
  Settlements 81
  The cultural landscape 92

5
The Middle Ages 109

6
The English Wars and Plantations 135

7

**The Making of the Modern Landscape:
The Post Plantation Period** 152
Introduction 152
Economic and demographic trends since the late
17th Century 154
The rural landscape 160
Industrial activities and the landscape 192

8

The Contemporary Rural Landscape 207
Population distribution and density, and land use . . . 207
Historical origins 211
Current and future change 233

9

Rural Buildings 244
Nature of vernacular architecture 244
Vernacular buildings in the British Isles 247
Irish vernacular 249
Irish non-vernacular buildings 258
Farm outbuildings 267

10

The Towns 269
Distribution, size and functions 269
Historical growth of towns 271
The four major cities 289

Consolidated Bibliography 313
Subject Index 335

List of Illustrations

Figures

(*Frontispiece*) Provinces and counties of Irish Republic and Northern Ireland. ii

1: Geology. 11

2: Major relief and drainage. Structural regions. . . 12

3: **a** Glacial features and **b** major soil types. . . . 21

4: Climatic features. 25

5: Chronological framework of climatic, vegetational and cultural changes since the last major glacial period. . . 38

6: Distribution of major mesolithic sites. . . . 43

7: Distribution of megalithic tombs. 52

8: Bronze Age burials in relation to relief and esker and kame deposits. 64

9: Distribution of raths, hill-forts and Iron Age royal sites. 83

10: Ancient (Iron Age, Early Christian) settlement patterns. **a** Two mile Stone, Co. Donegal and **b** Beginish, Co. Kerry. 98

11: Distribution of medieval motes, rectangular earthworks and major castles: Irish enclaves in 14th Century: English pale at end of 15th Century. 110

12: Distribution of tower houses and deserted medieval settlements 119

13: The effects of 17th Century confiscations on catholic ownership of land and present-day distribution of protestants 149

14: Roads, settlement and farm boundaries at Ballylynan, Co. Laois, in 1704 and 1855 161

15: Open-field strip holdings: eastern Ireland. . . 172

16: Fossil strip fields and enclosure patterns on commons: eastern Ireland. 178

17: Changes in the rural settlement pattern during the 19th Century, Co. Mayo. 185

18: Consolidation of rundale holdings in the 19th Century, Co. Donegal. 186

19: **a** Rural population distribution and **b** average farm size.   209
20: Settlement and field patterns.   216
21: Farm clusters.   221
22: Regional farmhouse styles.   251
23: Possible evolution of western house.   255
24: Characteristic plan forms of Irish towns.   .   .   .   272
25: Origins of towns (of over 1,500 inhabitants in 1971).   .   274
26: Maynooth, Co. Kildare, 1757 and 1821.   .   .   .   282
27: Site and growth of **a** Dublin and **b** Belfast.   .   .   290

Plates

1: **a** Brandon mountain, Co. Kerry (Bord Failte); **b** coastal
lowland near Letterfrack, Co. Galway (J. K. St. Joseph). .   15
2: **a** Benbane Head, Co. Antrim (J. K. St. Joseph); **b** the
Burren, Co. Clare (Bord Failte).   18
3: **a** Dissected limestone plateau, King's mountain, Co. Sligo
(Board Failte). **b** Glen of Aherlow, Co. Tipperary (Bord
Failte).   19
4: **a** Central Lowlands, Co. Offaly, with esker ridge (J. K. St.
Joseph); **b** drumlin landscape, Co. Monaghan (Bord Failte).   22
5: Megaliths. **a** Wedge tomb, **b** court tomb, **c** stone circle
(Bord Failte).   54
6: Early Irish monasteries. **a** Inchcleraun, Co. Longford (J. K.
St. Joseph); **b** round tower, Kilmacduagh, Co. Galway (Bord
Failte).   78
7: **a** Raths, near Oldcastle, Co. Meath (J. K. St. Joseph); **b**
earthworks, near Fethard, Co. Tipperary (J. K. St. Joseph).   82
8: Medieval castle and monastery. **a** Trim castle, Co. Meath
(Bord Failte); **b** Jerpoint Abbey, Co. Kilkenny (Bord Failte).   118
9: **a** Late medieval tower house, Co. Cork; **b** corbelled dry
stone hut (clochan), Co. Kerry; **c** Burncourt, Co. Tipperary.   125
10: Demesnes. **a** Painting of Westport House, Co. Mayo (1760)
(Bord Failte); **b** gardens and ornamental woodland,
Powerscourt House, Enniskerry, Co. Wicklow (Bord Failte).   168
11: Rundale relics, Clare Island, Co. Mayo (J. K. St. Joseph).   170
12: **a** Small fields divided mainly by banks of sod and stone, Co.
Kerry (Bord Failte); **b** small fields divided by dry stone walls,
Co. Galway (Bord Failte).   174

13: **a** Large fields divided by banks, hedges and frequent trees, Co. Kildare; **b** medium-sized fields divided by banks overgrown by gorse, Co. Wexford (Bord Failte).   175

14: **a** A modern industrial estate, Galway city (I. D. A.); **b** Clonsast bog, Co. Offaly (Bord na Mona).   .   .   .   201

15: **a** Eastern-farmhouse, Co. Meath (Bord Failte); **b** western-farmhouse, Co. Kerry (Bord Failte).   252

16: **a** Large thatched farmhouse, Co. Limerick (K. Danaher); **b** two-storey house with slated roof, West Cork.   .   .   260

17: **a** Estate cottage, Co. Donegal; **b** 'georgian' farmhouse, Co. Wicklow; **c** Co. Council cottage, Co. Wicklow.   .   .   262

18: **a** West Cork. Two-storey stone farmhouses (Bord Failte); **b** the Rosses, Co. Donegal. A cluster of single-storey three-roomed houses (Radio Eireann).   263

19: **a** Enniscorthy, Co. Wexford (Bord Failte); **b** Strokestown, Co. Roscommon (Bord Failte).   276

20: **a** View of central Dublin and Liffey quays (Rex Roberts Studios); **b** Dublin, south of the Liffey. Georgian squares and terraces (Rex Roberts Studios).   293

21: **a** Cork city and the river Lee (Bord Failte); **b** Londonderry city (J. K. St. Joseph).   303

22: Belfast. Aerial view of South-west city (B. K. S.).   .   308

Introduction

Natural landscapes are the product of geological, climatic and biological processes operating independently of human influences. In long and widely settled areas, such as Ireland, the natural features have often been strongly modified by human agency and masked by man-made features to form a distinctive "cultural landscape". The main purpose of this book is to describe the cultural landscape of Ireland and its evolution since the first arrival of men in the country some eight thousand years ago. Cultural or humanized landscapes include all parts of the earth's surface where the natural physical and biotic world has been modified if not wholly transformed by human activity; they include too all the artificial constructions or features that man builds or lays out on the earth's surface in the course of his economic life or to accommodate his social activities. In closely settled areas these artificial features can exist in profusion, can coalesce and form a continuous layer overlying the natural landscape.

The most widespread elements of the Irish cultural landscape, such as the mosaic of enclosed fields and the profusion of scattered farmsteads, were made to meet the needs of farming people whose major interest has always been to produce food and organic raw materials. Although the landscape is predominantly rural it is, nevertheless, man-made. The farmlands, for example, have been won by clearance of the natural forest vegetation. The very raw materials of farming, the cereals and animals, were most of them introduced by man and at a very early period in the history of human occupancy. Natural materials have been used for economic and social ends; rocks, soil and plants are all used to form distinctive human structures. The farmland is sub-divided into fields defined by earth and stone boundaries; copses and woodland have been planted to beautify the landscape, or to supply timber, to provide windbreaks and a habitat for game; stone, straw and mud have traditionally been used for rural buildings. However, it is not always possible to distinguish clearly between natural and cultural features because the force and range of the impact of human activity on the biophysical environment is not fully understood. Thus, some landscape features often deemed

1

natural, such as the peat bogs, may be the outcome, in part at least, of human interference with the natural habitat, perhaps interference in remote historical periods whose effects are now hard to discern and verify.

The natural environment has inevitably influenced the broad course of agricultural history and the cultural landscapes which are residual from it. But the cultural landscape is in no sense an inevitable "response" to physical environment. In the analysis of rural landscapes there is always a risk of lapsing into simplistic determinism, especially when peasant communities are involved which are widely but erroneously interpreted as "controlled" by their environmental setting. The many and often fundamental ways in which the cultural landscape has changed through prehistoric and historic time, while the natural environment, the geological and climatic surroundings, has been more or less constant, is sufficient counter to crude notions of environmental determinism. As Wagner (1961) has cogently argued, human societies use the available resources of a country selectively in accordance with their cultural preferences and their technological capacity up to the limits imposed by environmental conditions. The selection and use of particular resources implies geographical patterning of population and settlement. Within the areas which man selects for exploitation and settlement he "makes himself at home" by arranging and changing the surroundings as far as he is capable to suit his needs. The cultural landscape or man-modified landscape is thus the product of selection and transformation. Given the cultural preferences of a society it is of course possible to discern environmental influences, especially in the case of peasant cultivators whose livelihood depends on an intimate relationship with the land and its varied resources. But the culture of the community, its agricultural skills and social organization are not a direct product of the environment, rather they determine the environment selected and the way it is used. The physical components of the cultural landscape such as settlement forms, field patterns and house styles, are in large measure ordained by the preconceptions and traditions of the community; adjustments of form are doubtless made according to local environmental conditions but cultural concepts must exist before they can be adjusted.

While the physical basis of the landscape may be relatively stable, the cultural landscape is a dynamic entity whose appearance is continually changing as cultural and technological developments alter the pattern of relationships between man and his environment. The cultural landscape is not simply the product of contemporary human activities. Many phases of human activity have modified the surface of the country in ways still partially visible. A cultural landscape thus shows the accumulated works of man over long periods of time and in long compounded patterns; it cannot be fully understood without deep historical and prehistorical perspectives. Certain features have been inherited relatively unchanged from remote periods of the past and, more important, the contemporary arrangement of the major elements of the landscape, the settlement patterns, field systems and communication network, is the end product of a long process of development in which each successive phase has conditioned the next. Even when radical transformation of the landscape has been undertaken, the precedents are important because the new pattern may be partly a reaction to the old.

Much attention must therefore be focussed on the past. But the subject matter under consideration, namely the natural environment and man's material culture, are unfamiliar in conventional history and so too is the perspective on history which must often be adopted, the concern with what the French historian, F. Braudel, describes as "geographical time" and "social time". Braudel in his writings dissects history into various planes and talks of three kinds of historical time: "geographical time" which is the almost timeless history of man in relation to his environment; "social time", history with slow but perceptible rhythms, the history of social groups and groupings; and, finally, "individual time", which is the traditional type of history on the scale not of man but of individual men, the history of events which are simply the surface manifestations of larger movements. The geographer when describing the evolution of the cultural landscape is involved to some extent with all three historical planes but chiefly with geographical and social time. It is at the level of geographical time that man's basic adaptation to local environment and his utilization of the resources available there can be described; indeed, owing to the nature of available evidence in the prehistoric periods, this is almost inevitably the level of observation. Attempts to reconstruct the cultural landscape of prehistoric periods and the economic and social activities which shaped it are based on inferences from limited archaeological and palaeobotanical data. Written evidence is unavailable and it is rarely that material remains can be attributed with certainty to identifiable individuals or groups. The archaeological and palaeobotanical evidence must be interpreted in terms of our knowledge of ecological, cultural and social systems, knowledge which includes both observed and documented patterns among contemporary and past peoples. Inevitably, there is a considerable element of speculation in this interpretation and it is essential that speculation be identified as such and distinguished from the limited amount of hard data. In Ireland the historical geographer is confronted with an exceptional abundance of archaeological sites, especially from prehistory. Such an abundance of material can, however, be an embarrassment in the absence of extensive archaeological survey to determine clearly the function and chronology of the sites. Given reasonable assumptions about the purpose and age of sites it is possible to make interesting deductions about the general distribution of human activities and this assists understanding of the evolution and appearance of past landscapes, but the underlying assumptions and uncertainties must not be forgotten.

In the historical periods, documentary and literary sources are available but the bulk of them are of limited use to the historical geographer. These sources are concerned mainly with political, military and religious affairs and contain little of direct relevance to an understanding of the landscape or the routine economic and social activities which moulded it. Furthermore, archaeological evidence for the historical periods is relatively slight. Hence, our knowledge of the appearance of the landscape in the Middle Ages is regrettably limited and not significantly better than that for prehistoric periods. The situation does not improve appreciably until the 17th Century when, with the plantations, substantial written information first becomes available, in the form of geographical descriptions and surveys, about the character of the landscape in defined geographical areas. It was also at this time that cadastral mapping began, to facilitate the massive land transfers from Irish owners to English and Scots settlers. The primary concern of the early cadastral maps, however, is to show property boundaries, and as sources of landscape information they are disappointing. It was not until the 18th and 19th Centuries, when maps were specifically prepared for the purposes of estate management and agricultural improvement schemes, that any systematic attempt was made to depict settlement and field patterns in any detail or with reasonable accuracy.

It has been possible to establish within Irish prehistory a broad succession of cultural "stages", the succession which is typical of most European countries. The earliest stage is a Mesolithic or Middle Stone Age culture characterized by a simple hunting and collecting economy. Subsequently in the New Stone Age or Neolithic period, a food-producing economy was introduced and man first became a settled farmer. Agriculture with an emphasis on livestock farming remained the basis of society, but in the succeeding Bronze and Iron Ages numerous technical advances, particularly a knowledge of metals, gave man enhanced ability to control and modify the environment. There is no reason to suppose abrupt transitions between the major cultural stages. Usually the prehistoric evidence points to gradual transformation, and sometimes striking continuity of particular cultural elements can be discerned. Moreover, the pace and intensity of cultural change must always have varied locally and regionally.

Little progress has been made in identifying the causes underlying change in prehistoric society, but the problem here is a general one found in all attempts to explicate cultural change and not linked particularly to any peculiarities of the Irish situation or limitations in the Irish data. It is frequently difficult in the case of prehistoric societies to determine whether changes have resulted from a group of invaders or simply from the transmission of ideas. Traditionally there has been a tendency in British prehistory to attribute all changes, even in details of ornamentation, to different groups of invaders. A more balanced attitude is now evident in which continuity of population is more readily admitted, with ideas and techniques originating from outside. Throughout Irish prehistory there appears to have been considerable indigenous cultural development but also a succession of immigrant groups at increasingly advanced cultural levels. The first Mesolithic settlers were of course immigrants, probably from Britain. Neolithic economy and culture seems to have been introduced by immigrant groups from a variety of outside sources but there was no sharp termination of the older Mesolithic ways. In the Bronze and Iron Ages there is certainly evidence of considerable cultural continuity as well as important innovation and change. It is hard in these periods to determine how far innovation and change are the result of immigrant groups, of acculturation by influences from abroad or the outcome of strictly indigenous processes.

Cultural advance, however caused, seems to have been accompanied by changing assessments of environmental resources and growing capability to modify and remodel the natural environment. Each culture "responds" differently to the environment and utilizes different physical resources, or at least different combinations of these resources. For example, Mesolithic groups inhabited mainly the raised beaches and lake shores, while Neolithic communities spread widely inland, although with a preference for upland margins. Later in the Bronze Age and in the Iron Age there was a recognizable tendency for farmers to spread onto the extensive areas of lowland which occupy the central portions of the country, and the higher hill flanks were abandoned or declined in relative importance as areas of settlement. This basic ecological adjustment has persisted down to modern times.

Although less influence may now be accorded to invading groups during prehistoric times, there is no question but that they were of major importance in the historical period which has been characterized by a succession of immigrant waves. The invaders, however, were never able to swamp indigenous culture; their influence was confined to particular regions of the country and served essentially to colour and diversify the basic Irish culture rather than replace it. Viking settlers first introduced urban life and commercial traditions, but only to the coasts; the Anglo-Normans established their villages and towns mainly in the south and east of the country and even here their cultural identity was eventually eroded. The large-scale plantation of English and Scots settlers in the 16th and 17th Centuries produced a distinctive community only in the north; elsewhere the planters usually formed a small and thinly spread class of landowners, powerful but eventually destined to derogation and partial absorption into the larger Irish community.

Internal forces, as well as the impact of intrusive cultures, have moulded the landscape in important ways during historic times. The development of Irish agriculture and, to a lesser extent, industry and commerce produced many changes. For example, widespread agrarian improvements and town building enterprises, often sponsored by local landlords, influenced almost all parts of Ireland in the 18th and 19th Centuries and had a decisive role in the formation of the contemporary landscape. The importance of demographic forces can also be clearly seen. Sharp population growth in the 18th and early 19th Century, for example, led to expansion and intensified use of the improved land, while population decline during the last century and a half, resulting from heavy emigration and high rates of celibacy, has greatly reduced population pressure in the rural areas and led to the widespread abandonment of fields and farms. Economic and social forces continue to modify the landscape in the towns and in the countryside. An attempt is made in this book to describe the most important contemporary changes and, tentatively, to discern future trends.

Although cultural preferences and technological skills enable man to select particular portions of the natural habitat for his use and to transform them, it is clear in the Irish context that certain features of the geographical environment have had a profound and persistent influence on human activities. The insular character of the country and its peripheral position on the Atlantic edge of Europe, for example, are of fundamental importance. Ireland has often lain outside the mainstreams of European history or experienced major continental developments in a weakened or diluted form: it escaped, for example, the embrace of the Roman Empire; the feudal system was confined to the south and east of the country and the cultural forces of the Reformation and the Enlightenment made little headway. Close relationships between Ireland and her larger island neighbour have been inescapable; they were not confined to colonial exploitation but involved intense and fruitful interconnections of people and ideas. Whilst the colonization of Ireland by the English and Scots is a well-known feature of her history, there have been important population flows in the other direction. Irishmen, for example, settled widely in Wales and Scotland in the Dark Ages and in modern times millions of Irishmen have settled in the industrial cities of England and Scotland. Many major cultural innovations in Ireland have originated in Britain or, if they have spread from Europe, have been "filtered" through Britain; the feudal system, for example, most of the medieval monasteries, urban life, patterns of government at local and national level, the universities and the ideas of agricultural improvement in the 18th and 19th Centuries.

The peripheral position of Ireland in Europe is associated with the notable preservation of older customs, skills and ways of life, especially in the remote rural areas. Much of this ancient legacy has dramatically disappeared during the last 50 years or so with growing affluence, improved communications and the spread of factory work and mechanization, but it is clear that study of the vestiges of the material and spiritual traditions of rural Ireland can throw light on the distant past and the evolution of peasant communities in Britain and western Europe generally. This theme has been most notably developed in the writings of Evans (1957) where there is constant and valuable emphasis on the "timelessness" of traditional rural life, an approach which has much validity in the study of many rural activities and customs. However, the "time immemorial" thesis must be applied with caution to the cultural landscape. There is evidence that the cultural landscape of Ireland has experienced a series of important changes, sometimes concentrated in relatively brief periods of history. Continuity in peasant traditions has thus occurred despite changes in the cultural landscape and physical framework of rural life.

As well as the marginal position and insular character of Ireland, several other features of its geographical environment have exerted a pronounced influence on the basic pattern of human activities and the evolution of the cultural landscape. The first is the oceanic climate, especially the mild winter temperatures and high to medium precipitation, with which are associated the plentiful growth of vegetation, especially grassland, the wide development of peat bogs, and soils generally impoverished by leaching. Many long-standing features of Irish society are, in large measure, adaptations to this oceanic fringe environment. The mild, moist climate, combined with the predominantly low-lying relief of the country, provided an environment which, before the advent of man, supported a dense cover of deciduous woodland. However, once the woodlands were cleared for human usage, the land was best suited to the development of pastoralism rather than to crop growth for which the high rainfall is a hindrance. Deep-rooted pastoral traditions, along with other factors, have encouraged the dispersed pattern of settlement evident in many periods, for example the raths of the Iron Age and Early Christian period, the medieval tower houses and, to some extent, the dispersed farmsteads of the present-day landscape. The pastoral emphasis of early Irish society probably inhibited the acceptance and assimilation of urban life, although the cultural isolation of the country may also have been influential here.

Major regional contrasts exist within the country. There is, first of all, the contrast between the poorer western portion of the country beyond the Shannon, with its wide extents of barren upland and blanket bog, higher rainfall and strongly leached soils, and the more accessible and physically well-endowed eastern portions of the country, with a drier climate and extensive drift-covered lowlands. Especially in the historic period, immigrant peoples, Anglo-Normans and English planters, have been drawn to the richer lands of the east and cultural factors have thus reinforced natural contrasts. Equally striking is the persistent tendency of the north to stand apart culturally from the rest of the country. Northern separateness, noticeable even in prehistoric times, has resulted largely from the region's proximity to, and close cultural associations with, Scotland and the relative isolation from the remainder of Ireland produced by the ill-drained drumlin belt, mountains and lakes.

1
The Natural Habitat

In a long-occupied and widely settled country, such as Ireland, the landscape is a synthesis of natural and cultural elements. The natural elements, especially the underlying rocks and the relief features developed on them, are the product of processes operating independently of man over vast periods of time. Cultural elements, although relatively recent in origin, are now predominant, as the natural habitat has been intensively used and transformed by man's economic and social activities, making it difficult to envisage the appearance of the landscape before the coming of man. In this book the central concern is the way in which the cultural landscape has evolved, but the analysis must commence with an account of the geological, climatic, soil and biotic resources which have provided the background for and materially influenced man's economic and social activities. The basic features of the natural habitat are described chiefly from the standpoint of human usage; the emphasis is on description and no detailed attempt is made to explain the evolution of the geological structure and relief features, for example, or to investigate the underlying causes of climatic phenomena. A more detailed account of the development of the vegetation cover since the retreat of the last ice sheet is necessary, emphasizing the long sequence of changes and the progressive reduction of the natural forest cover which have resulted not only from secular climatic variations but from human activities. Natural and human causes are indeed often difficult to disentangle.

Physiography, Glaciation, Climate and Soils

Physiography

Ireland is a country of ancient rocks. With the major exception of Cainozoic basalts in the north-east, the rocks date from the Palaeozoic era and they are comparable in age and related structurally to the rocks of highland Britain. Ireland was influenced by the large-scale folding and

9

faulting of the Caledonian (Devonian-Silurian period) and Armorican (Permian-Carboniferous period) mountain building phases which formed the structural framework of north-western Europe. The Caledonian and Armorican mountain belts converge in the country, but owing to prolonged denudation the major part of Ireland is now lowland with approximately three quarters of the country below 500 ft (152·5m) and almost 95% lying below 1000 ft (305m). Existing relief variations are related more to the differing resistance of rock types to weathering and erosion than to tectonic forces. However, in the north and west of Ireland and in the Leinster Mountains and the Newry Axis the relief features often have a discernible north-east to south-west grain which is a legacy of Caledonian folding, while Armorican folding is responsible for the conspicuous east–west orientation of the parallel ridges and valleys of southern Ireland.

The extensive Central Lowland, underlain mainly by Carboniferous rocks, is the dominant physical feature of the island (Figs 1, 2). It lies for the most part between 200 and 400 ft (61 and 122m), stretches for approximately 120 miles (193km) from east to west and covers an area of some 8000 sq. miles (20 720km²). Around the margins of the country pre-Carboniferous rocks are exposed in a number of detached upland areas to which differential erosion and faulting have often given strong definition. Only in the east between Dundalk and Dublin is the upland perimeter completely absent; here the lowlands reach to the coast. Elsewhere, easy communication from the Central Lowlands to the sea is provided by corridors between the upland areas. The Moy Valley and the lowlands behind Galway Bay and Clew Bay, for example, are major avenues to the Atlantic, and the Slaney, Barrow, Nore and Suir Valleys are traditional avenues of communication to the south coast.

The upland areas fall into four main groups broadly distinguished by age, structure and the character of their surface relief. They include the Caledonian highlands of the north-west, Caledonian structures in the east, the Armorican hills and valleys of the south and the Cainozoic basaltic province in the north-east. With the Central Lowland, therefore, the country can be divided into five major physiographic regions (Fig. 2). The essential characteristics of each region are described below.

The Central Lowlands, underlain by Carboniferous limestones, is the only place in the British Isles where Palaeozoic rocks come to the surface in an extensive lowland. The lowland is best developed and most continuous north of a line from Galway to Dublin and south of the Newry Axis. To the north and south of this belt the lowland relief is frequently

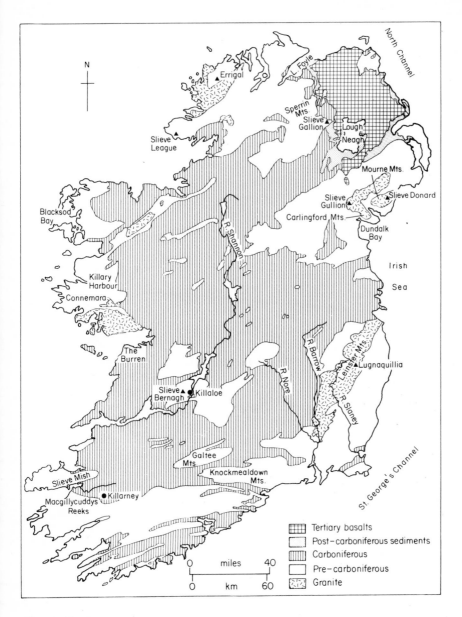

Fig. 1: Geology

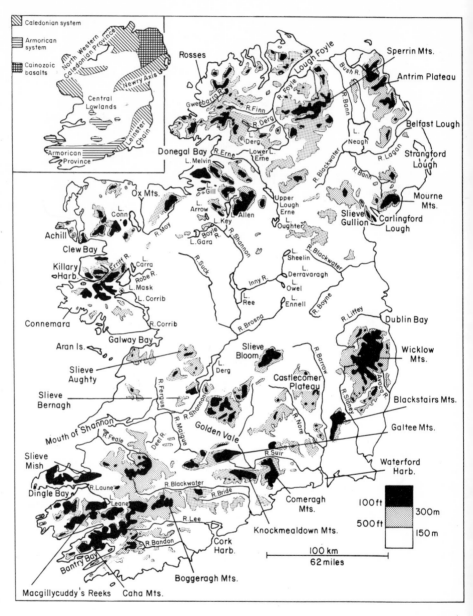

Fig. 2: Major relief and drainage. Structural regions (inset).

interrupted by two types of upland area; first, by residual plateaux of Upper Carboniferous shales, grits and thin coal seams which are younger than the limestone and, second, by isolated mountain ranges formed on anticlinal inliers of the resistant Old Red Sandstone and Silurian slates and shales which underlie the Carboniferous. The mountain ranges, such as Slieve Bloom, Slieve Aughty, Slieve Bernagh, the Devilsbit Mountain, Silvermine Mountains and the Galtee Mountains (Plate 3b), are more numerous to the south where they provide some of the most striking landscape elements, often rising abruptly from the level lowlands to over 1000 ft (305m) and in some places 2000 ft (610m). Although developed on Armorican folds, these mountains have a clear north–east south–west trend which suggests the indirect influence of Caledonian structures. Carboniferous uplands include the Castlecomer Plateau and Slieve Ardagh Escarpment in Co. Kilkenny, whose poorly drained surfaces rise to over 1000 ft, the lower but scenically similar plateau surfaces around the Shannon Estuary, and the striking plateaux of Leitrim, Sligo and Fermanagh (Plate 3) which have been deeply dissected into a number of steep-sided blocks with flat, bog-covered summits lying between 1500 and 2000 ft (457·5 and 610m).

Most of the Carboniferous limestone in the Central Lowlands is entirely concealed by a heavy mantle of recent glacial deposits and peat bogs, whose major characteristics are described at a later stage. The cover of glacial drift is of great thickness in the east but thins out markedly west of the Shannon where the bare limestone is sometimes exposed at the surface. On these exposures the dominant landforms have been produced by solution of the rocks and distinctive karstic landscapes have developed of both an upland and lowland character. The desolate rocky upland of the Burren in north Co. Clare is a classic area of upland karst with scarp slopes, dry valleys, enclosed depressions, disappearing streams, caves and subterranean drainage, and bare, fissured limestone pavements (Plate 2b). Some of these features recur in the karstic landscape of the Marble Arch Upland in Co. Fermanagh. Lowland karsts are well developed in east Co. Galway and on the Aran Islands with pavements, solution lakes and turloughs (small basins, seldom more than 1km^2, containing lakes which fluctuate seasonally in size and sometimes disappear). The large lakes of Corrib and Mask, which lie along the junction of the limestone lowlands and the Caledonian rocks of west Connacht, probably occupy solution hollows which have been enlarged by ice erosion. Karstic features may well be widely developed on the solid geology of the Central Lowlands but, owing to the extensive superficial glacial deposits, the dominant aspect of the lowland is that of a plain of glacial deposition with young morainic landforms.

The major drainage channel of the Central Lowlands is the River Shannon, which exceeds 200 miles (322km) in length, and its tributaries. Along its course the slow-moving river sometimes broadens into many channels as it penetrates drumlin swarms and elsewhere it expands into lakes, the largest of which are Loughs Allen, Ree and Derg. To the south of Lough Derg the Shannon enters the Killaloe Gap before reaching the extensive tidal estuary. Like many Irish rivers which flow across the Central Lowlands, the channel is markedly narrowed and occupies an impressive gap where it runs through the resistant rocks of the peripheral uplands.

The Caledonian country of the north and west falls into two parts, west Connacht and Donegal, which are separated by Carboniferous rocks around Donegal Bay but possess striking similarities. Both contain ancient Palaeozoic rocks forming scattered mountain ranges separated by lowland corridors. The rock surfaces are barren and rugged, especially in the mountainous portions which have been intensely glaciated. Corries with arêtes, ribbon lakes, ice-smoothed surfaces, roches moutonnées, and fiordic inlets like Killary Harbour and Lough Swilly are among the variety of glacial landforms. Individual peaks rise to over 2000 ft (610m) but there are also fragmented upland plateaux and areas of low ground, particularly along the coasts, from which the mountains often rise abruptly (Plate 1b). Major relief features can be largely explained in terms of rock character and especially resistance to denuding forces. Quartzites and granites characteristically form the mountains while the lowlands and valleys have developed on less resistant rocks, such as the schists, and along faults. The inhospitable physical character of the region is accentuated by the high rainfall, leached soils and exposure to Atlantic gales.

West Connacht contains essentially two mountainous peninsulas separated by Clew Bay and standing in strong contrast to the limestone plain to the east. Much of it, even the low-lying portions, is devoid of soil and the surfaces are festooned by bog patches and innumerable lakes which may lie in rock basins or depressions in the peat. Human settlement here is markedly coastal and the interior almost desolate. The coastline facing the Atlantic is picturesque, varied and irregular, with high promontories, steep cliffs and fiordic inlets alternating with coastal lowlands fringed by sandy bays and offshore islands. In Donegal the Caledonian folding is clearly evident in the north-east, south-west trend of the rugged mountains and many of the valleys, such as the Gweebarra, Foyle and

Plate 1a: Brandon mountain (3127 ft), Co. Kerry. Looking north, north-west: Lough Cruttia in the foreground and an ascending succession of corrie basins with spectacular crags.

Plate 1b: Coastal lowland near Letterfrack, Co. Galway, with rock exposures, bog patches and scattered farms. The quartzitic peaks of the Twelve Bens rise abruptly from the inland edge of the lowland.

Swilly. The ancient rocks are concealed beneath drift deposits in the lowlands of the Foyle and its tributaries but outcrop again along the Tyrone-Derry border where the rounded summits of the Sperrins rise to more than 2000 ft (610m) above wide valleys and form a barrier between the eastern and western lowlands of Ulster, the former centred on Lough Neagh and the latter on the Foyle.

In the east the Caledonian country forms two dissimilar areas—the Newry Axis and the Leinster Chain. The Newry Axis lies athwart the boundary between Northern Ireland and the Republic, forming a rough triangle with its sides running from Belfast Lough to Longford in the interior and thence approximately to Drogheda and the coast. In this region the Lower Palaeozoic slates, shales and sandstones form mainly low, rolling country rarely exceeding 1000 ft (305m) and widely covered by drumlinized glacial drift. Mountains have been formed by younger igneous intrusions of granite and gabbro. The complex igneous masses of the Mourne and Carlingford Mountains and of Slieve Gullion, with their distinctive ring-dykes, are located around the deep fiordic inlet of Carlingford Lough and rise abruptly from the surrounding lowlands.

The Leinster Mountain Chain, the second Caledonian unit in the east, is essentially a north-east to south-west trending ridge developed on a granite batholith originally intruded into overlying Ordovician strata. The unroofed granite now extends from Dublin Bay almost to the Barrow Estuary in Co. Waterford and forms the most extensive tract of high ground in the country. Over 200 sq. miles (518km^2) lie above 1000 ft (305m). The most characteristic topographic forms are dome-shaped granite mountains, many of them rising above 2000 ft (610m). However, there are also extensive level surfaces within the mountain chain, such as the Calary Plateau and Blessington Basin, and deep, steep-sided glens and precipitous corrie basins. Around the granite core the indurated Ordovician shales and slates form a narrow line of ragged, fringing uplands. To the south-east of the mountain chain in north Co. Wexford, the Ordovician and other rocks underlie an area which is essentially lowland but much diversified by a scatter of volcanic and quartzite hills aligned along the Caledonian axis.

In the parallel ridges and valleys of the south of Ireland the Armorican east–west grain is displayed with exceptional clarity. However, although Armorican folding has been influential, the present relief features are essentially the product of differential denudation. The Carboniferous limestones and the Old Red Sandstone which underlies them were originally folded into a series of well-marked, east to west trending anticlines and synclines. Today, however, the Carboniferous rocks occupy the valleys and the older sandstones the ridges; denudation has removed the Carboniferous cover, exposing the Old Red Sandstones which, as they are more resistant, have remained upstanding.

Most of the valleys of the Armorican zone are drained by streams flowing eastwards, some of which turn abruptly southwards before they reach the sea. Recent submergence has drowned the lower parts of the valleys and the resulting inlets provide fine natural harbours. The ridges of the south of Ireland are of varying altitude. In southern Co. Cork and Waterford a striking characteristic of the relief is the development, over hundreds of square miles, of level surfaces at a general elevation of 600–800 ft (180–240m) on the ridge summits, and again at 200–400 ft (60–120m). However, there are peaks of over 2000 ft (610m) in the Comeraghs and Knockmealdowns. In Co. Kerry and west Co. Cork the Armorican uplands broaden and increase their elevation, and the grandeur of the topography has been accentuated by features of glacial erosion. Some of the highest mountains and most spectacular landscapes of Ireland occur here, including the Dingle Peninsula (Plate 1a), Macgillycuddy's Reeks and the Upper Lake of Killarney. Towards the Atlantic the limestone valleys have been partially submerged by the sea to form deep rias separated by high mountainous peninsulas.

Early Cainozoic basalts, the eroded remnants of much more extensive lava floods, occupy an area of some 1550 sq. miles (4000km^2) in the north-eastern corner of Ireland. The bleak uneventful surface of the Antrim Plateau is developed on thick, gently sloping basaltic sheets which rise above 1200 ft (366m) over wide areas. In the east the lava flows have been deeply dissected into the isolated seaward-facing Glens of Antrim and on the east and north often terminate abruptly in steep cliffs (Plate 2b). To the west the basaltic sheets are downwarped beneath Lough Neagh (155 sq. miles; 400 km^2), the largest freshwater body in the British Isles, and the drift-filled valley of the Bann, but they reappear on the western side and terminate above the River Roe in a bold escarpment which is a topographical continuation of the Sperrin arc.

Glaciation

Although the solid geology is of great age, most of the landforms with which man is in direct contact have been moulded by recent geological processes. Within the last 200 000 years the country has experienced at

Plate 2a: Benbane Head, Co. Antrim. The level, uneventful surface of the Cainozoic basaltic plateau terminates here in steep cliffs. Giant's Causeway in the foreground and Rathlin Island on the horizon.

Plate 2b: The Burren, Co. Clare. Bare limestone upland with extensive pavements. Galway Bay and Connemara on the horizon.

Plate 3a: Dissected limestone plateau: King's mountain, Co. Sligo. "Striped" holdings and dispersed farms at the foot of the plateau below the scree-covered slopes.

Plate 3b: Glen of Aherlow, Co. Tipperary. Well-enclosed farmland on Carboniferous lowland. Galtic Mountains in the background developed on Old Red Sandstone and Silurian rocks, with open moorland and recent afforestation.

least two major glaciations—the Munsterian and Midlandian, which correspond to the Riss and Würm glaciations in the Alps, and glacial and peri-glacial activities have modified the surface in many important ways. In the first glaciation (the Munsterian or Eastern General) the whole of Ireland, with the possible exception of nunataks in the west and southwest, was covered by ice. During the second glaciation (the Midlandian or Midland General), which had more influence in shaping the present landscape, ice covered the northern and central parts of the country. A subsidiary ice mass was generated in the highlands of Kerry and West Cork, from which ice lobes spread into the surrounding lowlands to form the magnificent bow moraines which stretch from Castlemaine to Killarney, but a wide ice-free zone extended from the Dingle peninsula to Wexford in which tundra conditions and solifluction processes prevailed (Fig. 3a). The ice finally melted away from the country about 12 000 years ago, leaving the surface relief much as it is today although coastline outlines have been significantly altered by a Post Glacial rise of sea-level caused by the melting of the ice sheets (Synge and Stephens, 1960; Mitchell, 1976).

On the limestone lowlands the dominant action of the ice was the deposition of drift sheets from which most of the productive soils of the country have developed. The distribution, constitution and surface morphology of the drift have had a marked influence on the landscape and on patterns of land utilization. Although it generally reflects the characteristics of the rocks over which the ice sheets moved, the drift cover is variable in composition, ranging from irregular deposits of till or boulder clay to water-sorted sand and gravels. It is, moreover, smeared unevenly over the solid geology, reaching a thickness of over 200 ft (60 m) in the east of the Central Lowlands but thinning out to the west into a discontinuous blanket with sporadic outcrops of solid rock. The drift has been moulded into a variety of landforms. It sometimes forms gently undulating surfaces, as in the Curragh in Co. Kildare and in the Dublin region, but elsewhere the surface can be highly irregular. It may, for example, be diversified by meltwater deposits, such as the long gravel ridges, or eskers, which are especially numerous in the Midlands where they provide routeways through the lowland bogs and the Shannon callows (Plate 4a). In some areas there is a confusing assortment of hummocky kame, meltwater channels and retreat moraines. On the northern and western fringes of the Central Lowlands the drift is frequently moulded into a tightly packed mass of rounded, steepsided hillocks, called drumlins, with a multitude of lakes and bog patches in the

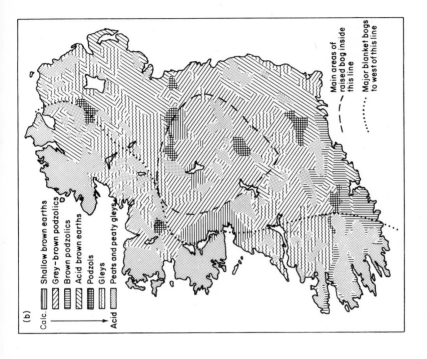

(b)

Calc.

▨ Shallow brown earths

▥ Grey-brown podzolics

▤ Brown podzolics

▧ Acid brown earths

▦ Podzols

░ Gleys

Acid

▓ Peats and peaty gleys

– – – Main areas of raised bog inside this line

········ Major blanket bogs to west of this line

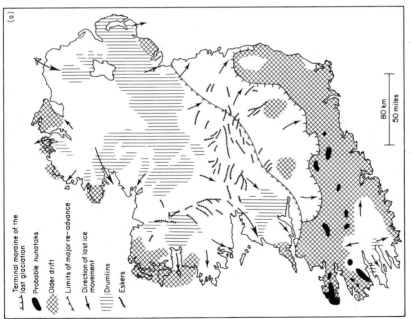

(a)

⊥⊥⊥ Terminal moraine of the last glaciation

⬬ Probable nunataks

⬚ Older drift

⌣ Limits of major re-advance

→ Direction of last ice movement

▥ Drumlins

〰 Eskers

80 km
50 miles

Fig. 3: a Glacial features. **b** Major soil types. (An Foras Talúntais and H. M. S. Miller.)

Plate 4a: Central Lowlands, Co. Offaly. A prominent esker ridge in the foreground. The River Shannon and its wide floodplain visible in the background.

Plate 4b: Drumlin landscape, Co. Monaghan.

inter-drumlin hollows (Plate 4b). This highly distinctive drumlin topography is best developed in a broad, almost continuous belt stretching across the country from Strangford Lough in north-eastern Ireland to Sligo and Donegal Bay on the Atlantic coast. Owing to the poor drainage and irregular terrain, the drumlin belt has been a barrier to communication and a major cultural divide in the country since prehistoric times. Smaller drumlin swarms occur in the Bann Valley, in east Co. Clare, and in central Co. Mayo where, at its western extremity, the submerged drumlin swarm forms a remarkable archipelago in Clew Bay. In the areas of Munster which were not covered by Midlandian ice, the older Munsterian drifts are exposed; the glacial landforms have a more weathered and rounded appearance and occur along with more recent peri-glacial features such as accumulations of head formed under freeze-thaw conditions by the mass downhill movement of unsorted, weathered materials.

Owing to the moist climate, low relief and limited permeability of many parent materials, the drainage of the drift deposits is generally poor. Surface streams are irregular and ill-defined and numerous lakes occur, often merely the remnants of larger water bodies which have been progressively reduced in size by fen and bog growth. Some of the lakes occupy hollows in the drift surface and others lie in solution hollows in the limestone. Waterlogging in the drift hollows has encouraged the growth of extensive peat bogs. Sand and gravel sheets, which originated as out-wash plains or deltaic deposits in pro-glacial lakes, are more freely drained than the areas of boulder clay.

In the uplands the rock surfaces were scoured by ice and denuded of their soil. Spectacular corrie basins were formed on the mountain sides, whose present freshness of relief has resulted from renewed corrie sapping during cold periods after the retreat of the main ice sheet. Valleys were also deepened and widened although the bottoms of the glacial troughs have often been concealed by later soliflucted head deposits and river alluvium. Glacial action, on the whole, has increased the contrasts between the uplands and the lowlands. Erosion impoverished the uplands leaving them with spectacular relief features but often devoid of soil. In the lowlands the deposition of the soil-forming tills and the concealment of the inhospitable karsts have been the major consequences. Tongues of drift often extend up the glaciated valleys but on the flanks of the uplands the drift cover rarely extends beyond 600–800 ft (180–240 m) above sea level and its upper boundary often forms an important scenic and cultural divide by determining the altitudinal limits of improved land and farming.

Climate

Exposure to prevailing westerly winds blowing in from the warm waters of the North Atlantic Drift ensures that Ireland has a markedly oceanic climate with frequent showers, high relative humidity and low annual ranges of temperature. Cool cloudy summers are followed by winters which are damp but exceptionally mild for the latitude. Maritime influences are most marked near the Atlantic coast but the Irish Sea also has a warming influence so that the Midlands are slightly colder than the rest of the country. Regional differences in temperature, however, are not great, with the average ranging from 9°C in the north-east to 10·5°C in the south-west. Annual temperature ranges are everywhere slight. At Valentia on the south-west coast the annual range of temperature is 8°C and at Dublin 10°C. Temperature extremes and harsh frosts are rare.

Owing to the prevalence of moist westerly winds, rainfall is generally higher in the west (Fig. 4). Even over the low ground there is a general fall in totals from west to east, from 40 inches (1000 mm) in the west of the Central Lowlands to under 30 inches (800 mm) on the east coast. Most of the rainfall in the country is frontal in origin but orographic effects are also important and accentuate the rainfall gradient from west to east. High mountains on the west coast intercept the eastward moving air and rainfall is markedly concentrated on their seaward-facing slopes. The west receives between 40 inches and 60 inches of rainfall on average with totals of over 100 inches (2540 mm) on the higher mountains. Most of the eastern half of the country has between 30 and 40 inches although sharp rises are recorded in mountainous areas. The coastal lowlands between Dublin and Drogheda have the lowest rainfall totals in Ireland. Everywhere the frequency of rain and cloud limits the duration of sunshine hours, but the south-east is rather more favoured than the remainder of the country, and sunshine totals tend to decline towards the north-west and over high ground.

The extreme moistness of the soil environment is owing to cloudiness and low summer temperatures, which check evaporation rates, as well as to the persistent rainfall, impeded drainage or the impermeable materials from which much of the soil cover is derived. On the east coast there is considerable loss of moisture from the soil in summer but on the west coast there are extensive areas, corresponding largely to the blanket bog areas, where the precipitation-evaporation ratio always favours precipitation. Frequent winds of moderate to severe strength are a

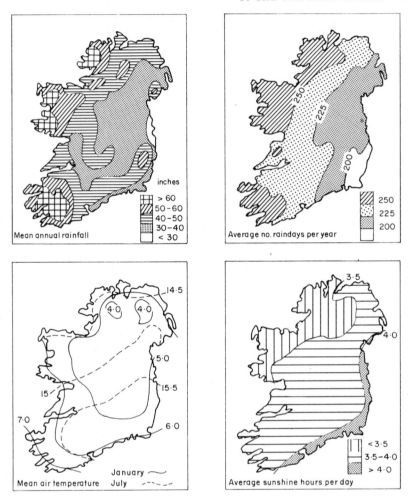

Fig. 4: Climatic features.

characteristic of the western seaboard of the country but their drying efficiency is reduced by the high moisture content of the air itself.

The proverbial changeability of Irish weather from day to day and even hour to hour is basically the result of the frequent movement across the country of frontal depressions embedded in the westerly air stream. Passage of a depression brings a rapid succession of rainfall belts, contrasting air masses and changing wind directions. More stable, high pressure conditions with drier air sometimes extend from the continent over the eastern parts of the country and deflect the depressions but unsettled weather with cloudy or overcast skies and periodic showers is most characteristic. Much of the character and kaleidoscopic beauty of the Irish landscape derive from constant variations in the strength and quality of the light. The frequent haziness of the atmosphere, which is largely owing to water vapour, mutes the colours of the landscape and produces many subtle shades of green, blue and brown. Mountain areas in particular have a peculiar beauty and variety of colouring associated with the filtering of sunlight through moving banks of cloud or falling rain. In spells of clear air and direct sunlight, the landscape, especially the lush grass and foliage, springs into vivid, almost lurid, colours.

Soils

Irish soils are a sensitive response to climatic conditions, the calibre of parent materials, local relief and drainage conditions and the length of time during which pedogenic processes have operated. In the cool, moist climate, leaching is the predominant soil-forming process, leading to widespread podsolization and soil acidity, especially in the wetter west and in upland areas. Poor natural drainage in the lowland areas frequently produces waterlogging which encourages the spread of peat and gleying of the soils. Owing to Ireland's long and complicated glacial history, most of the soils are derived from glacial drifts. Generally these superficial deposits are relatively local in origin and thus reflect some of the characteristics of the underlying rocks, but there is often some admixture with materials transported by glaciers from different locations. The variable constitution and structure of the drift, as well as the topographical forms developed on it, are related largely to the depositional behaviour of the ice sheets as they traversed the lowlands. In upland areas glacial erosion often removed the loose surface materials and soils are mainly confined to patches of glacial drift on the valley sides, restricted areas of recent alluvium and head deposits.

The soils have been considerably changed from their natural state by a long period of human interference. Much of the soil cover developed originally under forest vegetation before the advent of farming, and with the removal of the trees the soils were more exposed to leaching and progressively degraded, while better opportunities for the spread of peat were also provided. Intensive grazing, trampling and dunging by herds of cattle must also have had a significant influence at least on the surface layers of the soil. Cultivation too has disturbed the natural profiles; hard-pans, for example, have been broken and ploughed up and soil nutrients absorbed by crops. New materials and fertilizers have been deliberately added to the soil. The wide distribution of 18th and 19th Century lime kilns is a reminder of the determined application of lime to counteract soil acidity, and sand and seaweed have been extensively applied to the soils in the coastal areas. Bog clearance and drainage of the land have been important too for many centuries, especially in the eastern areas where the intensity of human improvements has generally tended to reinforce the natural superiority of the soils.

The major soil types are described below and their distribution shown in Fig. 3. Alkaline brown earths have developed only where there is a thin drift cover over limestone lowlands, chiefly in east Co. Galway and north Co. Clare. Brown and grey-brown podzols, with patches of peat and peaty gleys, are the most widespread soil types, originating from deep lowland drifts and covering over one quarter of the country. Heavier than the brown earths but generally well-drained and of medium base status, they include the most fertile soils in the country. However, they are variable in quality; they possess, for example, a high base status when developed on fluvio-glacial outwash deposits, and gleying tends to increase towards the north and west. Grey-brown podzols are best developed on calcareous drift in the Midlands and east of Ireland. Brown podzols, which are rather less fertile, have developed on less calcareous parent materials and are confined to the older drift of Munsterian age in southern Ireland where the deposits have been exposed to longer periods of leaching.

Acid brown earths are especially characteristic of the Foyle lowland and the Caledonian areas of the east, the Newry Axis and Leinster granite. They form on lime-deficient parent materials such as granites, basalts, sandstones, shales and slates. If their natural deficiencies are corrected by liming and fertilizing, the acid brown earths can make useful agricultural soils. Gleys or waterlogged soils have developed widely on the stiff clayey tills of the drumlin belt and on the fine-textured impervious drift of the Upper Carboniferous plateaux to the south of the Shannon Estuary.

Podsols, with raw humus at the surface, upper horizons impoverished by the washing out of soluble salts and well-cemented layers of pan at the base, are widely distributed, especially in the west and in upland areas. They have typically developed on lime-deficient parent materials under intense leaching. Often they underlie peat bogs where the hard pan horizon may have contributed to the impeded drainage conditions. Peat and peaty soils are also widespread in conditions of extreme wetness. Peat is wholly an accumulation of plant material without mineral content and is therefore described later under the heading of vegetation. But it is often present in normal soils producing peaty podzols or peaty gleys. These peaty soils are characteristic of mountainous areas, especially on the western seaboard; they are widely developed on the highlands of Kerry for example and on the mountainous areas of Donegal and west Connacht.

The Evolution of the Vegetation Pattern

It would be misleading to consider the activities and distribution patterns of prehistoric man in relation to present environmental conditions. Throughout their long period of settlement, human beings have been involved in a continuing if uneven process of transforming the natural landscape and replacing it with a cultural landscape which is essentially a human artifact. The appearance of the landscape at the beginning of the prehistoric period was thus substantially different from that of today. Furthermore, our attempts to understand man's relationship to the environment during the early stages of settlement are complicated by a succession of natural changes in the environment itself. These changes were basically produced by secular, climatic variations which were linked both to far-reaching changes in the natural vegetation cover and to movements of sea-level with resulting changes in shoreline configuration. Particular attention must be paid to the history of the natural vegetation cover as it was this which dominated the landscape before the advent of man and indeed long after his arrival.

Major stages of vegetational history have been distinguished mainly through the analysis of fossil pollen (Smith, 1970). In normal conditions large quantities of wind-blown pollen grains from trees fall on the surface of the ground and decay there. However, in Ireland this "pollen rain" has been unusually well preserved in the anaerobic conditions of the peat bogs which have long formed a major element of the landscape. As the bogs themselves grow upwards naturally through continued surface accumulation of only partially decayed bog moss and other organic material, the older bogs incorporate a record of vegetational changes in the surrounding areas (Mitchell, 1956, 1965). Careful study of a vertical series of pollen samples through a bog will thus illustrate the changing composition of the vegetation cover. Pollen analysis has indeed permitted the subdivision of the Late Glacial and Post Glacial periods into zones defined by major changes in the composition of the pollen rain, zones which themselves reflect vegetational changes (Fig. 5). Large-scale vegetational changes must be associated with climatic changes effective over wide regions. The quasi-contemporaneity of pollen zones can therefore be reasonably assumed, especially within an area as small as Ireland. Recently the increased use of radiocarbon dating has provided a better basis for the absolute dating of the zones (Walker and West, 1970).

Clearly, the vegetational stages identified by pollen analysis have climatic implications, but it needs emphasis that all evidence for past climatic change is indirect and must be interpreted. There is a particular lack of precise information about the climatic tolerance of species, which prevents the making of clear climatic deductions from the observed vegetational changes. Quantitative assessment is especially controversial. There is, however, no major disagreement about the broad qualitative pattern of climatic events until Atlantic times. Exceptional complications then arise because the advent of farming people leads to a marked increase in the degree of human interference with the environment and to the large-scale depletion of the natural vegetation cover in order to provide open areas for cultivation and livestock grazing. In such circumstances it becomes more difficult to distinguish or disentangle climatic causes from human interventions.

With technological advance and the related growth of population, the natural vegetation cover has been progressively removed and the cultural landscape, over the long term, has grown more extensive and more complete. But the process of clearance was not a simple or even development. There is evidence, in some areas, of human colonization and a subsequent withdrawal, and even a succession of such phases. In other areas, human attempts to colonize and utilize the land were clearly not successful but nevertheless produced far-reaching deleterious changes and the development of new types of vegetation cover, such as the moorland on the mountains and, in some places, the quickening of bog growth (Mitchell, 1965; Case et al., 1969; Moore et al., 1975).

The flora of Ireland, and indeed of extensive areas of western Europe, was largely eliminated during the last glaciation, although cold-tolerant species may have survived in the unglaciated southern portions of the country and on larger "nunataks" elsewhere. The level of the sea relative to the land fell during the last glacial epoch by several hundred feet because vast quantities of water were locked up in the greatly enlarged ice sheets. Ireland had an open connection with Britain during some part of the time and Britain in turn was linked to the continental mainland. Most of the vegetation which developed in Ireland, as the Post Glacial climatic amelioration made growth again possible, entered the country by the temporary land-bridges. However, as the ice sheets continued to melt, sea-levels rose and by around 5000 B.C. Ireland had again been severed from Britain and the coasts had assumed approximately their present outline. Many plant and animal species which succeeded in migrating from the European mainland into Britain were unable to reach Ireland owing to the newly-formed sea barrier. This, it seems, is the major reason why Ireland possesses a very limited range of flora and fauna, compared with that of Britain, and is even poorer in comparison with neighbouring continental countries. However, the ecological homogeneity of the country, linked especially to the overriding influence of a damp, mild, oceanic climate, also limits its biotic diversity. There are, with the exception of the considerable rainfall decline from west to east, no major climatic contrasts within the country; the altitude of the mountains is not great enough to permit the development of tundra-like vegetation and extensive areas of geologically undifferentiated lowlands occur, especially in the interior of the country, which support a markedly restricted range of plant communities (Webb, 1957). The number of recorded species of both plants and animals in Ireland is less than one-third of the number occurring in north-western Europe. For example, beech, which dominates the woodlands of western Europe, is a notable absentee, as well as numerous shrubs which characteristically develop under a beech canopy. Reptiles, roe deer and the common shrew are conspicuously absent. A considerable variety of plants has been introduced into certain localities of Ireland within recent centuries, especially by large landowners interested in the commercial development and beautification of their estates and gardens (McCracken, 1965). These include many species which have been widely planted, such as beech, lime, chestnut, a wide range of coniferous trees and fuschia. Despite this recent enrichment, the biotic range in Ireland remains markedly low in relation to neighbouring countries.

Towards the end of the Pleistocene Ice Age, in the Late Glacial period, the lowland areas of Britain and western Europe were for a time (approximately 10 000–9000 B.C.) covered by open tundra-like vegetation which had gradually established itself in the wake of the retreating ice. In Ireland the extensive Central Lowland areas were similarly covered by grassy tundra: only a very limited variety of trees were able to establish themselves, mainly birch copses, and these were restricted to scattered sheltered situations. The vegetation records indicate that somewhat warmer conditions prevailed in the middle of the Late Glacial period (Allerød oscillation) with a corresponding increase in the variety and amount of plant and animal life. Large herds of reindeer, the giant Irish deer and other herbivores grazed the stretches of open country (Mitchell, 1949). Towards the west, patches of sub-arctic heath prevailed with dwarf willow, crowberry and juniper (Watts, 1963).

Although the conditions in Ireland seem to have been well suited to hunting communities, there is no evidence of contemporary human settlements. Elsewhere in western Europe and certainly in adjacent Britain there is evidence that Palaeolithic hunting groups were following and living upon the migratory herds of bison, wild horse and reindeer which grazed the open tundra. In Ireland, however, there is no unequivocal record of man until well after the climatic improvement at the beginning of the Post Glacial period, around 8500 B.C. A Palaeolithic worked flint recently found in glacial gravels near Drogheda, Co. Louth (Mitchell, 1974) appears to have been deposited by ice advancing southwards down the Irish Sea. It does not demonstrate the presence of Palaeolithic man within Ireland but does suggest that he migrated as far west as the basin of the Irish Sea. The virtual absence of Palaeolithic settlers was probably mainly owing to the insular nature of the country and its remoteness from the continental mainland; both these factors diminished the probability of visits by migrant hunting groups.

At the end of the Late Glacial period there was a recognizable deterioration of climate (Younger Dryas) with corresponding impoverishment of the flora and restriction of the extent of tree growth. However, with the transition from Late Glacial time to the warmer conditions of the Post Glacial, a forest vegetation began to develop and, once established, it survived until cleared away by man. Though the forests persisted, it is clear from pollen analysis that the trees within them varied considerably in relative importance. The sequence of change in forest vegetation which has been worked out relates essentially to the central lowland areas of the country. Firm evidence about altitudinal variations in vegetation is limited but reasonable inferences can be made. Throughout the Post Glacial period, changes in the composition of the forests were related to the changing climates and the existence of the land-bridge to Britain along which the migration of new plants was possible. First, there was a noticeable spread of birch trees and, with progressive amelioration of the climate, these were supplemented by the vanguard of hazel and pine forests, and in time by elm and oak. Eventually, the birch woods were completely replaced by newer arrivals which formed into dense continuous forests. By the Boreal period (c. 7500-5500 B.C.) it appears that the country was already covered by deciduous forests, with the possible exception of the mountain tops, lakes and swamps. It was this extensive and undisturbed forest which formed the habitat of early man in Ireland. The herds of large herbivores that flourished in Late Glacial times had become extinct and the first human society had to adjust to the forest environment and live by exploiting its economic resources.

With the transition from the Boreal to the warmer and wetter Atlantic period around 5500–5000 B.C., the oak and the elm came to occupy a dominant place in the forest vegetation, with alder as a major component in the damper areas. This vegetational pattern appears to have been relatively stable, and had it not been for human interference, might have persisted essentially unchanged down to the present day. In the first place, the severance of the land links to Britain, which followed on the Post Glacial warming, checked further plant immigration and, second, it seems possible that the Atlantic period, although sometimes referred to as the period of "climatic optimum", was not climatically very different from today, with temperature and precipitation means only marginally higher. A succession of minor climatic variations have occurred since the Atlantic period but none of them were great enough to induce marked changes in the character of the natural vegetation cover.

Towards the end of the Atlantic period there was a sharp temporary decline of elm, a phenomenon that appeared widely in western Europe at this time. Simultaneously there was a fleeting appearance of plantain, a plant which thrives in open surroundings. The elm decline may reflect the advent of farming groups and in particular the presence of domesticated grazing animals which browsed on the elm shoots. However, the dramatic nature of the elm decline would imply a large-scale colonization of farmers over a very short period of time, which seems unlikely from a variety of other viewpoints (Watts, 1961). In particular, the elm recovers its former importance before the middle of the third millenium, which is hard to explain if the initial decline was owing to the impact of a farming economy. It has been suggested that the temporary decimation of the tree may have been associated with widespread elm disease rather than human intervention or climatic change, and that at a later stage farmers could simply have exploited the forest openings cleared by disease and pasture weeds would have accompanied them. Later, with the elm recovery, the forest re-asserted itself and the clearings and the weeds disappeared. Shortly before the second millenium, the elm began a second trend of decline which is permanent and unambiguously linked to the far-reaching and long-term ecological changes wrought by an expanding agricultural economy. The decline of elm is accompanied by the spread of secondary woodland dominated by ash, a tree favoured by human activity whose pollen is infrequent before post-Atlantic times. Bog stratigraphy frequently shows evidence of an abrupt forest clearance, with the decline of elm accompanied by the spread of ash and the appearance of such pasture plants as plantain, cereals and weed species (Smith and Willis, 1961/2). Such abrupt clearances, often associated with evidence of burning, must surely point to the sudden incursion of farming groups. Evidence also exists for a cyclic process of local forest clearance followed by farming and, ultimately, forest regeneration; a pattern which suggests the practice of shifting cultivation or slash-and-burn agriculture. Thus, excavation of a Neolithic habitation site (Eogan, 1963) at Townley Hall in Co. Meath indicates prolonged settlement, but the numerous hearths and stake holes (some located below hearths) surrounded by occupation debris seem to imply a pattern of intermittent occupation. Samples of charcoal showed clearly that fuel was derived from scrub, such as hazel or hawthorn, which may well have colonized clearances made for temporary cultivation purposes, and forest trees, such as oak and elm, seem to have been eliminated before the settlement was established.

The original forest ecosystems of Ireland have long since been destroyed or at best persist in highly modified form. Man's removal of the natural forest vegetation was a lengthy and complicated process to which further reference will be made in the later discussion of the major phases of human settlement in the prehistoric and historic periods. Centuries of farming activity, including cultivation and pastoralism, have left Ireland with a conspicuously low percentage cover of natural woodland, probably lower than any other European country. At the present day, even if the recently planted coniferous forests are included, only some 3% of the total area is under woodland. The forest was eventually replaced mainly by grassland on the better lowland soils, by moorland on the uplands, and by peatland communities which flourish both in lowland and upland conditions. It is these three types of vegetation cover which now dominate the landscape, and fragments of natural woodland survive mainly in places unsuited to farming. The peatlands are both of limited agricultural value and unsuited to tree growth, being without soil development. They support at best a narrow range of specialized shrubs on the drier bog margins and provide some rough grazing for mountain sheep and hardy cattle. The grasslands are the focus of agricultural activity, and on them, understandably, woodland is scarce, confined to windbreaks and the parklands around large estates. However, one of the most striking characteristics of farmed areas is their subdivision into many small fields most commonly separated by low banks colonized by hawthorn, blackthorn, gorse and sporadic trees.

Hence, from ground level the farmed landscape often appears relatively well wooded but this impression is misleading.

Moorland vegetation, made up of rough bent grass, heather, gorse and bracken, is typical of the scattered hills and mountain masses which surround the central plain. Calcareous till, so plentiful on the lowlands, rarely extends above 800 ft and the peripheral hill country is frequently developed on acid rocks, such as granite. Altitude accentuates rainfall and lowers temperatures, and the cool damp environment of the hills produces soil impoverishment and a general tendency towards water surpluses and peat formation. Blanket bog can develop but more often there are wide areas of thin acid soil. Podzolization is the principal soil forming process and illuviation of iron and aluminium is accompanied by the accumulation of raw humus in the surface soil horizons.

Woodlands were once widely developed on the mountains, although the exposure and low summer temperatures perhaps limited the density of the growth and the highest summits were probably always above the tree line (Smith, 1972). The clearance of the woodland was initiated by farmers in the prehistoric period and achieved slowly by a combination of burning, felling and animal grazing. Systematic clearances occurred in the 16th, 17th and 18th Centuries A.D., owing to the intensified use of timber as an industrial fuel and as a building material, but also for military-strategic reasons and to create agricultural land, sheep grazing and grouse moors (Andrews, 1956; Leister, 1963; McCracken, 1958–59). Burning of heather to facilitate new spring growth is still widely practised by farmers in hill country. Bracken and gorse have probably increased their hold in the hill areas as deforestation proceeded. These plants are kept in a subservient position by tree cover but are aggressive species in open country; burning is particularly favourable to their spread as it eliminates the main competitors. The present moorland vegetation cover of the hill country, therefore, is very much a product of human interference. Picturesque though it may be, it possesses very little feeding value for animals and represents an unsatisfactory form of ecological balance between man and nature.

The grassland communities are developed in a wide range of conditions, ranging from deep calcareous soils in the eastern lowlands to shallow peaty soils which are developed at low altitudes in the moister north-west and west of the country but found mainly on the foothills of mountain masses elsewhere in the country. Grassland, however, flourishes best on limestone soils such as are characteristic of the central and eastern lowlands. These lowlands, although covered by calcareous soils, are in many areas poorly drained; their soils are often rich in clay and relatively impermeable, and the undulating glacial topography with numerous enclosed hollows, a topography typical of young glacial landscapes, provides a milieu favourable to bog formation. Thus, a recurrent feature of the Central Lowlands is a mosaic of bog and grassland, the brown bog occupies the hollows while the dry ridges and eminences are clothed in vivid green grass.

A precondition of the establishment of a productive blanket of grassland in the lowland areas was the clearance of the forest vegetation and of the boulders and stones frequently incorporated in the morainic soils. The bulk of the boulders have over the centuries been laboriously built into field boundaries where they are now frequently concealed by sods and vegetation. Often surplus stones can be found piled up in mounds or ''consumption dykes'' within the fields. Many of the field boundaries are of relatively recent origin and the consumption dykes may often have been larger than at present and provided a ready source of materials for walling. The layers of sod which characteristically cover the stone cores of the field boundaries are usually derived from shallow drainage ditches which flank the walls and are probably in most cases contemporary with them.

Two main categories of bog exist; raised bogs, which are most widely developed on the Central Lowlands, and blanket bogs, most characteristic of the western highlands. These bog types differ in their mode of formation and, despite their visual similarity, possess differences of floristic composition. The main component of both the bog types is sphagnum moss but the remainder of the vegetation in each type has a distinctive character.

Bog growth began at different times in different regions and in particular sites. In some locations there is evidence that blanket bogs had begun to form as early as 2000 B.C. However, this is not conclusive evidence for climatic change. Climatic conditions favourable for peat formation may have existed for some time before, and the beginning of bog accumulations may have been the culmination of a long period of soil impoverishment by natural or human agencies. During the Sub Atlantic period temperatures fell slightly and rainfall increased and the climatic deterioration is thought to have been a cause of the rapid growth of the ombrogenous sphagnum peats of the upper horizons of the raised bogs. In the lower layers, the plant remains are much decayed and are considered to have developed slowly under relatively warm and dry conditions (Mitchell, 1945). At some sites the initial bog growth may well be attributable to changes following on man's removal of the forest cover for tillage purposes and for grazing. Blanket bogs, for example, are frequently developed over a layer of tree stumps, especially pine. Deforested soils would have been exposed to heavy rainfall, especially during Sub Atlantic times, with consequent hard-pan development and waterlogging providing conditions in which rushes and mosses grew abundantly and eventually accumulated into bogs.

The evolution of the extensive blanket bogs on the lowlands of north-western Mayo well illustrates the complex history of bog development (Moore *et al.*, 1975). This area today is one of the most desolate and uneventful landscapes in Ireland but it has experienced a succession of marked changes in its vegetation cover in which human activity has clearly played an important part. The original Post Glacial ecosystem was coniferous woodland with oak patches in the valleys, but this woodland was drastically reduced at some time during the 4th and 5th millenium B.C., perhaps by burning. No cultural remains have been found from this early stage but it is likely that farmers were responsible for this primary clearance. With the removal of the forest, peat growth ensued which was in turn colonized by pine forest. The erection of megalithic tombs in the area may have commenced in the second half of the 4th millenium. Many of the tombs have survived but are partially buried under layers of much later peat growth. Field boundaries have also been unearthed under the peat which may be associated with Bronze Age farming. About 2300 B.C. a massive destruction of the second pine forest took place by burning; indeed, charcoal fragments in the peat suggest that sporadic fires have been a regular feature since Neolithic times. After this widespread destruction the woodland did not regenerate and eventually the peat cover extended and encroached even on the better-drained, farmed areas. The whole region, with the exception of a narrow coastal strip, has remained largely peat-covered and uninhabited, although limited colonization and bog clearance occurred during the marked growth of population in the 18th and 19th Centuries A.D. Investigations at Glenamoy in north-western Mayo show that in recent centuries the flatter areas of bog have been accumulating at a rate of 10 cm per century.

The raised bogs, or lowland bogs, are natural organic accumulations made up chiefly of sphagnum moss, a plant which flourishes in semi-aquatic surroundings. Post Glacial lakes and ill-drained hollows in the young undulating drift surface acted as focal points for bog growth. In section, the typical raised bog comprises a thick layer of acid peat, consisting mainly of humified sphagnum together with remnants of heather and sedges, overlying a peat layer consisting of woody and fen plant remains formed under base-rich conditions. It appears, therefore, that, in the first place, fen peat developed in the damp basins, similar to the contemporary and extensive fen peat stretches around the ill-drained southern shore of Lough Neagh, and that, later, sphagnum accumulated. Once established, the bog creates conditions favourable to its further growth, as drainage channels are progressively blocked and waterlogging is accentuated. In the acid anaerobic conditions of the bog, organisms of decay cannot flourish and there is a resulting steady accumulation of plant debris. The depth of this organic material varies greatly from site to site from a few feet to as much as 30 feet (9·1 m). The bog surfaces have frequently grown upwards above the general level of the surrounding lowland and the bog margins have expanded peripherally from their lake foci onto the adjoining tills. Local topography and drainage conditions determine the extent of lateral expansion and the areal extent of the bog surfaces varies greatly from an acre or two to many square miles.

Blanket bogs have developed primarily as a response to climate and grow more extensively in western and northern areas with high rainfall (usually 12·7 cm +) and waterlogged, acid parent materials. The peat layers are thin in comparison with the raised bogs of the Midlands. Unlike the raised bogs they are found in elevated positions as well as lowlands, and can develop on sloping sites (not on slopes over 15°) from sea-level up to high altitudes. Many of the mountain tops of Kerry, Mayo and Galway are covered with blanket bog. In Northern Ireland there are extensive areas of blanket peat on the Sperrin Mountains, on the level, waterlogged surfaces of the Antrim Plateau and in the Mournes. Blanket bogs are slow to accumulate on well-drained slopes or base-rich materials but, with sufficiently high rainfall, they can develop on limestone slopes and on base-rich surfaces such as the basalts of the Antrim Plateau.

Human activity has probably been even more important in reducing the area of bog than in stimulating its growth. Considerable areas of woodland still existed in the Middle Ages but forest clearance for commercial and military-strategic reasons culminated in almost complete forest destruction by the 18th Century. As the woodlands dwindled the bogs were increasingly used as an alternative to timber for domestic fuel and as building material for poorer farmhouses, barns and field boundaries. The fossil wood preserved in the bogs also came into use. Population pressure in the 18th and 19th Centuries led to intensified use of the peat resources and to the reclamation of "cut away" bog for agricultural purposes. This process was particularly important in the lowlands where workable peat lies upon potentially fertile soil. On the higher land the soil underlying the

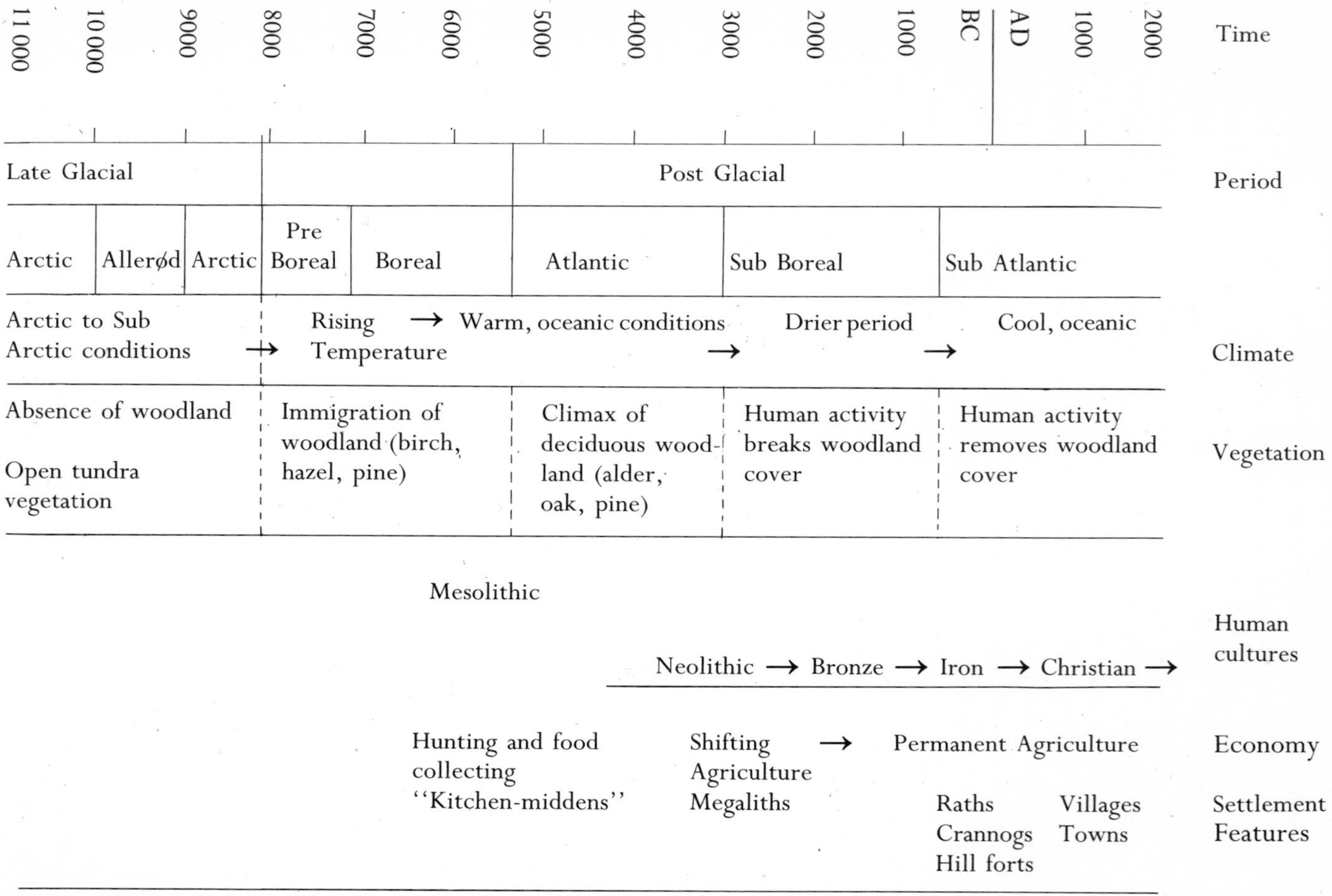

Time	Period			Climate	Vegetation	Human cultures	Economy	Settlement Features
2000 AD	Post Glacial	Sub Atlantic		Cool, oceanic	Human activity removes woodland cover	Christian ↑	Permanent Agriculture	Villages Towns
1000						Iron ↑		Raths Crannogs Hill forts
AD / BC								
1000		Sub Boreal		Drier period ↑	Human activity breaks woodland cover	Bronze ↑		
2000						Neolithic ↑	Shifting Agriculture Megaliths ↑	
3000								
4000		Atlantic		Warm, oceanic conditions ↑	Climax of deciduous woodland (alder, oak, pine)			
5000						Mesolithic	Hunting and food collecting "Kitchen-middens"	
6000		Boreal		Rising ↑ Temperature	Immigration of woodland (birch, hazel, pine)			
7000		Pre Boreal						
8000				Arctic to Sub Arctic conditions ↑	Absence of woodland			
9000	Late Glacial	Arctic	Allerød	Arctic		Open tundra vegetation			
10 000								
11 000								

Fig. 5. [caption partially illegible] ... relation ... climatic ...

blanket bogs is of poor potential. The extent of the lowland bog surfaces had thus been considerably reduced before the commencement of commercialized and mechanized peat cutting in the 20th Century (Plate 14). Commercial exploitation, if continued at present rates, will lead to virtual depletion of the major lowland peat resources within a few decades. At high levels, the blanket bogs have shown evidence of natural shrinkage in the present century and in many areas the formerly continuous peat cover has been reduced to a series of islands or "hags", sometimes revealing the stumps of prehistoric woodlands. This phenomenon of shrinkage has been observed elsewhere in Britain but general knowledge of blanket bogs is limited and the real causes of shrinkage are as yet unknown (Bower, 1962). Blanket peat may be an inherently unstable system in which erosion ultimately occurs as the outcome of accumulation. Various biotic activities, such as sheep grazing and trampling, may encourage erosion; they could be major causes or merely trigger factors accentuating the inevitable.

2
The Mesolithic and Neolithic Periods

Mesolithic Ireland: The First Settlers

When the first human groups migrated into Ireland about 8000 years ago, the country, like Britain and the greater part of temperate Europe, was covered by dense deciduous forests. The only important exceptions to this were the highest mountains, the lakes and marshes. The first communities (known to archaeologists as Mesolithic or Middle Stone Age communities) were not based upon a farming way of life but upon a food collecting and hunting economy, exploiting in particular the food resources of the shoreline and coastal waters. Mesolithic man was a pioneer entering and settling a land well populated by plants and animals but previously unvisited by human beings. His primitive form of economy did not lead to any significant interference with the natural forest ecosystem. Mesolithic ways of life persisted alone for over 2000 years before the knowledge of domestication of animals and plants became widespread in Ireland during the 4th millenium B.C. and clear evidence is available of the destruction of the natural woodlands by burning and animal depredations. Equally important, however, was the substantial continuity of the Mesolithic ways of life after the time when the first farmers began to settle in the country. Indeed, the bulk of the Mesolithic material is late and overlaps with the period of early Neolithic influences. This point is becoming clearer as radiocarbon dating revises our estimates of the date of the arrival of the first Neolithic settlers. The tendency has been for this date to be pushed steadily back in time. As recently as the 1960s it was customary to date the beginning of the Neolithic period at around 2000 B.C. but present evidence points to origins in the 4th millenium, probably even earlier than 3500 B.C.

No Mesolithic graves have been found to excavate and the remains of recognizable huts or houses are very rare, perhaps because, as with many hunting and collecting groups, the buildings used were flimsy and impermanent and have thus left few physical traces for the archaeologist to uncover. One interesting exception is the Mesolithic site at Mount Sandel in Derry where recent excavations have revealed the post holes of several huts and associated features such as pits and hearths. The huts possess round plans, approximately 20 ft (6 m) across, with central hearths. It has been suggested that the buildings may have been part of a winter settlement site where the dwellings were more substantial and durable than those used at other times of the year (Woodman, 1973).

The main body of Mesolithic remains to have been identified and excavated in Ireland is in the form of rubbish dumps. These are mainly located in northern and especially north-eastern Ireland and are typically sited along the coasts and on the banks of rivers and lakes. The dumps are usually buried beneath recent marine deposits and consist of food debris (the remnants of molluscs and crustaceans, fish, birds and occasionally fragments of mammal bones), a few crude stone implements and stone chippings produced in the course of tool-making operations. Some of the dumps or middens are large and must represent long periods of accumulation. Such sites, even when carefully excavated, provide little direct evidence of the material culture and, of course, virtually no guide to the ethnic composition or non-material aspects of the prevailing culture, such as language or religion. The conditions in which the Mesolithic remains are preserved have also seriously hampered attempts to reconstruct a picture of the culture in Ireland. Few undisturbed or primary sites exist, because the major settlement zones have been submerged by Post Glacial marine trangressions and the habitation refuse scattered by the sea and redistributed. The Mesolithic culture survived over a very long period. It was first established along the coasts during the Boreal period but in the subsequent warmer and wetter Atlantic period sea levels rose, following the continued release of water hitherto contained in the ice sheets, and beaches were formed at new levels. Eventually, delayed isostatic readjustments have led to a rise in the level of the land and the beaches formed during the Atlantic period now lie inland. Mesolithic remains are usually found incorporated in the sand and gravel deposits of the raised beaches, especially the best developed beach which lies at approximately 25 ft (7·6 m) above present sea-level. This, however, is probably not always their primary position. The materials may well have been washed up into the raised beaches and thus be in derived or secondary contexts. Given such disturbances of the environment, it is, of course, highly likely that the known remains are very incompletely representative. Dating Mesolithic material is further complicated by the problems of correlating the various beaches and the realization that the features are not of uniform age along their length owing to regional contrasts in isostatic recovery from north to south. In the southern portion of the beaches, along the coasts of north Leinster, isostatic recovery was less marked than farther north, and indeed south of Dublin raised beaches are absent. The probability is that the beaches are youngest in the south and oldest in the north.

Despite the limited cultural content of the Mesolithic sites in Ireland and their disturbed physical contexts, a study of the available remains does permit some useful insights into the origin, geographical distribution and environmental adjustments of the Mesolithic communities (Woodman, 1973–4). In the first place, even if we allow the possibility that for these remote millenia the ratio of known to unknown sites is seriously small, there is a noteworthy concentration of finds in north and north-eastern Ireland, especially along the coasts and the banks of major rivers and lakes. We can reasonably conclude that the bulk of the population must have lived in the northern region and that the settlements, whatever form they may have taken, would have been close to the rubbish middens. In addition, the extent of the middens suggests that the related settlements may have been relatively permanent and that considerable food supplies were to be found more or less in situ in the coastal locations. There is a marked absence of Mesolithic finds from upland areas and this is in contrast to England where Mesolithic finds are numerous in hill areas, such as the Pennines, which probably served as summer hunting grounds. Raised beaches along the coasts of north-eastern Ireland seem to have been particularly important foci of settlement, and it is from such a site at Larne, Co. Antrim, that the Mesolithic culture derived its title ''Larnian'' (Movius, 1953). Mesolithic sites are particularly prolific on the shores of Strangford and Belfast Loughs in Co. Down (Stephens and Collins, 1960; Morrison, 1961) but coastal sites are known as far west as the Inishowen Peninsula (Addyman and Vernon, 1966) and as far south as Dublin Bay (Liversage, 1968). The Bann Valley is also an important source of Mesolithic finds; the settlements here were located on the edges of a series of lakes which occupied the valley floor but whose basins have subsequently been silted up or filled by peat. There is also evidence of Mesolithic penetration far inland, to the shores of the Inny Lakes in Co. Westmeath, for example, and to Lough Allen and Lough Gara in Co. Sligo and Co. Leitrim, respectively (Raftery, 1944). As emphasized above, all the available evidence of Mesolithic settlements is from the northern half of Ireland. Once again we must admit the possibility of incomplete

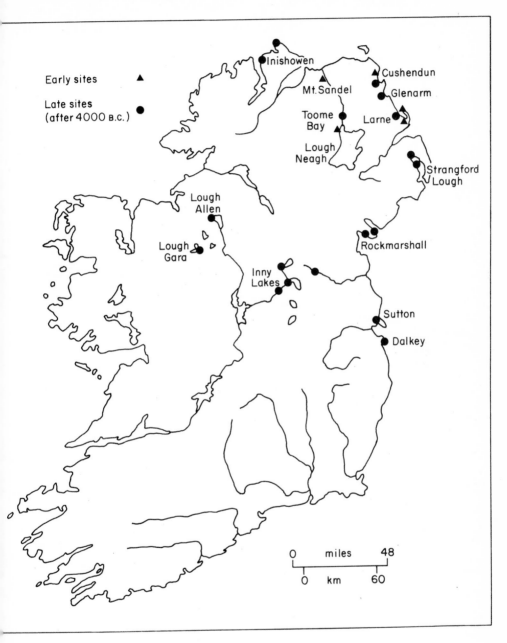

Early sites ▲

Late sites (after 4000 B.C.) ●

Inishowen

Cushendun

Mt. Sandel

Glenarm

Toome Bay

Larne

Lough Neagh

Strangford Lough

Lough Allen

Rockmarshall

Lough Gara

Inny Lakes

Sutton

Dalkey

| 0 | miles | 48 |
| 0 | km | 60 |

g. 6: Distribution of major mesolithic sites (Mitchell, 1970).

knowledge. Many inland sites may be obscured by bogs which have typically developed since Sub Atlantic times in ancient lakes and water courses, precisely the places to which Mesolithic communities would have been attracted. One positive advantage of north-eastern Ireland for Mesolithic man was the abundant flint resources of the Cretaceous chalk deposits, deposits unknown elsewhere in Ireland but in the north-east exposed intermittently between beds of Tertiary lava from Lough Neagh to Belfast Lough. There is certainly plentiful evidence of early flint working, and the attraction of flint resources, combined with the food resources of coastal and inland waters, must have made the north-eastern corner of Ireland an exceptionally favoured environment for Mesolithic man.

Ancient shell mounds and dark habitation layers occur in sandhills and other recent deposits at numerous locations along the coasts of Ireland, especially the southern and western coasts, but they appear to be distinct from the Mesolithic sites of the north-eastern parts of the country. The main constituents of the mounds are oyster, cockle and periwinkle shells, many of which have been opened and their contents clearly used as human food. The occurrence of stone hearths, charcoal and pottery fragments within the shell layers seems to exclude the possibility that the mounds were merely rubbish dumps. In many places the sites were clearly occupied, although perhaps only on a seasonal basis. On the whole, little datable evidence survives within the mounds and, owing to the absence of Late and Post Glacial raised shorelines in the southern parts of the country, the physical context of the deposits does not provide a rough chronological framework. There are, however, suggestions that in many places the mounds have accumulated within historic times and were being added to down to recent centuries. On Beginish Island, Co. Kerry (O'Kelly, 1956), there is evidence that shellfish were an important dietary item of the farming community in the Early Middle Ages and a shell mound at Carrigtohill on the shores of Cork Harbour, a locality where numerous other shell mounds have been recorded, contained early medieval pottery. The shell mound under Sunday's Well, Cork City, seems to date from the 17th and 18th Centuries A.D. (O'Kelly, 1955; Coleman, 1938). Shell mounds occur at a number of coastal sites in Connemara, Co. Galway, and may vary in date from the Iron Age to the medieval period (Kinahan, 1872–3). In Co. Donegal, several coastal localities show evidence of occupation in the form of shell mounds and habitation layers and for the most part they seem to date from the early Christian period. The habitation layers in the sandhills of Dundrum Bay, Co. Down, have yielded archaeological material ranging in date from the Neolithic to medieval times (Collins, 1952). Many of the shell mounds and habitation layers of the Irish coasts are thus not of Mesolithic origin but they are interesting in indicating that the gathering of sea food was an important and long-standing feature of peasant life in coastal areas. The gathering was probably a seasonal occupation and, in a manner reminiscent of the Mesolithic, accompanied by temporary settlements.

The Irish Mesolithic appears as the most westerly extension in Europe of a primitive pattern of life that was widely developed over the North German Plain in the Boreal and Atlantic periods. In the East Baltic the Kunda culture is representative and in Denmark the Maglemose and Ertebølle cultures. Very similar to the Irish Mesolithic is the Mesolithic culture of western Scotland generally referred to as "Obanian" after the important discoveries at Oban in Argyllshire. Shell middens are characteristic here and, as in Ireland, they cluster around the major Post Glacial shoreline. A recurrent feature of the Mesolithic culture province of northern Europe is an association of settlement with the sea shore (especially shallow and sheltered inlets) or inland lakes and rivers, all of which provided plentiful food, particularly oysters and shell fish. Exploitation of local flint resources and the production of coarse pottery are also widespread characteristics. The extension of Mesolithic culture into the British Isles was probably facilitated by the contemporary existence of a land-bridge between south-eastern England and north-western France, and, possibly, a continuous or near-continuous land link between Denmark and north-eastern England via the Dogger Bank. The likelihood is that Mesolithic man did undertake sea voyages but that his craft were very primitive, probably only skin-clad coracles similar to those which have survived in a number of localities in Britain down to recent times and to the curraghs of western Ireland and the coracles of the River Boyne. Lengthy voyages would have been impractical and the existence of land-bridges or shallow and narrow strips of water may well have been an important determinant of the direction and scale of migratory movements.

In many regions there is evidence of considerable continuity of Mesolithic culture and population elements into the Neolithic era. A merging of cultures occurs with attendant problems of definition of archaeological materials. This is well illustrated in the Danish Ertebølle culture, where the contents of the coastal kitchen-middens reveal a slow transformation of the Mesolithic culture under influences from Neolithic groups living in the country (Troels-Smith, 1953). Inevitably, problems of definition arise in the ultimate stages of the Erteb∅lle. As previously indicated, many of the Irish middens normally accorded the title of Mesolithic overlap chronologically with the onset of Neolithic influences. There seems indeed to have been considerable merging of the culture traditions, so much so that the middens have been described as para Neolithic and doubts raised as to their Mesolithic status (Herity, 1970). It cannot be contested, however, that some of the Irish midden material does substantially antedate the arrival of Neolithic influences (Mitchell, 1970, 1971). The sites at Islandmagee and Cushendun on the coasts of Co. Antrim, for example, as well as the site at Toome Bay, Co. Londonderry, are of Boreal age datable to the first half of the 6th millenium B.C. The contents of the post-Atlantic middens provide evidence of interaction and acculturation between Mesolithic and Neolithic peoples, including, for example, polished stone axes, pottery, flints of Neolithic type and, occasionally, domestic animal bones. Although much modified, it seems likely that this later culture is a direct development from the early traditions of the Boreal. In the first place some of the implements in the later middens (such as flakes, Bann flakes and scrapers) continue the technological traditions of the Boreal sites. Second, the pattern of distribution and particularly the siting of the middens exhibits consistent features over the whole chronological range. There is at all times a link with shorelines and river banks, and thus a strong contrast with the main body of Neolithic settlement evidence which is essentially inland and upland.

Most of the Irish Mesolithic material and certainly the earliest finds are confined to the north-eastern corner of Ireland suggesting that it was probably from Scotland that Mesolithic man made the first entrance into Ireland, travelling across the narrow North Channel which, in the Boreal period, was even smaller and narrower than at present. The north-east, perhaps largely owing to its valuable flint resources, seems to have long remained the focus of Mesolithic culture and the area settled was not greatly extended until around the time that Neolithic influences were spreading; the Mesolithic people then seem to have experienced some sort of population explosion and widely extended their range of settlement on sea and lake shores in the northern half of Ireland. We can only speculate on the basic reasons for this expansion but it may be that the adoption of certain Neolithic innovations invigorated the Mesolithic culture or that the complementary nature of their economies permitted useful trading links to develop between the indigenous peoples and the new farming groups, the former flourishing as specialized fishermen and hunters.

Ultimately, the Irish Mesolithic folk were absorbed into the Neolithic way of life but there could have been a long period of relatively independent existence. The different economic orientation of the two cultures and their dependence on different physical resources may have removed any basis for serious conflict, indeed, as previously suggested, mutually useful exchange of produce could well have taken place.

The Mesolithic mode of land exploitation was extensive rather than intensive, the population at any one time was doubtless small (to be numbered in hundreds rather than thousands) and much of their food was obtained along sea and lake shores. Forest plants may have been collected and forest animals hunted but, save around the encampments, there was no reason to clear away or interfere with the forest cover of the island. The stone tools of the early inhabitants were primitive but this in itself is not the reason why they did not undertake major environmental transformations. As with most hunting and collecting communities, their minor impact on the environment was the product of their basic economic stance and the limited demographic pressures existing within the community. They used existing natural resources and did not transform the prevailing ecosystem in order to achieve higher productivity. Given this passive relationship with the environment, the human impact on the natural landscape was almost certainly slight even within the limited areas that were settled and not withstanding the long period of occupancy. Recent investigations suggest that pre-Neolithic settlers in the British Isles may have interfered with the natural woodland on a greater scale than hitherto envisaged, perhaps by burning of the vegetation cover (Walker and West, 1970), but palaeobotanic evidence in Ireland, with the possible exception of the findings in north-west Mayo (Moore et al., 1975), shows no signs of significant cultural interference with the natural vegetation until the advent of Neolithic influences in the 4th millenium. Changes in the vegetation cover did occur between the Boreal and Atlantic periods but they are such as can be convincingly explained in terms of secular climatic change.

The Neolithic Period and the Spread of Farming

Few Neolithic settlement sites have been discovered or excavated in Ireland but the remains of the massive stone tombs or "megaliths" erected by early farming communities can be found in many parts of the island. About 1200 tombs have been recognized and classified (De Valera and O'Nuallain, 1961, 1964, 1971). These tombs, which are the first surviving architectural monuments in the country, have a wide distribution but are noticeably concentrated on the fringes of the major hill areas, on what is today regarded as marginal land. Megalithic distributions provide a basis for generalizations about the geographical spread of the Neolithic population and, less securely, for the size of this population; they are also a central concern in our attempts to elucidate the basic ecological adaptions of prehistoric farming communities and to assess their impact on the landscape. Palaeobotanical evidence, supported by radiocarbon measurements, provides a further important source of evidence about landscape developments in the Neolithic period, especially when considered in conjunction with the distributional evidence of the megaliths. However, owing to prevailing uncertainties about radiocarbon dating, it is not possible to ascribe dates to the palaeobotanical or to the archaeological evidence with any precision or finality. Research in dendrochronology (tree-ring dating), commenced in the 1960s, indicates that all established radiocarbon dates before about 1000 B.C. are too recent (Renfrew, 1973). The precise calibration which should be applied to the dates is not yet clear but it seems that the notional radiocarbon years must be corrected by a significant amount, amounting to some seven or eight centuries at 3000 B.C., in order to convert them into true dates in calendar years. The convention generally adopted is to use "b.c." for uncalibrated radiocarbon dates and B.C. for dates expressed in calendar years after calibration. Tree-ring calibration thus has the effect of significantly "stretching" the duration of the Neolithic period, but it is advisable at this stage to avoid undue emphasis or reliance on individual dates and to proceed with an approximate and provisional chronology, remembering that future developments in radiocarbon age determination may lead to yet further adjustments in prehistoric dating.

Making reasonable allowance for the tree-ring calibration of radiocarbon dates it would appear that the first attacks by farmers on the woodlands took place in the first half of the 4th millenium and some sporadic attacks perhaps slightly before 4000 B.C. Thus, at Ballynagilly, Co. Tyrone, where an early Neolithic house and evidence of the burning of natural vegetation have been excavated (ApSimon, 1969), the land clearance appears around 3200 b.c., implying a calibrated date of c. 4000 B.C., and the clearance horizon in Fallahogy bog, Co. Londonderry (Smith and Willis, 1961/62) would also seem to belong to this early period. Indeed, clearance horizons of a broadly similar date (falling within the date brackets 3400–3000 b.c.) have been identified in a number of Irish bog deposits, mainly located in the area north of the central plain. It seems likely therefore that burning of natural vegetation and ensuing cultivation was occurring on a considerable scale and by the middle of the fourth millenium Neolithic farming must have been making a real impact on the environment.

Relatively few of the Irish megalithic tombs have been accurately dated but the available radiocarbon evidence points to origins mainly in the late 4th and the 3rd millenium. The first Neolithic land clearances thus appear to antedate considerably the widespread building of megaliths. It is difficult, however, in the present state of knowledge to establish whether the first farmers were culturally distinct from the megalith builders or whether there was a continuity of farming population but with a long pioneering phase before a relatively stable pattern of settlement was achieved and conditions became conducive to large-scale ritual expression. Some recent research indeed hints that the earliest Neolithic settlers in the British Isles may have built timber mortuary monuments with inconspicuous overlying mounds which were the ephemeral precursors of the durable stone tombs. The stone tombs are envisaged as developments from timber prototypes originating ultimately in central Europe. A transformation from timber to stone occurred after the burial customs had been adopted by the communities in the islands and stony uplands along the Atlantic edge of Europe (Powell, 1969). But the existence of distinct megalithic building styles in Ireland with, to a significant degree, complementary geographical distributions, could be taken to imply the existence of diverse immigrant streams possessing, on arrival, their own well developed megalithic traditions, and, if that is the case, it suggests a separate origin for any pre-megalithic farmers who may have existed. The early land clearances and the megaliths are located in similar environments on the lighter soils and hill slopes and if the megalith builders were secondary migrants then the districts which they colonized may have been pioneered and already partially cleared of their original forest cover by the earlier settlers.

The impressive scale of the megalithic tombs has facilitated the study of their geographical distribution, while the durability of the structures provides us with an assurance that the present pattern is a good indication of the original distribution. It is true that during the historic periods the bulk of the Irish population has been settled on the lowlands but it is unlikely that land clearance and farming activities there have led to the destruction of many megalithic tombs. As will be demonstrated below, our understanding of the nature of Neolithic society and its environmental requirements makes it seem unlikely that the lowland areas were settled to any great extent, and the general colonization of the lowlands was probably not started until the Bronze Age and not completed until the Iron Age. If the distribution of tombs was ever wider than the surviving pattern, then we have to envisage a remarkably thorough-going process of destruction involving, moreover, a series of very durable structures. This seems unlikely in Ireland. The survival of a wealth of field monuments is one of the most striking features of the Irish landscape and where a major category of monument is absent over an extensive region it is highly probable that it never‘ existed there. There are thus good reasons to maintain that the present essentially upland concentration of megalithic tombs is the original and total distribution, and not simply the mutilated edge of a once more extensive distribution pattern.

How far the megaliths can be used as a reliable guide to the distribution of population and settlement is of crucial importance to the student of prehistoric geography. It is indeed highly probable that the tombs were located close to the builders' settlements, even although few of the latter have as yet been discovered. However, this spatial association of tomb and settlement is often too readily assumed, and the validity of the evidence supporting such an association needs to be carefully examined. In the first place, the tombs are concentrated in areas which, from a variety of standpoints, but particularly in terms of soil and drainage characteristics, were probably well suited to the needs of early farmers. Light, free-draining soils were available on the hill slopes and the natural forest vegetation there was probably thinner and less continuous. Clearing the vegetation cover for crop growth was thus not too laborious, given the limited range of tools available, and elaborate drainage of the soil was not required. Moreover, the open scrub and heaths of the windy summit areas above the zone of settlement may have been the only places where open grazing for livestock was available at the time. The megaliths, in short, are associated with the areas likely to have provided suitable agricultural resources for the Neolithic population and it is of course improbable that the dwelling places of an agricultural people would have been separated from the land which they worked.

This general argument is persuasive but it needs to be supplemented by evidence of actual habitation sites. The number of excavated Neolithic houses in Ireland, as indeed throughout Britain, remains small. However, the evidence from them does point to a close geographical association of tombs and habitations. There are, first, excavated houses which, while they are not intimately connected with a megalith, do lie at the same altitude and possess a similar site ecology. Second, there are a few house sites which abut on or even underlie megalithic tombs.

The most substantial body of evidence relating to prehistoric settlement and houses was provided by the famous excavations on Knockadoon Peninsula in Lough Gur, about 12 miles (19·7 km) south of Limerick city (Ó Ríordáin, 1954). Indeed, this excavation, conducted mainly in the 1930s and 40s, was the first in Ireland to reveal domestic structures of Neolithic and Bronze Age date, and there have in fact been no subsequent major additions to our knowledge. Houses with rectangular and round or curvilinear plans occurred, probably the homes of small farmers. The basic physical features of the district are a group of bare and irregular limestone hills with a sporadic cover of thin, light soil, contrasting strongly with the heavy wet soils of the surrounding Limerick plain. The suitability of the area for early farmers is attested by the rich accumulation of field antiquities dating from the early Neolithic to the Bronze Age and including stone circles, megaliths, barrows, crude lynchets and other sites. In this district then there is an association of megaliths and house sites within a defined area of settlement. The early Neolithic house excavated at Ballynagilly, Co. Tyrone lies at the same general elevation (approximately 650 ft) as the nearest megaliths and is typically sited on a low hill of glacial sand and gravel. One striking illustration of the close relation of tomb and settlement occurs at Ballyglass, Co. Mayo where a rectangular timber house was excavated (Ó Nualláin, 1972) underneath the western end of a court-tomb—indeed the house may have been intentionally demolished to make way for the construction of the tomb. Excavations at Townley Hall, Co. Louth (Eogan, 1963), have shown that a passage tomb was constructed on top of a Neolithic habitation site. Habitation refuse has indeed been found under a number of excavated tombs in various parts of Ireland.

There is general acceptance of the view that the major features of the Neolithic culture in Ireland were introduced by successive bands of immigrants from a variety of outside sources. Regional variations in megalithic tomb styles in particular suggest the existence of numerous cultural strains among the early farming populations. Classifications based on megalithic architecture correspond broadly with differences in the assemblages of grave-goods associated with each architectural type, thus supporting the inference that megalithic building styles are a reliable indicator of basic cultural variations. The distributions of the various megalithic styles overlap considerably but there is also an unmistakable tendency for certain styles to concentrate in particular regions (Fig. 7).

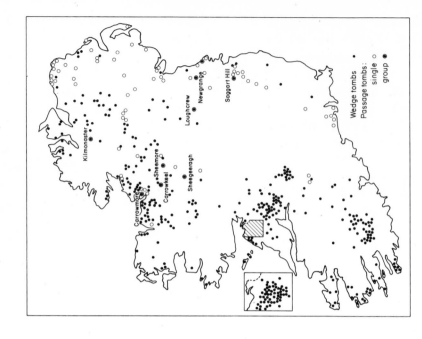

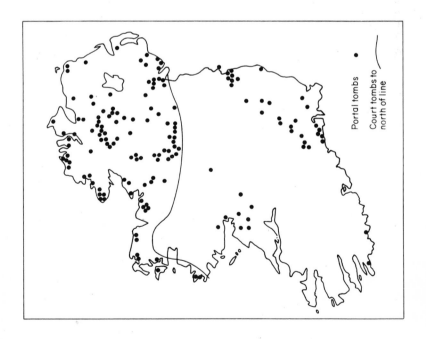

Fig. 7: Distribution of megalithic tombs. (Based on De Valera, Ó Nualláin, Herity.)

The recurrent feature of the tombs is the provision of a burial chamber constructed with enormous undressed stones (Plate 5). This feature is often covered by a large artificial earthen mound or barrow but many of the Irish stone chambers are free-standing. The absence of barrows may have resulted from natural denudation of the mound materials but it may also reflect either a national practice of building without barrows or simply that many tombs were never completed. It is most probable that the tombs were dynastic burial places, the foci of ritual activity over long periods of time, and at some sites there is evidence that the structures were remodelled to meet changing needs. The builders appear to have had some astronomical interests and abilities. At Newgrange passage tomb, for example, on the morning of the winter solstice the sun's rays shine through a specially contrived slit in the roof along a passage 19 m in length to illuminate the central burial chamber (Patrick, 1974). It is not yet clear how far astronomical considerations as distinct from ecological considerations may have influenced the pattern of megalith distribution. Perhaps the most that can presently be claimed is that astronomical criteria may have influenced the detailed siting and the orientation of monuments but that the general situation was selected on ecological grounds. Other forms of megalithic monuments include single standing stones (which are commonly called gallauns in southern Ireland) and grouped stones, usually in linear or circular (henge) arrangements, which are believed to have had sacred functions (Plate 5). One variety of stone circle, the recumbent-stone circle, was astronomically orientated and seemingly used to determine the time of equinoxes and solstices. The standing stones are usually in proximity to tombs but are much less widespread. Most of the henge monuments, for example, are found in the south-western peninsulas of Ireland, on the bog-covered spurs of the Sperrin Mountains in Co. Tyrone and in the borderlands of Co. Wicklow and Co. Kildare. It is uncertain too how many of the standing stones or stone circles are of Neolithic, Bronze Age or even Iron Age provenance. Some of the single stones may have been erected as late as the Christian period.

The Irish megalithic tombs fall into four classes, distinguished by tomb morphology and the shape of the barrow (De Valera, 1961). Relatively few tombs are intermediate in type and the various classes can be readily distinguished on the ground usually without excavation. Moreover, the main outlines of the geographical distribution of each type have been reliably established.

The first and the best studied category are the court tombs. These tombs consist of an orthostatically defined court or courts giving access to

c

Plate 5: Megaliths. **a** Wedge tomb, on the Burren, Co. Clare. **b** Court tomb (the "Broad stone"), Co. Antrim. **c** Stone circle, Drombeg, Co. Cork.

long, segmented burial chambers normally roofed by corbelling. Overlying the tomb are long, usually trapezoidal, cairns or barrows. Over 300 court tombs have been identified, with the overwhelming majority located in Ulster. The northern portion of Ireland, beyond the barrier of the ill-drained drumlin belt, thus seems to have been culturally distinctive even at this early stage and it is an identity which has frequently asserted itself throughout history.

Megalithic structures similar to court tombs exist in south-western Scotland, the Isle of Man, the Yorkshire wolds, the Cotswolds and South Wales, while some authorities stress the affinity of the court tombs with structures in Brittany and the Loire Estuary. However, the question of external relationship remains a point of debate. Court tombs concentrate markedly on light upland soils, on the fringes of the major mountain areas near the upper limits of present-day cultivation or, in smaller numbers, on isolated hills and eminences within the lowland areas. They do not occupy truly mountain sites. The 1000 ft (305 m) contour is a clear upper limit but there is no lower limiting contour. A preponderance of sites lies between 400 and 800 ft (120 and 240 m) but they are frequent right down to sea-level wherever well-drained soils occur, such as on the low drift-free coastlands of north Antrim or Lecale (east Down). However, study of Neolithic colonization in north-eastern Ireland (Watson, 1956) indicates that areas of light, well-drained soils away from mountain masses failed to attract their fair share of settlement and the mountain areas may well have had some special attraction. Possibly this was the open upland grazings for cattle and sheep or perhaps simply a cultural preference for living with the security and vistas of the hills. Court tombs are conspicuously few in the central lowland of north-eastern Ireland, the Lough Neagh Basin. Most of the scattered sites there seem to be located in proximity to flint supplies or related to isolated tracts of driftless land which formed ancient routeways across the ill-drained river basins.

Conspicuous concentrations of elaborate court tombs occur west of the Erne on the west coast of Ireland between Mayo and Sligo, particularly around shallow sheltered bays such as Bunatrahir and Ballysad. De Valera (1960) has argued that these western concentrations of tombs reflect the history of Neolithic migration and settlement. He envisages a colonization movement of court tomb builders from overseas, probably France, using the Atlantic seaway. The shallow north-western bays were the first major points of access for migrants travelling northwards along the mountainous and sometimes cliffbound coast of western Ireland; they became primary foci of entry for the new culture and the tombs show a tendency to muster at the north-western entrance points. From there, it is argued, the tomb building traditions spread towards the east, along recognizable channels determined by geographical factors and particularly by the distribution of uplands, and ultimately were diffused to Scotland and even to Wales. However, other origins have been urged for the court-tomb builders. Some investigators have seen the court tombs as part of a thallasic Neolithic culture province—the Clyde–Carlingford culture—which had the Irish Sea and particularly the Northern Channel as its cultural focus (Evans, 1953). One recent commentator (Case, 1969) suggests, on the evidence of similarities in pottery and tomb-building traditions, that the court-tomb builders are more likely to have come from or through the Yorkshire wolds than from elsewhere in the British Isles or the continent of Europe. At present, however, there is simply insufficient evidence to establish the place of origin or the mode of entry (Collins, 1973).

The most impressive category of megalithic tombs are the passage tombs. In these structures the burial chambers are approached by passages and the whole monument is covered by a substantial circular cairn defined by large kerb stones. There are over 300 examples in Ireland and most of them, unlike the other megalithic tombs, are found grouped together in cemeteries and regularly sited on hilltops or other prominent places. The sites are widely dispersed over the northern half of the Central Lowlands and noticeably absent in the south of the country. The main centre of gravity of distribution is east and central Ireland, a region which contains the great passage tombs at Dowth, Knowth and New Grange in the Boyne Valley in Co. Meath, and the passage-tomb cemetery on the Loughcrew hills, Co. Meath, which alone contains 30 cairns (Eogan, 1968; Evans, 1953; O'Kelly, 1967). Further impressive examples of passage tombs are found at Carrowmore and Carrowkeel in Co. Sligo and on the summits of the Dublin mountains. Within the cemeteries variations in tomb size suggest the existence of different social rank groups but the nature of these groups is impossible to determine and it is dangerous to project historically known groups back into the remote periods of prehistory.

The larger Irish passage tombs are among the most splendid and awe-inspiring of the monuments of prehistory in western Europe. Erected first in the Neolithic, they continued to be used and perhaps even built in the succeeding Bronze Age. The technical mastery exhibited in their construction, the artistic decoration on their stones and the very scale of the structures point unmistakably to the existence of complex and prosperous communities which could have been supported only if considerable areas of land had been cleared of forest and occupied for agriculture. The hilltop sites where the passage tombs are found were probably selected for their suitability as prestige burial grounds and may not be sensitive indicators of the location of settlements. It is odd, however, that no settlements associated with the populations who built the tombs have as yet been found.

The strong association of these great tombs with the east coast lowlands may well be significant. This is the driest part of Ireland and although generally low-lying it possesses relatively well-drained soils. It is the area where enterprising elements among the early farming community, anxious to move from the easily worked but relatively unproductive soils of the hill margins, may well have made their first inroads on to the potentially more productive lowland soils. Herity (1974) has argued that the builders of the Boyne tombs were skilled and dynamic settlers from the Gulf of Morbihan district in Brittany who settled in the Boyne Valley around 2500 B.C. and later penetrated to other parts of Ireland. This is an interesting and rather persuasive speculation but, once again, it is hard to know with certainty whether the great tombs are evidence of the arrival of a significant number of immigrants or simply of cultural borrowings by an already established Neolithic population. Materials from the Newgrange passage tomb have yielded uncalibrated radiocarbon dates of around 2500 B.C. (O'Kelly, 1972), indicating that the monument may have been built during the last two centuries of the 4th millenium. Pollen study of the turves which are incorporated in the barrow overlying the tomb has revealed the presence of wheat pollen (triticum). The turf in which the pollen occurred had been stripped from a field formerly tilled but which had reverted to a scrub condition. It seems therefore that cereals were being cultivated in the Boyne Valley at or before the time when Newgrange was being built and this implies colonization and farming of the eastern lowlands well within the Neolithic period. Such progress probably had to await a certain level of technological achievement, the formation of well-organized, hierarchical societies and the growth of a considerable population from which an adequate labour force could be drawn for the onerous task of forest clearance and land drainage. Once the lowlands were colonized their economic productivity would of course have reinforced the superior·economic and social status of the settlers. The fertile lowlands of north Leinster have often in Irish history emerged as an important focus of settlement and advanced culture, and their prominence seems to have been asserted at a relatively early stage in the Neolithic period. Perhaps the settlement pattern laid down by the first colonists was an enduring one and their domestic structures have not readily come to light because they are buried beneath the later settlements in the area.

Portal tombs typically consist of a simple chamber with an imposing entry formed of two tall portal stones and covered normally by an enormous capstone sloping down to the rear of the chamber. The general distribution of the court tombs and the portal tombs shows considerable overlap and both are associated with long barrows, but the portal tombs are located further towards the plains pointing to a greater penetration of woodland than is suggested by the typical elevation of the court tombs (De Valera, 1960). De Valera has proposed that the portal tombs are a derivation from the court tombs and some relationship is certainly suggested by the morphology and distribution of the tombs as well as the finds from them. However, the problem of origins remains largely unresolved and firm conclusions must await a great deal more evidence (Herity, 1964). The portal tombs extend far outside the court tomb province with important clusters occurring on the northern and western slopes of the Wicklow Mountains and in the hinterland of Waterford. They are, however, noticeably absent from western Ireland. Numerous examples are found around the eastern shores of the Irish Sea especially in Wales and Cornwall. The portal tomb is indeed the principal tomb-building tradition around the coastlands of North Wales where it seems also to be the earliest definable type of megalithic tomb (Lynch, 1969). Powell (1969) has suggested that the portal tombs are versions in stone of older timber prototypes, "sepulchral fossils of now invisible prototypes and related to, but of more archaic heritage than the 'long tumulus' complex".

Wedge tombs form the fourth major class of megalithic tomb. The "wedges" consist of a single main chamber with walls and ceiling formed of stone slabs. The chamber is basically rectangular in plan but narrowed at one end to produce a characteristic wedge shape. Almost 400 sites have been recorded. Their distribution is predominantly south-western. The wedge tombs are not only the most numerous category of megalithic tomb, they also exhibit a higher degree of territorial exclusiveness. To some extent the wedges overlap the court tomb province in the north but the grave-goods do not suggest any significant fusion of the cultures. Indeed the wedge tombs may have been built at a later period: they seem to be contemporary with the Bronze Age cist graves which, being confined mainly to the north and east of the country, exhibit a roughly complementary distribution (Fig. 8). The concentration of the wedge tombs in the relatively flint-poor south of Ireland suggests that many of them may have been built by metal-dependent communities. Bronze implements are found in the tombs and there is a particularly interesting pattern of wedge tomb distribution in the south-western peninsulas of Co. Kerry and in West Cork where the wedges occur in marked concentrations near copper deposits. The clusters of tombs at Allihes in the Caha Peninsula north of Bantry Bay, Co. Cork, are noteworthy examples of this tendency. It may well be that the wedge builders were one of the first groups to practise metal working in Ireland. It is highly likely too that the farming economy of the wedge builders was more dependent on cattle and grazing than that of the court-tomb builders. The wedges are noticeably concentrated on light well-drained soils and avoid the drift cover.

Impressive concentrations of tombs occur in north-west Clare on the high karstic plateaux of the Burren district (De Valera, 1961). The forbidding appearance of the Burren and the evident attraction of these bare areas for early farmers has led to the suggestion that the limestone plateaux may earlier have possessed a more extensive cover of drift which has been progressively denuded in Post Glacial times. Although palaeobotanical data are scarce the picture of the vegetation cover is that, at least up to the Boreal and Atlantic periods, there was a more or less complete cover of pine with subsidiary hazel and yew (Watts, 1963). It may thus well have been human interference which led to removal of the tree cover, ensuing soil erosion and the ultimate exposure of the bare limestone. But it is not necessary to invoke a more extensive cover of vegetation and soil in order to explain the remarkable concentration of prehistoric monuments. Despite their superficially forbidding appearance, the large expanses of bare limestone pavements are in fact valuable grazing areas and could have provided an attractive habitat for farmers dependent mainly on their livestock. Vegetation flourishes in the sheltered micro-climates existing in the multitudes of grykes and other forms of solution hollow, and some basis for livestock grazing is thereby provided throughout the year. Prehistoric settlers must have valued the stony tracts in much the same way as present-day cattle farmers. It is significant, for example, that the tombs invariably avoid the existing pockets of drift scattered over the limestone surface. A plentiful supply of tabular limestone slabs is available from the disintegrating pavements and provides a ready source of building materials. The slabs are often inserted upright into the narrow deep grykes to form solid if rudimentary fences. This mode of forming enclosures is still practised and may indeed always have been necessary for efficient cattle keeping in this irregular terrain. The slabs have also been used ingeniously and aesthetically to form the walls and roofs of the numerous, wedge-shaped tombs.

3
The Bronze Age

The Bronze Age in Ireland, which stretches throughout the second millenium and the greater part of the first millenium B.C., was clearly a period of considerable technological advance. There is plentiful evidence for the development of vigorous traditions of working in bronze and gold, traditions which flourished despite the absence of rich indigenous metal resources. Tin, for example, was imported, and considerable quantities of gold used during the period may not have been of native origin (Raftery, 1971; Harbison, 1971). The use and production of metal goods spread throughout the country and in the Middle and Late Bronze Ages metal craftsmen attained a conspicuously high level of technical and artistic achievement (Eogan 1962, 1964; Harbison, 1969). However, there is a serious lack of knowledge about basic economic and social organization during the Bronze Age period. Surprisingly little can be ascertained about population distribution, settlement patterns, building styles and domestic arrangements, or, save by implication, about basic economic activities. Moreover, there are few useful radiocarbon dates with which to establish a clear internal chronology. Understanding of the ecological system in the Neolithic and in the 1st millenium A.D. is significantly better. The megalithic tombs provide evidence of population distribution in the Neolithic, and from the Iron Age and Early Christian period there is an abundant legacy of easily recognized settlement sites. A broad comparison of conditions in the Neolithic and Iron Age shows that Irish society and its relationship to the environment had undergone fundamental changes inevitably accompanied by important developments in the cultural landscape. Ireland in the 1st millenium A.D. is a more populous place and the major concentration of settlement has shifted from upland areas to the lowlands, implying that the thick forests which covered lowland areas had been breached and cleared. But efforts to understand how this crucial transition occurred are seriously hindered by imperfect knowledge of the intervening Bronze Age.

The chronological subdivisions of the Bronze Age (Early, Middle and Late) have been based on stylistic changes in bronze and other metal work and in ceramics, along with evidence of change in burial customs. It is uncertain how far these changes are related to more fundamental economic and social developments in, for example, settlement patterns, house styles and features connected with agriculture. Pottery and bronzes are artifacts of potentially swift stylistic change and their study may not permit recognition of more deep-seated economic and social developments. Burial traditions are admittedly of more import as they reflect fundamental cultural attitudes; sharp changes, such as that from communal burial practices to single burials, very probably imply the arrival of culturally distinctive immigrant groups. Minor changes of style, for instance within the single-burial tradition, are harder to interpret and may reflect shifts in religious outlook among the existing population rather than the arrival of new communities.

The first introduction of bronze working is usually attributed to immigrant groups known as "beaker people" from their distinctive beaker-like pots (Case, 1966). Although occasionally using the megalithic tombs, the beaker people did not practise communal burial and their descendants buried their dead singly accompanied by pottery food vessels in shallow cist graves. Probably immigrants from Britain, the beaker peoples are evident in the north and east of Ireland around the end of the 3rd millenium and from this time the Bronze Age in Ireland is customarily dated (Harbison, 1973). It is likely, however, that the beaker folk supplemented rather than supplanted the existing populations of the country. Knowledge of metallurgy was soon adopted by the indigenous communities and the continuation of megalithic burial practices thereafter suggests that the innovation did not bring about an abrupt break in traditions and patterns of life. Food vessels and bronze artifacts found in megalithic tombs show that the tombs continued to be used and probably built in the Bronze Age. The farms excavated at Lough Gur in Munster suggest that farmers and herdsmen dwelt in the locality from the Neolithic to the Bronze Age period and there is no evidence of any sudden economic or cultural changes during this long period. Moreover, knowledge of metallurgy may have reached Ireland in different ways and from a variety of sources. It is likely, for example, that the entry of the beaker people was roughly contemporary with that of the wedge-tomb builders into south-western Ireland and these people also used bronze implements; indeed, to judge from the proximity of their megaliths to copper deposits, they may well have been bronze producers. The complementary geographical distribution of cist graves and wedge-shaped megalithic tombs is particularly noticeable in the south of the country, suggesting their association with contemporary but distinctive cultures. The building of the wedge tombs in the Early Bronze Age is a further important reminder that megalithic burial customs were not confined to the Neolithic period. But as the Bronze Age period proceeded, the old megalithic burial traditions must have gradually lost their appeal and there is evidence that Bronze Age cist burials were sometimes inserted into pre-existing megalithic barrows and cairns. However, the megalithic cults left an important legacy of lore and superstition connected with the tombs and the standing stones. The incising of crosses on old standing stones, for example, suggests that they retained some religious or superstitious potency as late as the Christian era. Indeed, certain superstitions associated with megaliths have lingered on to the present day.

Single burial in cists or pits was the most general Bronze Age burial custom. In the early Bronze Age a new form of single burial in cinerary urns appeared, probably diffused from northern Britain, which eventually superseded the food vessel style where single cremations were placed in cists and accompanied by an ornamented bowl. This change in burial customs might again indicate the arrival of new immigrants, but perhaps it is not conclusive evidence and the new rites may result simply from changes of religious outlook among the existing inhabitants.

Because of the paucity of known settlement sites, the pattern of population distribution in the Bronze Ages can only be tentatively deduced, mainly from the distribution of graves and, to a lesser extent, metal finds. Pollen records also help to gauge the population situation but contribute more directly to an understanding of the pattern of contemporary farming and hence of the appearance of the landscape in general. Burial sites, where they occur in considerable numbers, are an indication of the presence of population and a complete map of burial sites over an extensive area will be suggestive of gross regional patterns of population distribution. However, the known burials must be representative of the total original pattern, and not a geographically biased sample whose distribution has been governed by accidental discoveries made, for example, in the course of quarrying, building or agricultural activities. This pre-condition is reasonably met in the case of the megalithic tombs in the Neolithic period but does not apply so readily to the Bronze Age when, in the first place, megaliths are simply one component of the total range of burial types with importance only in the earlier phases and, second, the distribution of the remainder of burial places is, for a variety of reasons, imperfectly understood.

The single burials which chiefly characterize the Bronze Age were either isolated or in cemeteries. Some were made in earthen tumuli or in stone cairns which were frequently sited on hill tops and still form conspicuous landmarks in many parts of the country. Probably the majority of burials, however, were in the flat earth and, save in a few cases where they are marked by pillar stones, no surface manifestations occur. Lacking clear surface indications of the distribution of burials we are, to some degree, dependent upon chance finds and the pattern of recorded sites may be misleading as a key to the full distribution. There is, for example, a tendency for known Bronze Age burials to concentrate in areas where glacial sands and gravels are abundant, especially in kame and esker formations (Weddell, 1970). This pattern of finds might simply reflect the distribution of commercial sand and gravel quarrying and thus be of limited value in attempting to understand the basic settlement ecology of the period. An element of fortuity cannot be discounted, but it is nevertheless probable that the distribution is indicative of real settlement patterns. The drier sand and gravel belts perhaps served first as routeways helping to link up the separate "islands" of Neolithic population established on the flanks of the main hill masses. Later, they seem to have provided one of the first major footholds for permanent settlement in the generally damp and forested lowland areas. The clustering of Bronze Age sites on the lowlands of Kildare and Carlow is associated with the diffuse belt of kame deposits and deltaic sands and gravels which marks the extremity of the Midlandian ice sheet along the western flanks of the Leinster mountain chain. Other areas where Bronze Age tombs are noticeably concentrated are the kame and esker belt of Co. Westmeath and the extensive kame deposits of Co. Tyrone and the Foyle Valley in northern Ireland. A concentration of tombs in the lowlands of eastern Galway is also noticeable. In this area the underlying limestones are covered only by a thin and discontinuous mantle of glacial drift and outwash materials, and soil management and drainage problems would not therefore have posed a serious obstacle to Bronze Age farming (Fig. 8).

Finds of Bronze Age tools and ornaments, often occurring in hoards, have a widespread distribution in Ireland (Eogan, 1969) but the discoveries are accidental and the pattern of them unlikely to be of great significance. The majority have been found in the Midlands and East Leinster, although Northern Ireland is also well furnished with finds, with Co. Antrim and northern Co. Down emerging as a major focus. Relatively few finds are known from Munster, yet, paradoxically, this is the region which possessed the major copper resources. In general, no clear-cut regional patterns emerge either in the frequency or the character of

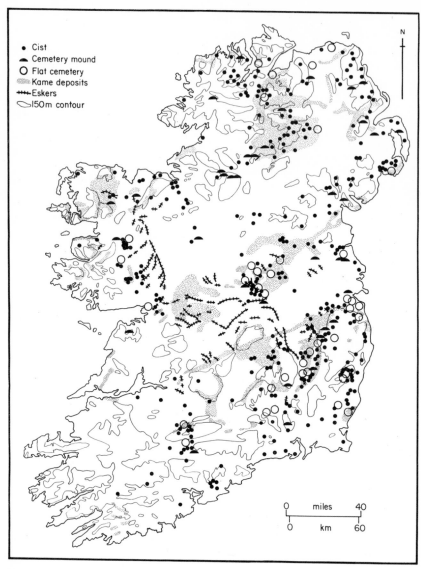

Fig. 8: Bronze Age burials (Weddell, 1970) in relation to relief and esker and kame deposits.

bronze finds. It seems that metal craft was practised widely throughout the country and for the most part national rather than regional styles prevailed.

Ceramic materials, obtained mainly from graves, suggest a rich diversity of traditions. How far these traditions represent distinct intrusive communities is difficult to determine. The ceramic forms, at least in northern Ireland where the distribution of early Bronze Age material has been mapped (ApSimon, 1969), exhibit a complex geographical distribution which could be interpreted as a mosaic of distinct communities or, perhaps more realistically, simply as a basically homogenous culture utilizing in different places and times a wide range of pottery from a variety of external sources. Given the highly developed metal industries and the evidence of extensive trade contacts, it is only reasonable to anticipate a rich miscellany of domestic and ritual artifacts in the country. Pottery in these circumstances seems unsatisfactory as an indicator of regional cultural divisions. The existence of such divisions must be established at a more fundamental level.

Although firm economic and social data are few, there can be no doubt that farming remained the fundamental basis of livelihood during the Bronze Age. It is evident that cattle played a central part in the farm economy but pig breeding seems to have increased in importance relative to the Neolithic period, and it is possible that the domestic horse was introduced into Ireland by Beaker immigrants (Wijngaarden-Bakker, 1974). Livestock raising was accompanied by some cereal production. Oats, more tolerant of humid conditions than other cereals, became established as a major crop at this period and there is also evidence of wheat, rye and barley growing. In the Bronze Age and in the succeeding Iron Age, aristocratic groups may have followed the footloose existence characteristic of warrior herdsmen but the great bulk of society was probably dependent upon mixed farming. The organization of agriculture and the associated settlement system may well have undergone important change but attempts to reconstruct the pattern of change are, inevitably, to a large degree speculative. What is proposed here is that shifting cultivation with impermanent settlements occurred in a mainly forested environment during the Neolithic period, although shifting cultivation may not have been universal. This system of agricultural organization, probably similar to contemporary swidden cultivation in tropical areas, seems to have been widespread among the pioneer agricultural communities of the European temperate forest belt. Crops were planted in clearances made in the woodlands by burning and felling; when the local soil fertility was exhausted the clearances were abandoned and the natural vegetation re-asserted itself. It is proposed that subsequent to the Neolithic there was in Ireland a gradual transition, occupying essentially the Bronze Age, towards a rural economy in the Iron Age which was centred on livestock and supplemented by crop growth, with extensive open grazing areas established in forest clearances, relatively permanent settlements and some fixed fields. It is wise, however, to stress the problems of generalizing about the Bronze Age as a whole. The economic organization of different social groups perhaps differed, regional contrasts must have existed then as now, and the period seems to have been one of numerous cultural vicissitudes.

The declining proportion of tree pollen in the deposits of the Bronze Age is evidence that the process of forest clearance was continued and there seems to have been an expansion of farmed land with sporadic incursions into the ill-drained and previously forested lowlands. As clearance for cultivation purposes continued and grazing pressures increased, the forest began to disappear from the landscape and the pollen record shows a compensating increase of grass and herb pollen. Around the clearings in the high forest, many of the shrubs and bushes which are characteristic of the present-day rural scene, such as hawthorn, gorse and broom, were able to flourish and spread.

Palaeobotanic evidence clearly points to an expansion of farmed land and reduction of the forest cover but it indicates too a complex pattern of vegetation in this period and the succeeding Iron Age; the area of farmed land expands and contracts considerably through time, and at any one time areas of virgin forest are mixed with areas of tillage and of secondary forest in various stages of regeneration (Mitchell, 1954–6; 1965). The general situation is typified by the Early Bronze Age settlement site at "the Corbie", Ballynagilly, Co. Tyrone (one of the few Bronze Age habitation sites to have received large-scale excavation) where pollen analysis in the surrounding bog clearly indicates a complicated sequence of forest clearance. Several phases of agricultural activity and forest regeneration seem to have occurred here but with a long term tendency to progressive deforestation (ApSimon, 1969). All of this is certainly highly consistent with the existence of shifting agriculture even if it does not conclusively demonstrate its existence.

Broad trends are evident from the pollen record, such as the gradual removal of the original forest cover, phases of farming settlement and, sometimes, the temporary restoration of the woodland cover, but it does not seem that we can identify with any certainty the detailed workings of the farming economy or greatly illuminate the relationships between agrarian organization and settlement patterns. At Beaghmore in Co. Tyrone, for example, a palaeoecological study (Pilcher, 1969) suggests a cyclic system of shifting agriculture with lengthy cycles of use and fallow. The sequence is dated to the end of the 4th millenium and implies a period with phases of cereal agriculture and grazing lasting some 200 years followed by a grazing phase of similar length and, ultimately, a phase of forest regeneration lasting around 50 years. Were these lengthy phases of farming associated with extensive continuously farmed clearances or is it rather the sum of a succession of small short-term clearings which is recorded in the pollen diagram? This problem of interpretation arises at Beaghmore and with the pollen record from other sites, and in the present state of knowledge it is impossible to prove the issue decisively one way or the other. Conditions in prehistoric Ireland may have been unusual: the presence of numerous livestock and a mild moist environment may have made possible the prolonged use of extensive areas of land, and a migratory pattern characterized by a long-term ''drift'' of the farming communities from one part of the country to another could well have emerged rather than a highly mobile system where small patches were used for only a few years. Moreover, some of the archaeological evidence also suggests significant continuity and stability of settlement. The existence of the megaliths and other substantial burial monuments in the Neolithic and Early Bronze Age, for example, as well as the clear evidence of technological advances during the Bronze Ages and the implied existence of specialized craftsmen and traders, are all consonant with well established communities living in relatively permanent settlements and providing a surplus of food over and above the needs of the farmers themselves. It must be noted, however, that surprisingly little archaeological evidence of settlements has as yet come to light.

Settlement studies in many parts of the world have shown that a functional relationship exists between farming systems and the pattern and permanence of settlements (Allan, 1972; Harris, 1972), but it is a loose relationship and consequently hard to propose reasonable generalizations let alone rigid rules. Thus, even if plentiful evidence about settlements in the Neolithic and Bronze Ages were available to us, it would still be difficult to make inferences from it about agricultural organization. Studies of agricultural systems in many different parts of the world suggest that the simplest forms of shifting agriculture, the swidden systems, which today survive mainly in tropical areas, are typically associated with long fallowing and temporary village settlements. More advanced and more productive patterns of shifting agriculture can however develop, often under the pressure of growing population, which are characterized by short periods of fallow and permit semi-permanent or near-permanent settlements. The most productive forms of shifting agriculture can support substantial village settlements which are virtually permanent. A sedentary pattern of farming, within a framework of fixed farms and defined cultivation areas, represents the most advanced stage of agrarian development, and is typical of peasant communities living within centrally organized states and usually within reach of cities and towns (Wolf, 1966). Cognizance of this broad sequence of development in agricultural systems and its relationship to settlement patterns is helpful in the interpretation of Irish archaeological evidence but, clearly, caution is needed in making comparisons between contemporary and prehistoric situations or between areas where the basic environmental conditions in which farmers operate differ enormously.

The great dynastic stone tombs of the Neolithic period in Ireland seem to suggest considerable stability of settlement at a very early stage but evidence of actual Neolithic habitations is limited. The famous excavations on the peninsula of Knockadoon on Lough Gur, Co. Limerick, which provide the best evidence of early settlement conditions, show that the locality was occupied from the Neolithic to the Middle Bronze Age. There may, however, have been short-term cycles of use. Some of the individual houses were occupied only for short periods and, while on the other habitation sites there was no clear indication of interruption of settlement, it is hard to state positively that no breaks occurred. Moreover, considerable stability of settlement sites is not inconsistent with some form of shifting agriculture, and pollen analysis of the lacustrine deposits in Lough Gur, close to Knockadoon, has indeed provided evidence of phases of farming settlement followed by periods when trees invaded the former open areas (Mitchell, 1959). Some fixed fields seem to have existed in Ireland during the Neolithic and the Bronze Age and their stone boundaries have been identified under peat bogs at about 30 locations in the north and west of the country and partially excavated in a number of places (Herity, 1971; Caulfield, 1974). It is not yet clear whether these fields were integral to a widespread system of sedentary farming, but such seems to be unlikely in view of the growing body of palaeobotanic evidence from many parts of the country which shows a complex sequence of expansion and contraction of the farmed areas and hence points to the existence of shifting agriculture. It seems most likely that the early enclosed fields were scattered, localized developments built, perhaps, to facilitate the combination of stock-rearing and crop-raising and not remnants of an extensive and continuous pattern of enclosures.

Studies of contemporary swidden systems have shown that they are best adapted to forest ecosystems, being dependent on the regeneration of woodland vegetation to restore the soil nutrients to exhausted cultivation plots (Harris, 1972). But the contemporary systems are normally heavily based on crop staples and do not involve animals to any important degree. In the Irish context, livestock appears to have been important from the very beginning of farming. Livestock grazing curtailed the regeneration of the forest cover but, nevertheless, the productivity of the arable could be enhanced by manuring and thus a close interdependence of livestock and crops may have been established at an early date. The natural environment of Ireland, especially the mild and moist climate, was best suited to livestock and they became of decisive importance in the rural economy and in the evolution of the cultural landscape. Animals were not only a major source of food and integral to crop production, they also had a key ecological role. Reduction of the Irish forest cover, while facilitated by the provision of more efficient tools such as bronze sickles and improved bronze axes, must have resulted partly from population growth and a related demand for larger areas of cultivation, but the most extensive forest reduction may have been caused inadvertently by the grazing of livestock, particularly cattle and goats, around the cultivated patches and over the deserted patches. Grazing activity would have checked the rate of forest regeneration, tending to produce open areas or an impoverished cover of bushes and scrub, and thus have eliminated the ordinary means whereby swidden clearances are able to recover their original fertility. However, the cattle not only reduced the forest cover and thereby provided more and more productive land, they could also by manuring the land serve as a complete and effective replacement for the forest's role in restoring fertility to cultivated areas. Almost inevitably there would have been a transition to new and more productive patterns of land use and food production centred on livestock, patterns which were well suited to Irish environmental conditions.

The cattle would have naturally flourished more than the crops in the mild and moist Irish environment and by the Bronze Age intensified grazing would have accelerated the conversion of forest into scrub but also into open areas which included rough grassland. It is noticeable in the pollen records of the period that as the forest cover diminished there was a matching expansion of hazel scrub, of the kind which still flourishes in calcareous regions of the west today, and an increase in the incidence of grass and herbaceous pollens suggestive of open grazing areas. Great increases of animal density were made possible in the grazing clearances where a much larger proportion of the vegetation could be eaten as compared with the forest environment proper. Thus progressive opening of the landscape by cattle was a self-reinforcing trend. Specialized pastoralism was inhibited in the early stages of forest clearance and only when open country was established could there have been motive and opportunity for the thorough-going development of pastoralism (Fleming, 1972). Dependence on pastoralism, it needs to be emphasized, and an associated opening of the countryside were highly likely developments in Ireland where the long growing season and mild oceanic climate provides very favourable conditions for grassland growth. Land, especially that on limestone subsoil, reverts with remarkable rapidity to good pasture even when it has been exhausted by long periods of tillage. Cattle were to remain the predominant basis of the Irish rural economy throughout most of the prehistoric and early historic period, and it is not until the Middle Ages that a more even balance was struck between the proportion of land devoted to crops on the one hand and livestock on the other.

The expansion of pastoralism must also have led to changes in the methods of crop cultivation, although it is difficult to set a time-scale on developments. Controlled livestock grazing and intensive manuring of cultivated areas would in time emerge as an alternative to the habit of allowing natural vegetation to recolonize fields in order to restore soil fertility. The countryside outside the remaining areas of natural forest could thus take on a permanently open appearance, much of it devoted to the pastoral activities for which its natural conditions are best suited. Tillage areas would normally be sited in localities with fertile well-drained soils, and their productivity could be greatly enhanced by manuring. Relatively limited areas of tillage land would have sufficed the population provided that cattle from the wide surrounding grazing areas were given regular access to the tilled land during the winter months. Such islands or "infields" of productive and intensively manured land could then provide a base for more permanent settlement. The raths, which were the dominant settlement units during the 1st millenium A.D., were probably settlements of this kind. Their occupants (as will be described more fully at a later stage) practised a mixed type of farming although with a distinct pastoral emphasis, and around the raths there are traces of small areas of fields probably used for intensive tillage and defined by banks which permitted control of livestock. But these enclosed areas were only a very limited portion of the total landscape. Much of the countryside as late as the Middle Ages remained open grazing with few fences or enclosures and there were extensive tracts of forest and secondary scrub which harboured wolves and other wild animals.

This tentative and inescapably speculative outline of the ecological adjustment of prehistoric societies to the Irish environment and of the early emergence of the cultural landscape emphasizes the close and lasting integration of arable and livestock farming and especially the pastoralist element. It may be that the infield and outfield system of land use which was dominant during the historic period emerged at an early stage as the natural means of spatially organizing the pattern of mixed farming, especially in an environment where small patches of cultivable land lay scattered amid extensive tracts best suited to grazing. In places the grazing areas could be cleared for temporary crop growth and, no doubt, as population increased the permanent infields were progressively expanded. However, grazing remained the major land use and the extensive permanent pastures which today dominate rural land use have grown from the open grazing areas first established during these early periods. The Irish pasture lands are in fact a biological sub-climax that developed in association with cattle (O'Sullivan, 1963). Brush and tree vegetation would rapidly recolonize the land if the animals were removed or the intensity of grazing substantially reduced. Indeed, where grazing land is neglected at the present day, low shrubby species frequently invade and indicate the early stages of the succession back to woodland.

The agricultural colonization of Ireland was not an even process characterized by a steady transformation of the natural landscape into farmed land. Shifting cultivation itself entailed a cyclic pattern of land use and it seems that some areas were adversely affected. The massive spread of peat bogs in particular, which may have been partly initiated by human activity, certainly led to a loss of potential agricultural resources. Growth of the great bog systems of Ireland has been a long and complicated process commencing at different times in different regions and locations. The basal layer of some bogs dates from Late Glacial times and they preserve in their stratigraphy a record of vegetation changes before and after the coming of men. It is noticeable that the major part of the growth has occurred since human occupation of the country and human interference with drainage conditions in the course of agricultural activity may have been one cause of the rapid expansion of peat. However, the precise importance of human activity is not completely clear. It is possible that deforestation could have led to soil podsolization and impeded drainage (especially in the cooler and moister climate of the Sub Atlantic period) and thus have induced a rapid growth of bogs. Such a development is indicated in the history of land use reconstructed by palynology in Goodland townland, Co. Antrim (Case *et al.*, 1969), where, after Neolithic agriculture in the 3rd millenium B.C., the quality of soil deteriorates. Podsolization led to iron-pan formation, at least in hollows, and rushes spread over the abandoned cultivation patches further impeding the drainage and leading to the establishment of blanket bog. However, soils beneath the bogs elsewhere in Ireland have not always revealed evidence of fossil podsols or hard-pan development and it may have been that the bogs were already spreading when agriculturalists were clearing the forests and that human activity generally facilitated rather than initiated the bog growth. Thus, accumulations of blanket peat may have taken place on the hillsides as these areas, from which the forest cover had been removed by early farmers, were progressively abandoned in the Bronze Ages during the general shift of settlement to lowland environments.

There is evidence of a general decline in agricultural activity and of deterioration in the environment as a whole in the latter half of the first millenium B.C., a trend which continues into the first two or three centuries A.D. (Mitchell, 1965). Bog growth continued and the evidence of herbs and grasses falls markedly; elm began to re-establish itself, suggesting that even the better soils were being abandoned, and ash also increased, indicating a considerable re-expansion of secondary woodland. It is difficult to know how all this should be explained and a very complicated web of interacting human and environmental factors may be involved. The climatic deterioration of the Sub Atlantic period may have been a contributing factor: rainfall increased and average temperatures appear to have declined, but the precise magnitude of these climatic changes and their significance for vegetational change remains a matter of controversy. In all probability the changes in climate and their effects were slight. The frequency with which gold ornaments were deliberately buried in hoards during this period (Eogan, 1964) has suggested to some interpreters that political unrest, perhaps associated with the incursion of warlike groups, may have brought about an agricultural collapse. However, Irish society seems to have been characterized by endemic tribal warfare and political anarchy over long periods of time and perhaps no external threat needs to be invoked in order to explain the habit of burying gold objects in bogs. The notable absence of settlement sites from the later stages of the Bronze Age could be related to the expansion of woodland and scrub. The regenerating woodland may have submerged the vast majority of the settlements and when, several centuries later, the woodland was again cleared, all traces of the settlements could have been simultaneously removed.

The evidence of cattle keeping and the conspicuous sparseness of settlement remains from the Bronze Age, and especially from its closing stages, have sometimes been taken to imply the widespread existence of nomadic pastoralism in the country, a way of life involving regular seasonal movements of herds and humans and typically associated with light, movable, residential structures made of perishable materials. Some of the archaeological findings would seem to support this interpretation but the evidence, in total, is limited. The idea, however, needs attention if only to illustrate further the wide range of interpretative theory which can arise when the available archaeological evidence is not plentiful or convincing enough to commend clearly one particular explanation. A Late Bronze Age settlement at Ballinderry crannog in Co. Offaly (Hencken, 1942), for example, contained the remains of a number of light wicker huts the fragile character of which seems more consistent with the needs of a mobile population than a sedentary one. The structures, however, are small and may not have been intended for human use. The existence of nomadic people is also suggested at a hill settlement excavated at Piperstown, Co. Dublin, and ascribed with reasonable certainty to the Late Neolithic or Early Bronze Age (Rynne, 1965). It consists of eight burial cairns and the foundations of six circular habitation sites, the foundations of which were simply loose stones perhaps intended only to hold down the edges of a skin covering supported by light stakes. The enigmatic "village" settlement situated near the famous Carrowkeel passage tombs in the Brickslieve Mountains of Co. Sligo has certain resemblances to Piperstown. This "village" consists of nearly 50 stone rings on a bare limestone ridge almost 800 ft above sea level. It is tempting to associate the "village" with the great passage tombs nearby but there is in fact no means of dating the village structures or even of conclusively proving that they were habitations. As they lack doorways and are too large to be roofed, the rings, it has been surmised, may have served as protective sites for the tents or other light structures built by periodic visitors, perhaps the tomb builders or perhaps herdsmen of much later or even of earlier date (Macalister, 1912). Aerial photography has recently shown that similar circular foundations, some 50 in number, lie on the peat-covered surface of Knocknashee Mountain in Co. Sligo at the same altitude as a number of megalithic cairns (Norman and St. Joseph, 1969).

Thus, some of the settlement remains from different parts of the country do suggest the work of mobile people but the dating of the evidence is rather insecure and the evidence in total is not convincing or plentiful enough to justify ideas of general nomadism. The importance of livestock was great and may well have increased as the Bronze Age proceeded but the existence of nomadism is belied by the evidence that crop production did occur, indicating a sedentary existence for at least part of the year: it is also hard to reconcile nomadism with the existence of massive burial monuments. It is worth noting too that the insubstantial houses which have been excavated could have been associated with trans-humant herders, carrying out seasonal excursions to unimproved tracts of land but based normally in more permanent settlements, rather than with strictly nomadic groups. Transhumance was a deeply established custom in Ireland and there are indications that it was practised in many parts of western Europe from a very early period (Hicks, 1972–3; Dehn, 1972). As late as the 16th and 17 Centuries A.D., outside observers, superficially acquainted with the summer migrations of herds and herdsmen, were led to describe Irish society as a whole, and especially the communities in the remoter northern and western portions of the country, as "nomadic". It is an error that prehistorians, seeking to interpret archaeological material in terms of economic activities, could profitably mark.

4
The Iron Age and Early Christian Period

It is difficult to determine a clear starting point for the Iron Age in Ireland. A small number of objects decorated in the Halstatt and La Tène styles which characterized the iron-using Celts of the continent can be discerned in Ireland during the last few centuries B.C. (Rynne, 1958; Harbison, 1971). Thereafter, iron technology came into general use with the new metal used for every-day tools and bronze reserved mainly for ornaments. Apart from these changes there is continuity of the indigenous Bronze Age culture, little trace of invaders and certainly no evidence to suggest a wholesale replacement of the native population. Some small immigrant groups either from Britain or directly from the continent may have arrived, but essentially there appears to have been a survival and development of indigenous Bronze Age cultural traditions into a period contemporary with the far-reaching cultural changes of the Iron Age in southern Britain. Much of the Irish Iron Age culture is so distinctive that it could hardly have been derived from elsewhere. The dominant settlement forms—the raths, cashels and crannogs—are almost peculiar to the island and a growing body of evidence suggests that some of their roots are deep in the Bronze Age and perhaps even earlier (O'Kelly, 1970). Moreover, widespread Iron Age forms in Britain, such as the vitrified and multivallate forts, are almost wholly absent in Ireland. So too are many of the characteristics, for example of burial and pottery, which make up the known La Tène culture on the continent. The distinctiveness of Iron Age Ireland must have evolved; there is no evidence of a wholesale importation of culture and no obvious source of origin outside the country.

The inception of the Irish Iron Age is inextricably linked with the confusing and still obscure issue of when and how the Celtic languages were introduced into the country. The Iron Age has been persistently associated with, and sometimes described by, the linguistic label "Celtic". This labelling has meant that a material culture and a language have been identified and, moreover, the label seems to imply that anything before the Iron Age is not Celtic. However, as observed above, the use of iron marked a technological innovation rather than the coming of a new people. Technological change does not need a language change and the introduction of the Celtic language may well have occurred at a much earlier stage than the introduction of iron, probably in the Bronze Age. If the La Tène invasions involved only small groups, as the archaeological evidence suggests, then it is hard to see how they were solely responsible in such a short time for the wholesale celticization of the country in language, customs and literature, a process certainly completed by the beginning of the Christian period in the 5th Century A.D. and perhaps achieved considerably earlier. Earliest records, such as the Massiliote Periplus, as well as linguistic evidence, suggest that by 500 B.C. the inhabitants of Britain and Ireland were already Celtic speaking and organized in basically the same way as the related continental communities. The problem thus seems to be to find a period of prehistory which shows the marks of population migrations sufficiently large to diffuse the Celts or proto-Celts throughout large tracts of central Europe and bring them into Britain and Ireland. Perhaps the crucial phase was the time of the so-called Beaker people—i.e. around 2000 B.C.—and, after this "völkerwanderüng", populations were relatively stable and social and economic development throughout the widespread Celtic realm progressed along lines that were broadly parallel yet in some important respects divergent (Dillon and Chadwick, 1965).

Certainly Ireland, along with much of western and trans-Alpine Europe, shared the Celtic language and some similarities of life-style and material culture during the early centuries of the last millenium before Christ (Raftery, 1964). In Britain and on the continent Celtic polity was virtually terminated by the Roman imperial expansion but it was able to continue unbroken in Ireland, where the Romans never penetrated, down to the Middle Ages. Only in Ireland could there survive a language and literature developed directly from the ancient Celts. The Celtic tongue in western Scotland was introduced by Irish invaders only shortly before the Christian period. In Wales the indigenous Celtic tradition waned through the period of romanization and much of surviving Welsh tradition stems from Irish infusions during the closing phases of the Roman occupation.

The Celtic society, whose foundations were probably laid in the Bronze Age, was to dominate Ireland for over 1000 years, down to the Middle Ages. It is customary to use the spreading of Christianity in the 5th Century A.D. to divide this long period into two parts—the Iron Age and the Early Christian period. Over the entire period, however, there was substantial cultural continuity, evident particularly in basic economy and settlement forms. Society remained tribal and rural; pastoral activities were important and the pattern of settlement essentially scattered, the dominant settlement form was the independent single farmstead surrounded by a circular earthwork. Save for a limited number of coastal trading centres established by Viking settlers, Ireland remained devoid of towns until the Middle Ages and trade was mainly transacted at seasonal fairs.

The coming of Christianity to Ireland in the 5th Century A.D. and the associated strong development of eremiticism and monasticism were no doubt important departures, but there are earlier signs of cultural and economic quickening from about A.D. 100 onwards, reflecting perhaps the cumulative benefits of technological advances but probably associated too with influences from the Roman world and particularly contacts with neighbouring Roman Britain. There was no Roman occupation of Ireland but the links with Roman Britain were obviously close and varied (Ó Ríordáin, 1947; Bateson, 1973). Groups of British refugees displaced by the Roman occupation may well have arrived in Ireland, although the main migratory movements were in the opposite direction, and in the Late Roman period there is evidence of widespread colonization by Irishmen in the western districts of Britain, in Wales, the Isle of Man and western Scotland (Jackson, 1964). Many objects from Roman Britain, particularly metalwork, reached Ireland, and Irish dogs, cattle and hides were exported to Britain. Trading contacts were responsible for some of the interchange but piracy and slave-raiding were also prevalent around the Irish Sea, particularly as Roman authority in Britain declined.

The influence of neighbouring Roman Britain may have been responsible for a number of cultural developments in Ireland, some of which contributed to the formation of landscape features. The erection of long linear frontier earthworks, such as the Black Pig's Dyke in Co. Monaghan and Co. Leitrim, the Dorsey in Co. Armagh and the Claidhe Dubh in east Cork, may have been inspired by knowledge of Roman frontier fortifications in Britain, fortifications such as Hadrian's Wall in northern Britain and the Antonine Wall in southern Scotland. However, this interpretation of the Irish linear earthworks is speculative: the Black Pig's Dyke may have been built by Ulstermen to protect their southern boundary but nothing definite is known of its age or purpose. Pollen analysis suggests that forest clearance was quickened in the early centuries of the 1st millenium A.D. and tillage and fixed settlement came to play a

Plate 6: Early Irish monasteries. **a** Inchcleraun, monastic site on island, Upper Lough Ree, Co. Longford. Traces of the circular monastic enclosure can be seen and of ancient fields perhaps associated with the monastery. **b** Round tower (over 100 ft high, 30·5 m) on monastic site at Kilmacduagh, Co. Galway.

larger role than before (Watts, 1961; Mitchell, 1965). Ash is substantially reduced in the pollen record and elm becomes extremely rare. This is probably owing to forest clearance on the calcareous drifts of the lowlands, areas in which archaeological evidence also suggests a decisive expansion of permanent settlement by communities who by this time were equipped with iron tools and probably using a heavy plough, drawn by an ox team, for tillage. There is, however, an increase in birch and alder, linked probably to the prolific generation of these trees from seeds and their capacity to recover from fire and browsing damage. The improvements in rural economy at this period may have been introduced under the influence of neighbouring Roman Britain. In time, the Christianization of Ireland and the organization associated with the new faith, particularly with the monasteries, seem also to have encouraged cultural and economic development and sustained the process of landscape transformation. References to ploughs drawn by teams of oxen, and thus presumably of a heavy variety and perhaps equipped with an iron coulter and a mould board, occur in writings of the Early Christian period (Lucas, 1972, 1973). No historical sources have survived from earlier periods and it is possible that the heavy plough was introduced into Ireland some time before the first written references to its use. However, this introducthon is unlikely to have taken place before the beginning of the Iron Age, if one can judge from the evidence about ploughs in the British Isles as a whole (Bowen, 1961). Unfortunately, little is known of the form and appearance of the early Irish ploughs; the literary references are not specific and no representations of ploughs are available until after the Middle Ages. Moreover, few remains of ploughs have been discovered in datable archaeological contexts. It is noteworthy too that the fragmentary fields which have survived from the Iron Age and Early Christian period are small and have roughly rectangular or rounded shapes; heavy ploughs would have been difficult to manoeuvre in such fields and their shape seems more consistent with the use of light manoeuvrable ploughs of ard type. Perhaps, however, these ancient fields were used by livestock and the tillage areas were not enclosed; cropping may have been carried out on open "outfields" amenable to the use of heavy ploughs. There may have also been a lengthy period of time when light and heavy ploughs were in simultaneous use.

The reconstruction of developments in the prehistoric period must rely for the most part on inferences from archaeological data. With the Iron Age, however, we come tentatively within the scope of documentary history. Little of Irish history or mythology was actually written down until the coming of Christianity, when the monks devoted themselves to the recording of secular events and traditions as well as religious and biblical material. But, because of the remarkable continuity and archaism of Irish traditions, the monkish writings shed light on life and institutions in much earlier periods, almost certainly back to the beginnings of the Iron Age (Dillon, 1954; Jackson, 1964). The continuity and conservation of Irish tradition, however, has relevance outside the island. Ireland possessed institutions, customs and language, once common to the whole of Celtic Europe. Only in the peripheral island, isolated from the cultural changes and population replacement at the centre of the continent, could the old ways of life survive so long. In Ireland a European barbaric society was preserved down into late historic times, thus providing a unique opportunity to perceive at close quarters the conditions from which broader European society has grown. This is true of institutions and customs and perhaps also of the cultural landscape, of the husbandry, settlements patterns and field systems which it is the particular task of the historical geographer to reconstruct as far as possible.

In the Iron Age and especially the succeeding Early Christian period, there is evidence that Ireland was not only culturally vigorous but also more intensively settled than ever before. Unlike the preceding Bronze and Neolithic Ages, habitation sites are very numerous while the burial monuments are scarce. The outstanding features of the surviving settlement sites are the enclosing earthworks, which are almost invariably circular in plan. Within the majority of the earthworks few or no structural remains survive above the surface of the ground, although excavation can often reveal the foundations of buildings. The survival of such a vast number of earthworks has been favoured in a country with long-standing pastoral traditions, where most of the productive land is kept in pasture and the impact of ploughing is relatively slight. One author has indeed remarked that "nowhere else in western Europe are the corrugations of the surface representing activities of ancient man so clearly visible over large areas" (Norman and St. Joseph, 1969). Many of the earthworks have been further protected by superstitions about their fairy origins, superstitions strong enough to prevent their molestation even in a nation of small, land-hungry farmers. However, present day attitudes are different and many earthworks are now being destroyed by land reclamation, building development, quarrying and road-building. An ancient settlement pattern, perhaps unique in Europe for its remarkable state of completeness, is now endangered, and the very profusion of the sites provides an embarrassment to preservationists.

The surviving earthworks from the period vary greatly in size and in the kinds of location which they occupy, and it is unsatisfactory to lump them together. Classification, however, is made difficult by the great number of the sites, many of them completely unstudied. Satisfactory classification must clearly await more detailed surveys and systematic excavation. In the following discussion four main types of settlement are described, following the categories presently recognized by most Irish archaeologists; raths, promontory forts, crannogs and hill-forts.

Settlements

Raths

The principal form of settlement from the period, indeed the most numerous and widely distributed of any of the field monuments of antiquity, is the rath or "celtic ring-fort", a distinctively Irish form, almost unknown elsewhere in the British Isles. There are well over 30 000 surviving raths scattered over the Irish countryside (Plate 7). A typical rath comprises a small level area enclosed by a circular earthen bank and fosse, with the diameter of the sites varying between 50 and 150 feet (15 and 47 m). Some very large examples can be found, however, with diameters exceeding 300 feet (91 m). As well as "rath", the terms "dun", "lios" and "cathair" are used to describe the sites and anglicized forms of these various terms are very frequently found as place-name elements, often in localities where no earthworks can be seen and thus suggesting that the raths were formerly even more widespread than today. In stony areas a stone wall is often found in place of the earthen bank and the sites known as cashels, the anglicized version of "caiseal".

Although the general distribution of the raths has been mapped with reasonable accuracy (Fig. 9), only a small proportion of the total number has been excavated and consequently caution is needed in generalizing about the origin and function of the raths as a whole. The 60 or so excavated sites may be an unrepresentative sample. Most writers have tended to ascribe the majority of the raths to the Early Christian period but this is a reasonable working hypothesis and no more, and strictly the evidence is insufficient even to warrant this sort of approximation. The Early Christian period may have been the most important stage in the history of the raths, but raths were not restricted to that period. On some excavated sites there is an absence of convincingly datable finds, and the

Plate 7a: Raths, near Oldcastle, Co. Meath. Underlying the straight, present-day field boundaries are the outlines of older irregular fields perhaps associated with the raths.

Plate 7b: Earthworks, near Fethard, Co. Tipperary. Probably the site of a deserted medieval village. Only two farms and an ancient, ruined church survive on the site.

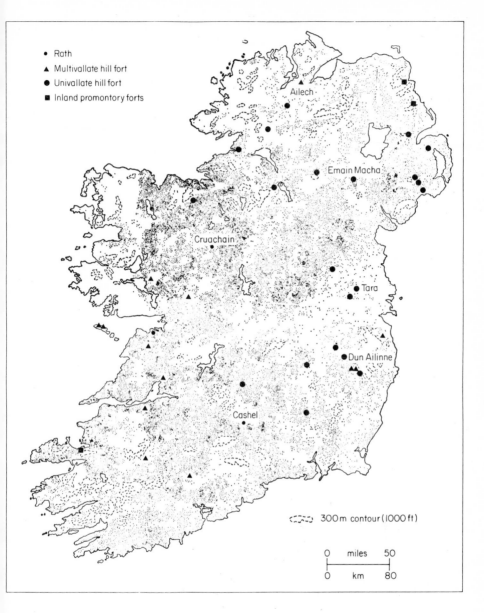

Fig. 9: Distribution of raths, hill forts and Iron Age royal sites. (Based on McCourt, 1970; Raftery, 1972.)

datable finds, as well as historical evidence, suggest that some raths were used over a very long period of time, from the Late Bronze Age down to the end of the Middle Ages, and even as late as the 17th Century in some locations. A rath-like structure at Carrigillihy, Co. Cork (O'Kelly, 1951), has been attributed to the Early Bronze Age, although this early dating has occasioned some controversy. Ó Ríordáin (1940) placed the earliest rath excavated at Cush, Co. Limerick, in the later stages of the Bronze Age as it was used for Bronze Age urn burials after it had gone out of use as a dwelling place. At the other end of the time-scale the maps and diagrams of R. Barthelet, a military cartographer of the early 17th Century, show that the raths and the related forms, the crannogs, were still inhabited in northern Ireland at the time of the Ulster Plantation (Hayes-McCoy, 1964).

It is a reasonable assumption, however, that the main mass of the raths date from the 1st millenium A.D. Survival of so many settlement sites from this period permits a tentative reconstruction of the general population distribution. The rath-dwelling population was obviously widely distributed throughout Ireland, but, in contrast to the Neolithic period, settlement in general has moved to lower altitudes, shifting from the uplands to the lower hill flanks and the lowlands, much as at present. Raths are particularly numerous on the lowlands around the Shannon Estuary and on the lowlands of eastern Connaught. The penetration, widespread clearance and settlement of the damp forested lowlands, which in earlier periods had been a barrier to settlement, was a notable achievement perhaps facilitated by the introduction of superior metal equipment and farming tools.

It is clear from investigation of the site characteristics of the raths, from surviving surface features and from excavations, that the raths were not strictly forts. In the majority of cases they mark the sites of single family farms, a mundane origin indeed considering the strong superstitions everywhere connected with them in the minds of country folk. The circular earthworks are simply the perimeter walls of the farmyards, sufficient to keep domestic animals in or out and perhaps provide some shelter from wind and rain but not formidable enough to provide other than peace-time protection to the house. Variations in rath size perhaps reflect the social status of the farmers, although there are grounds for believing that the raths were generally the residences of substantial farmers. Excavations, such as those at Garryduff, Co. Cork (O'Kelly, 1963), Letterkeen, Co. Mayo (Ó Ríordáin and MacDermott, 1952), and Ballypalady, Co. Antrim (Waterman, 1972), illustrate that the raths accommodated people who practised metalcraft in iron and bronze probably within the rath walls and possessed articles which were derived from foreign sources, such as pottery, beads and bracelets of glass and jet. In general, raths seem to concentrate at intermediate lowland levels, between approximately 100 and 400 feet (30 and 1200 m), and to be sited on slopes rather than flat land or summit sites. Unlike the hillforts, which clearly had some defensive role, the raths are not usually found in dominant or commanding positions, save in ill-drained districts such as the drumlin belt where only elevated sites were suitable for habitation. Typically, the raths occur in sheltered positions just below the summits of lowland eminences. Defensive considerations were thus not of great importance. Within the lowlands the rath dwellers showed a clear preference for the better quality soils; they avoided areas where gley or podzol soils occur and where gravelly soils or blanket bog are found. The situation, site and soil preferences of the raths thus strongly suggest an agricultural orientation for their occupants.

The economy of the rath farmers was based, primarily, on livestock and, secondarily, on crop growth (Proudfoot, 1961). Indeed the emphasis on cattle-raising, which normally makes necessary a close relationship between farm and fields, may in part explain the markedly dispersed nature of the rath settlement pattern. The raths sometimes exhibit a tendency to occur in loose groupings but this probably reflects a preference for particular soil conditions, and the distribution pattern remains diffuse, suggestive always of single independent farms rather than communal or village type organization. In a few of the stone-built cashels ruined stone structures are visible. Within the raths there is a notable scarcity of structural remains but vestigial foundations are sometimes traceable and archaeological excavations have provided useful information about the farmhouses and other buildings. The majority of the buildings were probably timber-frame constructions with walls of turf or wattle and daub; rounded and rectangular forms co-existed but rounded structures were most common. The concentric post-holes at Lissue Rath, Co. Antrim, were interpreted (Bersu, 1947) as the supports of a mushroom-shaped roof covering the entire area of the rath. However, little evidence for this sort of structure has been found at other sites and it seems likely that in most raths the buildings were small, free-standing structures. Souterrains or stone-lined subterranean chambers, similar to the fogous of Cornwall and the weems of Scotland, frequently occur within the raths. These features probably served as refuge places and for food storage. They are also found independently of raths, especially in north Co. Louth, and may

D

perhaps mark the sites of undefended farmsteads of which no other trace has survived.

Often the structures within the raths seem to have been irregular and the foundations constructed with poor masonry. Excavations have sometimes revealed a lack of clear-cut order in the lay-out of post-holes, and numerous apparently ephemeral features exist which suggest that some raths were places only for temporary occupation (Ó Ríordáin and Hartnett, 1943; Harper, 1973). A number of excavated raths have revealed very little trace of human habitation and it is probable that they served simply as cattle pounds. At Ballypalady, Co. Antrim, at Garryduff, Co. Cork, and at Lisduggan, Co. Cork, all places where groups of raths occurred, the excavations revealed that one rath in the group showed little trace of habitation and probably served as an enclosure for the cattle of the owners of the occupied raths. The number of raths in a locality may therefore be misleading as an indication of human population density. More needs to be known of the pattern of rath use before adequate generalizations about national or regional population size are possible on the basis of rath numbers.

The two most striking features of rath settlements are the general emphasis on circularity in building plans and the location of buildings within prominent enclosures. This Iron Age and Early Christian custom of building within conspicuous circular enclosures appears to have been the secular development of an extremely ancient religious tradition, and the forerunners of the raths are perhaps the sacred enclosures erected around megalithic burial sites, such as the Giants' Ring at Ballynahatty, Co. Down, which encloses a megalithic tomb, or the Longstone Rath, Co. Kildare, which encloses a granitic monolith probably of Bronze Age date. At Carrigillihy, Co. Cork, the circular stone bank of the excavated rath incorporates some large orthostats and suggests a direct development from megalithic sepulchral monuments.

Circular and rectangular building plans are to be found in all the main periods of Irish prehistory but a strong emphasis on circular plans, both for domestic buildings and their enclosing earthworks, is a conspicuous feature of Irish settlement throughout the Iron Age and the succeeding Early Christian period, indeed into the Middle Ages. Britain and Ireland were exceptional in their retention of traditional customs of building with circular plans throughout the Bronze and Early Iron Age, that is at a time when rectangular forms were dominant on the continental mainland. However, after the Romano-British period in Britain, and perhaps partly as a result of Roman influence, rectangular forms tended increasingly to be adopted and to replace circular forms, while Ireland perpetuated circular forms long after their eclipse elsewhere in the British Isles.

Promontory Forts

Promontory forts form a further and clearly definable group of settlement sites which appear to correspond roughly in age to the hill-forts and the raths. Coastal promontory forts are very numerous. Approximately 200 sites have been recorded, most abundantly in the south and south-west, but a few related structures exist inland on mountain spurs and cliff edges. The purpose of the promontory forts is clearly defensive. Typically, they comprise small level areas on cliff-defined promontories, protected on the landward side by ramparts and ditches. However, there is a notable scarcity of internal structures and habitation refuse. Souterrains sometimes occur and tumbled stone foundations but investigation of the interior of the structures has thrown remarkably little light on their function and age (Childe, 1936; O'Kelly, 1952). It is not even clear where the builders lived. Perhaps the forts were erected to meet some short-lived emergency defensive or aggressive, but, like so many impressive military systems, little use was ever made of them. Structural resemblances to sites in Brittany, the Isle of Man and south-western Britain suggest an Iron Age date. Some finds from the forts also indicate an Iron Age date and even medieval occupation.

Crannogs

Crannogs are lake dwellings built on artificial islands constructed of stones and brushwood and consolidated by wattle fences and piles driven into the lake bottom. Comparable in size to the raths, the crannogs were also roughly circular in shape and served as the sites of single farmsteads. The occupants of the crannogs appear to have farmed the adjacent lake shores and to have lived on the islands for security. Causeways sometimes provided links to the shore but dug-out wooden boats were also used. Most of the material from Irish crannogs dates from Early Christian times but there is evidence of crannog building as early as the Neolithic period; indeed Ó Ríordáin (1943) has speculated that the crannogs represent a fusion of the old Mesolithic lakeside settlements with a Neolithic way of life. The tradition of building lake dwellings is one of the most persistent in the history of Irish settlement and it is known that some crannogs were still inhabited in the 17th Century A.D. Crannog dwellings were well suited to the lake-strewn marshy environment of the country, especially in the west and north-west, and this fact, as well as the deep cultural conservatism of Ireland, may explain why the fashion of crannog dwelling seems to have persisted and to have become important at several points in history, especially in the Iron Age and Early Christian period when the largest and most elaborate sites were constructed. At Island McHugh in Lough Catherine, Co. Tyrone, the crannog was constructed in Neolithic times, occupied throughout the Bronze Age, extended in the Early Christian period and, ultimately, utilized as the site for a castle in the Late Medieval period; a castle which was occupied until the 16th Century. The well known site in Ballinderry Lough, Co. Offaly, described by Wood-Martin in the 19th Century and later excavated by O'Neill Hencken, comprised two super-imposed occupations (Hencken, 1941–2). The lower settlement dated from the Late Bronze Age and consisted of a number of tiny circular wicker huts as well as a larger wooden structure located on the lake side. This early occupation was terminated by a rise in lake level which deposited a layer of mud over the island settlement. Settlers in the Early Christian period built a crannog on the same spot which was an extension of a natural island rather than a completely artificial one. However, another excavated crannog in Ballinderry Lough (Hencken, 1953), and the Lagore crannog in Co. Meath (Hencken, 1950–1) were on completely artificial islands.

Hill-Forts

In Ireland the study of hill-forts has been, until very recently, almost completely neglected; indeed it was commonly held that hill-forts were rare or even absent. However, a variety of sites do exist which seem to qualify broadly for the title "hill-fort". These sites are usually larger than the raths, occupy defensible elevated positions and possess considerable ramparts of earth or stone. Some element of defence is clearly suggested by their lay-out and siting but there may be different categories of settlement involved, and the precise uses to which they were put, as well as the dates of erection, are largely conjectural. Further archaeological investigations will no doubt lead to improved classification and terminology, but in the meantime the term "hill-fort" can be used as a convenient and not too misleading blanket title which serves at least to differentiate the sites from the more numerous lowland raths.

Structurally, the Irish hill-forts are, in the main, strikingly simple. The great Celtic hill-forts, characterized by closely-set, stepped multivallation, which are found in lowland England and on the European mainland, have no counterpart in Ireland. Complex multivallation is found in Ireland only at a few northern sites and these, oddly, are modest lowland structures with the proportions of raths rather than hill-forts. The Irish hill-forts are much less spectacular and, moreover, are limited in number relative to the size of the country and the vast quantity of earthworks of other categories deemed to be roughly contemporary with them. Study of their morphological characteristics (Raftery, 1972) has shown that the bulk of the hill-forts fall into two main categories with roughly complementary distributions (Fig. 9). There are, first, the univallate hill-forts, with an easterly distribution. Their essential features are the enclosure of extensive hill top areas or other defensible natural positions by a rampart of earth which is usually roughly circular in shape and follows the contours below the summit. A number of these hill-forts are distinguished by the presence within the enclosure of megalithic burial mounds, which are probably older than the enclosures themselves and presumably date from the Neolithic or Bronze Age. Apart from the rampart and the tomb, few surface remains of any antiquity survive in these sites except for occasional enigmatic grass-grown irregularities. It is not clear whether the sites were intended for permanent settlement or temporary refuge, whether indeed they were basically defensive at all. Ritual functions as well as defensive may have been important and the frequent linkage with tombs suggests that the sites may have possessed long-standing sanctity or prestige.

The second and less numerous category of forts possesses widely-spaced multivallate defences constructed either with dry stone or earth. Most of these forts possess a small inner enclosure or "citadel" with a number of outer and roughly concentric ramparts. The forts have a westerly distribution and are mainly concentrated in the south-west of the country where univallate sites have not been recorded. Some of the most impressive examples are stone cashel structures such as Grianan of Ailech in Co. Donegal (Bernard, 1879), which comprises an impressive central cashel with traces of three denuded earthworks surrounding it, or the stone fort of Cahercommaun in Co. Clare (Hencken, 1938), which consists of a massive inner "citadel" with two outer enclosures. There are resemblances with Spanish Iron Age forts and it has been suggested that the multivallate defences reflect connections between Iberia and Western Ireland in the Iron Ages, involving either immigrant groups or simply cultural influences spreading in the traditional manner along the Atlantic seaways. The occurrence of the distinctive "chevaux-de-frise" defences at four western sites is also suggestive, as this feature is unknown elsewhere save in the Iberian Peninsula. The eastern univallate forts, on the other hand, do not appear to have structural parallels elsewhere and their frequent association with megaliths suggests an indigenous evolution.

The sites here loosely described as hill-forts are usually ascribed to the Iron Age but there is often uncertainty as to the date of the structures and the precise use to which they were put. Excavated sites are few and the references in early Irish literature, even when they can be confidently tied to known sites, are of limited value. Excavations of the hill-fort at Freestone Hill, Co. Kilkenny, produced evidence for its construction and occupation in the 4th Century A.D. (Raftery, 1969). Current excavations at Dun Aillinne, Co. Kildare, and Rathgall, Co. Wicklow, demonstrate occupation in the Late Bronze Age, the Iron Age, and into the Middle Ages (Wailes, 1974; Raftery, 1971). The occupations, however, may not have been continuous. Excavations at Navan Fort in Co. Armagh suggest that the main features date from the Iron Age (Waterman, 1970). The principal sites referred to in early literature are the famous royal sites with an important place in Celtic mythology; these include Tara, Co. Meath, Navan Fort (Emain Macha) in Co. Armagh, Dun Ailinne in Co. Kildare and Grianan Ailech in Co. Donegal. These sites, however, are exceptional ones. With the exception of Grianan Ailech, they are not located on commanding hills but on eminences in fertile lowland areas which, although they permit broad vistas, have little defensive value. A ritual or ceremonial function seems therefore the most likely interpretation. There is no evidence that any of the Irish hill-forts, even the major royal centres, possessed urban functions; indeed, as previously indicated, the use of the Irish hill-forts and related structures remains generally obscure. In some cases they may have served merely as refuges for the local population and have had few permanent inhabitants. The frequent absence of surface structures lends some weight to this interpretation. Other sites may have served as ritual centres or the residences of minor kings, indeed the two functions may have been combined.

In barbarian societies, ceremonial centres with religio-administrative functions have sometimes developed into cities but this did not materialize in Ireland because underlying conditions were not favourable to the transformation. Town life develops most naturally in a sedentary society based on agriculture, especially if a food surplus is available to support the urban population. The nucleated settlements characteristic of cultivators provide focal points for urban genesis through the selective growth of favoured settlements or synoecism of several adjacent villages. However, the incentive to urban growth and the pace of the development appears to depend heavily on the pre-existence of appropriate social institutions and patterns of leadership. In Ireland the main emphasis of the rural economy was towards pastoralism and scattered habitations, and there is a likelihood that the élite of the society were themselves identified with a pastoral and mobile way of life and their traditions thus inimical to urban living. Moreover, the chronic political instability which reigned in the country may well have been a deterrent to urban genesis. Ireland in the Iron Age was divided into hundreds of small petty kingdoms or tuaths whose inhabitants appear to have engaged in regular warfare and predation on their neighbours. Owing to the low productivity of farming, extensive rural hinterlands were required to sustain urban settlements in early times and such hinterlands could not be effectively organized in Ireland while stable and centralized political institutions were absent. Some of the Celtic hill-forts or ''oppida'' on the continent eventually took on certain urban functions, but this was probably under cultural influences from the city states established by Greek traders in the western Mediterranean (Pounds, 1969). Ireland, however, was much too remote to feel the impact of these civilizing influences. For a variety of reasons, therefore, Irish native society did not spontaneously generate town life. Even the most illustrious of the Iron Age royal sites and hill-forts were eclipsed shortly after the advent of Christianity into the country. The major monastic centres, such as Monasterboice and Glendalough, replaced them and were usually built on new sites. At a few places, such as Downpatrick, Co. Down, and Cashel in Co. Tipperary, major political sites developed into monastic centres but in most cases the founders of monasteries avoided the pre-existing political capitals. Moreover, even the largest and most celebrated of the monastic centres failed in their turn to grow into urban communities. A system of urban settlement was eventually introduced into the country by Vikings traders in the 9th Century and, more extensively, by Anglo-Norman colonizers in the Middle Ages. This imported system was to provide an influential and enduring ingredient of the national life. It needs emphasis that the considerable artistic and technical achievements of Iron Age and Early Christian society, especially in metalcrafts, as well as the existence of traders and craftsmen, were supported throughout the first millenium without any urban infra-structure.

The Cultural Landscape

Despite the survival of so many individual settlement sites, there is no clear knowledge of the appearance of the cultural landscape as a whole during the Iron Age and Early Christian period. Were there, for example, extensive areas of improved grassland and were there many enclosed fields as we know them today? The available evidence suggests that the rural landscape of these remote periods did not bear significant resemblance to the contemporary rural scene. Pollen analysis indicates that much of the landscape was covered by woodland, and especially degraded secondary woodland, during the periods when the raths were occupied. Almost certainly, therefore, the area of the farmed land was much less extensive than today. Recent aerial photography has shown that the raths are sometimes associated with limited areas of small block-like fields (Norman and St. Joseph, 1969). The outline of these field boundaries can in some instances be traced on the ground but typically they are evident only on aerial photographs and underlie the present-day enclosures (Plate 7a). Modern fields are much larger in area, more rectangular and even-shaped. The underlying fields are thus clearly older than the present pattern and seem to belong to a quite different order of agrarian organization. That the raths and juxtaposed enclosures are contemporary is suggested by their contiguity and also consistent with the prevailing view of the raths as ''einzelhöfe'' from which farming of a mixed (arable-livestock) character was practised. It is notable, however, that the fixed fields are evident only in the immediate vicinity of the raths, and thus there is no reason to suppose that extensive areas of landscape were enclosed. Although in some localities the number of raths roughly equals that of modern farmsteads, this may not necessarily imply a comparable intensity of land occupation. It needs to be remembered that the raths date from many different periods and, although indicative of the broad distribution of population in the country as a whole, the actual number of raths in a defined area may be misleading as a guide to population density at any one time. Moreover, although there is evidence that crop growth was carried out from raths, some of them may have been only the temporary abodes of a cattle-keeping people, or indeed mere cattle enclosures in a predominantly wooded landscape.

Not only was the extent and general appearance of the farmed land in Iron Age and Early Christian Ireland very different from today, there is also no clear evidence of any significant degree of continuity of major landscape elements. Neither the contemporary settlement pattern nor the field patterns can be seen as a heritage from the period of Celtic occupation. Ethnologists and folk-life students have been impressed with the sometimes remarkable survivals in both the oral and literary traditions and the material culture of the Irish countryside (Evans, 1957; Macneill, 1962). The survival of the Celtic tongue within Ireland, however tenuously, is a further illustration of remarkable continuity. It has been easy, where many social traditions are demonstrably of such high antiquity, uncritically to accept that the character of the cultural landscape has also survived unchanged from "time immemorial". Such a viewpoint has been almost unconsciously reinforced by modern Irish nationalism which has tended to emphasize and encourage belief in the continuity of Celtic traditions within the country, partly to establish a separate national identity and thus counter the influence of anglicization and substantiate the movement to political independence. It is true that the vast majority of place-names in Ireland are of Celtic origin, even if heavily anglicized, but the significance of this is often misunderstood. The repetition of the same place-name elements throughout Ireland (e.g. bally, rath, lis, kill, dun, drum, knock, ard) is indicative of the country's early cultural identity and uniformity but it is not evidence of continuity in the cultural landscape. Old place-names have survived in plenty because in general they are the names not of settlements and other visible components of the landscape but of small land units known as townlands into which, since at least the Medieval period, every county and parish has been divided, and which at an early date gained legal and therefore lasting significance. The townlands are of ancient but obscure origin, formerly called by a wide variety of local names such as "balliboes" in parts of Ulster and "ploughlands" in parts of Munster. There are in all over 62 000 townlands in the country. They vary considerably in size but are usually large enough to contain several small farms. Despite frequent enlargement and division of individual townlands, this basic system of territorial divisions has remained as an enduring pattern while the morphological features of the landscape, such as settlement units and fields, have undergone a succession of far-reaching changes. Place-name evidence offers little help in dating the actual settlement units. Save in the anglicized east, few of the farms in the Irish countryside have individual names. They are traditionally referred to simply by the names of their owners and the townlands in which they lie. Many of the surviving farm clusters, or clachans, bear the same name as the townlands in which they are located but in such circumstances it is difficult to determine whether the settlement or the territorial unit is older. The place-name may often appear in ancient documents but this is not evidence that the present-day settlements were then in existence.

The similarity between the dispersed pattern of contemporary rural settlement and the diffuse distribution of the raths is frequently referred to in discussions of landscape continuity. Like the rath, the single family farmstead, which is the characteristic settlement unit of the Irish landscape today, stands on its own land at some distance from its nearest neighbours. Moreover, both settlement patterns are associated with an economic organization based heavily on animal husbandry. But it is unsafe to assume any direct continuity between the two patterns. Earlier scholars believed that there was continuity, that the present-day scattering of farms, which is such an emphatic feature of the landscape, was an arrested stage of development, an expression of age-long Celtic pastoralism. Such a pattern of rural living, independent, pastoral, was clearly in strong contrast with English rural traditions where village life predominated with an emphasis on communal organization and arable farming. It was a contrast which could readily be seen as deep-rooted because it seemed consistent with certain myths about the national character of the Irish and the English, the former independent and fractious, almost anarchic, the latter revelling in well-ordered ways, restrained and docile. However, it is striking that very few of the farmsteads occupied today appear to lie in rath sites; the occasional occurrence of cottages and other farm buildings within rath walls may imply some continuity of habitation from the time that the earthworks were built, but this is uncertain as the population pressure of the early 19th Century may sometimes have led to re-occupation of rath sites which had been deserted for many centuries. More important, it has been conclusively established that over wide areas the diffuse patterns of farms, each held in severalty (i.e. individual or unshared tenure of a piece of land), is of relatively recent origin and was preceded in the 18th and 19th Centuries by small nucleated settlements or farm clusters which were the centres of open-field systems worked by several farm families. Although a number of the old farm clusters and vestiges of the associated field system still survive today, especially in remote districts or in areas with poor soils which have escaped agricultural reforms, there has clearly been a very thoroughgoing transformation of the basic rural settlement pattern and the agrarian organization which sustained it. The transformation is recent enough to have left recoverable evidence in the landscape and to have been amply recorded in literary and cartographic sources.

While the dispersed farms of the Irish countryside can no longer be viewed as a pattern of long standing, it has been argued by some geographers that the farm clusters, or "clachans", represent a settlement pattern of great antiquity; indeed the possibility has been raised that farm clusters co-existed with the raths, as the nuclei of primitive open-field systems and the settlements of inferior cultivators perhaps subservient to the rath dwellers. Evans and others have seen the origins of the clachan and its rundale background as far back as the Neolithic period and viewed the settlement form as a basic and enduring institution in the rural organization of the whole of Atlantic Europe (Evans, 1939: Proudfoot, 1959). However, as yet no firm evidence can be presented for this view. Early Irish literary sources have not provided clear evidence for the pre-medieval existence of clachans or open-field agriculture, and archaeological evidence lends little support to the idea, indeed it contradicts rather than supports it. There are, however, a number of suggestive hints from the study of settlement history in other countries, such as Wales, and in various aspects of the place-name distribution in Ireland. A dichotomy between pastoral warrior overlords holding land individually and a ground mass of subservient cultivators has been seen by numerous prehistorians as a fundamental trait of Indo-European society (Palmer, 1953), and such a dichotomy may well have persisted into historic times in remote peripheral areas of the continent such as Ireland. Celtic society in Wales possessed a pastoral warrior aristocracy along with an unfree majority of bondmen whose economy had a stronger arable bias than that of their overlords. These bondmen lived in small nucleated settlements each with a corporately worked infield and their livestock grazed common pastures. By the 16th Century, however, the farm clusters and open fields had been replaced by isolated farms and enclosed fields (Jones, 1959). Welsh conditions were perhaps broadly comparable to those in Ireland but there may also have been important differences: the striking abundance of raths in Ireland, for example, is not matched in Wales even within the productive lowland areas.

It has been suggested (MacAirt, 1955) that the two most common Irish place-name elements, rath and baile (anglicized as bally), referred originally to distinct types of settlement, single isolated dwellings and clustered dwellings, with distinct ethnic origins. Where baile place-names are common, the pre-Celtic farmers had perhaps been left in occupation of the land, even if relegated to bondmen, while raths accommodated the Celtic immigrant population who were generally freemen of superior social status. If this interpretation were true then the distribution of baile place-names might provide a rough indication of the local distribution of early farm clusters. The only area where this view has been tested is Co. Down (Proudfoot, 1959), and in that area there is a rough but arresting tendency for raths and baile place-names to exhibit complementary distributions. Raths are less numerous in the eastern areas of the county where baile is strongly represented in place-names, and rath and baile place-names combined give a more complete picture of settlement as a whole, corresponding with that suggested by the distribution of churches and later Anglo-Norman settlements.

The distribution of raths, even on relatively homogeneous lowland areas, is uneven and we may therefore speculate that other forms of settlement once existed in the gaps even though these settlements, unlike the raths, have left no trace in the landscape. Perhaps subservient elements of society lived in undefended house clusters in the localities devoid of raths; that is, the free and unfree components of society lived not only in different types of settlement but also in different areas. This interpretation remains an intriguing possibility which only future archaeological investigation can demonstrate conclusively. Indeed all attempts significantly to deepen understanding of Irish settlement history must rely on archaeological progress. Place-name evidence has proved, in the main, unrewarding. Gaelic place-name elements simply do not fall into chronological groups in the same way as German, English or Scandinavian place-names, and thus do not help us to reconstruct the historic growth and spread of settlement. The significance attached by MacAirt and others to the baile place-names is questionable. Price (1963) has argued that in medieval documents the meaning of ''baile'' seems to be simply a ''piece of land'' and cannot be tied to the meaning ''hamlet'' or ''group of houses''. Moreover, he claims that there is no evidence of its use in the formation of place-names before the middle of the 12th Century A.D.; by the 16th Century, however, the use of baile had been greatly extended in place-names. Often in the period of Irish recovery in the 14th Century A.D. English settlements were overrun and their names translated into Irish: where the name contained the word town, baile would be substituted for it. Hence, Price argues, the proportion of baile names is greatest in the parts of Ireland which were conquered by the Anglo-Normans in the Middle Ages but later came back into Irish occupation, the Midlands, the south-east and the north-east.

No clear archaeological evidence has been found for the existence of clachans in the Pre-Medieval period. However, the evidence from Duneight rath near Lisburn, in Co. Down, is of interest (Waterman, 1963). Outside the rath and close to the entrance were found traces of occupation which may have been the remains of a dependent settlement. The *Annals of Ireland* refer to the destruction in 1010 of the fort and town of Duneight. This is indeed one of the few cases where an early Irish literary source has assisted the interpretation of an excavation. But the morphology of the "town" and the character of its buildings were not revealed by the excavation. Perhaps the destroyed settlement was originally a farm cluster or clachan occupied by bondsmen, but the evidence is not conclusive. Apart from Duneight there is no archaeological evidence for the existence of clustered settlements or for open-field cultivation; indeed wherever any evidence is available about settlements other than the raths it again suggests the prevalence of dispersed settlements with patches of enclosed fields—the very antithesis of nuclei and open-fields. At the site at Twomile Stone in south Co. Donegal (Davies, 1942) two cashels are associated with a scatter of stone huts set amid the relics of a pattern of irregular fields defined by banks of stone and earth (Fig. 10). This, as the excavator believed, may well be a settlement of free farmers and attendant bondsmen from the latest centuries of paganism, but the dwelling places are scattered and not nucleated and the enclosure pattern of walled fields further suggests individual holdings rather than communal cultivation and open fields. The huts here are small, roughly rectangular structures set in mounds of stone and earth with the floors partially excavated in the solid rock. In two cases the huts possessed stone-lined entrance passages almost 10 feet long. One of the older huts may have been a pit dwelling. The settlement studied and excavated on Beginish, Co. Kerry (O'Kelly, 1956), and most probably dating from the late Christian era or perhaps even the Early Middle Ages, presents a similar pattern of dispersed houses and small irregular fields enclosed by stone walls (Fig. 10). The houses here were stone-walled, circular structures, built partly underground and roofed with timber beams and thatch. The semi-subterranean nature of the dwellings may be linked to the exposed position of the settlement on the windswept Atlantic coast. Rather similar houses were excavated from another and probably roughly contemporary island site—Iniskea North, on the coast of Co. Mayo (Henry, 1954); they have a similar dispersed distribution. The ancient settlement of Lissachiggel in the Carlingford Mountains. Co. Down (Davies, 1939–40), consists of a cashel and a number of adjacent huts and field walls which may all be roughly contemporary and attributable to the Pre Christian Iron Age. A number of hut sites, with irregular plans, stand within the cashel or lie against its walls. There are also hut sites, resembling those in the cashel, on the surrounding open

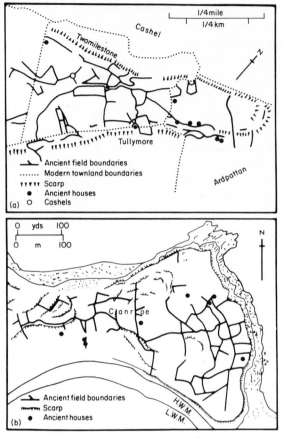

Fig. 10: Ancient (Iron Age, Early Christian) settlement patterns. **a** Twomile Stone, Co. Donegal (Davies, 1942) and **b** Beginish, Co. Kerry (O'Kelly, 1956).

moor, and the fragmentary remains of field walls built partly of upright boulders which suggest that some cultivation was carried on by the hut occupants. The huts outside the cashel, if they are to be interpreted as the residences of servile familes, are conspicuously scattered. There is no approach to clachan form and some of the huts lie several hundred feet apart.

The idea of a deep-seated dichotomy, with ethnic implications, between dispersed and nucleated settlements may be rather misleading and more recent studies have tended to emphasize the flexibility and fluidity of the settlement pattern. McCourt (1971) and others have shown how in recent centuries single farms have developed into nucleated groups, and nuclei themselves fluctuated in size with the ebb and flow of population and changes in agrarian organization and farming techniques. Such flexibility may indeed have been inherent in the settlement system from early times; rather than opposing and unchanging types of settlement there may be a single dynamic scheme within which dispersal and nucleation are alternative developments. Thus, the clachan type of settlement with open-fields can perhaps develop from ''einzelhöfe'' at any time: some of the clachans which existed in Ireland during the 17th and 18th Centuries evolved from an earlier pattern of dispersed single holdings, perhaps in some instances from the raths as the rural population gradually increased during the Middle Ages. The reverse process is not unknown and is indeed well exemplified during the last two centuries when a predominantly nucleated pattern gave way to a dispersed pattern under the influence of improving landlords and new scientific conceptions of agricultural practice. Recognition of the fluidity of the settlement pattern and the possibilities of regional variations in this pattern makes it difficult to arrive at an estimate of average conditions at any period of history and certainly undermines simplified interpretations of settlement evolution. It is probably safest to assume that the rural settlement pattern in each major period has comprised of both nucleated and dispersed elements. In the Iron Ages, for example, there were dispersed raths, and also, perhaps, dependent settlements some of which may have been nucleated. In the Medieval period there were certainly numerous dispersed holdings. Some of the raths would fall into this category as well as the monastic granges and the hundreds of isolated tower-houses whose remains are scattered over the Irish landscape. Co-existing with the tower-houses were, first, the clachans, containing groups of small farmers, and, second, the larger nucleated villages of the feudalized east and south with churches and other institutions and a differentiated social structure.

The widespread pattern of rectangular fields enclosed by banks and hedges which today forms one of the most conspicuous features of the rural scene has often been viewed as an inheritance from prehistoric times. Campbell, the distinguished Swedish ethnologist, wrote of the contemporary Irish fields as a Celtic legacy, linked with ancient pastoral traditions (Campbell, 1935), and numerous other writers, especially in the 19th and early 20th Century, tended to regard the Irish fields as of lengthy but unspecified age. However, most research since the 1930s indicates that the enclosure pattern is of comparatively recent origin, most of it having been formed since the late 17th Century. During the Middle Ages, open-field systems (organized either on an infield-outfield basis or on a three-field system) were widespread and these survived in many areas down to recent times. Some degree of enclosure, however, especially in the immediate vicinity of settlements, must always have existed. Enclosures have been noted already in association with the raths and there is evidence that fields with fixed boundaries existed in some places in the Neolithic period. There is no reason, however, to suppose that extensive tracts of landscape were systematically enclosed and it is difficult to demonstrate any continuity of these ancient field patterns down to the present day. The famous excavations at Cush in Co. Limerick (Ó'Ríordáin, 1940) are of particular importance in discussions of landscape continuity, as they appear to show that enclosures with low banks of stone and sod, identical with those existing widely in the present landscape, were associated with the raths. This, however, may not be an illustration of absolute continuity but rather a case of similar needs in different periods producing similar results. The extent of enclosure in the Irish landscape may well have varied considerably from one major historical period to another depending on the changing balance between agricultural and pastoral influences. Thus if, as can be reasonably demonstrated, a new system of enclosure was introduced after the medieval open-field systems declined, it could be a case of a lengthy history repeating itself, with the important qualification that the area of land covered by enclosures in prehistoric periods was not remotely comparable with the area covered by enclosures at the present day.

Christianity

Christianity spread rapidly throughout the country and soon occupied a central role in social and cultural life, but it was obliged to come to terms with the peculiarities of Irish conditions. Pagan and Christian ideas were frequently fused: many of the sacred sites of pagan times were adopted by the new religion (as at Kildare and Croagh Patrick), and Irish Christian art, although it received foreign influences, continued to exhibit markedly its Celtic origins. The spread of the new faith if it did not directly inspire was certainly accompanied by a quickening of economic life which is reflected in the clearance of forests especially in the damp and difficult lowlands.

Traditional Roman Christianity, which was non-monastic at the time and organized by bishops within a diocesan framework, was diffused into Ireland in the 5th Century from Britain and Gaul. This influence was first decisively felt in the north and east of the country, probably as a result of the missionary activity of St. Patrick (a converted Briton) and Palladius (a

Gaulish bishop from Auxerre). The Roman model appears to have made little headway and in the 6th Century there was a decisive trend towards monasticism, a pattern which seems to have first influenced southern Ireland and became predominant throughout the country by the 7th century (Hughes, 1966: Hanson, 1968; Ó Fiaich, 1967). The Gallic Roman Church flourished best in civilized communities where urban centres could serve as nodal points in its territorial administration and as bases for missionary activities in the rural hinterlands ("paganus" = countryman). Ireland did not provide a favourable milieu. Having escaped the Roman imperial occupation the country did not possess an urban system to accommodate the new ecclesiastical organization; society remained tribal and exclusively rural. A federation of Celtic monastic communities developed in place of the Roman diocesan system. New monasteries were located in isolated rath settlements and thus Christianity became an essentially rural organization relating to rather than modifying the traditionally diffuse pattern of farm settlements. There was an absence in Ireland not only of towns to serve as ecclesiastical centres but of nucleated villages to provide natural nodes for the development of a parochial system. Save in the coastal towns established by the Vikings, there is no evidence for the existence of parochial organization until the Norman colonization in the 12th Century which also introduced manorial organization and village settlements into the eastern and southern parts of the country. In the north and west of the country, where Norman settlement was sparse, parochial development was even more belated.

The organization of the early Irish monasteries differed markedly from the mainstreams of monastic organization in Western Europe. There was little of the uniformity of discipline which was to become characteristic of the great continental orders such as the Cluniacs, Cistercians and Benedictines. The Irish pattern seems to have been one of variety and idiosyncracy, expressing native inclinations and institutions, deriving some of its inspiration from the eremitical movement of the Levant and Eastern Mediterranean but influenced too by Roman Christianity. In their physical lay-out the Irish monasteries were also distinctive, utilizing native building traditions to accommodate the new monastic organization (de Paor, 1964). The monks, for example, adopted the traditional habit of building within a circular rath or cashel (Plate 6), a form of enclosure used widely by contemporary secular settlements but also of long-standing use for religious purposes as is illustrated by the great enclosures which surround a number of Neolithic and Bronze Age megalithic tombs and standing stones. Within the monastic enclosures stood a small church of rectangular plan, while the monks lived in detached cells or circular huts made of corbelled dry stone or wood and wattles, structures which have been built for diverse functions in Ireland from the remotest periods of prehistory right down to the present century.

Hundreds of small monastic settlements grew up in all areas of the country. Only a select few developed into major centres: in these cases the buildings often overflowed the original cashel boundaries and a scatter of new churches and cells were built outside it. In the 9th Century a tall round tower was sometimes added to the collection of buildings, partly to serve as a campanile but also as a refuge from attacks by Vikings and Irish chieftains who were interested in the accumulated wealth of the monasteries (Plate 6). The larger and more famous monasteries were centres of learning and artistic endeavour of an order unprecedented in Ireland (Henry, 1954; Bieler, 1963). They were also self-supporting institutions economically, producing their own food by farming and fishing. The nationwide spread of monasteries must have brought land clearance and productive activity into many hitherto unsettled areas, especially as many of the early communities deliberately selected sites of extreme remoteness such as off-shore islands and inaccessible mountain glens. Scores of monastic settlements were also built in lowland areas which previously had been forested and little occupied. Many of the most inception. It is likely that the prefix ''kil'' (cill = church), found widely Clonfert and Clonmacnoise, are located in the central belt of Ireland in areas which by nature were damp and thickly wooded. Here the monasteries may well have pioneered the ground, preparing the way for the spread of farming folk and the building of raths.

Eremiticism was an integral part of Irish monasticism from its inception. It is likely that the prefix ''kil'' (cil = church), found widely as an element in place-names, is in many places associated with the tiny churches or oratories which the eremites built. Many of these structures must have been small and made with perishable materials; frequently all traces have disappeared but in a few localities with long traditions of building in stone, such as the Dingle peninsula in Co. Kerry, the oratories have survived. Sometimes, if the sanctity of the eremite was sufficient, he attracted followers who, in time, built their cells and oratories near his, and many major monastic centres, such as Glendalough and Clonmacnoise, developed in this uncoordinated way around the cells of distinguished ''sancti''.

Archaeological remains and place-names from the Early Christian period are very numerous but by no means uniform in character throughout the country. Significant regional variations perhaps reflect missionary efforts which reached the country from a variety of sources or, alternatively, represent the merging or colouring of the new Christianity with pre-existing regional cultures. Among the archaeological remains of the period which exhibit geographical concentration are killeens and ogham stones. Killeens are small rath-like enclosures whose boundaries are characteristically formed by field walls. The killeens, however, are in most cases considerably older than the field boundaries which have probably accommodated the killeen sites in the course of their recent expansion. Within the killeen enclosures there are frequently the remains of a church and numerous cross-inscribed stones. In recent centuries the enclosures have often been used as children's burial grounds, primarily for the burying of unbaptized or still-born children who were not permitted to be buried in consecrated ground, but originally many of the enclosures must have been church sites and perhaps associated with a very early phase of Christianity. The distribution of the killeens is essentially south-western but the complete distribution is not fully known; it may be that many more sites once existed elsewhere in the country and have been destroyed by field formation and recent enclosure movements as allegiance to the ancient customs associated with child burial withered away. Ogham is a peculiar script based on the Roman alphabet and belonging to a very early period of Irish Christianity. It was used for writing epitaphs and was frequently incised on memorial stones many of which have been preserved. The surviving inscriptions have a predominantly southern distribution in Ireland and indeed are often associated with the killeens.

Bowen (1969) has described how the place-name elements "diseart" and "teampall", although found over the whole of Ireland, have a predominantly southern location indicative again that a distinctive Christian ethos originally existed in the south of the country in those areas where the monastic ideal first gained a foothold and flourished. The prefix "diseart" is derived from "desertum", the original milieu of the eremitical movement, and its southerly distribution suggests the intrusive nature of monasticism and perhaps direct contact between southern Ireland and the eastern Mediterranean along the ancient Atlantic seaways and without the mediating influence of the Gallo-Roman world.

The monasteries replaced the old political centres such as Tara in Co. Meath and Cashel in Co. Tipperary and remained the main kind of settlement focus in the Irish landscape from the 5th and 6th Centuries down to the beginning of the Anglo-Norman colony. But even the largest monastic centres, which contained several hundred people, were not towns in any modern sense. They lacked, for example, regular commercial or industrial organization and do not seem to have possessed a clearly defined or regular street plan. Both on functional and morphological grounds they cannot properly be described as urban. The monasteries were numerous and widespread but the sites were generally ignored when the medieval network of towns was established by the Anglo-Normans. The break between the two systems was not complete, however, and a limited number of monastic sites, such as Trim, Kildare, Kells, Slane, Clondalkin and Downpatrick, re-emerged as medieval urban centres or important villages. At Kells the medieval town seems to have grown up among the remains of the famous Columban monastery but most often the medieval settlements have a slightly different "centre of gravity" from the ancient monasteries. In Downpatrick, Co. Down, for example, the ancient cathedral is located where the Patrician monastery stood but the town has grown on lower ground to the east. Likewise at Slane in Co. Meath, which is situated at a fording point of the River Boyne, the ancient monastery stands to the north of the settlement on a 500 feet (153 m) high hill. At Cashel too the town grew up close to but detached from the monastic "acropolis" which was located on a precipitous limestone outcrop. Whether at any sites there was direct continuity of settlement from the monastic to the medieval period is uncertain. Continuity of site is easy to establish; continuity of settlement is a different matter and harder to confirm.

There is much to suggest that Irish monasticism had lost its vigour and that many of the monasteries had decayed before the Normans arrived. This is not to argue that Irish society as a whole was in decline; indeed there is evidence in the 9th and 10th Centuries of a flourishing cultural life, and contact with Norse coastal trading bases quickened the commercial life of the country. But Norse raids had a serious effect on monastic culture and many monasteries both on the coast and inland were plundered repeatedly during the 9th Century. As the Viking crisis reached its peak there was mounting anarchy among the Irish themselves, and internal warfare also led to the destruction of many churches and settlements (de Paor, 1967; Lucas, 1967). Perhaps more important were the far-reaching ecclesiastical reforms carried out in the 12th Century, under the influence of the Hildebrandine reforms, before the coming of the Anglo-Normans. These reforms tended to diminish the status of the Irish monasteries. A series of synods in the first half of the 12th Century under the auspices of native chieftains and prelates promoted the establishment of diocesan organization in place of the old monastic organization (Hughes, 1966). The dioceses took on much the same form as they have today and Ireland was divided into four ecclesiastical provinces with archiepiscopal sees at Armagh, Dublin, Cashel and Tuam. Several decades later the great continental orders, led by the Benedictines and the Cistercians, were introduced into the country in order to further the reform of church life. With their subsequent and rapid spread the era of the older Irish monasteries was decisively ended. It was not only Viking aggression but the zeal and determination of native reformers which brought about the eclipse of the old order and introduced a new. This would help to explain the tendency for Norman towns to grow up on new sites. In the cases where there is a correspondence of site between the monastic and medieval settlements, the slight shift of settlement focus which often occurs may be diagnostic of a break in the continuity of habitation.

The Viking Settlement

The conventional image of the Vikings as warriors and pirates has obscured the important place which colonization and trade played in their political and economic life. Piracy was common in the early stages of Viking contact with the outside world but it was soon followed by colonization, settlement and peaceful commercial relationships. Once settled in a foreign country the Vikings developed local trade with their neighbours and their traditions of exploration and adventuring made them important agents of international trade also. Commerce on such a scale demanded large trading stations and it was from these that the first towns grew up, both in Scandinavia and in the Norse colonies (Foote and Wilson, 1970).

The earliest Viking contacts with Ireland were of a piratical nature and the onslaught was directed primarily at the wealth of the highly vulnerable Irish monasteries. The first recorded visitation of the Vikings to the Irish coasts was in 795 when the church of Rechru on Lambay Island off Dublin was plundered and burnt. There may, however, have been earlier and unrecorded raids. A period of raiding which involved monastic sites all around the Irish coasts was followed after the early years of the 9th Century by permanent settlement in fortified strongholds.

The Vikings could not effectively subjugate the country owing to the incoherent pattern of Irish society which was divided into hundreds of small kingdoms or tuaths with varying degrees of independence. Military victory against an individual tuath simply could not be consolidated. Had large kingdoms with centralized administrative structures existed the task would have been easier as the conquerors would have inherited machinery for enforcing their authority. However, if there were obstacles to general conquest, the absence of concentrated opposition did mean that the Norse were able easily to establish permanent footholds in the country. After a period of plundering, the Norse settled down in coastal strongholds from which they maintained strong links with the outside world as well as measured relationships with their Irish neighbours from whom they were separated by language, customs and economic interests. Considerable contact between the Norse and Irish did occur, political, economic and cultural, despite the general aloofness of the Norse community. Some Irish kings, for example, retained Norse mercenaries in their service and the Norsemen from the coastal strongholds sometimes allied themselves with one side or the other in the constant warfare and bickering between the Irish kings.

Viking settlement was focused initially in the west and especially in Limerick from which easy access along the Shannon was possible into the interior of the country (Young, 1950). Dublin was fortified in 841, and thereafter, throughout the 9th and 10th Centuries, Norse colonies, ruled by independent kings, were established along the eastern and southern coasts. Smaller settlements, perhaps only trading stations, existed inland, at Cashel and Thurles for example. The great ports of Southern Ireland, Dublin, Limerick, Waterford, Wexford and perhaps Cork, all owe their existence to the Vikings (Walsh, 1922). Small Irish settlements may have preexisted on or near the sites but they were not of an urban character. Dublin eventually became the principal Viking settlement; it was the centre from which the Irish sea was controlled, and an international port dealing with the exchange of commodities, such as slaves and silver, between northern Europe and the Mediterranean. It was perhaps people from the Dublin colony who settled in Cumbria and on the coasts of Lancashire and Cheshire in the early 10th Century where many of the place names betoken Norse settlers whose language had been modified by previous settlement in Gaelic areas (Wainwright, 1943). The Norse centres, although eventually brought under the nominal control of Irish kings, were never completely assimilated into Irish life and they retained a separate identity right up to the Anglo-Norman invasion. In the 10th Century there is evidence that the Norsemen in Ireland were being converted to Christianity but it is indicative of the separateness of the Norse settlers that the ecclesiastical links of Dublin and Waterford were with Canterbury rather than with the Irish church. The

Dublin Vikings or Ostmen remained of importance in the life of the city until 1171–72 when the city was handed over by Henry II to the men of Bristol, another great trading centre of the Irish sea which, like Dublin, had contained a colony of Viking merchants. After the Anglo-Norman conquest of Ireland the Norse communities in the coastal ports appear to have been settled in concentrations outside the walls of the cities. An identifiable Norse community can be traced around Limerick until at least the 13th Century.

The influence of the Vikings in Ireland was thus felt most directly in two very different ways: first, as a destructive influence on the traditional but perhaps already waning monastic culture, and, second, through the introduction of an urban tradition and the related quickening of commercial life and international ties. It may also be true that the Viking assaults generated for the first time within Ireland some sense of national identity (Binchy, 1962), as the Irish kings who provided effective opposition to the Vikings gained a new prestige among their countrymen which permitted them to claim authority over wide areas of the country. It was as a focus of resistance to the Vikings that the Tara monarchy, for example, grew to pre-eminence in Ireland. It is more certain that the prosperous trading towns must have had considerable impact upon the primitive pastoral economy of the Irish, forcing Irish society, at least in the south of the country, to adopt a more progressive commercial economy. The first coinage struck in Ireland was that of the Norse kingdom of Dublin (Dolley, 1965), and it is no accident that many of the Irish terms in shipbuilding, commerce and coinage are Norse loan words.

The Vikings do not seem to have settled to any significant extent outside their trading towns. The number of surviving Norse place-names is small and confined almost entirely to the urban centres and their immediate hinterland. Furthermore, the contemporary farming settlements of the Irish—the raths, crannogs and cashels—are notably free of objects showing contact with Viking civilization. There is, indeed, no clear indication in Ireland that Vikings ever became a rural peasantry as they did in the Shetland and Orkney Islands, the Western Isles of Scotland and the extensive Danelaw in eastern England. In Britain it is noteworthy that the Vikings were not town builders nor even, it would seem, town dwellers to any great extent. Moreover, when the Irish Viking community migrated to western Britain they apparently settled down there, despite their urban background, as a rural peasantry. The influence of the Vikings on Ireland was important; they introduced urban life and through their commercial linkages they brought the country, after a long period of isolation, into the mainstreams of European life. But the direct contribution of the Vikings to the landscape was limited to small coastal territories where their towns grew up. We cannot with certainty point to any rural landscape features which have been inherited from the Vikings.

5
The Middle Ages

The Anglo-Norman colonization in the latter half of the 12th Century was the first important immigrant movement to Ireland for more than a millenium and its consequences were far-reaching. Political conflicts ensued between native and settler, the latter often backed by English authority, which have remained the stuff of Irish history down to the present day. In terms also of the economic and social life of the country and its cultural landscape, the imprint of the colonization proved to be enduring even though much of the rural settlement pattern established by the immigrants was destroyed or obscured by later historical developments. The colony made its impact mainly in southern and eastern Ireland to which the immigrants, many of whom originated in adjacent Wales, were doubtless attracted by the existence of extensive and potentially rich agricultural lowlands. Here, improved methods of husbandry were introduced in association with new forms of rural settlement and, for the first time in inland areas, a network of urban centres was created. The introduction of castles, monasteries, friaries, manors, villages, parochial organization, improved agriculture and walled towns made the south and east of Ireland (see Fig. 11) an integral part of the feudal world of western Europe and gave the area a decisive commercial and cultural lead over the remainder of the country which it seems never to have lost until the advent of the 19th Century industrial revolution in eastern Ulster.

It is important to set the Anglo-Norman colonization of Ireland in a wide European context. Throughout Europe between the 11th and 13th Centuries fundamental economic and social developments were occurring; trade and industry were reviving, substantial population growth and migration are evident, and massive land reclamation was proceeding in many areas hitherto wooded and boggy. Improved methods of husbandry were introduced in both the old settled areas and the new, and new towns were founded on a great scale, especially in the eastern and western borderlands of Europe, in association with the marked expansion of farmed land and population (Mayhew, 1973). The Anglo-Norman

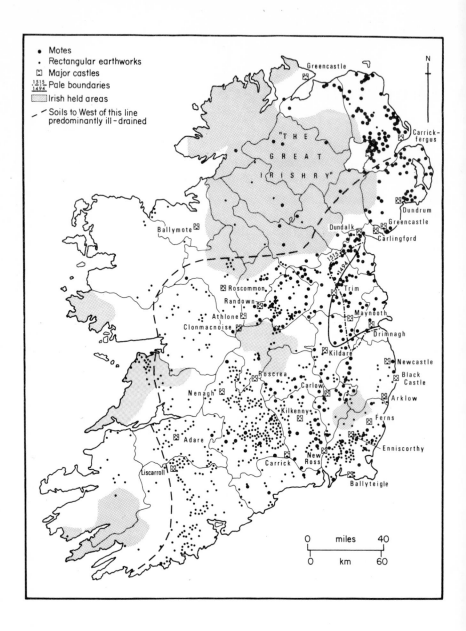

Fig. 11: Distribution of medieval motes, rectangular earthworks and major castles: Irish enclaves in the 14th Century: English pale at end of 15th Century. (Based mainly on Glasscock, 1970, 1975.)

conquest thus brought Ireland into the mainstreams of European development during a crucial phase of European history. Indeed, the conquest might be usefully seen as simply one of the wide variety of migratory movements in Europe which were linked to a general expansion of population and quickening of economic life on the continent. It is of interest too that the decline of the Anglo-Norman colony later in the Medieval period occurred at a time of widespread economic depression in western Europe. With the Anglo-Norman conquest therefore, the cultural and economic insularity of Ireland is terminated and secular trends in the economic life of the country begin to show a correspondence with general European developments.

The Norman settlement in Ireland, which commenced in 1167, over a century after the invasion of England, was not a centrally controlled campaign. Just as in lowland Scotland, the settlement resulted from the individual enterprise of ambitious barons. Those who ventured into Ireland were drawn mainly from the troubled marcher lands of Wales where during the previous century they had established themselves as a ruling military caste. Their military superiority enabled them rapidly to conquer the disunited Irish; almost two thirds of the country was occupied and divided up into extensive territories under the control of powerful families such as de Lacy in the ancient province of Meath, the Butlers in northern Munster and de Courcy in eastern Ulster. Military conquest was promptly followed by the establishment of effective administration within a new framework of manors, baronies and shires. This in turn produced an unprecedented degree of law and order under which commercial and cultural life flourished.

The English kings were obliged to intervene in Ireland to curtail the growing power and independence of its new lords. In 1171 Henry II visited Ireland with a powerful army and the troublesome "Lordship of Ireland" was established. The Norman lords henceforth were to hold their lands as the king's tenants and many of the Irish chieftains were also prepared to recognize Henry as overlord; but their was no decisive conquest of Ireland by the English monarchy. Allegiance to the English king was only acceptable to the Irish lords because it seemed some safeguard against the ambitions of their rivals. The allegiance was superficial and if English authority relaxed then most local magnates were ready to assert their independence. The fact that the colonial territories were conquered and developed by private enterprise helped to generate a strong tradition of independence among the Norman rulers, while, so far as the Irish chieftains were concerned, there was clearly no compelling reason for them to forget their ancient autonomy. The Anglo-Norman colony, like traditional Irish society, thus lacked any strong unified structure; its various parts were always inclined to assert their separateness and to engage in conflict with each other.

There was another and perhaps more crucial weakness in the basic structure of the colony, namely that Norman authority never extended over the whole of Ireland. The Norman adventurers were not attracted in any great numbers to the bleaker north and west of Ireland which was farthest removed from Wales and where agricultural resources were poorer than in the east. Here, native lords often remained in control of their ancestral territories, and a cultural redoubt existed from which at a later period in history a Gaelic resurgence and territorial expansion could be mounted. Connacht, it is true, was conquered but the influence of the Normans was mainly felt in the eastern lowlands of that province and, while numerous urban centres, such as Galway, Loughrea and Athenry, were established and important monasteries and friaries were founded, there is little evidence of lasting influence in the rural areas. The mountainous peninsulas of western Connacht and the ill-drained drumlin belt in the north-east of the province (approximately the area of the present-day counties of Leitrim and Roscommon) were left in the main to the Gaelic Irish, but Norman families eventually settled in a few locations even as far afield as the coastal lowlands of Erris in Co. Mayo, surely one of the loneliest locations in western Europe. The Normans made little headway in western Ulster and their footholds in eastern Ulster were always precarious. In the remote north-westerly parts of Ulster the life and archaic social institutions of the indigenous people were left untouched, and indeed remained undisturbed until the end of the 16th Century.

It is necessary here to describe briefly the long-term history of the colony before a fuller account is given of the nature of the settlement and cultural landscape within it. The eventual decline of the Anglo-Norman colony may seem an unexpected outcome. The Anglo-Normans were clearly superior to the Irish in military strength, capable of conquering, settling and administering the richest parts of the country, and enterprising enough to establish a network of fortified urban centres to protect their lands and serve as foci for commercial life. Their eventual cultural dominance might thus have been reasonably anticipated. However, a variety of external and internal circumstances and events led to a different outcome. There were, from the outset, certain weaknesses in the position of the colony *vis à vis* the Irish. First, the colonists were in a minority, so much so that economic cooperation with the Irish was essential from the earliest stages of settlement, even to work the manors effectively. Second, both the Irish and the Norman areas were fragmented. In the south and east, for example, the Anglo-Normans settled mainly on the richer lowlands, such as those in eastern Co. Kildare and in Co. Meath, in the wide fertile valleys of the Barrow, Nore and Slaney, and on level productive coastlands such as Cooley in Co. Louth, the plain of Mourne and the Ards in Co. Down, areas which could be protected by garrison towns and serviced by sea in the event of Irish attack. The unproductive hill areas and the surviving areas of woodland, as well as the extensive bog tracts, became the refuges of the native Irish. These refuge areas, especially the hill masses, often overlooked the feudalized lowlands. In times of unrest this haphazard arrangement meant that the colony could not be adequately protected, and in times of peace cultural borrowings could not be prevented. The more or less peaceful absorption of the colonists into Gaelic Ireland was the dominant trend, and this is understandable as the colonists were, after all, a minority existing in geographically scattered enclaves and, in view of their diverse origins, without any common cultural tradition of their own. Thus, in many areas, the colony was ultimately assimilated rather than decisively over-thrown. It was against this ethnic fusion that legislation such as the famous Statutes of Kilkenny in 1366, designed to keep the races apart and preserve intact the "English" character of the settlers, was enacted. The statutes, however, failed completely in their purpose and the process of assimilation went on.

By the beginning of the 14th Century the balance of forces within the country had begun to tip in favour of the native Irish. The separate identity of the colonists was increasingly diluted by acculturation and the frontiers of the colony were slowly pushed back not only by spasmodic warfare on the peripheries but by expansion of the Irish enclaves which had always existed within the colony. The so-called "Gaelic Revival," however, was always piecemeal and there was no concerted effort to consolidate and unite the Irish areas. Two events in the 14th century provided special opportunities for the resurgence of the native Irish population. The colony was, in the first place, seriously weakened by the Scottish invasion of Ireland in 1315 by Edward Bruce. Bruce was crowned High King of Ireland at Dundalk in 1316 but he had no solid native support and after a campaign of extreme ferocity, involving widespread destruction, he was deserted by his allies, overthrown and killed (Lydon, 1963). The violence and destruction of the Bruce invasion had a disturbing effect on the economic life and the morale of the colony. Villages, towns and lands were laid waste and many colonists drifted back to England and their lands were re-occupied by the Irish. Later in the 14th Century, the Black Death swept Ireland (Gwynn, 1935). In Ireland, as elsewhere in medieval Europe, the visitation of severe epidemics, especially bubonic plague, was a recurrent feature. The outbreaks were particularly severe during the 14th Century and they must have made some substantial inroads into the rural population, even to the extent of causing whole settlements to be abandoned. However, the available evidence is quite inadequate to permit a quantitative estimate of the demographic consequences of the Black Death in Ireland. In England it has been estimated that the Black Death and its sequelae may have reduced the population by half by the end of the 14th Century (Russell, 1948). The effect on the Anglo-Norman population may well have been similar, as their urban centres and cereal farming provided the conditions most conducive to the rat population and hence to the spread of plague. The pastoral economy and diffuse settlement pattern in the Irish areas provided some protection and, although it is clear that the Irish did suffer, their losses may have been proportionately less. The Anglo-Norman colony was thus weakened relative to the Irish, and contemporary accounts relate the wide extent of depopulation in the countryside and the tendency for the settlements of the colonists to be abandoned.

The declining fortunes of the Anglo-Norman colony occur at a time which seems to be one of general depression in western Europe, especially in rural areas. To a much greater extent than the Irish areas, the colony depended on external trade and it could therefore scarcely be immune to these wider economic developments. Settlement desertion and the expansion of woodland and waste at the expense of farmed land were, as will be described later, widespread phenomena in late medieval Europe. Developments in Ireland, therefore, may not be explicable solely in terms of internal events, but as yet Irish medieval historians have made little effort to set Irish developments in their wider European context and the importance of the international depression to the fortunes of the Anglo-Norman colony cannot be accurately assessed.

During most of the 15th Century the attention of the English and their resources in manpower and money were diverted to their monumental wars in France and their civil wars. The support of the Anglo-Norman colonists and the containment of the Irish along an extensive land frontier was not a priority. Nevertheless, the crown did not recognize the continued reduction of its territorial authority; it continued to claim the whole of Ireland even though, with the exception of the strong towns, its authority was limited to Dublin, Meath, Louth and Kildare. This group of counties was commonly called the ''Pale'' and it was only here that English customs and law were given any serious degree of respect. The geographical limits of effective English authority, however, fluctuated throughout the 15th Century and the Pale should not be envisaged as a stable administrative entity with well-defined boundaries. Outside the Pale, and in some places even within it, the great Anglo-Irish families, who were often of Norman-Irish descent, ruled their extensive territories in virtual independence of the English crown. Within the Pale itself there was often unrest, and cattle raiding was common especially by the Irish of the Leinster mountains who periodically plundered the adjacent lowlands and made forays to the vicinity of Dublin. Even within sight of the walls of the city it was the habit of landed families to dwell in tower houses for purposes of security. As the Middle Ages progress, the gulf between the Anglo-Normans and the English government widens. By the 15th Century the fusion of the Irish and the Anglo-Normans had proceeded so far that a new hybrid culture had emerged and it is almost pointless to argue which of the two groups ''triumphed'' over the other. The conflict between the English government and the Irish as a whole became of more moment than the differences between the colonists and the Gaelic Irish. However, the descendants of the more important Norman families retained some distinctiveness for many centuries. As late as the 17th Century they were still identified as the ''Old English'', and distinguished by their catholicism and deep roots in the country from the immigrant English landowners of the Tudor and Jacobean periods, new settlers whose protestantism marked them in an age when Irish nationalism became inextricably bound up with catholicism.

Although the outlines of the Anglo-Norman conquest and the broad pattern of settlement in the colony have been established by historians (Otway-Ruthven, 1968), there is relatively little detailed information available on the appearance of the medieval landscape. Historical geographers in Ireland have paid little attention to the medieval landscape, perhaps even less than the inherent difficulties of the subject justify. One basic cause of the poverty of research is the relative newness of geography as a subject in Irish universities but, quite apart from this, there are formidable problems to be faced in any attempt to reconstruct the geography of medieval Ireland. Relative, for example, to England there is a dearth of documentary material and a complete absence of cartographical sources. The Anglo-Norman settlement, unlike the later phases of colonial enterprise in Ireland, did not result in any significant attempts to record the geographical character of the occupied territories, or at least no such records have survived. Nothing remotely comparable to the Great English surveys, such as the Domesday Survey of 1086 or the Lay Subsidy of 1334, exists for medieval Ireland. The absence of comprehensive surveys is partly owing to the lack of a centralized government with the authority or resources to undertake them. The Anglo-Norman conquest was carried out by individual lords and conditions in the colony were perhaps too unsettled and the lords too concerned with their security to embark on systematic survey and mapping. What we particularly lack are comprehensive standardized surveys to act as a base-line in investigations, so that it could be clearly established over extensive geographical areas which settlements existed at a particular point of time. The older elements of the settlement pattern and the newer could then be broadly distinguished and the vexing question of how far there has been continuity of settlement might be partly resolved. Because of the limited documentary sources, archaeological investigation is potentially of high importance but archaeologists in Ireland, as elsewhere in the British Isles, have tended until very recently to ignore medieval material and to concentrate upon the monuments of prehistory. Our knowledge of medieval settlement patterns and field systems, indeed of the medieval cultural landscape as a whole, is thus in many respects unsatisfactory. Indeed knowledge is so poor that it is hard to provide preliminary orientation for archaeological investigation. It is clear that numerous medieval settlements had been deserted by the 15th and 16th Centuries but it is difficult to locate their positions. The problems of identification are particularly difficult in a countryside which abounds in ancient earthworks, many of which cannot be accurately dated.

As the Norman conquest proceeded, the subdued territories were secured by the building of numerous strongholds. During the initial phases of the settlement the most common form of stronghold was the mote-and-bailey earthwork (Orpen, 1907; Lawlor, 1938, 1939), a feature which often formed the focal point of new manors. There are almost 400 of these earthworks surviving in the present-day landscape and their distribution is a rough indication of the extent of Norman settlement (Glasscock, 1975). Mote-and-bailey earthworks follow a standard pattern. The main element is a flat-topped mound or mote (a derivation from the Norman-French word, "motte," which means a mound) on which wooden palisades and towers were erected. The mounds are usually artificial features built from ground level or added to pre-existing Irish earthworks; sometimes they are natural features, such as rock outcrops at Doonmore, Co. Antrim, and at Fore, Co. Westmeath, or esker ridges as at Middlemount, Co. Laois, and Cloonburren, Co. Roscommon. Baileys or courtyards of crescentic or rectangular plan were often built alongside the mote but at a lower level and usually but not always separated from it by a ditch. The great majority of the motes and mote-and-bailey earthworks were erected, probably hastily, during the early stages of the conquest and they were succeeded after about 1200 by the stone castles, as at Trim (Plate 8a), Carlow, Roscommon and Liscarroll, fewer in number than the motes but greatly superior in strength. It is possible that in some areas the motes continued in use until the 14th and even the early 15th Centuries. Stone castles were sometimes sited on top of motes but more generally they are located on new strategic sites, and under their protection new forms of settlement, the villages and towns, were able to develop.

Much of the Anglo-Norman settlement pattern in rural areas was subsequently swept away and the settlement features which have survived best and most profusely are the major fortified sites and the towns. These survivals give a misleading impression of the overall character of settlement in the colony. The Anglo-Norman settlers were not, as conventionally thought, predominantly urban or aristocratic. Farmers and artisans were involved; indeed the new settlement was largely rural in character, reminiscent of the large-scale colonization movements of peasant people occurring elsewhere in medieval Europe, especially in the east from Germanic to Slavic territories. Manorial organization, clearly modelled on English practice, was introduced into Ireland and considerable bodies of Welsh and English settlers, as well as Flemings from the Flemish settlements in Wales, were established in the countryside of south-eastern Ireland from Co. Kerry to Co. Louth, with an important outlier in the eastern areas of counties Down and Antrim.

Although no detailed map evidence survives from the Middle Ages there are many medieval inquisitions and deeds which show clearly that villages with open-fields and scattered strip holdings (Fig. 12), worked sometimes on a two or three field system, were of fundamental importance in the rural economy (Otway-Ruthven, 1951). These villages, especially in northern Leinster, might contain a medieval church and substantial houses, which after the 13th Century were replaced by tower-houses, and sometimes the settlements served as the centres for the developing parochial system. It is clear that it was the Normans who first undertook the task of organizing the countryside into parishes, and in the south and east of the country there is a close correspondence between the extent of secular manors and the new parochial boundaries. These

E

Plate 8: Medieval castle and monastery. **a** Trim castle, Co. Meath. The square keep, which is one of the most impressive examples of medieval military architecture in Ireland, dates from about 1200 and stands on the remnant of an earlier mote. Portions of the curtain wall, gatehouse and flanking towers also survive. **b** Jerpoint Abbey, Thomastown, Co. Kilkenny. A Cistercian foundation, once affiliated to Fountains Abbey, Yorkshire.

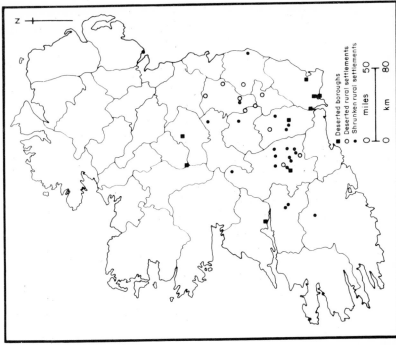

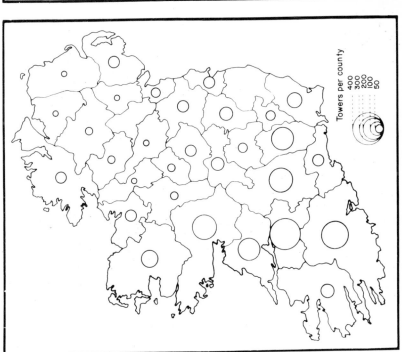

Fig. 12: Distribution of tower houses and deserted medieval settlements (Smith and Hayes, 1965; Glasscock, 1970).

medieval parishes have evolved, often through many amalgamations, into the present-day civil parishes and correspond closely with the ecclesiastical parishes of the Church of Ireland: the contemporary outlines of Roman Catholic parishes, however, derive from an 18th Century reorganization and diverge appreciably from the medieval pattern. Where the term ''manor'' occurs in medieval documents it does not always imply an estate worked on the medieval village pattern found, for example, in lowland England. Outside the south-eastern parts of Ireland, in the areas which the Anglo-Norman lords subjugated but did not intensively settle, manors were simply tracts of land, where the Irish pattern of life and settlement often continued unchanged: there is still however a close identity of manor and parish. Within the village communities of the south and east the demesne land of manorial lords seems often to have been a compact area entirely separate from the lands of other classes of the agricultural community. Besides the demesnes there were numerous other relatively large compact holdings. Some of these resulted from the engrossing of open-field strips, a process which was occurring piecemeal from the 13th Century onwards. Frequently in documents of the late medieval period there are references to ''imparking'' and to ''crofts'' and ''parks'' located among the ''acres'' and ''stangs'' which are the open-field strips. Other compact holdings, sometimes centred on isolated tower houses and the moated farmsteads, existed outside the framework of the villages, and probably originated in many cas 2s from individual enterprise in clearing the then widespread forest and bog for cultivation. However, any enclosure existing in association with compact holdings, either on village lands or outside them, seems to have been by ditches rather than fences and hedges. There is no evidence to suggest that enclosures existed on any appreciable scale and most of the arable land seems to have been laid out in open-fields.

The servile tenants (betaghs) who existed on many manors were, at least in the early medieval period, almost exclusively Irish. Sometimes the betagh community occupied a quite separate portion of the manor, perhaps a definite townland. Where the holdings of the betaghs were separate they may have been cultivated on a native open-field system smaller in scale and more fluid in pattern than the Anglo-Norman system and associated with small clusters of farms rather than villages. There may indeed be direct continuity between these farm clusters and the numerous clachans or farm clusters still surviving in many parts of south-eastern Ireland, especially in the counties of Wexford, Waterford and Kilkenny where the Norman settlement was first concentrated. However, as is indicated later, the precise ethnic origin of these and other similar settlement forms is difficult to determine conclusively.

The medieval rural organization and the cultural landscape of south-eastern Ireland was thus essentially similar to that in lowland England and indeed north-western Europe as a whole, with areas of open-field cultivation surrounding compact villages and interspersed with large consolidated holdings and patches of common grazing land and rough woodland. It is difficult to assess how much of the human geography of the Celtic periods survived the settlement of the Normans. There can be little doubt, however, that many of the native people continued to live within the confines of the colony. The marked persistence of Irish place-names and territorial divisions is evidence of this. The minor Irish kingdoms or tuaths, for example, often became the medieval baronies, and Irish estates often provided the territorial framework for the newly constituted manors and parishes. The survival of place-names and territorial boundaries is not, of course, evidence of the survival of the pre-Norman settlement pattern and route system. In the east of Ireland most of this seems to have rapidly withered away. Rath settlements disappeared and a new network of urban centres and routeways emerged. Villages and towns eclipsed the old monasteries as the chief focal points in the landscape, although a number of new settlements were at the sites of old monasteries, for example, Swords, Clondalkin and Tallaght, all in Co. Dublin, the town of Kilkenny, and Roscrea in Co. Tipperary.

Documented sites from the Middle Ages are usually Anglo-Norman and this tends to give an unbalanced view of prevailing conditions. In the extensive Irish areas beyond the colony and especially in the remote north-west, there was probably little fundamental change in the ancient pattern of life. Some Anglo-Norman settlement features were borrowed, but in the main the residents continued to hold their land in the old way. As the Middle Ages progressed, the raths and crannogs were gradually abandoned but many of the freemen must have continued the tradition of living in dispersed farmsteads and the working of compact holdings. We may tentatively conclude that the servile elements of society lived nearby in some other form of settlement, perhaps in farm clusters or clachans. In the purely Gaelic areas the only settlements which approached urban status were the episcopal centres such as Armagh and Rosscarbery in West Cork. At Sligo, however, it seems that the Anglo-Norman borough continued to exist throughout the Middle Ages even although under a Gaelic lord (Nichols, 1972).

It would be wrong to envisage medieval Ireland as simply divided into two antagonistic and self-contained culture regions. By the 13th Century there were communities with different degrees of Gaelic or Anglo-Norman orientation. Along the frontier lands the Norman settlers were slowly assimilated to Irish life and fashions, married into Gaelic families and adopted the Irish language, so that by the 14th Century they were scarcely distinguishable from their Gaelic neighbours. At the same time the independent Irish absorbed cultural elements from the Norman colonists, including the building of castles, tower houses and even, in some places, mote-and-bailey earthworks, and the colony therefore had some indirect influence on the cultural landscape of the Irish areas.

The establishment of the Anglo-Norman settlers led to considerable reclamation of new land, especially through deforestation. The virgin forests of the southern river valleys, such as the Barrow and Nore, were removed and the infamous territory of Gowran on the Leinster-Ossory marches, for example, was denuded of its abundant forest. In the territory of Hy Kinsella, in the south-eastern corner of Ireland, the extensive and dense forest of Duffry, which lay between the Mount Leinster Ridge and the River Slaney and provided a natural stronghold and rallying ground for defiant native bands, was progressively cleared. In Meath the Forest of Trim, which still existed in the early medieval period, was cleared away to provide agricultural land. Forest clearance not only provided new land for agriculture but was also undertaken to facilitate safe communication between settled areas, and the place-name element "pass" (as in Tyrrellspass and Milltownpass, Co. Westmeath, and Poyntzpass in Co. Armagh) came to connote an avenue of communication cleared through forest rather than a topographic corridor through hills. Efficient communications were sometimes difficult to establish owing to the numerous lakes, bogs and marshes as well as the forests. The River Shannon, with its flanking marshland, subject to periodic extensive flooding, was a particularly severe obstacle to east-west communication across the Central Lowlands. Centralized government even within the various regions of the country was difficult to enforce and the cultural distinctiveness of regions could survive, especially where physical features, such as hill barriers or bog tracts, reinforced the separateness of communities.

With the advent of the continental monastic orders from the 12th Century onwards, a new and dynamic force for change in the landscape was introduced. Benedictine foundations were comparatively few and the most numerous of the orders were the Cistercian and Augustinian. The Cistercians were the most enterprising order, establishing themselves in more than 35 abbeys. Many of the major English foundations established daughter houses in Ireland. Inch Abbey near Downpatrick, for example, and Grey Abbey in the Ards peninsula are daughter houses, respectively, of Furness Abbey in Lancashire, and Holm Cultrum in Cumberland. Tintern Abbey in Co. Wexford was an offshoot of Tintern Abbey in Monmouthshire and Duiske Abbey at Graiguenamanagh was linked to Stanley in Wiltshire. The Cistercian abbeys were usually located in isolated rural settings and sited along rivers. Typical sites include Mellifont, situated on a tributary of the River Boyne in Co. Meath and the first Cistercian house in Ireland, Bective, Co. Meath, which like Mellifont was situated near the Boyne, Jerpoint Abbey on the River Eoir in Co. Kilkenny (Plate 8b), and Holy Cross on the River Suir in Co. Tipperary. All these foundations are in fertile lowland areas but the Cistercians colonized harder environments too. Corcomroe Abbey, for example, stands on the flanks of the bare and inhospitable karst lands of north-west Clare and Baltinglass Abbey lies in the foothills of the Wicklow Mountains. The Cistercian houses were endowed with considerable estates usually granted by Norman lords and Irish chieftains. At their greatest extent the landed possessions of St. Mary's Abbey, Dublin, which was probably the leading house of the Cistercian order in Medieval Ireland, amounted to approximately 30 000 statute acres. The core of this great estate lay to the north of Dublin between the Rivers Liffey and Tolka but portions lay as far afield as West Cork, Galway, Mayo and Roscommon (O Conbhui, 1962). By the time of the dissolution of the abbey in 1539, however, much of the outlying estate had been alienated or lost to the Irish. The Cistercian monks as well as building their abbeys and barns were industrious farmers who skilfully exploited the various resources of their lands. Cereals, cattle and sheep were produced, fisheries developed and mills, bakeries and other local industries initiated (Carville, 1973). The monastic estates were organized into a number of granges or outlying farms worked by lay brothers. "Grange" still occurs frequently as a townland name, but rarely have the grange buildings survived into the present landscape.

The new orders of mendicant friars, Dominican and Franciscan, appeared in Ireland in the early 13th century very shortly after their foundation. They flourished most within the Anglo-Norman colony and favoured sites inside or just outside the walls of the towns. In time, however, they spread widely in Ireland, far beyond the confines of the colony and deep into Irish territories. The military orders, the Templars and Hospitallers, owned considerable estates and played an important part in the organization and defence of the colony. Their strongholds were powerful centres of English influence and often located in troubled marcher areas, such as

Kilteel on the Slievethoul Ridge between the palelands of Kildare and the Irish dominated hills of Wicklow, or Templetown on the plain of Cooley in Co. Louth, a fertile coastal lowland closely settled by the Anglo-Normans but repeatedly attacked by the Irish of the Carlingford Mountains. In the early 1540s, at the time of the dissolution of the monasteries, there were roughly 400 religious houses in Ireland, including the monasteries, friaries and the houses of regular canons. In the west of Ireland many establishments survived the suppression and continued to flourish until the end of the 16th Century.

Little is known about the dwelling-houses of the Middle Ages in either the Anglo-Norman colony or the Irish areas. Only the most substantial structures of the period have survived, buildings erected in stone, such as keeps, tower houses, churches and other prestigious buildings. It is highly unlikely that any extant farmhouses in Ireland pre-date the late 17th Century. The absence of ancient houses and the scarcity of archaeological evidence on the subject may mean that most medieval houses were insubstantial structures, made of perishable materials such as wood, clay or wattle and turf, and have thus left no tangible remains. The irregular and incomplete foundations which characterize the interior of the raths, many of which, at least in northern and western Ireland, were still occupied in the Middle Ages, certainly point to the existence of insubstantial and, in many cases, temporary buildings. It is unlikely that the style and structure of houses built within raths changed very much during the Early Christian and medieval periods. It is also relevant that there has been considerable continuity of occupation on many settlement sites since the Middle Ages, especially in the more settled eastern parts of the country, and the remains of older house structures may be buried beneath the present day settlements and thus difficult to discover or uncover by ordinary excavation.

Evidence of medieval vernacular structures is limited and almost wholly archaeological. Documentary sources have been disappointing in the amount of information they have revealed. Archaeological material, although limited, does suggest that a variety of house styles existed. Particularly in the west and south-west of the country, primitive buildings of clochan type were used, round in plan and with a domed exterior (Plate 9b). These were made entirely of stone and constructed without mortar by the corbelling method, a building technique utilized in Ireland from Neolithic times down to the present century. From the numerous surviving corbelled buildings a tentative reconstruction of development in their basic style can be made. This proceeds from the elementary circular

Plate 9: a Late medieval tower house, near Fermoy, Co. Cork. **b** Corbelled, dry stone hut (clochan), Dingle peninsula, Co. Kerry. Primitive structures like this one have been constructed from prehistoric times down to the present day as residences and outhouses. **c** Burncourt, Co. Tipperary, an embattled mansion built in 1641. Like many large houses of the 17th Century it was strongly influenced by defensive considerations.

clochan, whose interior plan conforms to the shape of the external wall, through circular clochans with rectangular interiors to elongated clochans with rectangular interiors and eventually to rectangular structures with ridged roofs of stone. Despite these stylistic developments, the elementary clochan form continued as a building style into the present century. Individual clochan structures are therefore very difficult to date and the forms of corbelled structures are not necessarily an indication of even their relative chronology. The elementary clochans lack windows and are too small in most cases to possess hearths. Nevertheless they do seem to have been used originally as residences by rural folk, although it is not clear that the clochan was ever the predominant building form even in western areas. It is only in post-medieval times that the clochan suffered a relegation in social status and came to be used mainly for lowly purposes, such as pigsties, hen-houses, booley huts, well covers and sweat-houses. Oral traditions suggest that in some remote, poor places clochans were still being used as homesteads in the 19th Century.

The largest surviving concentrations of clochans are in the south-western peninsulas of Ireland. Numerous corbelled stone huts are to be found here on ancient religious sites which in many cases are pre-medieval (Henry, 1957). The majority of clochan structures in the region, however, were secular dwellings and are found isolated or built in groups of two or three with a communicating passage: they lie close to and sometimes are physically linked with the remains of old field boundaries. Clochan building continued in the western peninsulas down almost to the present day, although the bulk of the more recent structures were not used as permanent residences but served as farm buildings and as shelters for herdsmen in the mountains and high valleys (Aalen, 1964). The purpose which the older structures served is not always clear, but it is highly likely that many of them were the residences of the peasantry of these parts both in medieval and earlier times (Macalister, 1899).

Structures similar to the clochans in plan and size but constructed with wood and wattles were probably used widely throughout the country both as houses and outbuildings and by transhumant herdsmen as temporary settlements or booleys. The maps and drawing of R. Barthelet, the Elizabethan cartographer, show that small houses with round or oval plans, wattled walls and dome-shaped thatched roofs were still common in Ulster around 1600 (Danaher, 1969). This region, because it was more isolated than other regions of Ireland from the mainstreams of European activity and relatively uninfluenced by the Anglo-Normans, was able to perpetuate indigenous building styles.

Two medieval farmhouses, rectangular in plan and similar in their general proportions to the residences of solid farmers at the present day, have been excavated at Caherguillamore, Co. Limerick (Ó Ríordáin and Hunt, 1942). These houses are substantial structures and their thick walls are faced with large stones and filled with rubble core. Inside, the walls had a wattle lining. The houses do not lie in raths but are part of a group of structures: the foundations of about a dozen houses are traceable, together with adjoining yards or gardens. It is tempting to regard these houses as the residences of Norman settlers arranged in a compact village-like form; certainly they represent a very different mode of settlement from the nearby raths, but if such substantial buildings were common to Norman settlers it is difficult to understand why more plentiful remains have not been found at other sites in eastern Ireland. Unfortunately, the excavations at Caherguillamore did not elucidate the relationships between the rectangular houses and other remains, such as the raths and the vestigial field boundaries apparently connected to them, which exist on the site. It is not known, for example, whether the raths were occupied contemporaneously with the houses. Increasing coverage of the Irish countryside by high quality aerial photographs (Norman and St. Joseph, 1969) has revealed over 40 sites which appear to be deserted villages or farm clusters. Most of these sites lie in eastern Ireland with a concentration in Co. Tipperary. The foundations and crop markings do not, however, in most cases add up to a very clear picture and only detailed archaeological investigation can confirm their true character and perhaps their date.

Two other important forms of medieval settlement merit attention—moated sites and tower houses. There are well over 700 square or rectangular moated sites in the country (Fig. 11). Farms survive in a few of these but the majority are empty. The typical site is a slightly raised rectangular platform, averaging perhaps 100 by 150 feet, surrounded by ditches and ramparts. These settlements have received little systematic investigation but they are very probably medieval in origin (Glasscock, 1970). In the first place they are found mainly in the south and east of the country where the Normans settled and, second, they are similar in size and shape to the many thousands of moated sites in England which can with reasonable confidence be ascribed to the Middle Ages (Emery, 1962), with a concentration between 1250 and 1350. Many of the Irish sites were probably the defended residences of Anglo-Norman settlers and were perhaps built, like the English examples, in the 13th and 14th Centuries when the colony was under pressure from the resurgent Irish. They are conspicuously absent within the Pale but notable concentrations occur in marcher zones, in, for example, Limerick, Tipperary, Clare and north Wexford where there would have been a special need for defensive settlements. Lowland sites are typical but there is wide variety in the physical conditions of the sites; some occur in poorly-drained, level areas and others on well-drained slopes, so that the raised platform and moat can scarcely be seen simply as an adaptation to ill-drained terrain.

In both the Anglo-Norman and the Irish areas the tower house became a familiar feature of the rural areas during the 15th and 16th Centuries (Leask, 1941), a symptom of the unrest and insecurity of the times and perhaps also, with its dispersed distribution, of a new emphasis on pastoral activities. Tower houses are small stone castles or keeps, three or four storeys in height, which accommodated the rural upper classes (Plate 9a). The family lived on the upper storeys and livestock were kept on the ground floor. There are suggestions that before the tower houses were introduced the rural upper classes had resided in hall dwellings of stone or timber (Waterman, 1959), each linked with a range of outbuildings arranged around a courtyard (O'Loan, 1961). Whether these hall dwellings were ever as widely distributed as the later tower houses is not yet clear. Several thousand tower houses, abandoned and decaying, still survive in the Irish countryside. There are over 400 tower houses in Co. Limerick alone and in Co. Tipperary some 250 examples (Fig. 12). Many of the towers, like the earlier hall dwellings, originally had courtyards or 'barmkins' attached to them but in most cases these have been completely destroyed. Tower houses were not confined to the countryside but were built as residences by important town families. Medieval towns such as Carrickfergus, Ardglass, Carlingford, Youghal and Galway possessed numerous tower houses interspersed among the low thatched cabins of the ordinary population. Tower houses are characteristic too of rural Scotland and the Anglo-Scottish border, areas which, like Ireland, continued to experience anarchic conditions through the Middle Ages. In most of England and Wales it is notable that tower houses are rare, a reflection of the greater political stability of these countries and the early existence of strong centralized government.

Town building was one of the major enterprises of the early Middle Ages in Europe, especially in association with colonial movements. In Ireland the Anglo-Normans undertook the formation of towns with vigour, creating an urban system in the country for the first time. The older Viking towns, such as Dublin, Wexford and Waterford, which were confined to the coasts, were taken over and developed but most of the

Anglo-Norman towns were settlements started from scratch under the auspices of feudal lords and endowed with privileges and rights that served to attract groups of craftsmen and merchants from abroad. Many of the settlements endowed with charters seem to have remained economically and socially torpid and did not develop beyond the status of mere villages, but there were others which flourished and some of these evolved into the major towns of the present day (Figs. 24, 25).

The successful Norman towns had a characteristic morphology and assemblage of features whose mature form is well illustrated, at least for the larger settlements, in the maps of the Elizabethan cartographer, John Speed. A castle built by the baronial founder of the town and strong encircling walls, either of stone or earth, were common. In Elizabethan Ireland there were still over 40 walled towns. The continental monastic orders were also represented in the Norman towns, and the friaries of the mendicant Dominican and Franciscan orders who favoured sites just outside the town walls. Earlier Irish monastic sites, where they existed in the vicinity of the new towns, were usually left outside the walls. The new towns served as parochial centres and possessed therefore parish churches. Some of these were clearly impressive structures, such as St. Nicholas' in Galway and St. Mary's in New Ross, Co. Wexford, both built in the Early English style with fine lancet windows; but, in general, church building did not evolve to the high architectural level attained in prosperous English and French merchant towns. Most of the towns possessed their own common fields as well as extensive liberties or communal grazing grounds. Agriculture and rural pursuits seem to have been part of the daily life of the townspeople.

Street plans in the Norman towns were typically winding and irregular and the streets narrow and dark, although there was provision of open spaces for markets and amusement. The walls and other fortifications imposed limits on town expansion but in the later Middle Ages squalid "Irish quarters" or "Irish towns" frequently grew up outside the walls, reflecting the colonial nature of the urban centres. Long before the end of the Middle Ages, substantial suburbs had developed around the major cities such as Dublin, Cork and Limerick. Thatched cabins accommodated the poorer elements of the urban population but in the larger centres, such as Dublin and Drogheda, more substantial timbered dwellings were also built, probably by the more well-to-do people. Little is known of the plan and lay-out of town houses or of domestic arrangements in general. Most of the houses were probably of wood, mud or other perishable materials, and have completely disappeared. In the later Middle Ages, however, the richer merchants often built substantial stone tower houses similar to those used by rural landowning classes and these towers very frequently have survived, although in a ruinous condition, to the present day.

Most of the largest and most successful towns lay in the southern and especially the south-eastern part of the country where the colonists made their initial entry (Fig. 25). Here, the invaders succeeded in establishing themselves widely in rural areas as well as in towns. The colony had greater stability here than elsewhere and its commercial life was able to benefit from the productive inter-relationships of town and country.

The prosperity of the most important Norman towns such as Dublin, Cork, Waterford, Youghal, Drogheda, Galway, Kilkenny and New Ross depended on long-distance trading as well as administrative and commercial links with the surrounding countryside. Almost all the towns had access to agriculturally productive hinterlands, and they were, significantly, located along the coasts, on navigable rivers or at important nodal points. Galway for example, established by the Normans in the 12th Century, stands strategically at the junction of contrasting natural regions but also has easy access to the Atlantic and developed strong trade links with Britain and the continent, especially Spain. The medieval town of Youghal, similarly an Anglo-Norman settlement, stood on the estuary of the River Blackwater and controlled access from the sea to the fertile valleys of the Blackwater and Bride. Youghal, like the other great southern ports, New Ross, Waterford and Cork, exported principally hides, skins and fish, and developed strong trade links with southern England and south-western France, but the full range of its trading activities extended from Scandinavia to Portugal. Kilkenny was one of the major inland towns. The settlement lies on the River Nore but did not possess port facilities; it lay, however, in a productive lowland area and controlled the gap between Slieve Ardagh and the Castlecomer Plateau, a strategic routeway between south-eastern Ireland and the central plain. Kilkenny is located at the site of the early church and monastery of St. Canice, but the medieval town grew up under the protection of a castle founded by the Marshal family and came in time to possess one of the finest medieval cathedrals in Ireland. Dublin was given a charter in 1171–2. A Viking settlement aready existed here as well as a number of early churches and monastic foundations but Dublin quickly developed as the main centre of Anglo-Norman authority and the leading city of Ireland. In it and the surrounding neighbourhood English influences could always be more or less preserved and direct contact with England ensured. The site is one of the few sheltered havens on the east coast of Ireland south of Carlingford Lough; it is thus the natural approach to and outlet from the eastern lowlands of Ireland which were the most prosperous portions of the country. In Ulster, Norman towns were confined to the east coast and all possessed port facilities; Carlingford, Strangford, Carrickfergus and Coleraine were the main centres. Away from the coasts the entire province lay throughout the Middle Ages under the control of the native Irish to whom town life had no appeal. With the possible exception of Armagh, where a small settlement grew up around the ancient archiepiscopal church, no towns existed in central or western Ulster until the arrival of Scottish and English settlers in the 17th Century.

It is clear that borough charters were granted to many places in the Early Middle Ages but often the settlements failed to develop commercial activities and, although burgesses are recorded in them, they remained, judged by their functions and size, effectively villages. Other boroughs, as well as villages, appear to have failed utterly and were eventually deserted (Glasscock, 1970; Fig. 12). The surprising feature is that almost all of the physical fabric of the deserted settlements has disappeared. Often where documentary sources indicate that a settlement once existed only a ruined castle or church survives today, isolated in the fields, and no other remains are discernible either on the ground or from the air (Plate 7). It is hard to believe that churches and castles would have been built in anticipation of settlers and the only conclusion can be that the settlements themselves were composed of very insubstantial structures.

The reasons for settlement decline and desertion were varied. In some instances it was owing to unfortunate or injudicious siting or simply that settlements became locationally obsolete as basic commercial or political forces changed. Thus, the spread of Anglo-Norman settlement and the eventual hegemony of Dublin must have diminished the status of some of the Norman towns established in the south-eastern corner of the country during the initial phase of the conquest. The town of Bannow, for example, on the Skar Estuary in Co. Wexford, was one of the first Norman corporate towns to be established and 160 burgages were recorded there in 1307. But before 1700 the site had been deserted and covered by drifting sand. The nearby Anglo-Norman port of Clonmines was also abandoned after its harbour silted up late in the medieval period. In the main, the cases of settlements that declined early in the Middle Ages, say before A.D. 1300, could well have resulted from general economic expansion and urban growth. As the larger towns expanded the economic base of neighbouring settlements was undermined and either their growth became impossible or the inhabitants moved into the towns. In other words, settlement growth and decline were probably proceeding in a natural manner and some adjustments were inevitable as an ordered hierarchy of settlements gradually evolved. Later in the Middle Ages, however, settlement decay and desertion seems to have been more widespread and it is hard to avoid the conclusion that the basic strength of the colony was declining. This dehabilitation must have provided opportunity for the resurgence of the native Irish population and in many places the Irish overran the Anglo-Norman areas and destroyed the towns and villages. Perhaps more often, the original Anglo-Norman community, as it weakened, lost its separate identity by gradual assimilation into Irish culture. This would have meant the degeneration rather than the disappearance of the Norman settlement pattern, a fusion of the native and colonial settlement traditions: final eradication of the Anglo-Norman settlements often had to await the energetic colonization and land reorganization undertaken by the new English settlers of the 16th and 17th Centuries. Consequently, in some regions it is either difficult or impossible to determine whether settlements are of native or medieval colonial origin. Are the clachans of south-eastern Ireland, numerous in the hilly areas of Wexford, Waterford and Kilkenny, for example, degenerate villages or are they Celtic? If the latter, should they be viewed as native copies of the Anglo-Norman villages or as survivors of a more ancient, indigenous settlement pattern? Similar problems of interpretation arise with nucleated settlements in areas peripheral to the Pale such as Co. Wicklow, Co. Westmeath, north Co. Louth and Lecale, Co. Down. It is doubtful whether even archaeological investigations could furnish the detailed evidence required to establish the ethnic origins of particular settlements. Pottery, for example, would not always be helpful because the Norman settlements sometimes lay beyond the commercial range of pottery imports from England and therefore they used native pottery and, as emphasized elsewhere, the houses of these periods, both Irish and Anglo-Norman, appear to have been insubstantial and very little of archaeological significance may survive.

Widespread desertion of settlements occurred in many parts of Europe during the Late Middle Ages and it seems prudent to view the experience of the Anglo-Norman colony in this wider context and not simply as the product of specifically Irish conditions. The colony was not a self-contained system; its towns drew agricultural produce from their surroundings and exported it to European countries in exchange for a wide variety of goods. Given these international linkages the economic welfare of the colony could not be insulated from the general rural depression in western Europe. In Germany, for example, after the great expansion of settlement in the High Medieval period there was a period when vast numbers of settlements were deserted from around A.D. 1300 to 1450. The desertion was accompanied by concentration of population in fewer and more favoured settlements, by some change from arable to pastoral farming and the expansion of forest and waste (Mayhew, 1973). It is now clear too that thousands of English villages were deserted in the Late Medieval period (Beresford and Hurst, 1971) and the desertion was accompanied by an increasing emphasis on pastoral farming and the spread of enclosures. Whether, in any country, the desertion of certain settlements was accompanied by an overall population decline is hard to establish owing to the scarcity of medieval population statistics and the difficulties of assessing the reliability of those which are available. Migration from some settlements may have led to the growth in others without overall growth of population. That considerable population movements from country to town occurred in Ireland is suggested by the growing number of Irishmen in the towns and cities as the Middle Ages proceeded. The Irish were numerous in the rural areas from the beginning of the Norman colony but the towns were established as colonial strongholds where the natives were initially not encouraged. An increased Irish population in the towns may simply reflect assimilation of the Irish into the Norman culture but, in view of the evidence for settlement desertion in rural areas, the likelihood of population movements cannot be overlooked.

Irish pollen records and documentary sources suggest a swing from arable to pastoral farming and an expansion of woodland and waste in the Late Middle Ages, which is consistent with the decline of the rural population and of the Norman village system, based as it was on arable farming, and the restoration of the Irish population with its ancient proclivities towards stock-rearing. The dispersed distribution of the many tower houses which were built in the Late Middle Ages may reflect the increasing emphasis on pastoral activities and it is noteworthy that these structures were widely used throughout Ireland both in Irish and Anglo-Norman districts. The swing away from arable farming to pastoral farming, the desertion of settlements and the general unrest of the times seem to be reflected in the vegetational changes recorded by pollen analysis. At Littleton Bog in Co. Tipperary (Mitchell, 1965), the initial wave of Anglo-Norman expansion in the 12th and 13th Centuries is marked in the pollen record by a decline of woodland and a matching expansion of cereal cultivation. After A.D. 1300 cereals contracted, grasses and plantain expanded and in places the hazel re-invaded the grasslands. It is of note that conditions changed again after around 1600 A.D. with the Tudor conquest, when clearance of the natural vegetation and particularly the remaining woodland commenced on an unprecedented scale. Interesting evidence of the return to grazing conditions in this same area of east Tipperary in the 14th Century is provided by the records of the medieval Manor of Lisronagh (Curtis, 1935–7) which lay some 20 miles to the south of Littleton Bog. The vegetational record at Goodland, Co. Antrim, (Case *et al.*, 1969) also shows that after expansion of farming and the field system in the Middle Ages the area reverted to rough grazing in the 15th and 16th Centuries and was used by transhumant herders.

6
The English Wars and Plantations

English motives for the final and complete subjugation of Ireland during the 16th and 17th Centuries and, perhaps more important, for the attempts to settle or ''plant'' large English communities in the country were many and mixed. A number of the more important motives are identified below but it is hard to place them in strict order of importance and impossible within the compass of a brief geographical work fully to consider their complex interrelationship. It does seem that English interest in a decisive conquest of Ireland was quickened by the religious conflicts in Europe, especially the rivalry between England and Spain which highlighted the strategic importance of Ireland's position in any conflict between maritime powers. Ireland's strategic significance to England was accentuated as the religious allegiance of the countries diverged and compounded the ancient political animosities. England accepted the Reformation but it was not welcomed in Ireland. Henry VIII and Elizabeth strove to further the Reformation within Ireland but the movement was resolutely resisted and catholicism soon emerged as a major unifying force among the Irish and a basis for resistance to English acculturation. Tudor English statesmen were keenly aware that Ireland might ally with the catholic powers and, if used as a base for England's enemies, would pose a serious threat to English security. This fear was clearly one of the strongest inducements to large-scale and decisive intervention.

Strategic considerations were of importance but the conquest of Ireland was influenced too by the character and attitudes of the Tudor monarchs of England, especially by their allegiance to the Renascence concept of strong centralized government. Powerful monarchs found it difficult to tolerate the partial independence of Ireland and they were angered and alarmed by the chronic if uncoordinated rebelliousness in the country during the 16th Century. Finally, the Elizabethan Age in England was one of considerable interest in colonial expansion and overseas settlement. Ireland was seen as a legitimate arena for these activities; indeed the

135

country became an area where valuable imperial experience was gained before the major English excursions in India and the New World. The eastern parts of Ireland, it was well known, had rich agricultural and forest resources which were an attraction for the entrepreneur. There was attraction too for the Elizabethan adventurer in Ireland, as the remoter parts of the country were relatively unknown and unexplored by Englishmen. Moreover, over much of the country authoritative rule seemed to be lacking; Ireland appeared as a land of warring chieftains and, according to some sources, profoundly primitive, a place which could well benefit from the "civilizing" influences of English cultural and commercial life.

Conquest and colonization were brought together in Ireland in a new way with the aim of simultaneously settling a variety of pressing problems; as a solution to England's security problem first and foremost, but also as the means whereby Ireland could be developed into a prosperous and useful colony where the new religion might flourish. A new policy of "plantation" emerged, in which conquest and colonization were closely linked, complementary processes, initiated and coordinated by the Government. It was reasoned that no conquest of Ireland could be effective unless followed by a large-scale settlement of English people. The loyalty of the "Old English" was uncertain; where they were not identified manifestly with the Irish interest, they seemed to dwell in a political and cultural limbo, tending to identify with England or Ireland according to their best interests at any particular time; their very catholicism made them suspect. A numerous "New English" community in Ireland would consolidate the conquest and provide the English authorities with an oasis of peace, economic progress and certain loyalty. Any English colony in Ireland would have to be strongly committed to support of the English interest, otherwise it could not be sure of its own security in a hostile land. These then were the main motives which prompted military conquest, which led to the seizure of Irish land and to the large-scale plantation of English settlers.

The wars of the Elizabethan period and the 17th Century, together with the land confiscations, so devastated the country that many features of traditional life were destroyed and by the end of the 17th Century the foundations of a new economic and social order had been laid. Accounts of the landscape and life of Ireland at the end of the 16th Century and the beginning of the 17th Century, especially those relating to the areas of relatively undisturbed Gaelic traditions, such as Ulster, are therefore of particular historical significance. Conquest and colonization generated a volume of descriptive material quite unprecedented both in quantity and in detail, but the accounts do come mainly from English sources and, as the English government was involved in a bitter and not always successful series of military campaigns against the Irish, allowance must be made for prejudice and propaganda. When justification is needed for an invasion or confiscation the Irish are readily described as barbarous and the land as wild and uncared for. If on the other hand the intention is to attract English settlers to Ireland then the country is presented in a favourable light.

The contemporary accounts show that Ireland around 1600 was, as a whole, far behind England in its agriculture and general economic life but was, nevertheless, a country of considerable contrasts in its human geography both at local and regional levels. The south-east (Leinster and east Munster) was a region with relatively rich land resources where the medieval Anglo-Norman colony had settled among and eventually fused with the Irish population to form a distinctive hybrid culture. This was a region with an urban tradition and some of the large towns, and especially Dublin, were comparable to the greater cities of England. Manorial village organization had once been widespread but this had been much modified and diluted in the later medieval period. Farming in the south-east and especially within the Pale was relatively progressive and carried out on a commercial basis. The cultural nerve centre of the region was the city of Dublin where life had much of the flavour of a large English city and trading connections with England were always close. The connections of eastern Ireland with England were to be strengthened during the 17th Century by the arrival of a new wave of English settlers and English influences. This new immigration was to have profound long-term implications for the landscape of the region and, in time, for the whole country.

In the north and the remoter western parts of the country, where Gaelic traditions were strongest, it is clear that at the end of the 16th Century agricultural methods were still generally primitive and cattle and cattle herding remained, as from ancient times, of major importance in the life and economy of the people. The word ''creaght'' (a version of the Irish word ''caoraigheacht'' which appears to imply a herd of animals) occurs frequently in English descriptions of these parts of Ireland in the 16th and 17th Centuries. In English sources the term ''creaghts'' is used to describe groups of wandering herdsmen and cattle, although sometimes the term is also used to describe the transportable wickerwork huts in which the herdsmen lived. English observers often saw the creaghts as part and parcel of a nomadic way of life. Nomadism however was a pejorative term: a nomadic way of life was judged to be inferior to one based on agriculture, and the epithet nomadism was perhaps too readily and glibly applied for that reason. It is unlikely that Irish society was nomadic in any strict sense of the term and the creaghts were probably groups of farmers who were summering their cattle on the mountains away from their permanent settlements. These summer excursions of cattle and herdsmen were the Irish version of the very widespread European custom called transhumance. In Ireland the transhumant movement was called "buailteachas" or, in its anglicized form, booleying. Booleying survived in many hill areas of Ireland until the 19th Century as an integral part of the Irish open-field or rundale system of tillage. The evidence indicates that the Irish had long been living in permanent settlements and nowhere were they wholly dependent on their cows. Surveys carried out in the early stages of the Ulster plantation reveal the existence within the province of a hierarchy of small territorial units with fixed boundaries, such as ploughlands, quarters and ballybetaghs, and the widespread use of a variety of land measures such as polls, tates and balliboes. The survey of Connacht in the 1630s showed that a similar pattern of land organization prevailed there. Such a degree of land division is inconsistent with a nomadic way of life: it points rather to a community firmly rooted to the soil and closely identified with particular small areas of land. There clearly was some tillage practised in the Irish areas of Ulster and Connacht but little evidence can be gleaned about it save that it was customary for English soldiers to devastate it along with the farm settlements so as to weaken Irish resistance. Dispossessed native groups retreated to the hills and waste lands with their livestock and they were sometimes able to survive there on their herds by extending the range of their customary grazing movements. Thus, although Irish society was predominantly pastoral, the degree of dependence on livestock at this time was probably exceptionally high and the creaghts a temporary development of an ancient transhumant tradition in order to survive the English wars of conquest and the ensuing disturbances during the plantations.

In describing Irish areas which had escaped the ravages of war the English commentators sometimes note with surprise the well-ordered landscape, the crops, fields and roads. The Irish chieftains commonly dwelt in stone tower houses and there are occasional references to stone houses being lived in by ordinary farmers, although wood and wattles appear to have been the main house building materials. Few vernacular structures have survived from the period and the limited information provided by contemporary accounts does not permit a balanced view of house styles in either the Irish or the English areas. Outside of the richer eastern areas it is likely that most of the Irish rural population lived in small wattle or clay cabins. The drawings by R. Barthelet, an English cartographer who worked in Ulster at the end of the 16th Century, show the wattle houses used in that region, houses with either oval or square plans and dome-shaped thatch (Danaher, 1969). In size they seem to approximate to the two-roomed houses still common in most parts of Ireland. A relic of these primitive wattle structures survived in the wattle and straw mat doors used on many stone farmhouses as late as the 19th Century (Lucas, 1956). Successive travellers and administrators vied with each other in their attempts to portray the poverty and squalor of the Irish houses. However, the devastation of incessant wars must be borne in mind: many of the permanent settlements had been destroyed and, as stated above, it is likely that Irish people in the war-stricken areas had adopted almost semi-nomadic ways and often lived in the inferior kind of huts that would normally have been used only by their transhumant herders.

With the plantations which followed the wars of conquest a new and more stable pattern of life ensued and the diet of the communities in the Irish areas and of the humbler elements of society throughout the country began to change fundamentally. Due to a combination of factors, environmental and cultural, the potato came to occupy a dominant place as a foodstuff. The potato was relatively new to Ireland and before the 17th Century it was the products of cattle, their milk and blood, along with oatmeal and oaten bread, which formed the basis of the Irish diet (Lucas, 1960–2). Milk was often made into butter, curds and a variety of cheeses, referred to collectively as whitemeats by English writers in the Elizabethan period. Following the introduction of the potato the ancient priority of milk in the Irish diet began to wane. The use of curds and cheese almost entirely died out during the 18th Century; milk and butter came to occupy a secondary place to the potato although they retained their traditional prestige as symbols of well being and good living.

The protracted warfare of the 17th Century which often forced the Irish to abandon their settlements and find refuge in the hills and bogs may have encouraged the use of the potato as an important item of diet. Potatoes required less attention and were less easily spoiled than cereals; they could be grown and concealed almost anywhere on mountain side or bog. Subsequently, with the growth of the landlord system and of commercial farming in the 18th Century, dry stock increased their economic importance over milch cattle, and the growth of rural population also favoured the spread of the potato as a major foodstuff. The potato fitted well in to the basically pastoral economy of Ireland and was ideally suited to the soils and climate. It is, as Salaman (1943) points out, an excellent crop to plant in freshly broken-up ground, peculiarly tolerant to the acidity which is characteristic of many Irish soils and it responds generously to the abundant and regular rainfall of the country. The agrarian and demographic importance of the potato may well have been exaggerated by historians, but it seems hard to deny the crucial role which the potato crop came to play during the period of rapid population growth in the late 18th Century. The plant was then able to sustain the poorer elements of rural society who were rapidly multiplying their numbers and provided the means whereby surplus population could expand into and settle poorly drained bog margins and the thin acid soils of the higher hill slopes.

In the century after the Ulster plantation, the north-east made considerable strides in its agriculture and began to benefit from the introduction of town life. Scots influence served to emphasize the regional distinctiveness of the province, but it did not create the separate identity of Ulster; essentially the plantation maintained and reinforced a long-standing separateness. Regional distinctiveness was not owing only to the internal barrier of the drumlin belt: short sea crossings made Ulster, even more than Leinster, the region of Ireland where intrusive cultural elements, particularly from Scotland and northern England, were strongest. Repeatedly in history immigrant elements have fused with native and given rise to distinctive regional cultures. There was, however, from the beginning of the Ulster plantation no cultural fusion between the protestant colonists and the catholic Irish, despite the similarity of their peasant backgrounds. The two groups existed together, but with little contact and with lively animosity. Contrasts within Ulster are important. The east, where the colonists were more numerous, shared the progressive agriculture of eastern Ireland generally and soon developed a vigorous urban life. Western Ulster on the other hand had a less hospitable environment and was, with notable exceptions such as the Lagan area, Co. Donegal, predominantly Irish; it shared many ethnic and environmental characteristics with Connacht and the west of Ireland as a whole. Ulster therefore had a distinct personality but it was, at the same time, a microcosm of the whole of Ireland with a richer east and a poorer, less hospitable west.

Ireland at the beginning of the modern period could thus be loosely divided into a south-eastern region where Irish and English influences intermingled and a north-western zone where Irish tradition was uppermost. After the Ulster plantation at the beginning of the 17th Century, Scots influence served to differentiate culturally the eastern parts of the northern province from the remainder of the country. In the middle of the 17th Century a French visitor to Ireland, Boullaye-Le-Gouz (Maxwell, 1923), wrote as follows: "The Irish of the southern and eastern coasts follow the customs of the English; those of the north the Scotch. The others are not very polished, and are called by the English, 'savages'." There is recognition in this simple statement that regional differentiation within 17th Century Ireland was rooted in the settlement traditions of three distinct ethnic groups. This threefold regional division (into east, west and north-east) provides a useful framework for discussion of the crucial developments in the cultural landscape from the 17th to the 19th Centuries which created the essentials of the modern scene. However, the boundaries between the regions were never sharply defined and there were many landscape features, such as the new estate towns and villages, common to the whole country, while other features occurred only in small localities within the major regions.

Pioneer attempts at planting English settlers in Ireland occurred in Laois and Offaly in the middle of the 16th Century and on a larger scale in Munster at the end of the century. Much was planned but neither scheme met with success and there is no clear evidence that they left much of enduring influence in the landscape. Laois and Offaly were inaccessible, thickly wooded areas notorious for their lawlessness, and their subjugation and settlement were important in order to secure the frontiers of the Pale. Attempts were made to establish garrisons after 1548 and the area was simultaneously surveyed (Curtis, 1930). These early enterprises failed and more determined efforts at plantation commenced in 1556 when the territories were shired and named, respectively, Queen's County and King's County (Dunlop, 1891). The towns of Maryborough and Philipstown (now Portlaoise and Daingean) were founded, and maintained thereafter a tenuous existence. Attempts to settle English and loyal Irish tenants in the rural areas led to prolonged struggle with the Irish who had been driven off the land, and it was not until the early 17th Century that the region was finally pacified and the last Irish resistance groups were transported to remote parts of Co. Kerry. The English settlement here was a protracted and troubled process, slow to take root. Clearance of the forests and the expansion of farmed land took place gradually during the 17th Century and it is uncertain how far the plantation episode in the 16th

Century can properly be seen as a turning point in the transformation of the landscape.

The plantation in Munster appears to have been, in part, an attempt to forestall a Spanish takeover of the southern parts of the country. A Spanish incursion, it was feared, would be a serious challenge to England and perhaps a prelude to the overthrow of the English state. The strategy in Munster was to attract colonists from England headed by a group of powerful landlord-undertakers and settle them on scattered fragments of land seized by the crown from Old English and Irish landowners. Those deprived of their land by the crown had been implicated in a rising of the Munster lords in 1579–83 against the attempts of Elizabeth I to extend and strengthen English administrative controls. The scale of planning for the plantation, much of it supervised by Lord Burghley, Queen Elizabeth's chief minister, was ambitious enough. Almost a quarter of a million acres of profitable land was involved, not including waste, mountain and bog. The population target for the plantation was perhaps between 15 000 and 25 000. Precisely how many planters actually arrived is unknown but there was obviously a considerable infusion of new population, especially onto the fertile lands of Waterford, Cork and Limerick, with lighter scattered settlement in the less hospitable lands of Kerry. It is clear that the English government saw the plantation as a major venture and important individuals such as Sir Walter Raleigh (Hennessey, 1883), Sir Richard Grenville and the poet Edmund Spenser (Judson, 1933) were among the settlers. But the difficulties of organization were great. In the first place the planters obviously received a hostile reception from the dispossessed Irish, most of whom were monoglot Gaelic speakers. The administrative situation was, in addition, very confused. No accurate maps of Munster existed, the precise extent of the land to be planted was rarely made clear and the validity of the titles to land was often uncertain. The estates of the planters were separated from each other and individual estates were often fragmented; even within the planted areas the English settlers were outnumbered by Irish and Old English and thus must have felt a high degree of insecurity which perhaps weakened their commitment to far-reaching changes. Nevertheless, on the more successful estates considerable improvements were carried out. Large stone manor houses of the Tudor style were built for the major families, often connected to the ruined tower houses of the dispossessed landowners, and frequently the tower houses themselves were occupied and refurbished. The economy of the plantation was almost entirely agricultural but little research has been carried out on the pattern of farming. Cereal growing and livestock production appear to have been involved with perhaps an emphasis on sheep and cattle which provided exports of wool, hides and tallow. New towns and villages were planned but it is not clear how many were actually built. Some enclosures were also erected, at least around the main centres (Quinn, 1966).

The short-lived but violent rising of the Irish against the planters in 1598 led to large-scale destruction of almost everything that had been achieved and the planters retreated to the major towns or fled back to England. The rising was, however, crushed by the English authorities and by the beginning of the 17th century order was restored and renewed efforts were being made to mount a second plantation. This appears to have had some limited success but was not as extensive as the first. There was some continuity of ownership between the two plantations but generally a new class of owners emerged and land became more markedly concentrated in a few hands. Richard Boyle, made Earl of Cork in 1622, and George Courtney between them owned almost one third of the new plantation lands. Absentee landlordism became a feature; the planters were a smaller minority than before, and the Old English and the Irish remained obdurately on the land. Without the enterprise and close guidance of the undertakers, economic development and landscape transformation were limited; more traditional modes of land usage re-asserted themselves and continuity rather than change became the rule—until life was again seriously disrupted by the insurrection of 1641 and the ensuing land confiscations. Some important and lasting changes were, however, introduced as a result of the plantation, especially by the energetic Earl of Cork who established iron works and built a number of towns where linen manufacturing was encouraged. Bandon, Clonakilty and Castletown were among these planned urban settlements, all of them bastions of protestantism and garrisons against the unpacified Irish in west Cork and Kerry.

The province of Ulster, which, apart from its east coast, had always remained independent and outside the sphere of English influence, was first conquered at the end of the 16th Century. In 1593 the earls of Tyrone and Tyrconnel joined forces against Queen Elizabeth, a long and fierce war ensuing which led to their defeat in 1603. Conquest was followed as in Munster by plantation, but the Ulster schemes of 1609–10 were more ambitious and thorough-going and they were to alter deeply and permanently the character of the north (Moody, 1939). Settlers drawn mainly from the lowlands of Scotland but also from England, almost all of them protestant, arrived in large numbers and settled in the countryside and in newly built towns. There had for many centuries been a steady but unregulated immigration from the west of Scotland into north-eastern Ulster but the early immigrants, who were catholics, had intermarried with the Irish and adapted to Irish culture. With the plantation a new culture as well as a new religious tradition was introduced into the province. The most traditional and Irish part of Ireland was transformed and made to accommodate a substantial but embattled outpost of British life. Ethnicity fatefully reinforced by religion provided a potent and lasting source of tension and internal conflict.

The major confiscations took place in the six ''escheated'' counties of Armagh, Cavan, Derry, Donegal, Fermanagh and Tyrone. Here much of the land was granted to English and Scottish ''undertakers'' in estates of from one to two thousand Irish acres. Those who obtained estates were obliged to import protestant tenants to work the land and defend it. The plantation schemes did not include the counties of Antrim, Down and Monaghan. Monaghan, apart from some local grants, was left to the native Irish and in Down the native catholic lords and the Old English, who survived mainly in the Ards and Lecale Peninsulas, were left in possession of their land. Antrim was granted to a Scottish Highland chief, Sir Randal MacDonnell, a catholic, who was later made Earl of Antrim. However, many of the colonists settled east of the Bann outside the counties of the official plantation project. New Scottish colonists, for example, soon established themselves as an influential element in north Down and south Antrim, an indication that there would have been a natural flow of Scottish emigrants into north-eastern Ireland even in the absence of planned immigration for the plantations. Eventually, indeed, it was ''Hither Ulster'', the territory east of the Bann, which became the stronghold of the immigrant population. This territory was not continuous with the ''Old English'' territories in north Leinster. Between the new and the old colonists there lay a broad strip of wild country, including the Carlingford mountains, Slieve Gullion and the ''Fews'' in south Armagh, where the dominance of the Irish population, their language and culture, was not seriously challenged.

In general the new settlers did take possession of much of the best land but there was no systematic expulsion of the Irish en masse to the worst land, as is popularly supposed. The main objective of the plantation was to establish viable protestant communities as islands of ''civility'' and loyalty amid the Irish population. As a result of the plantation some Irishmen were displaced and retreated to the hills and bogs of the province or migrated to Connacht, but many of the Irish remained in situ not only as labourers and leaseholders but as landowners. The wealthy city of London, for example, which was encouraged to participate in the plantation scheme by an exaggerated Government description of the natural resources in the area, obtained extensive estates in north Derry. Here the policy of the London companies was to leave the Irish on the land as tenantry. Similarly on the large estates granted to Trinity College, Dublin, in east Donegal, the Irish peasantry were, on the whole, left undisturbed. In the remote and rocky western seaboard of Donegal the colonial settlement was insignificant and, as in many of the poorer hill areas elsewhere in the province, the native population and ways of life remained unchanged. The catholic community in the province was, however, increasingly deprived of effective leadership. A considerable Gaelic and catholic aristocracy was left after the plantation, even in the escheated counties, but its members lived on usually in reduced circumstances; few of them were to survive the Cromwellian period and after 1690 they were virtually eliminated. As the protestant community strengthened its hold on the life of the province it came increasingly to dominate the richer low ground, especially of the Foyle, Bann and Lagan Valleys, while the catholics concentrated in the poorer upland areas such as the Mournes and the Sperrins. This areal and topographic segregation of the catholic and protestant population was not, however, envisaged in the original plantation scheme.

The new settlers applied themselves with vigour to the economic development of the province, and the landscape of the area, much of it still wild and wooded, was slowly but substantially remodelled. However, the colony did not proceed completely according to plan and its progress during the 17th Century was uneven. In the first two decades the rate at which British immigrants arrived fluctuated considerably; the undertakers on many estates failed to meet their obligations and insecurity of tenure was a serious impediment to settlement. In the 1630s, however, the flow of Scottish migrants began in earnest and reached unprecedented proportions, probably owing mainly to adverse economic conditions in Scotland, and the predominantly Scottish character of the Ulster immigrant community was decisively established (Perceval-Maxwell, 1973). Scotsmen were most numerous in Antrim, Derry, Donegal and Tyrone and the English in south Down, Armagh and Fermanagh. The economy of the province showed no striking momentum until well into the second half of the century. After the destruction of the Cromwellian wars economic recovery was slow. However, renewed efforts were made to attract British farmers and tradesmen to the north by landlords who needed them to rebuild and redevelop their damaged estates. These settlers engaged in the production of linen cloth on their farms and thus initiated the close combination of farming and domestic industry which was to become a distinctive feature of Ulster's economy and made the region, well before the 19th Century industrial revolution, into the most densely peopled part of the country. Puritan, Quaker and Flemish settlers later in the 17th Century made further important contributions to the development of linen production and thus quickened and enriched the economy of the province relative to the remainder of Ireland. By 1700 the linen industry was already established as an important element of the economy and it was to play a key role in the subsequent economic history of the province.

One of the most important results of the plantation was the creation, for the first time, of a system of urban centres in Ulster. The ambitious town building programme envisaged at the commencement of the plantation and encouraged by the government for strategic and economic purposes, was not fully carried out but nevertheless, most of the important Ulster towns of today had their origins with the plantation. The decayed medieval towns of Carrickfergus and Coleraine were revived and a network of more than a dozen towns, each protected by a castle and bawn and governed exclusively by British and protestant corporations, was established. The most impressive of the plantation towns was the walled city of Londonderry established on the River Foyle by the London companies as the focus of their estates, and the last great bastide town to be built in western Europe. Belfast, whose charter dates from 1613, had more modest beginnings as a market town and garrison. It did not grow sizeably until the 18th Century.

In the case of Ulster the English objectives were largely accomplished, but elsewhere in the country, with the exception of the Pale, a solution to the problem of securing the English interest had not been achieved. Experience in Ulster and Munster and in the less successful plantation schemes devised later in the reign of James I for various parts of Leinster and Co. Leitrim showed that sufficient Englishmen could not be found and moved to Ireland so as to outnumber the Irish and that the countryside could not realistically be emptied of its native population. Accordingly, during the remainder of the 17th Century, the concern of English governments shifted from plantation to the ownership of Irish land. Essentially, the ownership of land was changed but not the population who worked on it. The change in land ownership was a complicated process, still imperfectly understood. Only the major steps in the process are mentioned here, as it is the consequences of changing land ownership for the landscape which are of significance to the geographer rather than the detailed political and social forces which led to the changes.

In the 1630s an ambitious scheme for the plantation of a protestant community in Connacht was devised by the Lord Deputy, Thomas Wentworth, Earl of Strafford. This was the last occasion on which government interest was shown in the idea of large-scale plantation, but owing to the withdrawal of Wentworth from Ireland in 1639 the project was never completed. However, the detailed land survey accompanying the project, the so-called Strafford Survey made during 1636–7, has been partially preserved in the *Books of Survey and Distribution* and provides a valuable source of geographical information about an area where much that was of Gaelic origin had persisted, especially the patterns of land ownership by kinship groups and the widespread prevalence of transhumance (Graham, 1970). The Cromwellian confiscation of the 1650s was a more dramatic and far-reaching event affecting nearly half the country and carried out frankly on a religious basis. East and south of the Shannon virtually all catholics forfeited their land and no distinction was made between Old English and Gaels. The land in Connacht and Co. Clare was divided up between the indigenous proprietors and catholics transplanted from the east. The most far-reaching consequence of the Cromwellian confiscations was the intrusion of a numerous class of new English landowners into the richer eastern parts of the country. However, no systematic colonization occurred and, save for the major catholic landowners, few of the existing rural population were uprooted. Large estates passed into the hands of English settlers and they in time introduced numerous privileged tenants from England and Wales onto their estates, but there were no attempts to create self-contained or wholly protestant rural communities. Moreover, many of the Cromwellian planters soon abandoned their holdings and returned to Britain. The outcome therefore was very different from that in Ulster; a protestant upper class or ascendancy was created in the rural areas but not a viable protestant community.

With the Acts of Settlement and Explanation at the Restoration, the Cromwellian enactments were confirmed in most of their essentials but the catholic interest was partially restored. Thus, in the reign of Charles II there were still many important landed proprietors who were catholics and under whose patronage the traditional Irish pattern of life was able to survive. The Williamite Land Settlement at the end of the 17th Century clearly re-asserted protestant hegemony (Simms, 1958) although catholic ownership of land was not entirely eliminated (Fig. 13). After 1703 there were no more wholesale confiscations but, nevertheless, during the 18th Century the anti-catholic penal laws progressively reduced catholic owner-ship of land and by the end of the 18th Century scarcely 5% of Irish land was in catholic hands, although catholics must have constituted at least three quarters of the total population. Until the middle of the 19th Century the ownership of Irish land remained almost exclusively in protestant hands and the formation of large estates, achieved often through prudent marriages, was confined to enterprising protestant families and institutions. The Downshire family, for example, commenced as minor landowners in Ulster in the reign of Elizabeth I and came by the end of the 18th century to be one of the major landed families in the British Isles, owning some 100 000 statute acres mainly in Co. Down, Co. Wicklow and King's County (Maguire, 1972). Trinity College, Dublin, a bastion of the protestant ascendancy, derived a large part of its income from a considerable landed estate which was widely dispersed in Ireland (Aalen and Hunter, 1964). By the end of the 18th Century the College's estates were distributed in 16 counties and totalled around 200 000 acres. The bulk of this lay in Kerry and Donegal but substantial blocks also occurred in Armagh, Fermanagh and Longford.

Ireland at the end of the 16th Century was ill-mapped and the best available descriptions contain little useful geographical material. There were still, for example, widespread notions that Ireland was comparable in size to England; that large mysterious islands such as Hy Brazil and St. Brendan's Isle existed to the west, and that the interior of the country was more mountainous than the coasts. The north-western area of Ireland in particular was ''terra incognita'' so far as other European nations were concerned and even its coastal outlines were imperfectly charted. However, the English conquests, confiscations and plantations at the end of the 16th Century and throughout the 17th Century created an acute demand for accurate maps and geographical descriptions, and by the end of the century the situation had been dramatically reversed and Ireland was among the best mapped countries in the world. The story of mapping and geographical description in Ireland is inextricably interwoven with the process of English conquest and the transfer of the land to English and Scots owners (Andrews, 1961). However, the intellectual climate of the period was also influential in addition to military and administrative requirements. The widespread revival of learning which followed the Renascence led to a great improvement in the standards of geographical description and the 17th Century in particular was a period of growing

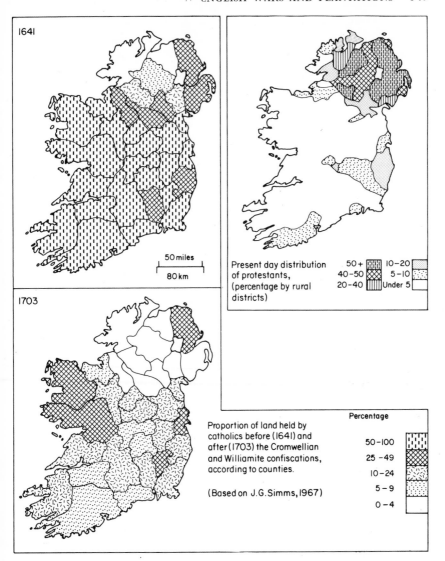

Fig. 13: The effects of 17th Century confiscations on catholic ownership of land, and present-day distribution of protestants.

interest in topographical and geographical writings among educated classes generally.

Survey work was carried out in association with the Munster plantation but the standard of work does not seem to have been high and few of the maps are still extant. The best known are the surveys of the confiscated

F

lands made by Francis Jobson who also produced a general map of the province of Munster and maps of individual counties within it. The survey and mapping which accompanied the Ulster War and plantation was more copious and thorough. Several map makers worked in the northern province but the most noteworthy are Richard Barthelet (Hayes-McCoy, 1964) and Sir Josias Bodley (Andrews, 1974). Barthelet accompanied the British army and made pictorial surveys of the areas over which the conflict was waged. His work is of absorbing geographical interest and includes detailed drawings of the landscape, its settlements, woodlands, farmland, houses, raths and crannogs. Bodley's survey carried out in 1609 is concerned with territorial divisions in the escheated counties and was clearly intended to facilitate the elaborate task of land apportionment among the new settlers. Twenty-eight of the barony maps survive covering the counties of Fermanagh, Tyrone, Cavan and Armagh. The division of Ulster into small units for plantation purposes demanded an amount of detailed topographical knowledge, not previously available, which could only be of practical value if plotted on maps. Bodley's survey, however, is not based on careful measurement but largely on verbal information which is presented in a rather crude diagrammatic form.

The major mapping enterprise of the 17th Century was carried out in association with the massive confiscations, affecting nearly half the country, which followed Cromwell's suppression of the rebellion of 1641. With the exception of certain parts of Connacht which had been surveyed and mapped earlier in the century during the viceroyalty of the Earl of Strafford, all the escheated or confiscated lands together with crown and church lands were surveyed under the direction of Dr. William Petty, an official in the Cromwellian army, between 1655 and 1659. Petty's maps, generally referred to as the "Down Survey", covered most parts of Ulster, Leinster and Munster, parish by parish, with an accuracy remarkable for their time and on a scale of either approximately six inches to one mile or three inches to one mile (Goblet, 1930; O Domhnaill, 1942). The Down Survey was the first cadastral survey of Ireland comprehensive enough to serve as the basis for a new, and vastly improved, small-scale map of the whole country and the accuracy of the survey at parish level made it a vital source for detailed administrative, legal and estate uses for nearly two centuries. As a source of information about the landscape it is disappointing; estate boundaries are clearly shown and an elementary land-use classification is used but little is shown of the settlement pattern, of the houses, of roads or the arrangement of fields. It is in the 18th Century with peaceful conditions and a new interest in the improvement of the agrarian economy that maps—and estate maps are especially important here—first begin to include a substantial amount of topographical information useful to the student of landscape evolution.

As the century proceeded there was a great improvement in the standard of topographical writings and it can be argued that regional geography first emerges in recognizable form. The first manifestation in Ireland of this new and more scientific approach to geographical description is the work of Gerard Boate, a Dutchman working for the British administration, who wrote *Ireland's Naturall History* in 1645. Even higher standards are set in the various writings and maps of William Petty, especially his *Political Anatomy of Ireland* (1672) and *Hiberniae Delineato* (1685). Petty's works are interesting for their analyses of the territorial statistics of the Cromwellian and Restoration settlements and in their attempts to estimate Ireland's population in the 17th Century. The work of William Molyneaux and the regional descriptions which he collected from correspondents in the 1680s represents the culmination of 17th Century geographical writing (Emery, 1958). Among the best known correspondents were Roderic O'Flaherty of Galway who wrote a description of the territory of West Connaught and Sir Henry Piers who described Co. Westmeath. O'Flaherty, for example, describes the custom of booleying or transhumance in the mountains of Connemara, and Piers provides an interesting account of the prevailing open-field agriculture in part of the Central Lowlands.

7

The Making of the Modern Landscape: The Post Plantation Period

Introduction

Ireland's economic history since the end of the 17th Century may be divided into two major periods. There was first a long period of economic, and especially agricultural, expansion which was accompanied by population growth. This was followed, after the early 19th Century, by a period of general economic decline and sustained depopulation, although in the 20th Century there has been some limited revival of economic life, particularly in eastern Ireland, and a long-term slowing down in the rates of depopulation. The growth patterns of numerous economic enterprises do not conform to these general trends and the character and pace of economic development has also varied regionally, with north-eastern Ireland in particular outstanding by virtue of its industrial progress in the 19th Century. Nevertheless, understanding of the contrasting pattern of economic and demographic developments in the two major periods is essential background to an interpretation of the modern landscape. The rural landscape, for example, and many of the towns went through their most formative evolutionary phase in the earlier period of economic growth, and, owing to the subsequent economic decline, most of these older landscape features have survived relatively unchanged down to the present day. On the other hand, most Irish industries and the limited areas of industrialized landscape originated in the 19th and 20th Centuries. A broad survey of economic and demographic trends over the entire modern period is therefore provided in the first section of this chapter, with emphasis upon those developments which had significant impact upon the landscape. In the two subsequent sections the evolution, first, of the rural landscape and, second, of the industrial scene are considered in more detail.

Information on economic and social matters in the 18th and 19th Centuries and on landscape developments is plentiful. The 18th Century sources include Grand Jury county maps, the abundant records associated with the organization of landed estates, and the many descriptions of Ireland provided by travellers, among the more interesting and informative of whom were Bishop Pococke, John Wesley, Arthur Young and Le Chevalier de la Tocnaye. Source materials for the 19th Century are especially abundant. Early in the century statistical surveys of the Irish counties by various authors, containing detailed economic and social reports along the lines of Sir John Sinclair's Statistical Accounts of Scotland, were published by the Dublin Society (Clarke, 1957), and William Shaw Mason assembled his three volumes of Irish parochial memoirs (1814–9). Some of the most important materials, for example the Parliamentary Papers, the Irish Ordnance Survey and the Irish censuses, are linked with the British administration in Ireland. British Parliamentary Papers, which run from the Act of Union in 1800 to 1921, are an immense and as yet far from fully exploited source of information on diverse matters such as administration, education, poverty, population, land holding and fishing. The mapping of Ireland by the Ordnance Survey commenced in 1831, chiefly to provide an accurate basis for an improved and standardized system of land valuation. By 1847 the whole country had been completely surveyed on a scale of six inches to one mile (Andrews, 1975). These maps provide a detailed, comprehensive and unprecedentedly accurate record of the landscape, including buildings, field divisions, antiquities and the boundary between cultivated and unimproved land, prior to the far-reaching changes which occurred in rural areas during the Great Famine and its aftermath. Subsequent revisions of the maps permit study of recent changes in the landscape, especially in the settlement pattern. The by-products of the Ordnance Survey, especially the letters and notes on place-names and social conditions, are also valuable sources of information for the historical geographer and local historian. In 1825 a new nationwide valuation scheme was commenced in connection with rating for the county cess and eventually all property in Ireland was mapped on the completed six-inch Ordnance Survey sheets.

The first complete official census was carried out in 1821. An incomplete census was taken in 1831 but fuller and more accurate information is given in the subsequent censuses carried out at 10 year intervals. The census volumes are a source of diverse social data as well as simply population totals. The 1841 census is particularly extensive and informative, providing a wealth of material on the condition of Ireland shortly before the Great Famine.

The writings of travellers, journalists and other visitors to Ireland in the

19th Century are plentiful but very varied in quality. In the pre-Famine period the works of Edward Wakefield (1812), C. Otway (1827, 1839, 1841), Prince H. Pückler-Muskau (1832), H. D. Inglis (1834), Mr. and Mrs. S. C. Hall (1841), W. M. Thackeray (1843) and J. G. Kohl (1844) are noteworthy, while later in the century the writings of H. Coulter (1862), N. W. Senior (1868), Thomas Carlyle (1882) and J. H. Tuke (1888) provide interesting descriptions of social conditions and the countryside, especially in the west of Ireland. Guide books for tourists, directories and gazeteers began to appear in considerable numbers from the end of the 18th Century, and Samuel Lewis' two-volume *Topographical Dictionary of Ireland* (1837) and the three-volume *Parliamentary Gazeteer of Ireland* (1846) in particular contain much diverse and valuable information. At the end of the century the *Base Line Reports* prepared by the officers of the Congested Districts Board provided detailed surveys of social conditions in the most depressed rural parts of western Ireland. The *Report of the Gaeltacht Commission* (Dublin, 1926) revealed that conditions along the western seaboard in the third decade of the 20th Century had changed little since the time of the Congested Districts Board.

Economic and Demographic Trends Since the Late 17th Century

The 17th Century saw the final reduction of all Ireland to English authority and in the relative peace and stability of the following century there was considerable economic expansion both in the agricultural and industrial sphere which continued into the first two decades of the 19th Century. The vast majority of the population, as in all other European countries, was engaged in agriculture and it was progress in farming which chiefly underlay the general economic advance. The catholic majority of the population was gravely disadvantaged by the penal legislation enacted between 1695 and 1727, especially the severe restrictions on catholic landownership, and a disproportionate amount of land and new wealth therefore accrued to the protestant ruling minority. Social justice apart, however, there is no doubt that the extent and the productivity of the agricultural land as a whole increased notably. The production of meat, cereals and dairy produce grew steadily under the stimulus of increasing demand in Britain. After the 1720s a favourable shift in the relative price of cattle gave a boost to livestock farming and encouraged the conversion of some of the traditional tillage lands to pasture. Between 1760 and the

1820s the volume and structure of Irish farm production again changed and in important ways. Population growth in Britain and Ireland, the Napoleonic wars and inflationary tendencies gave a decisive stimulus to food producers and encouraged more intensive use of the land. There was a marked increase in tillage, often at the expense of pasture, and the export of both grain and livestock products expanded considerably. At the close of the period Ireland was a substantial exporter of corn and live cattle. In the 1830s, however, there was a reversal to pastoral farming, a tendency which gained in momentum throughout the 19th Century.

Industrial progress was achieved in the 18th Century but the gains were not on the same scale as in agriculture. Textiles were the main growth industry. The linen industry in particular, which was operated mainly on a domestic basis, grew in importance in the rural areas not only of eastern Ulster but of Connaught and Leinster too and provided an economic mainstay in many towns such as Drogheda, Cork and Bandon, as well as Dublin. The spinning of woollen and worsted yarn, much of it for the English market, was an important form of domestic industry in the hinterland of Cork and in a number of southern towns such as Clonmel, Kilkenny and Carrick-on-Suir. Small-scale industries linked to agriculture, such as brewing, distilling, milling and tanning, existed in many towns but their production was mainly for the home market. It was chiefly the industries of the north-east, especially the linen industry, which had strong links with external markets and particularly with the English market. The creation of vastly improved road systems during the 18th Century, the building of canals and the improvement of inland waterways in the latter half of the century were further indications of economic advance and optimism. Use of the canals, however, declined markedly in the 19th Century owing to the competition of the railways.

Demographic growth accompanied the development of the economy. By the middle of the 18th Century the Irish population began to enlarge significantly and as the century proceeded numbers grew at a quickening rate. By the end of the century, it is estimated, numbers were expanding by over 15% a decade, a rate sufficient to ensure a doubling of the population in 50 years. In 1788 the population of Ireland was estimated as 3 750 000, and in 1821 the first census gave a figure of 6 802 000 which is probably reasonably accurate. In 1841 the first accurate census recorded a population in excess of eight millions and the total had probably increased to around eight and a half millions by the eve of the Great Famine in 1845.

The Irish economy remained relatively buoyant until the end of the Napoleonic wars in 1815 but the remainder of the 19th Century was characterized by economic decline or stagnation and, after the 1840s, by widespread depopulation. The reasons for this major reversal of fortune were numerous and are still not fully understood. It is clear, however, that with the growth of efficient modern transport systems based on the railways and cross-channel steamers many of the small-scale Irish industries were unable to withstand competition from the larger industries in the growing industrial districts of England where impressive internal and external economies of scale could be achieved. The Act of Union in 1801 aimed to make Britain and Ireland a common market and as the duties on trade were progressively reduced the rapid decay of many of the small Irish industries was inevitable. A further cause of Irish economic depression was the severe deflation which followed the amalgamation of the British and Irish currencies in 1825. Economic problems were severely compounded by population trends. The population increase which had been gathering momentum in the 18th Century continued into the 19th Century despite economic stagnation, with a marked growth in unemployment and poverty as consequences. The deep poverty of the peasantry in particular was universally commented on by visitors to Ireland during the first half of the 19th Century. Population increase was not checked until after the Great Famine of 1846–48 when a long-standing trend of severe population decline through large-scale emigration was initiated which reduced the population almost to half by the end of the century.

Outside of Ulster the textile industry had collapsed by the 1830s. It continued to flourish chiefly in Belfast where, between 1825 and 1850, the industry was revitalized and transformed from a domestic pursuit to a factory-based, machine-run enterprise. The Ulster linen industry was the only major Irish industry which was strong enough to survive and grow in the new economic environment, although in the mid 19th Century an important new development, iron shipbuilding, was added to linen as a mainstay of Belfast's industry. Unfortunately the great industries of Belfast imported most of their raw materials and sold their produce abroad. They were therefore unable to trigger off ancillary industrial growth in other parts of Ireland. Outside of Belfast and its surrounding towns there was little new industrial development in the 19th Century and the rural areas of Ulster declined in much the same way as the rest of Ireland.

With the general failure of industrialization, Irish economic activity was increasingly centred on food production, for which the country was geographically well endowed. In the 1830s there was a swing to pastoral farming and the tillage lands were encroached upon for cattle and sheep pastures. This was a trend which continued after the Great Famine when it was reinforced by heavy rural depopulation and a falling supply of labour. By the end of the 19th Century Irish agriculture had settled into a relatively stable pattern of extensive pastoralism based on permanent grassland, which, however inconsistent it may be with the prevailing structure of small to medium-sized holdings, has remained relatively unaltered down to the present time. Industrial growth in southern Ireland was slight until after the 1920s when a modest industrial expansion commenced which quickened appreciably in the 1960s and 70s. In the north, industrial development in the 20th Century has been much less marked than in the 19th and consequently the old disparity in the degree of industrial development in the two parts of Ireland has been reduced.

The remarkable population history of Ireland over the last two centuries merits closer consideration. Population trends are at once a response to changing economic and social conditions and serve as a formative influence upon them. Of particular consequence to the historical geographer is the important influence which demographic trends have had on the development of the landscape both in rural and urban areas. The causes of the upsurge in population in the 18th Century are still not clearly understood. Changes in either fertility or mortality or some combination of the two were immediately responsible for the increased rate of growth but the statistical records for the period are inadequate to allow measurement of even the relative importance of the two factors. As the demographic forces cannot be reliably measured it is extremely hard to interpret the precise economic and social factors behind the population change. Strong population growth was occurring widely in Europe in the second half of the 18th Century and the phenomenon still awaits an adequate explanation. It is perhaps unwise to seek the causes of Irish population growth solely in specifically Irish conditions such as the system of landholding or the growing dependence of the Irish peasantry upon potatoes for their food, although doubtless these were among a complex of interlocking forces and factors which contributed to the marked population growth.

Two interpretations of the population growth have been suggested. Connell's study of the period (1950) suggests that between 1750 and 1820 population growth resulted from increased fertility which in turn followed from high marriage rates and a fall in the age of marriage. It was changes in the structure of the rural economy at the end of the 18th Century which, Connell suggests, permitted a greater number of family farms and hence more and earlier marriage. The Napoleonic wars and the growth of population in Britain stimulated corn-growing in Ireland, and the substitution of arable for pasture encouraged smaller scale and more labour-intensive farming. This was a major stimulus to farm subdivision, which permitted more marriage and led to population growth. Population growth and farm subdivision, once commenced, reinforced each other in a cumulative way, and cause and effect are thus hard to separate. The growing availability of the potato also had important consequences, especially among the poorest classes and the landless people. With their limited aspirations the rural proletariat were able to survive with a small patch of potato ground and a cabin on inferior land while the better land was devoted to commercial grain growing. The importance which Connell attaches to early marriage in Ireland at this time has been questioned by Drake (1963) who stresses the importance of a decline in mortality brought about by the bountiful potato and other economic improvements. This interpretation, with its emphasis upon a decline in mortality as the basic force behind population growth, appears to bring the Irish demographic situation more into line with most other countries. Firm quantitative evidence, unfortunately, is not available to support decisively either interpretation and it is of course possible that both have some truth and validity.

The potato is inevitably involved in all interpretations of Irish demographic history but it seems likely that the wide adoption of the plant facilitated population growth rather than caused it. First, the prolific yield of the potato crop effectively delayed the high mortality which ineluctably follows rapid population growth unless there is a radical improvement in basic economic productivity and, second, the use of the potato permitted an expansion of population into boggy and hilly land which had been previously uncultivated. The potato yielded nourishing food from land which was of little value for alternative uses: in effect, therefore, it extended the ecological range of Irish rural society and especially of the poorer elements within it. Expansion of the settled areas in the 18th and 19th Centuries was facilitated by the potato itself, but in conjunction with the traditional farming practices of preparing "lazy-beds" and "paring and burning". The lazy-bed technique, which involved the planting of potatoes in raised ridges thrown up by the spade (Danaher, 1970), permitted potatoes to be grown successfully in poorly drained land and in areas with a thin soil cover, while paring and burning (Lucas, 1970) could increase the potato yield in marginal areas as the burning of the pared sods supplied phosphates to the acid soils. Benefits from burning, however, were short-term and the land had to revert to waste after a year or two.

Population increase was especially marked in the poorest stratum, the agricultural labourers, who by the 1840s constituted almost a quarter of the total population and subsisted largely on potatoes. The growing dependence of a large part of the population upon a single crop was clearly hazardous. Partial famines occurred ominously at least seven times between 1820 and 1845 and parliamentary enquiries were undertaken into the growing poverty of the rural population. Between 1845 and 1848 large-scale famine (commonly referred to by Irish historians as the Great Famine) occurred in the country owing to the general failure of the potato crop. The plant was severely affected by blight in the form of a fungus (*phytophthora infestans*) which flourished in the mild wet climate. The social consequences varied considerably from region to region and even parish to parish, but the overall impact was traumatic and horrific. Famines were of course common in Europe down to the 17th Century but the worst Irish experience occurred at a time when the likelihood of severe famines seemed to have receded. The event can rightly be described as one of the major tragedies ever to have struck a western nation in modern times (Edwards and Williams, 1956).

The Great Famine and its aftermath of disease, especially typhus and dysentry, led to massive mortality and emigration. It is difficult to estimate with any precision the number of deaths and migrants but perhaps a million died and another million left the country (Cousens, 1960–1). The losses in the 60 years following the Famine were very heavy and reduced the Irish population to less than half of its pre-Famine level; however numbers remained relatively stable after 1911 at almost three millions in the Republic and around 1·3 millions in Northern Ireland. Recent investigators have stressed that the long-term demographic significance of the Famine should not be over-emphasized and that the population would have declined even if the Famine had not happened; the Famine simply initiated the population exodus in a more abrupt and spectacular way than would have otherwise occurred (Kennedy, 1973; Lee, 1973). Populations do have a remarkable capacity to recover from the impact of famine and pestilence and the almost unbroken decline of the Irish population since the Great Famine must have resulted from long-standing deficiencies in the Irish economy. Growth of population occurred widely in Europe during the late 18th and the 19th Century. In most peasant societies population growth was normally accompanied by emigration, but modernization of the economy through industrialization eventually created sufficient employment to check large-scale emigration and allowed the population to stabilize or increase. The really exceptional feature of the Irish situation was not the Famine but the failure of the nation to expand its industries on a significant scale. Irish emigration consequently remained unchecked and proceeded at rates high enough to offset the natural increase of the population. Moreover, Ireland had close associations with the richest nations in the world, America and Britain, and consequently the disparity between economic aspirations and economic reality was greater than elsewhere in Europe. Emigration was thus intense. Industrial urban centres within Ireland did not grow sufficiently to absorb the rural outflow and losses from rural areas influenced the national total. In Northern Ireland the population rose before the Great Famine and fell afterwards, just as in Ireland as a whole, but the loss of population has not been so marked and during the 20th Century the population has shown a slight upward trend, so that it is now almost the same as the total reached in the mid-19th Century. Emigration has been a feature of Northern Ireland too but the exceptional development of industry and especially the growth of Belfast absorbed many of the migrants from the countryside and in time allowed the total population slowly to increase.

The Rural Landscape

The growth and development of agriculture which commenced after the plantations led to a reshaping of the whole pattern of the farmed landscape and of the location and structure of rural settlement; these changes continued into the early 19th Century and brought into existence much of the rural landscape as we know it today. In Ireland, as throughout western Europe, agricultural technology and attitudes towards the land changed very considerably over this period and a new pattern of farming emerged, more commercialized and scientifically based than hitherto. Open-field organization with intermixed holdings, where it still survived, was removed and holdings consolidated and sub-divided by enclosures. The remaining tracts of woodland and scrub were cleared and the land utilized for farming; many areas such as the medieval commons and the hill lands, traditionally used only for rough grazing, were transformed by liming and draining into productive farmland. Major landlords frequently built small towns, most of them with a remarkably uniform plan and architectural composition, to serve as the commercial centres of their estates and sometimes as a base for small-scale manufacturing, and a network of major roads and canals grew up to link together the new urban centres (Fig. 14).

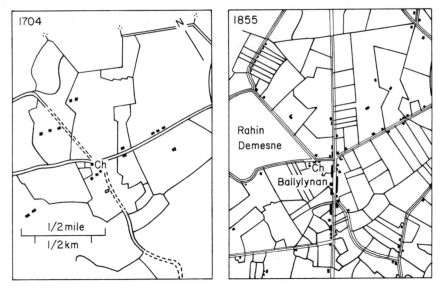

Fig. 14: Roads, settlement and farm boundaries at Ballylynan, Co. Laois, in 1704 and 1855. During this period new straight roads were built through the undeveloped countryside, to which new farm boundaries and enclosures were aligned. A new settlement pattern also emerged in which the dominant element is the "street village" of Ballylynan, built by the local landlords (Weldon family) to serve the estate. (Andrews, 1964).

The rural settlement pattern was extensively modified. Old nucleated villages and clachans which had been the foci of open-field systems lost their *raison d'etre* and were either abandoned or survived only in shrunken form. Rural settlement became increasingly dispersed, a trend encouraged by the building of the new road network and the colonization of hitherto waste lands. The spirit of improvement was responsible for many of the planned estates, ornamental demesnes and reconstructed farmhouses which still characterize the Irish countryside.

It was the new landowning class, mainly protestant and of English origin, which became the principal agent of landscape change. The new landowners were interested in their estates as a source of income and had usually acquired the land as payment for military services or as a business speculation. Large compact estates with autocratic owners could provide an effective framework for re-organization of the rural landscape. Standards of estate management, however, varied enormously. Clearly there was a great deal of neglect by indifferent or absentee landlords but on the larger, more efficient estates the scale of operations was impressive and often organized by professional land agents. Thus, a standard was set which could be followed, with varying degrees of effectiveness, by other smaller landowners and by enterprising farmers. Much of the enclosure and land improvement, for example, must have been undertaken locally by individual farmers. The landowners, especially in the east and south, frequently introduced privileged protestant tenantry from Britain on to their estates and established them on new compact holdings. It was held with deep conviction that protestantism and improvement went hand in hand and, besides the numerous British immigrants, groups of protestant farmers from continental countries were also encouraged to settle. Such, for example, were the Palatines who had fled from religious oppression in Germany and were settled by the Irish government in small scattered colonies in north Kerry, Limerick and Tipperary in 1709. These settlers retained their cultural individuality for some 200 years. They were noteworthy for their progressive farming and lived as a distinct people even after they lost their native language in about 1800 (Blume, 1952). There is evidence too of the importation of Dutch and French farmers and Huguenots, but their numbers were small and the Huguenots were mainly tradesmen and town dwellers.

One of the most important changes in the landscape since the 17th Century has been the spread of enclosures, a lengthy process which in some parts of the country was not completed until the 19th Century. At the present day the farmed land in Ireland is everywhere divided into small fields separated by substantial raised divisions or enclosures. These divisions are continuous and permanent and most commonly formed by banks constructed by piling up stones and sods. Where hedges exist they are usually grown on top of the banks. Enclosures are the most outstanding feature of the cultural landscape today but in most areas of Ireland very few enclosures seem to have existed down to the close of the 17th Century, and even in the areas which possessed them there was rarely a close regular network such as is characteristic today. Over wide areas of the east and west the farmland has only been reclaimed from moor, bog and forest since the 17th Century and the enclosures therefore cannot be of any great age, while in many of the long-settled areas open-field agriculture continued to exist until that time and the intermixed holdings were defined merely by "balks" or "mearings" which took the form of either unploughed strips, low mounds or stones placed at intervals. In the areas of very backward farming in the 17th Century there do not seem to have been fixed field boundaries and during periodic intakes from the grassland areas the crops were protected by temporary or purely seasonal fencing. On the thin soils of the mountain slopes and in certain stony lowland areas, such as the plains of east Galway, dry stone walls are the chief form of enclosure and some of these walls seem to be of long-standing, indeed certain areas may have been partially enclosed from prehistoric times. The remnants of old walls are frequently traceable around irregular or roughly oval areas which lie within and are considerably smaller than the modern rectangular fields.

Perhaps the most persuasive evidence for the relative recency of the enclosure pattern in Ireland can be derived from the accounts of travellers, topographers and agricultural improvers. A work entitled *Advertisements for Ireland*, published in 1623, states, "their fields lie open and unenclosed, where wood is plentiful they hedge in all their corn with stakes and bushes and pull them down in the winter and burn them". In 1641 there was a move in the Irish parliament to draw up a bill "for the mearing, and bounding, and inclosing of lands". No legislation appears to have followed, but clearly the subject was in the air at the time and there must have been a current need for enclosures. In a book entitled *A Brief Character of Ireland*, compiled in 1692 by an anonymous writer, it is stated that "enclosures are very rare amongst them, and those no better fenced than a midwife's toothless gums". A contemporary illustration of the Battle of the Boyne (1690) also shows a landscape of open, arable land without any enclosures. References in the topographical accounts collected by William Molyneux at the end of the 17th Century (MacLysaght, 1950) suggest that large areas of farmed land were still open or "champain" country. One of the contributors, Sir Henry Piers, in his detailed description of Co. Westmeath noted the absence of hedges and fences, "a defect which we cannot hope in our days to find how to be remedied unless our proprietors become inhabitants also". Piers explains that Irish farmers would erect only slight temporary fencing of the open arable areas in summer. However, in the same collection there are references to the well-hedged and fenced landscape in the Wexford baronies of Bargy and Forth, an important reminder of the regional variety of enclosure conditions. Thos. Molyneux (the brother of William) in his tour to Connaught in 1709 describes the Irish landscape as generally open and unenclosed, with the arable only fenced temporarily (Molyneux, 1846). However, he points out that around large towns, such as Limerick, there were some enclosures. The rural environs of Dublin were probably enclosed before the end of the 17th Century.

It is estimated that approximately an eighth of Ireland was still covered by woodland in 1600 (McCracken, 1971) and until the closing decades of the 17th Century most visitors to Ireland, and certainly those who applied standards derived from the English landscape, regarded the country as comparatively well wooded. By the beginning of the 18th Century, however, Ireland was virtually devoid of woodlands and visitors regularly commented on the treeless landscape. Large portions of Laois and Offaly, for example, counties which today are almost completely reclaimed and enclosed in medium and large-sized fields, were still well wooded at the time of their plantation in the late 16th Century. A survey, which preceded the plantation, referred to ''great woods'' shared in common by several communities (Curtis, 1930). Gerard Boate, writing in the middle of the 17th Century, points out that ''not withstanding the great destruction of woods in Ireland . . . there are still sundry great woods remaining . . . The County of Wicklow, King's County and Queen's County are throughout full of woods, some whereof are many miles long and broad''. It was still being stipulated in 18th Century leases granted to tenants in Queen's County (Laois) that several acres of woodland should be cut, burnt and destroyed to clear the land for the plough (O'Hanlon and O'Leary, 1907).

Most of the areas denuded of trees came to serve as farmed land but initially they were cleared for a variety of reasons. Military expediency was often important as the woods were notoriously a retreat for Irish rebels or ''wood-kernes'', especially in Ulster and West Munster. Ruthless clearing also occurred for the timber trade and to provide fuel for the numerous small-scale iron smelting furnaces, which were one of the most important industrial enterprises of the 17th Century and utilized the low-grade iron ores widely distributed in the country. As the forest resources began to dwindle both the timber trade and the iron industry declined and died. Deforested land was often used as rough grazing for the expanding livestock industry and until the 18th Century lacked enclosures and was very lightly settled. Extensive areas of the country, especially in Munster, in the 17th Century and the early 18th Century were used merely as unenclosed sheep and cattle runs (MacLysaght, 1950). In some areas, however, such as the Lagan Valley near Belfast whose clearance was undertaken by immigrant farmers, the removal of woodland provided land for intensive farming. The English conquests and land confiscations in the 16th and 17th Centuries led in the north and west of the country to a growing use of the hills and waste lands by dispossessed Irish groups who depended largely upon their cattle herds for a livelihood. Inevitably this must have meant destruction of the remaining woodland and thickets of these areas by more intensive livestock grazing. Such areas were generally unsuited to agricultural usage and once the natural vegetation cover was removed they usually degenerated to heath or bog. The bleak, treeless wastes of Connemara are a case in point. Portions of this area still retained a tree cover in the 17th Century even after centuries of seasonal grazing by transhumant herders, but from the 17th Century onwards the region was more intensively settled by refugee groups from other areas of Ireland and the remaining tree cover progressively eliminated. Today it is only on the small lake islands, which are inaccessible to cattle, that the original woodland vegetation has been preserved.

Apart from the considerable areas of Ireland where reclamation from woodland and moorland and the establishment of fields have been relatively recent there are extensive portions of the country which have unquestionably been settled and farmed from the medieval period and earlier. In these long-settled areas old nucleated settlements, whether of Anglo-Norman or native provenance, with their arable open-fields and commons remained an important ingredient of the landscape until the 17th and 18th Centuries. The processes by which the old farmed landscapes were transformed into the modern landscape of enclosed fields and predominantly scattered farms are of crucial importance to the historical geographer. However, a complete account of these changes cannot be provided as our knowledge of developments, particularly in eastern Ireland, is inadequate. There was nothing in Ireland equivalent to the parliamentary enclosure movement in England. The Irish enclosure pattern developed mainly as a result of local initiatives by landlords and farmers and, save for Co. Dublin and the old Pale areas, there seem to have been few acts of parliament passed in association with enclosures. In the richer lands of the east the enclosures and the pattern of dispersed farms appear to be older on the whole than in the west. A limited amount of enclosure had been occurring in the east from the late medieval period; the late 17th Century saw some quickening of the process but the main part of the enclosure pattern seems to have originated in the 18th Century. In northern and western Ireland the enclosures and the dispersed farms originated mainly in the late 18th and 19th Centuries and the process is relatively well understood; owing to their recency, the formation of the enclosures has been better recorded on modern maps and hence more actively and fully studied.

Between the late 17th and the 19th Centuries there were many far-reaching changes in the character and style of rural buildings, especially in the residences of the upper classes. Although the gentry were a small minority of the rural population their large houses had considerable scenic significance, especially as it became increasingly fashionable to build them within country parks or demesnes whose visual appearance was carefully designed as a setting for gracious living. As the 18th Century progressed these parks grew in number and scale to become important components of the total landscape, clearly distinguished from the utilitarian landscape of the surrounding farmlands (Malins and Knight of Glin, 1976).

The domestic architecture of the gentry changed radically in the late 17th Century. A few spacious manor houses were built by settlers in the early 17th Century, especially in Munster, but most of the gentry continued to live in tower houses until the middle of the century (Plate 9 p. 125). The leading settlers in the Ulster plantation built fortified residences with bawns and flanking towers sometimes of distinctly Scottish character as at Ballygally, Co. Antrim and Monea, Co. Fermanagh. After the Cromwellian wars, however, the protestant ascendancy in most areas began to build more elegant and spacious homes (Loeber, 1973). Frequently these new houses were attached to old tower houses, but many were completely new and their architecture undistorted by defensive considerations. Major seats were often surrounded by enclosed ornamental gardens, deerparks and waterworks. The houses, however, retained defensive enclosures, and leases to gentlemen tenants often included stipulations to protect the house with a wall or ditch. Fine examples of 17th Century mansions existed at Ballintober, Co. Cork, and at Blessington, Co. Wicklow, where the Hillsborough family maintained a large mansion. Both of these houses have been destroyed but their original character is clear from old prints. Perhaps the finest surviving house from the 17th Century is at Beaulieu, near Drogheda in Co. Louth. This tendency to build commodious houses was not confined to the richer south and east of Ireland. In Connaught and west Ulster important families followed the fashion. At Donegal Castle, for example, a large Jacobean mansion was added to an old O'Donnell tower house as early as 1615, and at Leamaneagh Castle in Co. Clare the O'Brien family added a large four-storey house onto a 15th Century tower house only shortly after the Cromwellian campaign.

Much of the late 17th Century building enterprise and improvements were destroyed in the Williamite war and it was not until the 1730s that the ascendancy landowners began again to invest their accumulated wealth from agricultural rents in large house building enterprises and at the same time to undertake the creation of elaborate and carefully designed demesnes as a setting for their great houses. The landlords had an influence on the landscape as a whole but it is in and around the great demesnes that their work can be most vividly seen.

Before 1730 many great houses possessed baroque formed gardens, but subsequently the primary influence on the Irish demesne is English gardening ideas as developed by William Kent, Alexander Pope and Humphrey Repton. The old formal gardens were swept away and extensive pieces of countryside, often up to 2 square miles (approximately 520 ha) in area, were transformed into picturesque parkland, at once highly artificial and naturalistic (Plate 10). The great demesne at Carton, Co. Kildare, was one of the first to be developed. Here between 1738 and 1757 over 1000 acres (approximately 420 ha) were assembled for the development of the demesne and enclosed by a great wall almost 5 miles (8 km) long (Horner, 1974–5). The formality and creative extravagance of the demesnes, and there are many hundreds of them, contrast sharply with the functional landscape and the humble farmsteads around them. Sometimes there is a discernible penumbra of well designed, substantial farmsteads and carefully located clumps of trees around the edges of the demesne, but often the demesnes are defined by massive stone walls and there is a striking contrast between the ordinary farmland and the demesne areas with their extensive lawns and ornamental woodlands. The great houses, built mainly in the Georgian style, and the demesne territories around them were often designed by leading architects and landscape gardeners from England, such as James Gandon, Richard Cassels, Francis Bindon, James Wyatt, John Nash and Thomas Cooley.

The second half of the 18th Century and early 19th Century was marked on larger farms by a widespread rebuilding of the old farmhouses and the erection of many new ones. Those of the 17th Century planters who were not major landowners settled first in stone, single or two-storied, thatched farmhouses with gable ends. These houses were usually free-standing but some examples can be found which were attached to abandoned medieval tower houses. Some fine examples of these original planter farmhouses still survive but many of them were extended and remodelled in the later 18th Century; slate roofs replaced the thatch and new rooms or even wings were added. However, it was more usual for the old houses to be replaced by new Georgian style houses which were small-scale models of large demesne houses and sometimes built according to contemporary pattern books. They were characterized by highly symmetrical façades and pretentious entrances with patterned oval fanlights over the door, a feature which became common in Irish houses of the late 18th or early 19th Century in both the countryside and the towns. The earliest planter

Plate 10: Demesnes **a** Painting of Westport House, Co. Mayo, by G. Moore (1760). A planned 18th Century demesne landscape. Clew Bay, with its archipelago of partially submerged drumlins, in the background. **b** Gardens and ornamental woodland, Powerscourt House, Enniskerry, Co. Wicklow.

farmsteads were commonly built on the courtyard plan with the house occupying one side of the yard. This arrangement has sometimes persisted down to the present day but if the fortunes of the farmer improved a new larger house was frequently built away from the farmyard, and the farm buildings might be concealed by curtain walls.

During the 18th and 19th Centuries the majority of the population in the rural areas of Leinster and eastern Munster dwelt in small single-storey houses with mud walls; hip-ended thatched roofs were characteristic with a two-roomed ground plan and central hearth. In most places the primitive oval plan of houses had been replaced by a rectangular form. Houses with these basic attributes are still widespread in the eastern lowlands. The basic central-hearth model was often used in the 19th Century for larger two-storey houses built by successful farmers and tradesmen. In Ulster the humbler elements of the planter population dwelt in small, two-roomed houses of the "but and ben" variety, comparable in size to the Irish houses but with stone walls and gable-end hearths. This was a house style common to the Scottish lowlands and perhaps introduced into Ulster by the Scots settlers. It was in time widely adopted by the Irish population of Ulster too. In western Ireland a common style of dwelling was the rectangular, stone-built long-house or byre-dwelling in which the humans and the cattle lived at opposite ends of a single undivided compartment. These unhygienic structures were, however, largely abandoned in the course of the 19th Century.

Regional Contrasts

The 20th Century rural landscape is essentially a legacy of a formative period of development in the late 17th, 18th and early 19th Centuries. Throughout the country the effects were broadly similar; the farmed landscape is covered by a patchwork pattern of enclosed fields, the settlement is highly dispersed in single farmsteads and the older nucleated farm settlements survive in only a few areas. However, broad regional differences do exist, especially between the east and the west of Ireland, and the north-east of the country also has some distinctive features. Evolution of the rural landscape during the 18th and 19th Centuries varied in the three regions owing to prior differences in historical development and regional differences in the force and timing of change. Agricultural improvement, the spread of enclosures and the establishment of a pattern of dispersed farms occurred on the whole earlier in the east than in the west. In the east the basic changes occurred in the late 17th and the 18th

Plate 11: Rundale relics, Clare Island, Co. Mayo. Rundale organization with nucleated farms and open-fields was terminated here probably in the late 19th Century and a new pattern of dispersed farms and narrow compact holdings, stretching from the coast to the interior hills, was established. Cultivation ridges (''lazy-beds'') formed during the rundale era are still evident underneath the modern field pattern.

Centuries, while in the west and the north-east changes tended to be delayed until the late 18th and 19th Centuries. The north-east was further distinguished by the successful growth of its industries, many of which had their origin in a rural domestic milieu. Each region merits separate consideration. Emphasis will be placed on basic developments in the pattern of fields and related developments in the settlement pattern. Developments in the east, which are more complex, will be described first.

Eastern Ireland (Leinster and Eastern Munster)

In the east there is evidence that engrossing of open-field strips had been occurring around the Anglo-Norman villages since the Late Medieval period, but before the middle part of the 17th Century there is no suggestion that the process of engrossing was anything other than a piecemeal operation involving the occasional transfer of strips between individual landholders. However, the cumulative results were considerable and where maps can be found that show strip fields (none of these are earlier than the mid 17th Century) the pattern is clearly a modified form of the medieval arrangement, comprising a mixture of rectangular, irregular and long narrow fields representing bundles of strips (Fig. 15). Piecemeal engrossing of strips on old open-field areas does not seem to have given rise to many enclosures and the growth of an extensive pattern of enclosed fields did not gain momentum until the 18th Century when enclosure became the hallmark of progressive farming. A number of exceptional, large villages in north-east Leinster, especially on the great estates of the Archbishops of Dublin (e.g. Tallaght, Rathcoole, Swords) and Armagh (e.g. Dromiskin, Termonfeckin) retained their open-fields until the late 18th Century. As late as 1825 the medieval strip fields survived in great numbers around the villages of Rathcoole, Dalkey and Saggart. Analogous survivals occurred in areas of poor physical endowment. Open-field organization, presumptively of rundale provenance, was long retained in the glens and isolated upland fringes of the Wicklow Mountains; in Glencullen until the present century, and until the late 19th Century on the Hillsborough Estates in West Wicklow. Similar late survivals could be found in the remote mountainous peninsula of Cooley in north Co. Louth.

Although many new compact holdings were being established in the latter half of the 17th Century there was no large-scale formation of enclosures. The boundaries of individual farms and townlands may increasingly have been fenced and ditched, following the establishment of

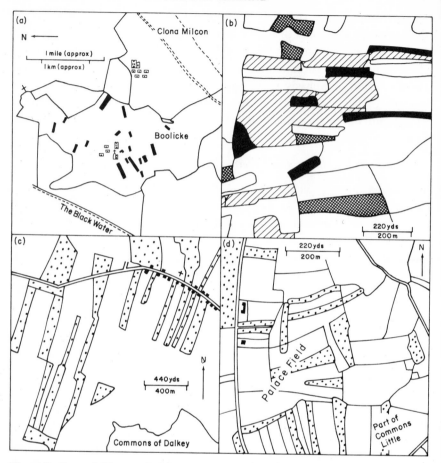

Fig. 15: Open-field strip holdings: eastern Ireland. **a** Parish of Boolicke, Co. Tipperary, in the mid 17th century; land belonging to the priest in black (Leister, 1963). **b** Part of the fields of Ballymore-Eustace, Co. Kildare, in the mid 17th Century; The scattered holdings of three tenants are shown (Down Survey). **c** Part of the fields of Dalkey, Co. Dublin, in the mid 19th Century; the holding of one tenant is shown (Otway-Ruthven, 1951). **d** Part of the fields of Newcastle, Co. Dublin; strips of one owner in 1765 are shaded and superimposed on modern field boundaries (National Library of Ireland and 6″ O.S. Sheet 21).

the ascendancy landlordry and the new planter class, but the general impression is still of a relatively open landscape with portions of the land used periodically for cultivation and grazing. Thus, while many areas of the east are described by contemporary writers as open or "champion" land, perhaps this need not always imply the prevalence of open-field systems *sensu stricto*. In lowland Ulster too there is evidence that, following the establishment of the new planters, there was a long delay before the enclosures were erected. The townlands here, as in many other parts of the country, were the primary units of enclosure; they were subsequently subdivided into farms whose boundaries were ditched and quickset. In the early 18th Century pasture land was fenced off from meadow and arable land, while the great hedgerows are the product of the landlord enclosure policy in and after the mid-18th Century (Crawford, 1964; Buchanan, 1970).

The spread of enclosures did not affect Ireland widely until the agrarian revolution in the 18th Century and early 19th Century. Especially in the latter half of the 18th Century the ideas of "agricultural improvement" and the "new husbandry" were gaining momentum in Ireland, as throughout Britain, and improvement was invariably coupled with enclosure. The estate structure with its autocratic landlords provided a framework within which changes in rural economy could be effectively and rapidly carried out, while the growth of a commercialized economy and the expansion of demand for foodstuffs stimulated the general introduction of improved farming methods. The new enclosures were primarily designed to provide a large number of small fields to suit the new forms of livestock husbandry made possible by improved pasture and the use of hay and roots for winter fodder. Enclosed fields both provided shelter for the livestock and effectively checked their movements, thus making it possible to rotate production with maximum flexibility round each farm. It was emphasized by the improvers that enclosure provided an opportunity to drain the land along the field boundaries so that ditching and the erection of enclosures were considered to be complementary operations. Even with the tillage boom during the Napoleonic wars cattle production remained an important farm enterprise; enclosures were particularly appropriate to mixed farming, and the rapidly growing rural populations and more intensive pattern of land use must have encouraged progressive parcellization of farms into small fields.

In eastern Ireland and especially on the best agricultural land the characteristic field boundary is a very substantial feature comprising a deep wide ditch and a bank of stone and sods with a hedgerow planted on it. Such features were a hallmark of *avant garde* improvers. In the 1770s Arthur Young, an intrepid and painstaking observer of agricultural developments at first hand in several countries, described in detail the formation of the new enclosures in a number of places in Dublin, Meath, Louth and Kildare. He relates that a Colonel Marlay of Celbridge (Co. Kildare)

Plate 12a: Small fields divided mainly by banks of sod and stone (Dingle Peninsula, Co. Kerry).

Plate 12b: Small fields divided by dry stone walls (Rossaveal, Co. Galway).

Plate 13a: Large fields divided by banks, hedges and frequent trees (Newcastle, Co. Kildare).

Plate 13b: Medium-sized fields divided by banks overgrown by gorse (near New Ross, Co. Wexford).

"practised husbandry with great success . . . his fences excellent, his ditches 5 by 6; the banks well made and planted with quicks". He describes similar features on the land of Mr. Clements at Killadoon; "he has been very attentive to bring his farm into neat order respecting fences, throwing down and levelling old banks, making new ditches, double ones 6 feet wide and 5 deep, with a large bank between for planting, more effectually than ever I saw in England". The same features had been established on reclaimed heath land at Grangegeeth near Drogheda where, Young states, "the fences about new inclosed pieces, and those made in general by gentlemen, are ditches 6 feet deep, 7 feet wide . . . with two rows of quick in the bank . . ." (Young, 1892).

There is no doubt that the spirit of "improvement" was making itself very widely felt in Ireland in the 18th Century, and eastern Ireland was ahead of the rest of the country both in the timing and quality of agricultural innovation. The eastern areas were not only among the most favoured from a physical standpoint, it was here also that the estate system was most firmly entrenched. J. Bush (1769) wrote that "the province of Leinster and the middle parts of the kingdom in general are the best cultivated and the most generally improved". This view is corroborated by Vallancey's *Royal Map of Ireland* (1785) which shows "improved land" by conventional fields defined by hedgerows, and the extent of land so covered corresponds generally with that stated by Bush.

The erection of enclosures was not only transforming the appearance of the traditional farmed lands in eastern Ireland, it is also clear that enclosed fields were spreading onto hitherto waste and rough lands. Arthur Young is again a key witness. He emphasizes that, in the late 18th Century, enclosures were in many places in Ireland creeping up formerly bare hillslopes, while lowland wastes and commons were being actively enclosed. At Kilfaine in Co. Kilkenny he writes "they are beginning to cultivate the mountains, the inclosures creep up the sides gradually" and in Ravensdale, in north Co. Louth, Young was "pleased to see the inclosures creeping high up the sides of the mountains stony as they are". The vast scale and thoroughness of these 18th Century enclosure projects, which often involved the establishment *ab initio* of the essentials of the present-day field patterns, are well illustrated by Young's account of developments on the estate of Baron Forster at Collen in Co. Meath. Forster's estate was some 5000 acres (approximately 2000 ha) which little over 20 years before had been waste sheep walk covered with heath, furze and fen. The improvements here were the greatest that even Young had ever met with. The land was wet and at the outset extensive drainage and liming operations were necessary. "The whole tract was inclosed in fields of about 10 acres each with ditches 7 feet wide and 6 deep at 1s a perch, the banks planted with quick and forest trees. Of these fences 70 000 perches were done". As part of the improvements roads were also made, new farmhouses built and a colony of French and English protestants settled on the land. The improvements at Collen were of course outstanding, but there were many others that were impressive and extensive. Young relates that Lord Bective of Headfort, near Kells in Co. Meath, had enclosed land on his Cavan estates with walling. Some 10 000 acres (approximately 4000 ha) of bog and rough land in Co. Cavan had been drained and improved by the Bective family and the dry rocky land divided with walls.

The essentially uniform character of the enclosure pattern now existing over most of eastern Ireland may be explained by the relatively short period during which the bulk of the enclosures was erected, the organization of the land within a framework of extensive estates, the scientific approach implicit in the "new husbandry" and the relatively level terrain. More complex and interesting field plans can be identified around some of the old villages and these are a legacy of a long gradual evolution as previously described. The old arable land in the immediate vicinity of the large villages of the Pale seems to have been peculiarly resistant to thorough-going engrossment and sometimes the only result of the improver movement was the erection of hedgerows along the old mearings which divided the strip holdings. Such a process has produced the remarkable linear fields of Rathcoole (Fig. 16). However, around other medieval villages, such as Whitestown in Co. Louth and Maynooth in Co. Kildare, there are regular fields apparently dating from the improvement and no existing signs of an evolved field pattern. In some of these villages old maps do show that the present field patterns have only recently replaced strip fields. In Fig. 16 a portion of the fields of Newcastle (originally a royal manor in Co. Dublin) as they exist today is compared with the same area as shown on a map of 1765. The latter map may well have been made to facilitate the enclosure of the remaining open-fields, and it is of particular importance in the study of eastern field-systems because it distinguishes and names three major areas around the village (the Pallace Field, Augh Mullin and Shiskeen Commons) which may well be the fundamental divisions of a three-field system. Enclosure thus did in some cases embrace old arable open-field tracts, involving not only the erection of hedgerows but the introduction of completely new field outlines. In the case of most villages there is a mixture including both the evolved field shapes and regular field outlines of more recent

(a) Rathcoole
Coolmine

(b) Bryanstown

(c) Boolyglass
750
800

(d) Carrickshock
Carrickshock
Commons
300
400

(e)

(f)

(g)

establishment, as at Crumlin, Swords, Rathcoole, Garristown and Ballymore-Eustace. The field patterns near Drogheda are instructive. Within the area of the old town-fields, which is still partly bounded by a deep ditch, the dominant field shape is elongated, with the slight curvature diagnostic of medieval plough strips. Outside the ditch there is an abrupt transition to regular block-type fields associated with the period of improvement (Fig. 16).

At the beginning of the 18th Century the commons were still an important element in the rural landscape of eastern Ireland. The existence of such open and unimproved areas was felt by many to be inconsistent with the prevailing spirit of agricultural improvement, and the increasing rural population pressure together with the decay of borough and manorial organization encouraged encroachment upon the commons both by landlord enclosure schemes and by squatter settlements. Enclosure on the private initiative of a landlord or, as occasionally happened in the area of the Pale, by Act of Parliament was often a single comprehensive project and the resulting field pattern is generally regular and geometrical, the fields being either very long, narrow and straight as on the commons of Garristown, Co. Dublin, enclosed in 1803, or squarish as on the commons of Dromiskin, Co. Louth, which were enclosed in 1801. On the other hand, commons which were encroached upon by illegal squatter settlement can often be distinguished from surrounding townlands today by their close pattern of small holdings and small irregular enclosures, representing uncoordinated and piecemeal enterprise e.g. Ballymore-Eustace (Fig. 16).

The study of "lost villages" which has proved so fruitful and interesting

Fig. 16: Fossil strip fields and enclosure patterns on commons: eastern Ireland. **a** Field pattern at Rathcoole, Co. Dublin, resulting largely from the enclosing of old open-field strips. Note the contrast between the narrow fields on the old arable area and the broader fields on the old commons (Coolmine). **b** Fields near Drogheda, Co. Louth. The narrow fields are located on the old town-fields whose ditched boundary is shown by the pecked line. **c** Fields at Booleyglass, Co. Kilkenny. Fossil strips to east of farm cluster. **d** Fields at Carrickshock, Co. Kilkenny. Fossil strips to east of farm cluster. **e** Narrow fields on Garristown Commons, Co. Dublin. Enclosed by Act of Parliament in 1803. **f** Regular rectangular fields on Dromiskin Commons, Co. Louth. Enclosed by Act of Parliament in 1801. **g** Broadleas Commons, Ballymore Eustace, Co. Kildare. Irregular enclosures associated with 19th Century squatter encroachments. (The scale of each drawing is $4\frac{1}{2}$ inches (115 mm) to 1 mile. (1·62 km). (Based on Ordnance Survey by permission of the Government, Permit No. 2999.)

in England has not been actively pursued in eastern Ireland, although it is clear that numerous villages have disappeared. The desertion of some villages occurred in the Late Medieval period (Chapter 7), but in some instances village dissolution may well have been more recent and associated with the plantations and the spread of compact holdings and enclosures. The old village communities must have suffered with the economic and social demise of the Old English, which was one of the major results of the Cromwellian conquest. As the descendants of the original settlers in the Anglo-Norman colony the Old England had substantial landed interests in eastern Ireland and were probably still the backbone of the surviving villages. They provided a focus of resistance to Cromwell and not unnaturally they suffered heavily in the subsequent land transfers. The formation of new compact holdings to accommodate Cromwellian settlers at the expense of open-field village lands is nicely illustrated by a surviving map of the manor of Drumcashel in Co. Louth, made in 1655—within a year of the manor's transfer to the new Cromwellian owners (O'Loan, 1959). In 1640 the manor belonged to John Roth, outlawed for participation in the 1641 rebellion. After confiscation the bulk of the manor was divided between two of Cromwell's officers, who received compact portions of 350 acres (140 ha) and 207 acres (83 ha), respectively. The remainder of the manor (some 200 acres or 80 ha) is clearly shown to be lying in open-field strips. A concentration of six houses and what appears to be the remains of a mote are shown near the centre of the manor and presumably represent the original medieval village. Where the open-fields once lay there are today large square fields and the site of the village is marked only by the mote and one large farmstead.

Lord Taaffe (1766) complained that he had seen the removal of many villages and their arable lands owing to enclosures for grazing. The decline of villages in the face of a grass farming economy is further referred to in a description of Mallow, Co. Cork and its neighbourhood in 1775 (Brookfield, 1952) which states that there were ''above a dozen villages in the parish of Mallow inhabited about 15 years ago by six or eight snug, warm cotters, and at present there is but one dairyman in each of the villages and in some few of them are one or two labourers''. Some old villages now exist in very vestigial form, perhaps only a farm or two adjacent to a ruined medieval church or motte, such as Tipper, Ardscull, Kilteel, Ardree, Glassely and Rathmore in Co. Kildare, Odagh in Co. Kilkenny, Kilmaclenine in Co. Cork, Ardmayle in Co. Tipperary, Salterstown in Co. Louth and Esker in Co. Dublin, or had become by the

19th Century simply the residence of agricultural labourers, as for example at Rathcor in Co. Louth. Other old settlements were improved and remodelled in the 18th Century to emerge as small towns with primarily commercial rather than agricultural functions, such as Maynooth and Ballymore-Eustace in Co. Kildare, and Donard in Co. Wicklow.

The isolated farmstead within a compact holding had for a variety of reasons become the most important element in the rural landscape of eastern Ireland by the early 18th Century, and most subsequent economic and social developments have tended to favour the predominance of this form of settlement. First, as has been already described, the medieval open-field systems and the associated villages were by the 17th Century much decayed and many dispersed farmsteads established in the Late Medieval period may have survived into the modern period. Certainly the planters were normally established on compact holdings and lived in isolated farmsteads. In Ulster it seems that the colonists were encouraged at the beginning to dwell in towns and villages for reasons of defence but a dispersed settlement pattern soon asserted itself. Planter farmsteads in Leinster and Munster were frequently located in the same general vicinity, perhaps for mutual protection, but the farms are not nucleated and there is no evidence of cooperative farming endeavour. Second, a pattern of isolated farms had been encouraged by the increasing emphasis in the late 17th Century on commercial livestock farming and the associated growth of large grazing farms, a trend which seems to have been particularly marked in southern Ireland. The development of a new and more efficient road system, which took place mainly in the 18th Century, had an important influence on the settlement pattern and tended to reinforce its dispersed nature (Fig. 14). New farms and roads were often established simultaneously and the farms located close to the roads, each holding standing at some distance from its neighbour and typically set back from the roadway by a field or two. Smallholdings and labourer's cottages, however, which became more numerous as the 18th Century progressed and the population grew, tended to locate haphazardly on the road sides. Finally, where land reclamation was carried out by landlords, where for example woodland was cleared or poor land made productive by liming, marling or drainage, the new settlement patterns were usually dispersed. In the case of poor marginal lands, however, which lay outside the close control of the improving landlords, colonization was often undertaken during the 18th Century by small farmers who rented the land and worked it in partnership. Their farmsteads were often built in small clusters in the rundale tradition, and individual holdings were frequently scattered but infield areas with unfenced and intermixed

G

holdings rarely developed around these new settlements. Holdings may have been scattered but fields were usually enclosed.

Estate organization, the growing commercialization of farming, and the spread of scientific agriculture all combined to order and rationalize the elements of the rural landscape. There was, however, an important countervailing force which, while its full consequences are sometimes hard to measure with precision, clearly had a pervasive and sometimes powerful effect. This was rapid population growth, a development which increased in strength towards the end of the 18th Century and assumed dramatic proportions in the early 19th Century. The impact of population growth on the landscape, however, varied considerably at local and regional levels. In western Ireland demographic pressures had marked and widespread effects on the landscape but on the richer lowland areas of eastern Ireland these pressures were generally held at bay. This was indicative of the powerful influence of the landlords in the east, of the existence of numerous large holdings which employed a large force of agricultural labourers, and of the long established custom of undivided inheritance of holdings. Population increase involved primarily the poorer elements of society and in the east this meant a marked growth in the number of agricultural labourers rather than of the farmers and thus the greater part of the population expansion did not directly influence the basic structure of landholding. The more numerous and larger towns in the east were able to absorb some of the population growth in their small-scale industrial enterprises, and emigration too provided some relief from population pressures. Emigration commenced from eastern areas in the late 18th Century and had gathered considerable momentum before the Great Famine of 1846–8; indeed, throughout most of the 19th Century, population losses were heavier in eastern Ireland than in the west. In the eastern landscape population pressure was revealed in the proliferation of smallholdings and cabins along the roadsides and evident too in the squatter colonies which grew up piecemeal on old commons, in poor hill country and along the edges of bogs. However, the orderly outlines of the improved landscape remained essentially intact. Haphazard growth was mainly evident in limited areas where it involved the poorest elements of society; the houses and holdings which the poor provided for themselves were insubstantial and often left few durable remains behind when the massive decline of population commenced after the Great Famine.

Western Ireland (Connacht, West Munster and West Donegal)

Agricultural improvement and the establishment of enclosures and dispersed farms occurred, on the whole, later in western than in eastern Ireland. Planter elements were fewer in the west and society more markedly polarized into a small group of powerful landowners and a mass of poor tenantry living on small farms often at little more than subsistence level. Demesnes were less common in the west and towns too were fewer and smaller in size. Before the 19th Century the ideas of agricultural improvement had made relatively little headway. The 18th Century expansion of pasture land for commercial livestock raising influenced some parts of the west and especially the lowlands of east Connacht where the limestone pastures were particularly well-suited to sheep farming. Here the formation of extensive livestock walks, as described by Arthur Young in his tours in the 1770s, may have involved the removal of earlier settlements and the displacement of population, although until the 19th Century it seems that the grazing areas were left open and without enclosures. Despite the occasional inroads of commercialized farming, which occurred mainly on the more productive lowlands and around the larger urban centres such as Limerick and Galway, traditional forms of nucleated settlement, inhabited by subsistence cultivators and associated usually with rundale organization, survived widely in the west until radical rural re-organization was carried out by landlords, sporadically at the end of the 18th Century but widely in the early 19th Century.

Rundale involved essentially the cooperative working of unenclosed arable and pasture land by several joint tenants who resided in farm clusters or "clachans". On the most productive land or "infield" connected to the farm cluster each farmer held his land in a number of scattered, unfenced fragments, often as many as 20 or 30, intermixed with the holdings of his neighbours. Around the infields were areas used in common for rough grazing, although some of the marginally productive land was periodically tilled on a shifting "outfield" basis (McCourt, 1954–5). The hills and boggy tracts were sometimes utilized by seasonal livestock movements known as "booleying", a traditional system of land utilization which served both to exploit the extensive areas of poor land suitable only for periodic grazing and to remove the animals from the vicinity of the arable patches while the crops were growing. The rundale system appears to have been endemic to western and northern Ireland (Evans, 1939; Flatrès, 1957). While it prevailed agricultural improvements were seriously impeded and the sharp population growth of the 19th Century led not only to smaller and smaller holdings but to increasing fragmentation of the arable land with resulting inconveniences, confusion and litigation. Yet so deep-rooted was the rundale system that its removal was usually opposed by the peasantry and could only be accomplished by the firm intervention of improving landlords and, eventually, government agencies.

Until the Great Famine equal sub-division of the farm holdings among co-heirs was still the prevailing custom in most western areas and population growth consequently led to extensive sub-division and acute fragmentation of holdings as well as disorderly expansion and congestion in the traditional farm clusters. Piecemeal and unplanned colonization of bog margins, poor hill lands and off-shore islands also occurred on a large scale. The urban infrastructure of western Ireland was very weak and in some areas non-existent, so that surplus population could not move into urban employment. Neither did emigration from the west serve as an important safety valve; indeed there was no post-Famine decline in total population until towards the end of the 19th Century and population growth continued in many western areas, including the most congested and depressed seaboard areas, until the 1880s. The conservatism of western peasant society and the associated retention of traditional standards and limited economic aspirations seem to be the crucial factors in explaining the sustained population growth. Despite harsh economic conditions neither the motivation nor the means to emigrate existed on any large scale. Some emigration was of course occurring in the post-Famine decades but unlike the eastern areas of Ireland it was not large enough to offset the gain by natural increase. The onset of population decline in the west was belated but, once initiated at the end of the 19th Century, the trend of decline was very severe and sustained.

Ultimately, the effects of rural re-organization in the west were broadly similar to those which had occurred somewhat earlier in the eastern parts of the country, but the process of landscape transformation tended to be more abrupt and in many areas was completed within the space of a few years. Intermixed holdings were consolidated and enclosures erected, while the number of single farmsteads increased greatly and nucleated farm settlements largely disappeared from most regions (Fig. 17). The custom of subdividing the holdings among co-heirs was also eliminated. Where the re-organized holdings were laid out in blocks an even spread of farmsteads was produced. This was a common method of farm consolidation in relatively level lowland areas. On hillsides and other areas where soil resources varied considerably over short distances the rundale holdings were re-arranged in narrow parallel strips and the farmsteads located in a linear manner along new roads which bisected the holdings (Figs 18, 20d; Plate 11). A greatly improved road network was built in

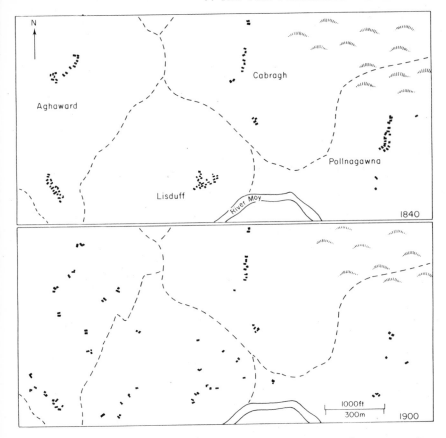

Fig. 17: Changes in the rural settlement pattern during the 19th Century: Co. Mayo. (1st and 2nd edns of 6″ O.S. Sheet 61). By the end of the century many new isolated farms had been established. Clachans became less conspicuous but the old nuclear areas of settlement were still discernible. (Based on the Ordnance Survey by permission of the Government, Permit No. 2999.)

many western areas during the 19th Century both in association with farm consolidation projects and in order to link up existing settlements, and roads for the first time penetrated the remote mountainous peninsulas of West Connacht and Co. Donegal. Small market towns were also established in many isolated rural areas which hitherto had lacked any form of urban life and small service centres grew spontaneously at nodes in the new road network.

Agrarian reforms tended to take place first on the better and more accessible land but much depended on the initiative and energy of individual landlords. Activity was particularly intense in the decades

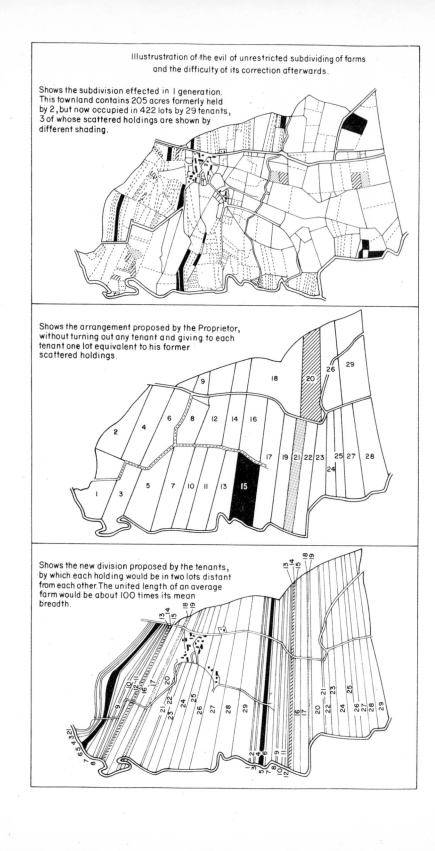

Illustrustration of the evil of unrestricted subdividing of farms and the difficulty of its correction afterwards.

Shows the subdivision effected in I generation. This townland contains 205 acres formerly held by 2, but now occupied in 422 lots by 29 tenants, 3 of whose scattered holdings are shown by different shading.

Shows the arrangement proposed by the Proprietor, without turning out any tenant and giving to each tenant one lot equivalent to his former scattered holdings.

Shows the new division proposed by the tenants, by which each holding would be in two lots distant from each other. The united length of an average farm would be about 100 times its mean breadth.

before and after the Great Famine. Immediately before the Famine population increase and congestion on the land were strong incentives to improvements, while after the Famine landlord projects could be promptly completed as the temporary reduction of population pressure eased the problems of rural re-organization. On many estates the rundale reforms were carried out swiftly by autocratic landlords. The large estates of the Bingham family around Castlebar and Ballinrobe in Co. Mayo were radically transformed in the 1840s; rundale organization was eliminated and new consolidated farms established, a process accompanied by large-scale, ruthless evictions of surplus population (Woodham-Smith, 1953). In west Donegal too there were far-reaching changes in the pre-Famine decade (McCourt, 1955). The much publicized improvements on the estate of Lord George Hill, on the boundary of Gweedore and the Rosses, were carried out, including the eradication of rundale organization which, Hill explained, "was a complete bar to any attempt at improvement". Many of the holdings on the 23 000 acre estate were consolidated, and fences, previously unknown in the district, were erected. Old house clusters were removed and new dispersed farmhouses built (Evans, 1971). Rundale reforms were proceeding at the same time on the neighbouring Dunlewy Estate and on the lands of the Marquis of Conyngham in the south of the Rosses. The Devon Commission in the 1840s reported that in south-west Donegal "the old landscape was daily being eradicated and improved". In the richer eastern parts of Donegal the rundale system was largely eliminated at the turn of the 18th Century when the farm clusters were said to be "dispersing daily into separate habitations and holdings" (McParlan, 1802). In Co. Roscommon the dissolution of rundale occurred mainly in the second decade of the 19th Century. Surveyors in the county were dismayed by the rapid change in the settlement pattern "owing to a great change of system, from tenants holding a farm in common, to each individual holding a farm of his own. Each of the tenants built a house on his farm, and the old villages were thrown down. This was in the years 1814-5-6," (Weld, 1832). The motives for landscape reform and its comprehensive character are very well summarized in the following account, taken from the voluminous report of the Devon Commission on the occupation of land in Ireland (Parliamentary Papers, 1845). The

Fig. 18: Consolidation of rundale holdings in the 19th Century. Proposals for reform at Glenfin, Co. Donegal. (Source: Devon Commission P.P. 1845, Appendix 14.)

changes referred to were carried out in the 1830s in the mountainous townland of Tullychar, the property of Sir R. A. Ferguson, near the Donegal-Tyrone border:

There were 12 tenants living on it, each holding a small share of the arable and meadow, with mountain grazing. As their houses were crowded together and their holdings much too small, and too intermixed to allow of their improving, it was necessary to make almost a total change; and the arable and meadow lands, with some of the mountain pasture were divided into eight farms; the remainder of the mountain pasture that appeared most capable of being brought into cultivation, was formed into six farms. . . . On each of the new farms a house was erected built of stone and lime and covered with Welsh slates. . . . The ditches on the old farms were all levelled, and the farms divided into five or six fields each, which contained from $2\frac{1}{2}$ to 6 acres each, by fences made with sods and sown on the top with furze (whin) seed. Roads were made for the accommodation of the farms generally, and branch roads struck off to each separate house and farm.

In some areas, however, rundale organization and the associated nucleated settlement pattern were particularly tenacious. Along the mountainous seaboard of west Connacht, for example, and the coastlands of Gweedore and the Rosses in Co. Donegal, rundale lingered on until the end of the 19th Century when its abolition became the responsibility of the Congested Districts Board, a government-sponsored planning authority with the task of rehabilitating the most depressed western regions (Freeman, 1943).

There are areas in the west where neither landlords nor government agencies have attempted any reform of the rundale holdings and certain localities too where their efforts were partial and pusillanimous. In these cases the consolidation of holdings and the erection of enclosures have sometimes been undertaken gradually by the farmers themselves especially when holdings were abandoned by emigrants, and the process of change has continued down to the present day. The typical outcome of this gradual organic development is a pattern of fragmented holdings less complex and confusing than the 19th Century situation but still highly inconvenient, with field walls and ditches which are often poorly constructed. New farmsteads have frequently been built away from the original clusters and the settlement pattern contains loose clusters of farms with a haphazard spread of farms around them tending to focus on the roads. Vestiges of the rundale era can thus still be traced in many western districts. The contemporary problem of farm fragmentation, for example, which bedevils western agriculture, although not nearly so acute as in the early 19th Century, is in large measure a legacy of the rundale era.

The planned re-organization of rundale holdings was usually accompanied by settlement dispersal and the rebuilding of the farmhouses in an improved style. The most common form of house in the west in the early 19th Century was the long-house or byre-dwelling, in which both animals and human beings were accommodated in one single compartment. Farm outbuildings were very poorly developed. Stone was the most common material used for house walls and the roofs of the houses were thatched and either hip or, more commonly, gable ended. As the 19th Century proceeded the habit of accommodating livestock within the house was gradually abandoned, although the custom lingered on in remote areas until the present century, and where landlords undertook extensive housing projects the farms were usually provided with barns and separate byres for the first time. In most places the rebuilt houses tended to preserve many of the features, such as thatched roofs and white-washed walls, and the general proportions of the older structures, but chimneys and flues were often added, slated roofs became more common and windows were made larger. In the present century two-storied stone houses with slate roofs have been widely built as farm residences and in some districts have almost completely replaced the older single-storey thatched houses. There was in the 19th Century and there still persists a great deal of uniformity in the style and size of western houses, more so than in the east where the planter element was more numerous and a more complex social structure existed.

Despite the reforming efforts of certain landlords the economic and social condition of western Ireland, and especially the seaboard areas, remained a serious problem in the second half of the 19th Century. Local increases of population had increased congestion and farm subdivision and the people were still precariously dependent upon the potato crop whose yield varied dramatically from year to year with partial famines resulting. Landlordism throughout Ireland had been severely weakened by the Great Famine, during and after which rents were not available, and on many estates bankruptcies occurred. In 1881, following a period of agrarian unrest, Gladstone's Land Act began the transfer of holdings from landlord to tenant, a process which was not completed for several decades. Although peasant proprietorship was no doubt a boon and perhaps ineluctable, fixity of tenure in western Ireland did mean that the smallholdings were stereotyped and in the main the new owners lacked any resources to initiate change—their main task was to keep alive. Inevitably, government agencies replaced the landlords as the only power which could bring about comprehensive change. A decent living could not be extracted from the small and fragmented holdings and in 1891 the British Government established the Congested Districts Board to have responsibility for the most depressed western areas which lay mainly in the counties of Donegal, Mayo, Galway and Kerry. The Board, which was in effect a pioneer attempt at comprehensive rural planning on a regional scale, included in its work the re-organization of the farm structure, enlargement and consolidation of holdings as far as possible and the encouragement of economic activities supplementary to farming, such as fishing and domestic industries. In 1923 the Board, after three decades of productive enterprise, was terminated and some of its responsibilities inherited by the Land Commission, a body which continues the work of reforming the farm structure, of enlarging uneconomic holdings, of consolidating scattered holdings and generally relieving congestion through re-settlement schemes. The main part of the Land Commission's work lies in the western Districts, especially those problem areas which had been the special responsibilty of the Congested Districts Board.

North-Eastern Ireland

The different physical, economic and social characteristics of the east and the west of Ireland and their contrasting historical development have made it essential to treat the two regions separately. North-eastern Ireland, however, also stands apart and merits separate consideration. The region involved here comprises the six counties which since partition in 1921 have formed the political unit of Northern Ireland. In this region, and especially in the three eastern counties (Down, Antrim and Armagh) which were the bastion of the protestant planter community, economic development in the last two centuries followed a course which by Irish standards was exceptional and the landscape was significantly differentiated. Population growth in the late 18th and the 19th Century was accompanied by agrarian reforms but, more significantly, by industrialization and rapid urbanization. At the beginning of the 19th Century the urban population of the region amounted to approximately 10% of the total but by 1926 the urban population had increased to nearly 75%. In the remainder of Ireland the urban population in 1926 did not amount to a half of the total and in some of the western counties it was below a quarter.

The protestant population of Ulster in 1800 accounted for almost half of the total population in the province but they were concentrated mainly in the three eastern counties: it was they who contributed most to the distinctive character of Ulster life. Their energy and self-reliance had not been inhibited in the 18th Century by the penal laws which were directed against catholics and had a depressing effect on social and economic life elsewhere in Ireland. Well before the 19th Century a prosperous and enterprising middle class had emerged in Ulster at a time when such a class scarcely existed elsewhere in Ireland save in Dublin and Cork. Moreover, relationships between Ulster landlords and their protestant tenants were less troubled than in most parts of Ireland, and the greater security of tenure and the right to compensation for any improvements made on the farms which was provided by the ''Ulster custom'', were also conducive to steady improvement in the rural economy. Linen weaving, which added to the prosperity of the farming people and was to be important in the early stages of Ulster's industrial revolution, originated as a domestic enterprise undertaken by Scottish settlers on their farms and was greatly encouraged by the arrival in the 17th Century of Huguenot refugees who were skilled weavers.

At the end of the 18th Century only the richer lowland areas most strongly settled by planters, such as the Lagan Valley, had been influenced by the changes associated with the agricultural improvement. Here the fields were often hedged in and the settlers lived in scattered, single farmsteads, but most of the countryside elsewhere was still unenclosed and many of the farmers still lived in compact but untidy farm clusters of up to half a dozen farms, known variously as closes, onsets, towns or, in a few localities, as clachans. Indeed the very success of the 18th Century domestic linen industry may have led to a lack of interest in progressive farming. In the early 19th Century and especially in the decade following the Famine there were far-reaching changes in the rural landscape of many areas carried out by the local landlords. The dispersal of farmsteads from the old farm clusters and the general adoption of enclosure, hedging and improved methods of cultivation transformed the traditional scene and gave Ulster a landscape which in essentials has changed little since. Small fields surrounded by hedged banks and averaging about 2 acres in size became almost universal. Field shapes vary considerably but the dominant shape is rectangular with the length approximately one and a half times the breadth, proportions advocated by the agricultural improvers of the time. Only in some remote localities, and especially in and around the Sperrin mountains, farm clusters and rundale organization have survived the agricultural changes of the 19th Century and are still to be found in varying degrees of preservation (McCourt, 1954).

Throughout rural Ireland both the landlord system and pressure of population declined during the latter half of the 19th Century. By the 20th Century the estate system was defunct and population pressure had been replaced by population decline. No new powerful influences have emerged to transform the rural scene, save around the largest cities. In the main the dwindling rural population has continued to function within the old framework of farms and fields. The failure of Irish industry to grow on any large scale in the 19th Century has also helped to preserve the landscape in its traditional mould both in the countryside and in many of the towns. Even in the north-east no extensive industrialized belts have emerged and outside of Belfast industry is largely confined to the scattered towns which are separated by tracts of countryside where the lay-out of the fields and the farms is mainly the product of planned changes carried out in the first half of the 19th Century.

Thus, although a variety of forces, including arterial drainage, housing improvements, modern industry, tourism and agricultural technology, are transforming many of its aspects the 20th Century rural landscape is essentially a product of developments in the 18th and early 19th Centuries. This is true of both the east and the west of Ireland and of the north-east of the country. The pace and timing of change in the rural landscape varied somewhat in the three regions but throughout the country the effects were broadly similar. Everywhere in Ireland the farmed landscape is now covered by a patchwork of enclosed fields; the farm settlement is highly dispersed and few of the older nucleated agricultural settlements have survived. Almost all the cultivable land is utilized for farming and the main gaps in the extent of the farmed lands correspond to bog areas and mountain masses.

Industrial Activities and the Landscape

The influence of industrial activity on the Irish landscape has been marginal. Major coal and iron resources are absent and this has hindered the development of extensive concentrations of heavy industry. Most manufacturing enterprises have operated on a small scale and have been widely scattered over the landscape. Their direct visual impact is consequently slight but they have had a significant influence on the settlement pattern, especially the growth of towns, and on the development of the communication network.

Industrial growth over the last two and a half centuries has experienced numerous vicissitudes and differed regionally in its character and extent. The 18th Century and the first two decades of the 19th Century was a time of general economic growth in which a variety of manufacturing enterprises existed. Subsequently, in Southern Ireland there was a reversal of economic fortunes; a long-term decline in industrial and manufacturing activities commenced which was not arrested until well into the 20th Century. The pattern of industrial development in north-eastern Ireland followed a distinctive course in the 19th Century. An industrial revolution of sorts occurred which permanently differentiated the economy and, to some degree, the landscape of the region from the remainder of Ireland.

Eighteenth and Early 19th Centuries

An early phase of industrial activity, conducted either on a domestic basis or in small-scale factory enterprises which were often supported by local landlords and located in their newly-built estate towns, influenced most parts of Ireland in the 18th Century. Promising developments occurred in a diversity of manufacturing activities, and especially in textiles. The domestic linen industry was particularly widespread, in Connacht, in the towns of south Munster and the east-coast towns, as well as in Ulster. But this early phase of industrial development ended rather abruptly with the general economic decline in the 19th Century and, save in the north, few of the early enterprises were able to survive into the present century. One major exception is the Guinness brewery in Dublin which began in 1759 and continued to expand and flourish, until in the 20th Century it had become one of the world's largest breweries. Its extensive buildings and warehouses on the south bank of the Liffey, which were linked to the Grand Canal, constitute an important element of the Dublin industrial scene and the brewery has provided a bastion of economic stability and employment in the generally precarious economic life of the Republic.

One legacy from this industrial epoch is a scatter of defunct installations such as water-wheels, the stumps of windmills, decayed factories and mills. However, these, while of interest to the industrial archaeologist, do not constitute a major ingredient of the landscape. The two most important and enduring legacies from the period are, first, the vastly improved and sometimes completely new urban settlements and, second, the new system of communications, on both of which industrial developments had a considerable influence. The major cities of Ireland, Dublin, Cork, Limerick and Waterford, expanded considerably at this time and greatly enhanced their appearance. In these centres economic development was based on both manufacturing growth and the expanding provisions trade with England, from which, owing to their port facilities and positions, the cities were well placed to benefit. Dublin, as the undisputed economic and political centre, profited most. A period of extensive rebuilding and expansion of the city took place in the late 18th and early 19th Centuries, its main legacies being the elegant Georgian architecture which still characterizes the centre of Dublin and the reclamation of land in Dublin Bay for the expansion of the docks and of industry. Dublin developed a more complex industrial structure than the other towns in the 18th Century with a variety of skilled luxury enterprises, including glass, books and furniture, as well as the basic textile and trading activities.

A number of Irish towns and villages, such as Birr, Westport, Fermoy, Hillsborough, Stradbally and Kenmare, were first established by landlords during this period of economic expansion and population growth, while many more towns were rebuilt or expanded, including Armagh, Tralee, Newry, Mitchelstown, Blessington, Dunlavin, Maynooth, Belfast and most of the other 17th Century plantation towns of Ulster. Many of these new or rehabilitated towns, it is true, were built to serve as the commercial centres of large rural estates but industry was usually an important ingredient of their economies and in some cases the backbone. Blarney in Co. Cork, for example, was converted by its proprietors, the Jefferyes family, from an impoverished village into a thriving manufacturing town based largely on linen, while Mountmellick, a Quaker colony in Co. Laois, became a prosperous town through its linen spinning, shipping its goods by a branch of the Grand Canal to Dublin. Other settlements such as Portlaw, Bessborough and Statford-on-Slaney, were specifically built as model industrial villages.

Apart from the fabric of many towns the most important scenic legacy from the period of economic advance in the 18th and early 19th Centuries is an elaborate communication system of roads and canals. The Irish road network was largely completed by the mid 19th Century. Built to link together the older centres of settlement and the numerous new estate towns and to serve the diffuse pattern of rural settlement when population was almost twice as large as at present, the road network is remarkably complex and fine-grained, especially in the lowland areas. Some of the most impressive road-building enterprises, however, were in highland areas. The most ambitious project was the Military Road built through the heart of the Wicklow Mountains after the 1798 rebellion to facilitate easy movement of troops in an area which hitherto had been relatively inaccessible and a traditional base for Irish resistance groups. Running for much of its course at over 1000 ft (305 m) through wild, bog-strewn country it has come in the present century to provide an important tourist route.

Canal building was energetically carried out in Ireland mainly during the 18th and, to a lesser extent, the 19th Centuries. Most Irish rivers, with the exception of the Shannon, lower Bann and Barrow, permit only limited access to the interior of the country. The relatively level relief of central Ireland provided good conditions for canal building while, in view of the numerous lakes and bogs, it was sometimes problematic for road building. Basically, the aim of the canal builders was to link up the principal natural waterways and connect Dublin with the Shannon and, thereby, with the Atlantic. This was largely achieved by the construction of the Royal Canal (1789–1817) and the Grand Canal (1756–1804) which linked Dublin to the Shannon and, via an offshoot of the Grand Canal, to the River Barrow. Canals were also excavated alongside unnavigable stretches of key rivers such as the Barrow and the Lagan. In Co. Galway a canal three quarters of a mile long linked Galway city to Lough Corrib, and the Cong Canal was built as a famine relief project in an attempt to link Lough Corrib to Lough Mask and thus further enlarge Galway's trade hinterland by permitting hookers to penetrate far inland on the lakes. The Cong enterprise was a complete failure; the canal was excavated in porous limestone and never held any water. In Ulster, Lough Neagh became the focus of the new waterways. The lough was linked to the north coast by the navigable lower Bann, to Carlingford Lough by the Newry Canal (1731–61), to Belfast Lough by the Lagan Navigation (1756–93) and to the headwaters of the Shannon by the Ulster Canal and the Ballinamore and Ballyconnell Canal (1847–58).

The canals were seen at the time of building as profitable ventures and as an important stimulus to the country's industrial and agricultural life. However, they did not measure up to expectations and the anticipated volume of traffic was rarely realized. The canals of the industrial northeast were the most successful. Most of the Irish canals were unable to compete successfully with the railway network built in the 19th Century and rapidly declined in importance, although desultory freight traffic continued until the 1950s on the Royal and Grand Canals. The inland waterways have recently experienced a limited revival with the development, mainly since the 1960s, of boating for pleasure purposes by tourists. Design standards on the canals were high and the substantial locks and harbours have survived along with the derelict canal hotels erected at passenger boat stages. Many of the houses built along the waterways for the canal employees are still inhabited. The coming of the canals brought new life to a limited number of old settlements, such as Rathangan and Monasterevan in Co. Kildare and, more impressively, to Newry in Co. Down which, after it was linked to Lough Neagh, became for a short period the major port of northern Ireland and still possesses a fine assembly of warehouses and other buildings dating from this period of prosperity. On the whole, however, the canals, like the railways, had little effect on settlement patterns and generally failed to create new settlements. A handful of quite new small settlements grew up at canal junctions or at passenger boat stages but most of the canal bridging points are devoid of habitation. Robertstown, Co. Kildare, owes its origin to the development of the Grand Canal; one mile east of the junction of the Athy and Shannon branches of the canal it was made the site of a canal hotel in 1801 and a small village quickly developed which had a population of 314 by 1841.

The Middle and Late 19th and 20th Centuries

It was in the 19th Century that the industrial life of northern Ireland diverged significantly from that in the rest of the country. Northern Ireland, and especially the three eastern counties, experienced an industrial revolution comparable in many respects to that of the industrial regions of England, Wales and Scotland, with a considerable growth of heavy industry and factory-based production chiefly concentrated in one major urban area. Elsewhere in the country, especially after the first two decades of the century, there was a deep and pervasive economic languor; it was not only that an industrial revolution failed to occur but that the earlier manufacturing enterprises initiated in the 18th Century tended to wither away. However, an industrial tradition did not altogether cease in the 19th Century, and in the 20th Century there has been a considerable revival and growth of industrial activity. Developments in industry during the 19th and 20th Centuries and their impact on the landscape outside of the industrialized north-east will be described first, that is in an area roughly equivalent to the present Republic and which for convenience is described here as "southern Ireland".

Southern Ireland

Industrial decline, and especially the collapse of the textile industry in the 1830s, had severe repercussions on the life of the southern towns, many of which were precipitated into deep poverty. The economic activities of most towns were increasingly confined to the provision of services to surrounding rural areas. There was little here to support a vigorous urban life as, after the Famine, the rural population experienced a rapid and sustained decline. Throughout the 19th Century and much of the 20th Century, therefore, the towns have either stagnated or declined. This long period of adversity is responsible for the widespread dilapidation and neglect which, despite the improvements of the last two decades, is still characteristic of many towns.

The industrial revolution may have had a meagre outcome in southern Ireland but significant developments occurred in communications and in mining. A network of railways was built in Ireland from the 1830s onwards. The south, despite its economic malaise, shared fully in the development, although northern Ireland with its industrial life and more numerous towns acquired a closer network of railways than elsewhere. The Belfast to Dublin line was completed in 1852 and by the 1860s most large towns had been connected by rail to Dublin or Belfast. Between 1860 and 1890 a number of light railways were built which linked even the remote western regions of Ireland to the basic rail network. Indeed, with its extensive roads, canals and railways, Ireland in the latter half of the 19th Century represented an underdeveloped economy with a highly developed transportation system. Like the canals before them, which they unexpectedly extinguished, the railways were enthusiastically developed as a panacea for economic ills and a means of breaking the isolation of remote towns and rural areas. However, no dramatic economic progress ensued, despite the energetic railway building activities. Improved communications could facilitate industrial growth but they could not generate it. Perhaps the major result of the railways was to increase economic centralization and enhance the already dominant status of Dublin and Belfast. The railway certainly led to considerable physical expansion of the two major cities. The building of a large harbour at Dun Laoghaire (Kingstown) and its linkage to Dublin by a passenger line in 1834 encouraged the southward spread of the city and the merging of the two settlements. In Belfast the building of railways between 1839 and 1850 from the city to Lisburn and other towns in the hinterland encouraged a comparable spread of the city's suburban areas.

Mining was actively pursued in Ireland in the 19th Century, although never on a scale large enough to support industrial developments. The resources of copper and lead were the major interest. In the 1880s Irish mining exploits experienced a general decline owing to competition from overseas producers and, in some cases, the exhausting of deposits. Their major contribution to the landscape is a variety of decayed installations often sited in lonely hill areas of outstanding natural beauty. Sometimes, however, the miners combined their activities with smallholdings and after the mines failed the farm settlements survived as "islands" in inhospitable hill areas. The most important mining developments occurred in the metalliferous belt of south-eastern Ireland along the flanks of the Leinster granitic outcrop. Here the most productive of the several ore bodies are the copper and iron ores of the Vale of Avoca and the lead and zinc ores of the Wicklow Glens, especially Glendalough, Glendasan and Glenmalure. The lead and zinc was worked sporadically during the 19th Century but all activity has now ceased and only ruined workings survive, most prominently in Glendasan where the adit mines, picking floors and sedimentation tanks can still be traced. Copper working at Avoca, although it declined in the late 19th Century, has revived in the post-war period and the abandoned and active workings are conspicuous scars in one of Ireland's most celebrated beauty spots.

The copper mines at Allihies on the Beara Peninsula, Co. Cork, were of importance during the first half of the 19th Century and employed over 1000 persons, but the mines declined in the face of foreign competition and closed in the 1880s. Subsequent attempts to revive them have not met with success. The main contributions to the landscape are the scattered tip heaps and the ruins of the village where the immigrant Cornish miners once lived. The Killaloe slate quarries in Co. Clare were opened in 1826 and employed about 700 workers in the 1840s; employment in them dwindled during the 19th Century but they continued in operation until the late 1950s.

Coalfields occur in Ireland in only a few scattered locations and their exploitation is rendered difficult by the faulted nature of the seams and the generally poor quality of the coal. Small-scale intermittent mining of the coal resources has taken place since the 17th Century but there was a recognizable expansion of activity in the 19th Century. Few industries sprang up in association with the mining but many of the abandoned workings and tips can be seen in the coal-bearing localities. The only Irish coalfield of significance lies on the Castlecomer Plateau, north of Kilkenny. Mining here of the small anthracite fields has had a chequered history of periodic closures, with expansion only in times of war when the competition of sea-borne coal was reduced. At present the main productive coalfield in the Republic of Ireland is a small area near Arigna, close to Lough Allen on the boundary of Co. Leitrim and Co.

Roscommon, where the semi-bituminous coals are worked by adits and are utilized mainly in a local power station.

Towards the end of the 19th Century the revival of woollen manufacturing, notably in the Athlone mills which had opened in 1859, and the advent of the co-operative creameries were the first indications of a long-term revival of economic fortunes and of the capabilities of the Irish economy outside of Ulster to adapt and respond to economic trends in the wider world. The number of woollen mills rose from 39 in 1861, to 74 in 1878 and 114 in 1899. Co-operative creameries were first established in the 1880s, following the campaign of Sir Horace Plunkett and the Agricultural Co-operative Movement to replace farmhouse butter by factory-produced butter in response to the competition of superior dairy products from Denmark and Holland. The creameries, which were inspired by Danish rural co-operative organizations, are one of the few illustrations in Ireland of co-operative economic enterprise in rural areas and the first important modern example of manufacturing growth in the countryside based on the processing of agricultural raw materials. They are most numerous in areas where dairy farming has been successfully developed, in particular the Munster lowlands and the lowlands around the head of Donegal Bay.

The bulk of southern industry has grown up since the 1920s, following the achievement of political independence by the 26 counties which now form the Republic of Ireland. Industrial growth was actively encouraged in the newly independent state in order to provide employment and check emigration. State intervention led to a major improvement in the industrial infrastructure of the country. In particular, increased supplies of power and light were provided by state sponsored hydro-electric schemes under the Electricity Supply Board and, later, by the large-scale development of the bogs under Bord na Mona. Indeed, the first public enterprise undertaken by the Irish state was the building of the hydro-station at Ardnacrusha on the River Shannon. Completed in 1929 it is still the largest of the nine hydro-electric stations built by the Electricity Supply Board on the Rivers Shannon, Erne, Liffey, Lee and Clady. Apart from the network of power lines and pylons, one of the most important scenic consequences of the hydro-electric schemes has been the creation of lakes, especially on the River Lee at Iniscarra, Co. Cork, and behind the dam at Poulaphouca in West Wicklow, where the Blessington Basin was flooded in the 1930s to form a storage reservoir almost 9 square miles ($12 \cdot 9$ km^2) in area.

Exploitation of bogs under Bord na Mona, the peat production board, has occurred mainly in the central lowlands, especially in Counties Offaly and Kildare. Here the extensive and level raised bogs are worked mechanically. The machine-cut turf is utilized for domestic fires and to feed a number of turf-burning power stations producing electricity for the national grid. Approximately one quarter of the electricity used in the Republic is generated at peat-fired stations. Of all the industrial activities of the 20th Century Bord na Mona's operations have had perhaps the most striking impact on the landscape. Bogs over many square miles have been stripped of their surface vegetation and the exposed peat provides a remarkably uniform vista, brown and level (Plate 14). This unusual landscape will, however, be transitory; by the end of the century the peat resources will be exhausted and the future appearance of the bog areas is difficult to envisage.

During the first three decades of independence progress in industrial development was not striking. In the 1930s a policy of wholesale tariff protection for Irish industries was commenced which proved effective in securing some new industrial growth, and a variety of noteworthy state enterprises commenced, including the Irish airline (Aer Lingus) and the Irish Sugar Company which manufactures sugar from home-grown beet at its factories in Carlow, Thurles, Mallow and Tuam. On the whole, however, the economic performance of the independent state was disappointing in both the industrial and agricultural sphere. A variety of political, economic and social factors hindered progress, including the civil war of 1922–3 which followed the war of independence, the world depression of the 1930s, and the World War in the 1940s. Able political and economic leadership was also very often lacking, and there was widespread pessimism and lack of initiative in Irish society which was encouraged by poor economic performance, by depopulation and a narrow, introspective intellectual climate. Since the late 1950s there has been a marked economic recovery which has led to a halt in the long-standing decline of population and a rapid rise in general living standards. Tariff protection has been reduced and industrial exports encouraged. Industrial development has been encouraged by generous grants and tax concessions to new factories. Between 1961 and 1971 alone, over 550 new industrial enterprises were established, of which 380 involved foreign participation. Thus, within the last 20 years the Irish industrial scene has changed appreciably; the quality and the range of industrial enterprises has notably increased, and export-orientated industries have grown as well as the amount of foreign participation in industry. The trend of economic transformation is clearly reflected in employment statistics. Employment

Plate 14a: A modern industrial estate, Galway city. The houses around the estate are typical of new residential developments throughout Ireland.

Plate 14b: Clonsast bog, Co. Offaly. Large-scale, mechanized exploitation of Midland raised-bog. Peat being loaded for delivery to power stations.

in the primary sector continues to decline rapidly. Between 1961 and 1971, for example, the number engaged in agriculture, forestry and fishing, fell from 379 500 to 282 000, the number of manufacturing jobs rose from 257 000 to 328 000 and the employment in services rose from 416 000 to 461 000.

The dominant feature of the distribution of industry in the Republic is the high concentration in the Dublin region, although other pockets of industrial concentration on a much smaller scale exist in Cork, the Limerick sub-region and Waterford. The great concentration of population in Dublin and the adjacent eastern counties, and the high *per capita* incomes in this region, constitute a major attraction for industrial activity. Dublin alone contains over a quarter of the total population of the Republic and is the major market centre and the only large pool of diverse labour skills. At Cork there is a variety of manufacturing concerns. Some of the new enterprises are located on industrial estates in the city suburbs but the most impressive feature of the city's industrial geography is the collection of major concerns sited on the shores of the outer harbour. Here a shipyard, steel mill, oil refinery and chemical plants make up the largest concentration of heavy industry in the Republic. Industrial growth in Limerick has been accompanied by development in the nearby town of Ennis and on the Shannon Free Airport Industrial Estate, a successful industrial development project about 15 miles (25 km) from Limerick. Factory development was encouraged near the airport in order to increase air traffic and thus counter any redundancies among the airport staff which might follow if Shannon Airport was overflown by long-range jet aircraft on the North-Atlantic routes. The planning of the industrial estate began in 1958 and the first factories moved to the site in 1960. Today there are over 40 firms in operation producing a variety of high value goods including electronic equipment and clothing. Shannon New Town, which has been built to accommodate the industrial labour force, consists mainly of a large modern housing estate adjacent to the industrial sites.

Outside of the four major coastal ports, Irish industries are not markedly concentrated in their distribution and being mainly small to medium-sized enterprises, few of which employ more than 500 people, they have minimal impact on the landscape. The food industries have a naturally even distribution and have made an important contribution to regional development although more factories are located in the east owing to the more productive agriculture. Many of the new industries established in the 1960s and 70s are of a foot-loose character and, given the widespread availability of electric power in the Republic, they are not tied to resources which are localized in their destribution. Owing to their frequent dependence on imported raw materials manufacturing industries have a tendency to cluster in the major ports, especially Dublin and to a lesser extent Cork, but many of the new industries have located in the small to medium-sized towns and this is a pattern which government policies have generally encouraged. A survey of over 400 new industries established during the 1960s with financial aid from the Industrial Development Authority, the state agency concerned with the promotion of industry, showed that there was a pronounced tendency for industrial establishments to locate in the smaller towns; nearly half located in towns of less than 3000 persons and two thirds located in towns of less than 10 000 (O hUiginn, 1972). The majority of the establishments were small. Over two thirds employed less than 10 persons and only 6% employed over 500 persons. In the late 1960s regional planning policies led to the establishment of compact industrial estates at Galway and Waterford (Plate 14) but, despite much contemporary discussion of industrial estates and "growth centres", there is no evidence of a decisive shift in government policies away from a wide dispersal of industry within the various planning regions.

One of the most important economic developments in modern Ireland has been the re-assessment of the geological resources of the country. During the first half of this century there was little mining of metals in Ireland but mining has now revived dramatically in the Republic. The application of new and sophisticated prospecting methods led in the 1960s and 70s to the discovery of large and valuable deposits of lead, zinc and copper in the Central Lowlands and the country promises to rank soon as Europe's largest base metal producer (Kearns, 1975). These newly developing resources will have considerable implications for the national economy and for the rural landscape, as they involve open-cast mining methods. There are possibilities that oil exists in commercial quantities under the sea-floor off the Irish coast. Most exploratory activity has so far centred on the south coast, but the extent of the resources is still unknown and there is no basis for predicting the pattern of future developments. Experience with North-Sea oil, however, shows that shore terminals and associated industries can have considerable impact on the coastal landscape and, unless considerable care is exercised, serious ecological damage can also be caused.

Northern Ireland (Counties of Antrim, Down, Armagh, Londonderry, Tyrone, Fermanagh)

In the north-eastern counties of Ireland, and especially in Belfast, there was a growing concentration throughout the 19th Century of industry and population. Despite the absence of local coal and iron deposits Belfast grew as rapidly in the 19th Century as the major industrial towns of Great Britain, increasing its population from 20 000 in 1800, when it was still a compact market town, to 350 000 in 1901 and almost half a million in 1951. Linen and cotton manufacturing provided the initial industrial base of the city but this was supplemented during the 19th Century by engineering, iron working, shipbuilding, and rope making, as well as by the growth of large port facilities. The port was especially vital to economic growth as it facilitated the import of essential industrial raw materials, such as coal and iron, which the province itself significantly lacked, and the export of the finished industrial products. Industrial growth and the spread of an impressive network of railways outwards from Belfast between 1840 and 1870 helped to promote the rise of industrial towns such as Lisburn, Lurgan, Ballymena and Portadown in the second half of the 19th Century. These new industrial towns were characterized by large mills, factories and uniform, brick-built areas of working-class houses. The railways also fostered the growth of the popular seaside resorts, such as Newcastle and Portrush, and the wide expansion of suburban Belfast.

Well before the 19th Century closed, eastern Ulster had emerged as a distinctive economic region within Ireland. Hitherto distinguished mainly by its ethnic composition and the relatively progressive agriculture of the planted lowland areas, it was now chiefly distinguished by the industrial emphasis of its economic life. Here alone in Ireland was a regional economy with a substantial industrial component and a landscape marked sporadically by the characteristic physical clutter of the industrial revolution, by clusters of factories, railways, ports and industrial housing. But eastern Ulster, like the remainder of Ireland, lacked coalfields to act as a magnet for extensive industrial and urban concentrations, and it was the resulting absence of large-scale external economies and of low transport costs which perhaps explains why Ulster has lacked the continuing dynamism which has characterized industrialization generally in the modern world. Outside the Belfast conurbation industrial enterprise is scattered in the small to medium-sized towns and between the towns the landscape remains unaltered and deeply rural.

In northern Ireland, despite the stronger growth of industry in the 19th Century, there was relatively little mining activity of any importance. The small-scale mining of iron ore and bauxite in the central and northern parts of the Antrim Plateau commenced in the 19th Century and continued until the inter-war period. Small amounts of low-grade bituminous coal have been mined since the 18th Century near Ballycastle, Co. Antrim and at Coalisland, Co. Tyrone, but in both places mining has stimulated only a limited amount of local urban and industrial growth and at Ballycastle the mines have now ceased to operate.

In the three western counties of Northern Ireland (Derry, Tyrone and Fermanagh) the imprint of 19th Century industrialization and indeed of the 17th Century plantation, the two most crucial phases of Ulster's history, is much less emphatic than in the three counties to the east. Protestant and catholic communities intermingle but catholics generally predominate. Industrial developments are few. The rural areas are intensively settled and dominated by small dispersed farms with only a scatter of small, sleepy market towns, their population rarely exceeding 10 000 and often numbering only a few hundred. The region is akin in many respects to the small farm areas of western Ireland, but at the same time, despite the absence of industry, it is recognizably a part of Ulster, neater, more prosperous, more uniform in its appearance and more consistent in its farming standards than the adjoining parts of the Republic.

Industry and economic life in the north have undergone far-reaching changes in the 20th Century and these have led to considerable modifications of the landscape, especially in the urban areas. During the first world war, boom conditions prevailed in the north-east, but the inter-war depression had severe consequences; the traditional industries, and especially shipbuilding, were markedly reduced and the unemployment rate, which in the 1930s averaged about 25% of the insured population, was unduly high in comparison with most of the other regions within the United Kingdom. There was a temporary improvement in linen and shipbuilding during the Second World War but subsequently the two industries have experienced a steady and apparently irreversible decline. Government policy in the post-war period has been directed towards the establishment of a range of new industries to replace the traditional ones and to provide the province with an industrial structure more diversified than hitherto and thus less vulnerable to economic recession. The new enterprises, most of which have been attracted from the overcrowded midlands and the south-east of England by the provision of generous government grants and cheap factory sites, include light engineering, electronics, oil refining, synthetic fibres, chemicals, clothing and food processing. This new industry, although of vital significance to the economy of the province, has not led to major shifts in the geographical distribution of economic activity but has tended rather to modify the character of the traditional industrial scene. Almost half of the new firms have located in the old industrial core region of Belfast and its vicinity, but unlike the traditional industries they are often clustered on large industrial estates and accommodated in spacious, modern style, one-storey factories which are in striking contrast to the storied mills and factories of the 19th Century.

Post-war modernization in the north, as in many of the depressed industrial regions of Britain, has had significant visual consequences. Modern motorways, radiating from Belfast, are a particularly striking innovation in the landscape and new housing estates, factories, schools and other public buildings are conspicuous amid the older fabric of the industrial towns. Taken as a whole, however, the urban industrial landscape is still dominated by the substantial legacy of 19th Century growth.

8
The Contemporary Rural Landscape

In this chapter the main ingredients of the contemporary cultural landscape in rural areas are described and the dominant forces which, over long periods of time, have moulded them. The present distribution and density of the rural population, the current rural economy and farm structure, and the extent and distribution of the farmed land within the total landscape are examined. Subsequently, the main emphasis is on the field patterns, including spatial variations in the size and shape of the fields and the methods and materials used to enclose them, and on the settlement pattern or characteristic distribution of the farms which is intimately connected with the field system and to the road network. Finally, there is consideration of the future changes which may occur in the landscape and the forces underlying them. A separate chapter is devoted to the buildings found in rural areas.

Population Distribution and Density, and Land Use

The population density for the whole of Ireland is 137 per square mile (52 per km^2) and for the Republic 108, a density which is markedly lower than that for England and Wales (790) and below the average for Europe as a whole. This light density is mainly due to the absence of large-scale industrialization but the pastoral emphasis of Irish farming, with an extensive rather than an intensive use of land, is an important contributory factor. Regional concentrations of industry in Ireland are few and rarely emphatic; indeed Belfast is the only centre where the lack of local coal and iron has been overcome and heavy industry grown up. Lacking heavily populated industrial belts, Ireland exhibits no very abrupt regional contrasts in population density. Mountains and bog tracts stand out almost everywhere as areas of low density, but the highland areas of Ireland are in the main small, compact hill masses, and, with the exception of the

Wicklow Mountains and the mountainous western seaboard in Donegal, west Mayo, west Galway and Kerry, there are no extensive areas unpopulated for relief reasons. About two thirds of Ireland is improved and farmed land on which there are approximately two million people living; the remaining third, classified as "other land", is unimproved land (mainly grazed and barren upland), bogs, lakes and built-up areas. Over the bulk of the country the rural population densities vary between 50 and 200 to the square mile. There is a noticeable relationship between rural population density and farm size. In general, average farm size is small to the north of a line drawn from approximately Galway to Dundalk, and holdings increase in size towards the south-east. Population densities tend to be higher in the areas dominated by small farms in the north and west (Fig. 19). In the richer agricultural areas of the south and east there are many small farms, but large farms occupy a significantly greater area of the total farmed land. Consequently, rural population densities are lower, usually below 100 to the square mile.

Ireland is unusual in having the highest rural densities of population on the poorest land. The most thickly populated agricultural areas of all occur along the western seaboards of Donegal, Mayo and Galway where the land is extremely poor and unproductive. The cultivable areas here are limited in extent, and within them the farms are so small and so close together that they sometimes form a loose but continuous agglomeration along the main coast roads. In the extreme east, on the other hand, and particularly in the rich agricultural counties of Meath, Louth and Kildare where the holdings are larger than elsewhere in Ireland and mainly devoted to pastoral activities, the farmsteads are widely scattered and, owing to the numerous hedgerows and trees, rarely intervisible. Here the rural landscape often gives an impression of profound emptiness and somnolence.

The dominant characteristic of the farm economy is the emphasis on livestock production based on permanent grassland. In 1970 there were over six and a half million cattle in the country and over six million sheep. About 70% of the farmed area, equivalent to almost half of the total land area, is at present devoted to permanent pasture. Hay occupies a further sixth of the farmed land and the remainder is devoted to a variety of crops, mainly cereals, potatoes and sugar beet. A high proportion of the remaining land (unimproved land which is not officially classified as farmland) forms rough hill and bog grazing for young cattle and hardy sheep. The following table indicates how the land of Ireland is presently used.

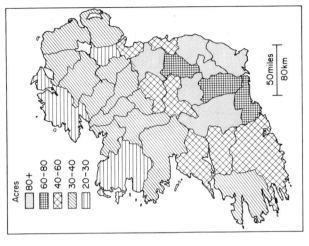

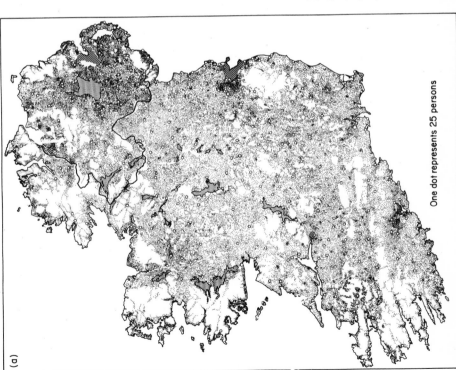

One dot represents 25 persons

Fig. 19: a Rural population distribution. **b** Average farm size. Population is widely and rather evenly distributed, especially in the lowland areas. The major gaps in the distribution coincide with mountain and bog tracts. Rural densities are highest in the north where the farms are smallest. Along the mountainous western seaboard in Kerry, Connacht and Donegal, the population is often confined to narrow coastal strips; here too the densities are high and the farms small. (Maps based on Colin Buchanan and Partners, 1968 and Gillmor, 1971.)

Acres
80+
60–80
40–60
30–40
20–30

50miles
80km

Table 1: Land Use, 1970 (million acres, to nearest 100 000 acre)

	Ireland	Republic	Northern Ireland
Pasture	9·6	8·4	1·2
Hay	2·8	2·2	0·6
Grain	1·1	0·9	0·2
Roots, green crops, fruit	0·4	0·4	0·05
Other land	6·4	5·1	1·3
Total Area	20·3	17·0	3·3

1 acre = 0·405 ha.

Livestock is dominant everywhere but the pattern of contemporary farming is typically mixed. Regional variations in the relative importance of individual agricultural enterprises, such as dairying, beef or crop production, provide a basis for dividing the country into agricultural regions (Gillmor, 1967), but differences are superimposed on a common pastoral basis and the prevalence of grassland and grazing cattle is everywhere an outstanding feature of the rural scene. Differences in farm economy do contribute to the differentiation of the rural scene but they do not produce marked differences save in the regions where tillage is important and in the limited areas devoted to fruit growing and market gardening. Little more than 10% of Irish agricultural land is tilled and most of this is concentrated in south-eastern Leinster, especially in Wexford, Carlow and south Kildare, although Louth and parts of east Ulster also have significant extents of tilled land. Rarely in these areas does the tillage make up more than a third of the total farmed land but the ploughed fields and the crops significantly diversify the rural scene, more care is lavished on the land and there is frequent trimming of hedgerows and banks. In north Co. Dublin there is a marked concentration of commercial vegetable growing along the coast near the village of Rush which has produced a distinctive landscape dominated by narrow fields and large glasshouses. The numerous apple and plum orchards lend a special character to the fruit-growing areas to the south of Lough Neagh in Co. Armagh.

The character and the regional distribution of agricultural production has varied in the past century in response to economic forces. The area under arable crops has been approximately halved during the last century while the number of cattle has roughly doubled. Increasing emphasis on pastoralism followed the adoption of Free-Trade policy in the 19th

Century and was reinforced by the growing competition of cheap grain imports from the New World in the 1880s. Grass growth in Ireland is favoured by the mild, moist climate, and livestock production for the large British market can be more cheaply based on grass than on tillage. However, these changes in farming have had little influence on the cultural landscape. Prevailing regional differences in rural population density, in farm size, settlement pattern and the shape and size of fields are a response to historical and social as well as strictly economic causes and, moreover, were established before the present pattern of land use developed at the end of the 19th Century. There is therefore little causal relationship between variations in farm economy and the basic lay-out and size of the fields and farms. Indeed in many areas today the pattern of farm production appears inconsistent with the land quality and farm structure. For example, most of the intensive arable farming in the Republic lies in south-east Leinster where the farms are among the largest in the country, while extensive livestock farming prevails on the smallholdings of western Ireland.

Historical Origins

There are resemblances between the rural landscapes of Ireland and large parts of Great Britain. Perhaps the major unifying feature is the almost universal patchwork pattern of enclosed fields in association with dispersed farms. Sometimes this is of long standing but more often it is the product of agrarian "improvements" carried out in recent centuries. However, the further back in time one proceeds the more evident is the distinctiveness of Ireland. The forces which created the towns and nucleated villages of the English lowlands and on much of the North German plain, for example, were never operative in Ireland. Ireland, moreover, escaped the embrace of the Roman empire and thus an early impetus to urban formation. At a later date it lay beyond the reach of the village-dwelling Anglo-Saxons. Villages were introduced by immigrants in the Medieval period but only into the south-eastern parts of the country, and their settlements were largely destroyed or decayed in later centuries. The pattern of Norse settlement was also exceptional. In the Danelaw of England and the Outer Isles of Scotland, where the Norse settled in great numbers, they formed a rural peasantry, but in Ireland they were mainly town dwellers and traders and made no lasting impression on the settlement geography of the rural interior of the country.

Landholding and the Estate System

In Ireland conflict between native and settler for the ownership of land has been a central issue of political and social history. Moreover, the system of landholding is a fundamental consideration in any analysis of the origin and character of the cultural landscape. Some elements of the landscape have been directly inherited from remote periods of history and these must be given due consideration, but it is the developments of recent centuries which have been most influential, especially the far-reaching changes of agrarian economy and of the rural landscape which occurred in the 18th and early 19th Centuries and were often carried out by major landlords within the framework of their large estates. However, in the history of landscape evolution it is almost always the case that earlier conditions influence later events in some way, direct or subtle, no matter how radical and comprehensive the events may appear at first sight. Estate planning was inspired by the widely prevalent ideas of ''agricultural improvement'' which emphasized a new commercialized and scientific pattern of farming operating within a reformed and rationalized landscape. This implied transformation of the older landscape elements inherited from medieval and earlier periods, but the new was normally conditioned to some degree by the old. New field patterns were influenced by the traditional field systems that they replaced and the inertia inherent in all settlements ensured that new settlement patterns incorporated elements of the old or reflected some degree of compromise with the traditional forms. Moreover, innovations had to be adapted to the unchanging physical realities of the country: hence, older regional contrasts sometimes emerged in a new guise, and despite the homogenizing tendencies of the great landscape transformations it is still possible to identify a persisting contrast between the landscape character of the richer east and poorer west of the country and to recognize the long-standing individuality of the north.

The system of large landed estates, which in the 18th and 19th Century embraced the whole country, has now been almost completely dissolved. Since the demise of the system in the late 19th Century almost all former estate tenants have become proprietors and many old demesne lands allocated among small farmers. This is in contrast to the remainder of the British Isles where substantial rural estates and tenant farmers are still numerous: in England, for example, about 60% of the farmland is rented by the occupiers. From being a classic illustration of a country dominated by great estates Ireland became by the 20th Century a country of small peasant proprietors. However, landlordism has had a profound effect on the rural landscape and many major elements of the rural scene today are residual from the time when the estate system flourished. In many areas the location of farms and routeways as well as the pattern of fields owe much to estate planning. Old demesnes with their high enclosing walls, ornamental woodlands and gardens remain in numerous places and contribute greatly to the richness and variety of the rural scene, even if the great houses have often been abandoned or converted to use as hotels, convents or government institutions. The slopes and terraces of river valleys such as the Boyne and Liffey, which provided vistas in a countryside generally rather level and uneventful, were favourite locations for demesne houses. Numerous market towns were also established, or substantially remodelled along contemporary lines, by local landlords to serve as the commercial centres of their estates (Chapter 10). Although urban in function, these settlements are limited in size, comparable in area and population to the larger villages of lowland England but distinguished from them by the absence of farms and, of course, by their wider spacing in the landscape. In lowland England there is, on average, a village every 2 miles (3·2 km) but the normal distance between Irish towns, disregarding here their status in the urban hierarchy, is some 5–10 miles (8–16 km).

The great landlords, who were most often English and protestant and thus divorced from their tenantry by language and religion, had been established in Ireland during the plantations of the late 16th and, more especially, the 17th Centuries. They replaced the older aristocracy who were either Gaels or Old English, i.e. descendants of the original settlers of the Anglo-Norman colony. Many privileged protestant tenants were introduced from Britain by the new landlords, especially onto the richer lands of the east where the landlord system was most deeply entrenched. This policy, combined with the long established eastern custom of undivided inheritance, helps to account for the greater number of big farms or rather the greater range of farm size in eastern Ireland today. The differentiated social structure associated with the medieval village communities which had been established by the Anglo-Normans in eastern and south-eastern Ireland has also been an important legacy and contributed to the development of a more complex pattern of farm sizes. Some of the larger holdings in eastern Ireland, however, were not originally associated with villages but, nevertheless, appear to have medieval antecedents such as feudal estates and monastic granges.

In the poorer west, especially in Connaught, there were fewer immigrant groups and the native Irish formed an overwhelming majority in the population. Although estates in the west were often very extensive, the bulk of the farm holdings there have always been small, probably owing to the indigenous custom of equal sub-division of land among co-heirs, which applied generally and with deleterious consequences for the expanding peasant populations of western Ireland until the period of the Great Famine of 1846–8. Thus in 1841 in each county of Connaught over 90% of the holdings were under 15 acres (6 ha). However, a similar pattern of uniformly small farms is characteristic of numerous poor hill and bog communities throughout the island where the egalitarian structure of native peasant society has been undisturbed by planter elements.

In Ulster there was, besides the indigenous Irish, a substantial community of vigorous Scottish and English settlers, and the widespread combination of intensive arable farming with the domestic linen industry seems to have allowed the subdivision of land during the period of marked population increase in the 18th and 19th Centuries to occur without any radical decline of living standards. Ulster farmers had the additional advantage of the "Ulster custom" or "Ulster tenant right" which provided them with reasonable security of tenure and compensation for any improvements which they made on their farms. In this respect the relationship between landlord and tenant differed significantly from that in most other parts of Ireland. A pattern of relatively prosperous small to medium farms came to characterize most parts of the northern province which allowed it to escape the worst effects of the Famine and provided a solid basis for the industrial developments of the 19th Century. The stimulus of an urban industrial market and, in the post-war period, extensive subsidization of agriculture by the United Kingdom government have helped to preserve the relative prosperity of the rural areas. A consistent air of modest well-being and neatness prevails which is in contrast with the decay and neglect frequently evident in the small farm areas of the Republic.

In the past century the traditional farm structure in western Ireland has been significantly modified through the sporadic enlargement of holdings made possible by massive rural emigration. The main change has been a sharp fall in the number of small farms (those under 15 acres), but the basic uniformity of holding size remains a distinctive feature with over half of the holdings still lying between 5 and 30 acres (2 and 12 ha). Sustained rural depopulation has of course deeply influenced rural society throughout Ireland. Thus in 1841 (before the Famine) only 7% of the farm holdings in Ireland exceeded 30 acres: by 1901 the percentage had risen to about 30 and at the present day it is almost 50%. Generally in Leinster and Munster the rural depopulation, although heavy, has involved the landless labouring classes rather than the landholders. The relative stability and prosperity of rural Leinster and Munster is owing both to the superior soil resources and to the more highly developed urban structure of the region. Contemporary economic changes are significantly altering the traditional character of rural Ireland. Small holdings are being rapidly reduced in number and the average size of holding continues to rise (Fennell, 1968). The changes are biting most deeply in the poorer small farm areas of western Ireland so that the long standing contrasts in farm structure between east and west are being eroded.

Fields

Ireland, relative to most European countries, possesses a much enclosed or "bocage" landscape. The widespread pattern of fields, roughly rectangular in shape and enclosed by banks, walls and hedges, forms one of the most conspicuous and ubiquitous elements of the cultural landscape and spatial variations in the shape and size of the fields contribute much to the distinctive character of the landscape in different parts of Ireland (Fig. 20, Plates 12, 13). In eastern areas not only are the farms larger but the fields are also more extensive in area and generally more regular in their outline (Flatrès, 1957). Two main types of field occur in the east, distinguished by size and by the form of enclosure: extensive tracts of countryside tend to be covered by one or other of the field types. First, large rectangular fields, averaging 8–10 acres (3·25–4 ha), predominate in central east Leinster with their classic development in Counties Meath, Kildare, Dublin and Louth. In most places these large fields seem to have originated during the era of the great landlords and are probably the product of estate planning or the work of substantial farmers. Enclosure is characteristically by a combination of deep drainage trenches and earthen banks planted with hedges. Generally throughout Ireland the crafts of hedging are poorly developed and the thorns are either profusely overgrown or ruthlessly pruned. Second, medium-sized fields, averaging 5–6 acres (2–2·5 ha), occupy most of the eastern areas, especially the south-east where they are well developed in the counties of Wexford and Waterford. These fields are often defined only by banks, some 4 or 5 feet (1·2 or 1·5 m) high, which are, rather misleadingly, called "ditches" by the Irish countryman. The banks typically contain a core of boulders and stones which have been cleared from the fields, and the layers of sod which

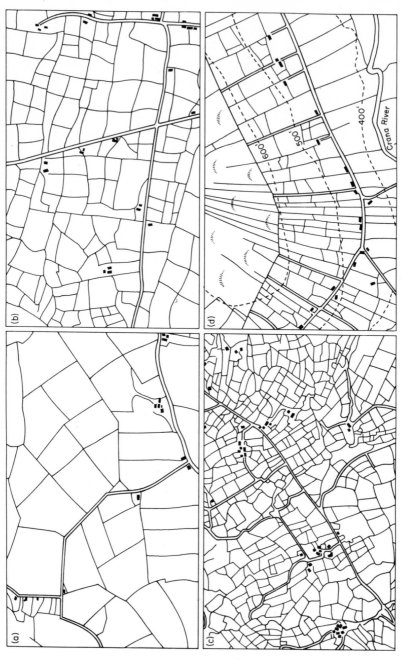

Fig. 20: Settlement and field patterns (scale: 3½ inches (89 mm) to 1 mile (1·62 km)). **a** Large regular fields, Co. Meath, with dispersed farms and roadside smallholdings. **b** Medium-size fields with dispersed farms, Co. Waterford. **c** Small, irregular fields, with clachans and dispersed farms, Co. Cork. **d** Highly regular fields associated with "striped" holdings, Co. Donegal. (Based on the Ordnance Survey by permission of the Government, Permit No. 2999.)

cover the stones are derived from shallow drainage ditches which flank the banks. Banks are a common form of enclosure in Ireland and occur widely in all regions, characteristically overgrown with a tangle of native trees and shrubs. The vegetation growing on the banks varies regionally according to soil and drainage conditions. On well-drained limestone soils hawthorn and ash are dominant with occasional clumps of hazel, but on inferior acid soils, hawthorn and gorse are dominant. Alder and willow increase in importance in very damp situations. Along the windswept western and southern coasts, the field banks are typically bare and trees and shrubs are scarce for several miles inland.

Although field boundaries are often poorly constructed many Irish farms possess substantial entrance gateways with tall stone pillars which may be circular with conical caps or rectangular and crowned with flat slabs of stone. Typically the pillars are painted white. Sometimes, especially on the larger farms of south-eastern Ireland, the pillars support wrought iron gates and have side walls of mortared stone. These impressive gateways are now rapidly disappearing from the countryside; they form an obstacle to the movement of modern farm machinery, tractors and lorries, and are consequently removed by the farmers.

In the west, with the major exception of the lowlands flanking the Shannon Estuary, large fields do not occupy extensive areas; fields tend to be medium or small while their shape varies from regular to highly irregular. Moreover, the field boundaries in western districts are generally less pronounced than in the east and the fields in most places defined only by low earthen and stone banks. The formation of fields in the west culminated in the 19th Century in a period when the rural population was much greater than today and the small size of the fields, averaging perhaps two to three acres, reflects the needs of small-scale peasant agriculture where the chief implement of cultivation was the spade. Such a field pattern is generally unsuited to the demands of advanced mechanized farming at the present day, but owing to the general economic inertia in western Ireland no dynamic forces have emerged to modify the inherited field pattern in any far-reaching way. Fields with regular outlines have resulted mainly from landlord planning in the 19th Century and, to a lesser extent, from the more recent work of government bodies, such as the Congested Districts Board and the Land Commission, responsible for the reform of farm structure. Long narrow fields with straight boundaries occur in some parts, especially on the hillsides, but, in the main, the planned fields are squarish or oblong. Field shapes are closely related to the basic methods of land consolidation and farm dispersal used during the period of agrarian reform and these methods will be described later and in more detail. Areas with irregular field outlines are mainly those which have escaped the reforming influence of the landlords. They are typically in areas of broken relief and poor soils to which the landlords paid little attention and where, very often, peasant colonization was a relatively recent and piecemeal process. The patchwork pattern of irregular small fields is both an adaption to the uneven topography and the outcome of intensive small-scale agriculture where every available patch of soil had to be exploited and demarcated. Such field patterns are to be found in many scattered localities in the west but they have their classic development in the thickly populated coastal areas of Connemara and west Mayo and on the extensive rock outcrops in south-west Cork.

The broad regional contrasts in field patterns which have been described above have only limited validity. The form of the fields has been influenced by a wide range of environmental and historical factors and considerable local variety can be found, sometimes even within the limited area of a single townland. For example, a recurrent contrast in the Irish fieldscape is that between substantial estate farms with their large regular fields, on the one hand, and, on the other, the smaller and more irregular fields associated with dependent small holdings which characteristically formed a belt or fringe at the edge of great estates. Occasionally too there are sharp local contrasts between fields which have evolved from old open-field strips and have a strikingly elongated form, and the more regular outlines of neighbouring fields established *ab initio* on commons or waste land (Fig. 16).

Variety is found not only in the shape of the fields, but also in the materials used to build field boundaries. Banks or ''ditches'' of earth and stone are the most common features but where soils are thin and the bedrock close to the surface the local stone is used for fencing and can give the fields a distinctive character. There are also considerable variations in the quality of dry walling from region to region. There are some fine examples of the craft but also many miles of poor loosely-constructed walls, especially in the west. In east Co. Galway the limestones are used to make the excellent and neat walled enclosures of the sheep-rearing country. In the karstic uplands of the Burren in Co. Clare there are dry stone walls of similar high quality, but there is plentiful evidence too of older and more elementary walling traditions involving limestone slabs which are derived from the decaying limestone pavements and simply inserted upright in the grykes or solution hollows. The gryke pattern has thus in some places had a formative influence on the evolution of the field pattern. In contrast, the field walls of the rocky western seaboard of Donegal are often constructed with granite boulders and have a more massive and irregular character. In the hill areas of West Wicklow large blocks of well-hewn granite from the granite quarries are sometimes used as the framework for field walls. Perhaps the most impressive walls in the Irish landscape are those which mark the boundaries of townlands in otherwise open hill areas: these walls are often over 6 ft (1·8 m) in thickness and march for miles over steep, wild terrain in order to define the areas of mountain which the farmers of each townland may use for common grazing. Striking examples exist in the Mourne Mountains of Co. Down and in the Connemara Mountains.

Examples can be found in Ireland of short stretches of stone wall which appear to be ancient, perhaps prehistoric (Davies, 1939). Certainly there has always been a tradition of building in dry stone, although it found its main expression in individual buildings such a megalithic tombs and clochan structures. It is unlikely, however, that the habit and specialized craft of making extensive field walls with interlocking dry stones originated before the late 18th century, when the attention of agriculturalists increasingly turned to the possibilities of exploiting poor moor and hill lands and there was a growing awareness that in an agricultural economy open lands were wasteful and too labour intensive. Traditionally, livestock on the mountains had had to be tended by herdsmen or tethered to prevent them straying or, when they were near settlements, to keep them away from growing crops.

The widespread pattern of enclosed fields in Ireland has sometimes been viewed as an inheritance from prehistoric times, perhaps linked with the pastoral traditions of the Celts. However, it is now clear that the essentials of the enclosure pattern are of comparatively recent origin and in most areas the fields have been formed since the late 17th Century, replacing medieval open-field systems or developing *ab initio* on land reclaimed from forest and bog. Aerial photography has shown that rath settlements, most of which date from the 1st millenium A.D., are sometimes associated with limited areas of small block-like fields and the raths and the fields may well be contemporary. Excavations at Cush in Co. Limerick suggested that field banks of stone and sod identical with those in the present landscape were associated with the raths. There is, however, no reason to suppose that extensive areas of landscape were enclosed during the period that the raths were inhabited (Chapter 4) and, moreover, there is no clear evidence of continuity of the old field network down to the present day. The method of building field walls with a stone core overlain by sods has clearly not changed since the Iron Ages and occasionally old field boundaries may be incorporated in the contemporary landscape, but modern fields are on the whole larger in area, more rectangular and even-shaped: the strong contrast between them suggests that the present enclosures were superimposed on the older system and did not evolve gradually from it. Similarities between the fields associated with raths and the present day fields may not be illustrative of absolute continuity but rather of similar agrarian needs in different periods producing similar results in the landscape.

On thin upland soils and in certain stony lowland areas where stone walls are often the chief form of enclosure, some of the field walls do seem to be of long standing and small areas here may have been enclosed from prehistoric times. This is especially true of the bare limestone uplands of north-west Clare and on the adjoining and almost equally bare Gort lowlands and the lowlands of east Galway. In these regions the rock debris, weathered from the limestone pavements, has been laboriously removed by man over many centuries in order to provide relatively level areas for grazing and for pedogenesis, a process which has been encouraged by the spreading of soil from the drift patches over the bare limestone, by animal dunging and, in coastal areas, by the spreading of sand, shells and seaweed. Masses of boulders have been piled up in the walls or into irregular heaps which have usually been overgrown by wild vegetation. The scattered deposits of glacial drift which form the best land and usually the only soils suitable for tillage were also full of boulders and these too had to be cleared away and built into the walls. Walls made of rounded ice-smoothed boulders mark off the drift patches from the limestone pavements where sharp angular material is incorporated in the walls. Reclamation and walling were inseparable operations in these regions. The extensive dry stone walls which today divide the farmlands into fields with regular outlines are rarely older than the 18th Century, but it is likely that some walled enclosures have long existed and that the fieldscape has evolved and grown gradually since the Neolithic period.

Settlement Patterns

The typical rural settlement pattern in Ireland is one of single dispersed farms, interconnected by an extremely close and complex network of roads and lanes, but clusters of farms occur in scattered localities (Fig. 21) and until the 19th Century were much more widespread in many parts of the country, particularly the north and west (Johnson, 1958, 1961). These

Fig. 21: Farm Clusters. **a** Cloonkeen, Co. Galway, with amorphous ground plan. **b** Luffany, Co. Kilkenny; farms, some of courtyard type, tightly packed at side of road. **c** Rushestown, Co. Galway, with farms strung out along one side of the road. **d** Derreen, Co. Galway; compact cluster with buildings arranged on either side of the road. **e** Lisdangan, Co. Kerry, a cluster of farms lying roughly parallel to each other. **f** Gorthadoo, Co. Kerry, a cluster of farms in parallel alignment. (The scale of the drawings is 5 inches (128 mm) to 1 mile, 1·62 km. (Based on Ordnance Survey by permission of the Government, Permit No. 2999.)

older settlements (to which some scholars have applied the Scots Gaelic term "clachan") were simply a collection of small farms, without a church or other institutions. True villages, which possessed an hierarchical social structure and served as centres for parishes and the provision of a limited range of rural services, occurred only in the east and south and were relatively few in number.

The farm clusters exhibit generally a concentrated but haphazard arrangement of buildings without any discernible overall plan (Proudfoot, 1959). This absence of spatial order seems to have been a fundamental characteristic of native Irish settlements. Interesting exceptions to the amorphous lay-out do, however, occur and are of two main kinds. In some old settlements in western Ireland the houses have a distinctive parallel alignment which seems to reflect an intimate connection between house type and settlement morphology. The traditional style of house, the long-house, incorporated both byre and dwelling in one single compartment and for hygienic reasons settlements were often deliberately located on sloping sites and the byre ends of the houses were pointed down the slope. In Irish farm clusters with a parallel alignment of houses, the orientation of the buildings is associated with the local slope and not the prevailing winds or any other identifiable factor. Often the orientation of the houses is completely different from one settlement to the next depending on the slope direction of the site. The alignment of the houses is not the outcome of settlement planning, it appears to have evolved naturally on relatively level sloping sites given the particular house style and hygienic constraints. Moreover, this lay-out may once have had a wider distribution than is now apparent. In many of the large farm clusters of the Dingle Peninsula in Co. Kerry, for example, it can be observed that the echelon arrangement has only recently been disrupted, usually when new two-storey houses were built in the present century and these, unlike the old long-houses, are characteristically built with their long axes along the contours. In general it seems that it is only where long-houses were inhabited down to a very recent period that their impress on settlement morphology can be clearly traced. The building of byres and outhouses separate from the house, which occurred widely in the 19th Century as the long-house tradition was dying, has frequently contributed to the confused lay-out of many surviving farm clusters.

Another type of farm cluster occurs with an ordered lay-out. Here the farms are usually arranged neatly on each side of the road or, less commonly, around a small and ill-defined central space, and the farmsteads are often of the courtyard type. Both the arrangement of the settlement and of the farmsteads suggests the influence of overall planning; landlord re-organization in the 18th and 19th Centuries might be responsible, indeed some of the settlements may even be a legacy of medieval feudal organization. No clear evidence is available on the question. Examples of these regular clusters can be found west of the Shannon, for example in east Galway, and occasionally they occur in the south-east of Ireland, especially the hill areas of south Kilkenny and Waterford.

The old farm clusters, whatever their morphology, were associated with open-field cultivation which involved the working by each farmer of a number of unfenced, scattered tillage plots close to the settlement. The grazing and bog land surrounding the arable area was held in common by all the farmers (Evans, 1939; Mcourt, 1954–5). There is almost everywhere a close identity between the townland and the farm cluster and its land, and they often had the same name. The combination of farm cluster with communal cultivation is termed the rundale system and it has largely disappeared from the Irish scene within the last two centuries. Because the fragmentation of holdings and the absence or inadequacy of enclosures retarded agricultural improvement, the rundale system has been eradicated by improving landlords, by the Congested Districts Board and its modern successor the Land Commission which is the state body with responsibility for land structural reform (Micks, 1925; Binns, 1950). In some remote areas, depopulation and roadbuilding have also led to the decline of rundale organization without the assistance of either landlord or government planning.

It is the planned elimination of rundale which has produced the present landscape of many areas. The bulk of the formerly fragmented holdings have now been wholly or partially consolidated, communal practices abandoned and fences erected to define the fields. Patches of old open-field arable land divided, as was traditional, by low "balks" or "mearings" (which were either unploughed strips, low mounds, or stones spaced at intervals) are now rarities in the landscape. In a number of cases the old farm clusters are still inhabited even though the open-fields have long been enclosed and most traces of communal agriculture have disappeared. But generally the clusters disintegrated when the agrarian organization sustaining them was reformed. The nuclei have been replaced by the present pattern of dispersed farms, usually conveniently aligned along new roads constructed at the same time as the rundale system was removed. The new patterns of farm distribution vary according to the basic mode of consolidation and enclosure. Improvers in the 18th and 19th Centuries distinguished between a "squaring" and a "striping". In the case of squaring the re-organized holdings were laid out in rectangular blocks so that a roughly grid-iron pattern of farm holdings was produced along with a rather even spread of farmsteads interconnected by a complex pattern of rough tracks or bohereens which linked to a framework of improved major roads. This approach to consolidation was commonly adopted on level lowlands with relatively uniform soil quality. The farmland was usually subdivided into a network of rectangular fields which reflects the larger framework of the holdings. With a striping, on the other hand, the old fragmented holdings were recreated as single narrow strips or stripes arranged in parallel rows (Figs 18, 20d). The new farmsteads are located along a single routeway which bisects the holdings, and the resulting farm pattern is thus markedly linear. Such a pattern of consolidation was well adapted to hilly lands where it permitted each farmer a share of the contrasting land resources ranging from rough hill grazing to arable patches in the valley; it also permitted considerable economies in road building. In many western areas, of course, the geometry of consolidation is a compromise and in some cases a combination of these two extreme forms, its detailed form depending on the local relief variations, the pre-enclosure pattern of farms and landlord policy.

In a few localities, especially of lowland Mayo and Galway, rundale organization and the associated farm clusters have survived essentially unchanged down to the present day, the clachans still dot the landscape and the reform of the complicated land-holding pattern, is one of the most arduous of the Land Commission's remaining tasks. Often indeed in this overcrowded countryside the necessary reorganization and enlargement of holdings can only be achieved if some tenants agree to migrate. Many of the displaced families have been resettled in groups on new holdings acquired by dividing up large estates in the eastern and midland counties.

In the east and south-east the landscape was enclosed at a slightly earlier period than the west (Aalen, 1965, 1970). How extensive rundale organization was in these eastern areas is uncertain but it clearly existed, e.g. in parts of Co. Kilkenny and around the Wicklow Mountains. There is also evidence in some eastern areas of an open-field organization more advanced and elaborate than rundale, which was very probably introduced into Ireland by Anglo-Norman settlers in the Middle Ages (Otway-Ruthven, 1951). With this were associated village settlements, larger and more complex than rundale clachans. The latter were simply clusters of small farms, while the villages, besides their farms, often originally contained tower houses (the fortified residences of upper-class people) and a medieval church. The extensive open-fields around the villages were, just as in lowland England and on the North German plain, divided into many long, narrow and unfenced strips with scattered ownership (Fig. 15). However, the medieval settlement patterns and field systems were in most areas destroyed or much modified during the decline of the Anglo-Norman colony in the Late Medieval period and during the large-scale re-organization of the countryside which followed the Tudor and Jacobean plantation schemes. In the late 17th and 18th Centuries a number of additional developments, especially the growth of enclosures and the decline of arable farming, caused further complete or partial decay of many of the remaining villages and their replacement by an almost ubiquitous pattern of isolated farmsteads. Around those few villages which have survived to the present day a field pattern clearly evolved from the old open-field strips can sometimes be traced, as for example at Rathcoole, Co. Dublin, where the extremely long narrow fields are simply the medieval strips with hedgerows around them (Fig. 16). But around other old villages, as over the eastern landscape in general, there are regular block-type fields which show no relationship to the earlier open-field strips which they replaced and appear to have been laid out mainly in the 17th and 18th Centuries. The framework of the new field systems was often the product of comprehensive estate planning by large landowners. However, it is very likely that much of the detail of the new enclosure pattern was the outcome of unco-ordinated efforts by individual farmers concerned to implement the new ideas of agricultural improvement, especially of crop rotation which implied the sub-division of the farm and the separation of livestock and crops.

Woodland

The Irish rural landscape is today singularly lacking in woodland. If we exclude the Government plantations started only in recent decades and confined mainly to marginal hill areas and patches of poor soils in the lowlands, the bareness of the scene is relieved only by farm windbreaks, scattered hedgerow trees, and occasional patches of ornamental demesne woodland, mainly mixed hardwoods, planted in the 18th and 19th Centuries by improving landlords. Owing to the numerous bushes and scattered trees in the field banks, the farmed landscape viewed from ground level often appears relatively well wooded but this impression is misleading. There were, however, still extensive areas of forest and scrub remaining in Ireland in the 16th Century (McCracken, 1971). Even after allowance has been made for any exaggeration in the contemporary descriptions, there can be little doubt that, prior to the extensive clearing and reclamation which followed the plantations at the end of the century, woodland and scrub were still important elements in the landscape. The counties of Laois and Offaly, for example, counties which today are almost completely reclaimed and enclosed, were still well wooded at the time of their plantation in the late 16th Century, and large areas of Ulster were still a wilderness of wolf-infested woodland and bog when the plantation of settlers from Scotland and England began there in the early 17th Century. But, with the plantations, colonization and commerce accelerated the pace of forest shrinkage (Crawford, 1964). The trees were removed for agricultural, commercial and military-strategic purposes. Most influential perhaps was the destructive exploitation of woodland for the charcoal pits of the small-scale but widely distributed 17th Century iron-smelting industry (Andrews, 1956). It is striking that by the middle of the 17th Century the destruction of the native forests was virtually complete, the farmed land was made more extensive and continuous and Ireland perhaps the least forested country in Europe.

Communications

Ireland possesses a road system of remarkable length and complexity, consistent with its diffuse pattern of settlement and the fact that the roads were built to serve a population much greater than the present. So close is the road network that it constitutes an important element of the landscape and some description of its nature and origin is therefore necessary. Much of the road system has evolved over long periods of history and in a piecemeal way to serve local needs: such roads form a close web adjusted to local topography, drainage conditions and long-standing features of the settlement pattern. Another distinctive and numerous class of roads can be discerned, usually straighter and more purposeful. These roads fall into two categories. The first was planned at a local level and in association with rundale reforms, as previously described. Roads in the second category provide direct links between established centres of population. They are the product of planning on a large scale to serve regional rather than purely local interests and date mainly from the 18th and early 19th Century (Andrews, 1964). Throughout this period road building was pursued zealously, and today, as a result, almost all areas, even the most remote, are well endowed with roads. It was strongly believed, and with some justification, that roads could stimulate economic development in a depressed and generally backward rural society. Moreover, road building materials were abundant in the Irish countryside and labour cheap and plentiful. In the 18th Century the Grand Juries, who were bodies of landowners providing local government within the baronies, financed the building of many roads to link up newly established estate towns and important demesnes. Frequently these roads are remarkably straight for many miles and they often cross extensive bogs and other difficult terrain. The Irish parliament also sponsored the building of trunk roads under turnpike trusts, work that was encouraged by the introduction of the first Irish mail coaches in 1790. However, attention to a system of trunk roads diminished in the 19th Century with the growth of railways which diverted heavy traffic from the roads and, at the same time, undercut the economic viability of the canals. In the early 19th Century the government sponsored numerous local road building schemes to provide employment in distressed areas or during famine periods, and the widespread distress prevalent in rural areas led to a plethora of ambitious, unco-ordinated and sometimes uncompleted projects.

The new routes, both the roads and, to a lesser extent, the canals and railways, had a considerable influence on settlement patterns: they were determinants of the settlement pattern as well as consequences. Old and new settlements tended to align along roads. This process was most marked in the west where old farm clusters were often abandoned by the farmers who built new residences conveniently located along the road-sides; this was a development often encouraged by landlords and government agencies but sometimes undertaken spontaneously by the farmers. Indeed the tendency for farms to shift from their traditional locations within clusters and relocate along the side of roads has continued down to the present day (MacAodha, 1965) and the resulting "ribbon development" is a marked feature of many small-farm areas and especially the western seaboard. The first roads ever to penetrate the remote peninsulas of the western seaboard, in Connemara and Kerry for example, were built as late as the 19th Century and were associated with the building of the first towns in these areas, such as Clifden (Connemara) c. 1820, Belmullet (Co. Mayo) in 1825 and Cahirciveen (Co. Kerry) in 1822. The penetration of roads and town life into these remote and deeply traditional areas served to assimilate them into the mainstream of Irish life and was a powerful factor in the decline of the last large Gaelic speaking communities.

The major part of the Irish road system was completed by the mid 19th Century and subsequent changes have generally involved improvements to the old roads rather than significant alterations or additions to the network. Road standards have been enhanced by widening and straightening and the improvement of the surfaces, especially since the 1950s when the number of motor cars began to increase appreciably and the tourist trade quickened. Motorways have been built in Northern Ireland to link Belfast to Dungannon and, eventually, to Derry.

The Limits of Improved Land

The area of farmed land was expanded considerably and its productive capacity much enhanced in the later 18th and early 19th Centuries as the new ideas of agricultural improvement were implemented. Contemporary accounts tell us that in many places new fields were being formed by landlords and enterprising farmers on formerly bare hillslopes, and the old common grazing lands were being improved and enclosed (Connell, 1950; Aalen, 1970). However, demographic forces were also important in moulding the landscape. The first accurate census of Ireland was taken in 1841, but there is evidence from earlier and less reliable censuses, as well as from other sources, such as the rent rolls and maps in estate records, and travellers' accounts, that the population grew very rapidly in the late 18th Century and the early 19th Century (Connell, 1950; Freeman, 1957). In the 60 years before the Great Famine of 1846–8 the population probably doubled and the countryside became increasingly overpopulated. By 1841 Ireland had over 8 million people, the greater proportion of whom were living off the land at bare subsistence level and heavily dependent on potatoes for their food. There were no important industrial resources or developments in Ireland—land was the only major resource and farms had to be divided again and again to accommodate the growing numbers, while a large landless class was also created. Emigration was for many the only alternative to growing poverty. The need for more farmland led to piecemeal peasant encroachment onto rough hill-slopes, commons and boglands. From this period may date the many small holdings which are located on the fringes of old commons in the eastern lowlands as well as the small impoverished farmsteads which still occupy remote locations in the midst of the extensive bog systems of central Ireland or lie along the upper limits of improved land in many hill areas in the east and west of the country.

With the Great Famine of 1846–8, when the potato crop failed absolutely, the long-standing but moderate flow of emigration became a great tide. Since then emigration has continued on such a vast scale that the total population has steadily declined. Normal excess of births over deaths would result in a steady growth of population were it not for this substantial emigration.

Emigration has been sustained by a number of forces but the major cause has been the poverty of an overcrowded countryside whose inhabitants could find easy access to relatively wealthy, industrialized economies in England and America (Kennedy, 1973). In rural areas the post-Famine declines of population have continued down to the present day and have led to some shrinkage of the area of farmed land. The effects of depopulation on the landscape can be best seen on poorer hill lands where there has sometimes been a downhill shift in the altitudinal limit of maintained fields. In lowland areas emigration has usually led to the sporadic abandonment of farms and, unless the land is utilized by neighbours, the buildings and fields are rapidly overgrown by gorse and bracken. The overall effects of depopulation on the landscape are most marked in the west and particularly the north-west as these are the areas which have experienced the heaviest losses of population. Here agricultural resources are generally poor, urban and industrial growth notably feeble and the economy over wide areas almost exclusively rural. The losses can be accounted for mainly by emigration although the rate of natural increase is also lower in western communities. County Leitrim, together with nearby parts of north Cavan, south Sligo and west Mayo, record the highest percentage fall and have long been the centres of gravity of population loss. Throughout the western regions there are abundant signs of economic and social decline, abandoned and broken farmhouses, neglected and overgrown fields, abandoned schools and churches. The west suffers not only from poor internal resources but also from an unfavourable farm structure of small and often fragmented holdings inherited from the peasant past. Moreover, the west's economic stagnation is linked with the region's remoteness from the expanding industrial, administrative and commercial cores of the country in and around Dublin and Belfast which consistently attract much the greater part of any new economic growth in the country.

Sloblands, Arterial Drainage and Modern Land Improvement

Although population decline in the 19th and 20th Centuries has led to the abandonment of some agricultural land, the losses have been in part offset by schemes to reclaim and improve certain areas. Polder schemes have not been undertaken on a large scale in Ireland but there were a number of scattered enterprises which merit mention. Efforts were made in the 18th Century to reclaim tidal areas, for example in Dublin Bay to facilitate the expansion of the city, and around the Shannon Estuary, but it was in the 19th Century, after the application of the steam engine to pumping equipment, that the most notable schemes were undertaken and tidal mudflats in a number of locations were embanked and artificially drained to provide productive farmland or "slobland". A number of 19th Century reclamation schemes, such as the North Slob near Youghal in the Blackwater Estuary and the drainage of the Fergus in Co. Clare, were begun as famine-relief projects. Drainage of the Wexford Slobs took place in the mid 19th Century. About 5000 a (2000 ha) were reclaimed in the North and South Slobs which today provide agricultural land and the site of a major bird sanctuary for geese, duck and waders of many varieties. Around 3500 acres (1400 ha) of saltmarsh and slobland were won by coastal reclamation on the shores of Lough Foyle in the early 19th Century. The seawalls around the reclaimed land were repaired in the 1950s and the deep silty soils of the enclosed areas are now some of the most productive in the north of Ireland.

Reclamation schemes have also taken place inland. An excess of surface water is a problem for agriculture almost everywhere in the country and removal of the water surplus is therefore basic to most reclamation projects. To be successful on any significant scale reclamation necessitates comprehensive action along extensive stretches of a river channel or even over an entire catchment area. The individual landowner can thus achieve little and effective schemes must rely upon government initiative. Numerous modern projects have been carried out by the governments of Northern Ireland and the Republic, (Common, 1970). In the Central Lowlands of Ulster the low gradient of the streams and derangement of drainage by glacial drift gives rise in many places to waterlogging, peat accumulation and periodic flooding, and there is extensive fenland on the southern shores of Lough Neagh. Since the 1930s, however, government-sponsored drainage projects have greatly improved the drainage situation, especially around Lough Neagh where the lake level has been lowered by increasing the discharge capacity of the River Bann. In the Republic too the government has undertaken important drainage and reclamation projects and the pace of developments has quickened in recent decades. By building embankments, straightening streams and increasing their drainage capacity, new farmlands have been created in many low-lying areas, notably along the Moy in Co. Mayo and in the ill-drained drumlin country of the Erne Basin in Co. Fermanagh where the problem of recurrent flooding was tackled by mutual agreements between the two governments over the use and control of water, and thousands of acres of land were made productive. The major flood and drainage problems of the Shannon catchment area, which covers some 15% of the area of the Republic, await comprehensive solutions and extensive winter flooding is still common on the "callows" or water meadows which flank the river. However, drainage schemes in various parts of the basin, for example along tributaries such as the Brosna and Suck, have significantly influenced the landscape and provided new agricultural land.

It is not only the water courses and valleys which have experienced modern reclamation. In the post-war period the substantial government grants made available to farmers who carry out reclamation projects and the advent of heavy machinery for land clearance have encouraged reclamation on farms in upland as well as lowland areas. Frequently this involves considerable amendment of the local environment, including the removal of scrub, boulders and old field walls, as well as general levelling if this is necessary to make cultivation possible. The provision of grants for fertilizers, especially lime, phosphates and potash, has permitted many farmers to further improve their land and increase their productivity. The effects of all this, however, are sporadic, dependent on the initiative of progressive farmers. Several million acres, it is estimated, are still capable of reclamation or improvement.

The Unimproved Lands

The largest gaps in the pattern of improved farmed land today correspond to the mountain areas. In the lowlands, variations in the proportion of land improved are explicable largely by the occurrence of bog land and, to a lesser degree, outcrops of bare rock. The vegetation of the mountains and bogs has been described in Chapter 2: here the emphasis is placed on the sparsely distributed but nevertheless varied forms of settlement associated with them. Large-scale use and consequent clearance of lowland peat bogs may well be a development only of recent centuries, a development encouraged by the eventual disappearance of the forests which had traditionally provided fuel and building materials for rural people. Generally the bogs have been unattractive to agricultural settlement: most of the bog surface is unenclosed and thinly populated while many of the small farms on the bog fringes have been established on patches of cut-away bog. Often the surface of the nearby bog lies above the field level and the straight junction of bog and field is clearly man-made. The modern mechanized cutting of the deep and extensive bogs of central Ireland by a large-scale government enterprise (Bord na Mona) has led to substantial changes in the landscape and ecology of these distinctive areas. Surface vegetation on the bogs must be largely removed and deep drainage channels dug in order to reduce the moisture content of the peat and facilitate the movement of heavy excavating machinery (Plate 14). Vast expanses of uniform brown peat have been exposed, over which the large peat cutting machines operate. The Board has acquired over 200 sq. miles (518 km²) of bogland, the great bulk of it located in the counties of Laois, Offaly, Roscommon, Westmeath, Longford and Kildare. Around the bogs there are a variety of industrial installations, including the peat burning power stations, briquette factories, workshops for the building and maintenance of peat working machinery, some 550 miles (880 km) of light railway to transport peat to factories and power stations, and housing estates built by Bord na Mona for its workers. Eight such estates now exist with a total of almost 600 houses. Coill Dubh, or Blackwood, in Co. Kildare is the largest of these settlements, planned and laid out in 1951–2 as a compact unit which now possesses 156 houses and a population of almost 800 people. The main mass of peat will eventually be removed (certainly by the end of the century at current rates of exploitation) and the economic future of the bog areas and hence their appearance is uncertain. Experiments suggest that the cut-away bogs could be successfully reclaimed for either agriculture or forestry.

The upper limit of farmed land in Ireland today lies at about 700 ft (213 m) and rarely rises above 1000 ft (304 m). Above this general level the glacial drifts, from which most productive Irish soils are derived, are usually absent or thin, while increased cloud and rainfall create difficulties for crop growth, and grass quality deteriorates rapidly. Because population pressure and agricultural expansion have tended in the past to push farming to the limits of the available soil resources, the upper limit of the drift is a very significant human boundary along which the often sharp contrast between improved and unimproved land provides a striking feature of the landscape. Below the boundary the land is enclosed and often closely settled while the drift-free upper slopes provide only rough unfenced grazing for sheep or are a source of turf supplies. The landscapes of the hill areas are singularly desolate and open. They are crossed by lonely roads, which were often built as famine relief projects, but traces of recent human activity and settlement are few, the most typical being occasional quarries and the sporadic remains of 18th and 19th Century mineral workings (lead and zinc). Prehistoric remains are rather more numerous. At high levels these include hill-top cairns from the Bronze Age and hill-forts of Bronze Age and Iron Age date, while at lower levels, and frequently just above the margins of present-day cultivation, are to be found the megalithic tombs erected by Neolithic farmers. In former centuries cattle were more important than sheep on the hill grazing where they were summered under the care of herdsmen who built temporary dwellings and resided with their herds. The remains of herdsmen's huts, usually only sod or stone foundations, can often be traced in remote hill locations—usually near streams and sheltered grassy slopes. Often, however, they have been much modified and incorporated into sheep folds and shelters by present-day sheep farmers. Temporary seasonal settlement on upland summer pastures was in fact a widespread custom among the peasant communities of Europe. In Ireland it was called "booleying" from an anglicization of the Irish world "buaile"— a cattle fold or milking place. Booleying largely died out in the 17th and 18th Centuries, probably owing to the growth of enclosures which permitted closer integration of livestock and crop production on the lowland farms, but the custom lingered on in remote areas until the 19th Century (Danachair, 1945; Graham, 1953–4; Aalen, 1964).

Today the unenclosed landscapes, which have traditionally provided common grazing, are being reduced by afforestation and, to a smaller extent, by reservoir building and the consolidation of ownership and improvement of accessible portions of hill pasture by enclosures, seeding and fertilizing. The forests are state plantations which when they have matured will considerably alter the landscape. In the present century almost half a million acres have been planted by the state in the Republic and Northern Ireland, the bulk of this since the Second World War. The newly created woodlands are coniferous, unlike the original natural deciduous forests of oak and ash. Spruce, pine, larch and fir are the main trees (Fitzpatrick, 1966), the most practicable types on podsolized, peaty and rocky soils. The state forests were developed initially for the single purpose of creating timber in the most efficient and profitable way but in both the Republic and Northern Ireland the forestry authorities have become increasingly sensitive to the demands of amenity, recreation and wildlife conservation. Multiple use is now a well-established principle and the forests, especially near Belfast and Dublin, are regularly frequented as places of relaxation by local people.

Current and Future Change

During the last two decades the economic life of the country has noticeably quickened, particularly in the Republic, and a variety of trends have emerged which if they gather momentum, as indeed seems likely, could materially change the appearance of the rural landscape during the remainder of the century. Recent economic expansion in the Republic has led to a substantial fall in emigration rates which now no longer exceed the natural increase in the population. Overall population decline has been checked and small increases in the national population have been recorded at each census since 1961. However, industrial expansion and population increase have not been evenly spread throughout the country. With the major exception of tourism the new economic activity and employment which has permitted the reduction of emigration is industrial and urban based, with the city of Dublin and the larger centres in the Dublin hinterland, such as Navan, Naas, Newbridge and Drogheda, providing for most of the economic growth and accommodating the bulk of the population increases. In most regions of Ireland the population in the open countryside has continued to dwindle and many of the smaller towns have merely maintained a rough stability in numbers. The growing pre-eminence of Dublin is very marked.

Population in Co. Dublin has approximately doubled in the present century and increased by almost 20% in the decade 1961–71. In Northern Ireland there has been a similar tendency for new growth to be regionally concentrated, with Belfast and the industrial towns of the east as the major foci. Although recent industrial growth around Cork Harbour and the Limerick-Ennis area has been noteworthy, it is mainly in the Dublin and Belfast regions that the quickening of industrial and urban activity has so far had appreciable impact on the rural landscape. Here it is not only the direct physical expansion of urban areas into the countryside which has been influential. Demands for rural recreational facilities, weekend cottages and parking areas, from a larger, more mobile and affluent urban community have increased land-use pressures in the rural hinterlands of the two metropolitan centres and these demands have been accentuated by a significant body of tourists from abroad. More consequential than recreational demands is the growth of permanent residence in the countryside by urban workers. Increasing mobility of urban workers makes it possible not only to weekend but also to live in rural areas and this latter trend is increasing. As a result population decline in the eastern countryside will not only be halted but even reversed, but this will be owing to an urban employed and orientated population settling in rural areas. Around Dublin the towns and villages located along the major arteries leading from the city have grown markedly. Commuter housing developments here have tended to follow the style of urban housing estates and contrast sharply with the already established buildings. Urban house styles have made some inroads in most rural areas of Ireland during the last decades, especially around large towns and near main roads, a reflection of the increasing re-orientation of the dwindling rural population towards the economic and cultural norms of the cities and towns.

Quarrying and Mining

An important recent development, with considerable implications for the landscape, is the revival of quarrying and mining. The growing demand for building materials and road metal has led to intensified quarrying of limestone, chalk, gravel and sand, and of igneous rock, especially dolerite and basalt. Sand and gravel deposits in commercial quantity are widespread in Ireland and quarries are a familiar feature of the landscape. There is a total of approximately 700 quarries in the Republic alone, 200 hard rock and 500 sand and gravel. The workings, however, are well scattered and, although they are more numerous in the hinterland of Dublin and Belfast, there are few areas of extensive devastation. The practice of removing, or mining, beach and dune sand is widespread, while, inland, pits are numerous along the terminal moraines of the last glaciation and on the sites of deltas formed in pro-glacial lakes. West Wicklow in particular has important sand and gravel quarries which supply the Dublin building trade. In Northern Ireland the Cainozoic basalts are quarried for road metals and the chalk outcrops for cement: granite is still worked in the Mourne Mountains, and at Coalisland, Co. Tyrone the landscape has been scarred by the open-cast mining of fireclays, brickclays, sand and gravel. The surface extraction of building materials, already an industry of importance, is likely to grow in the future, especially in the more highly urbanized parts of Northern Ireland. Future exploitation of sand and gravel deposits, facilitated by new and more economic methods of excavation and transportation, could severely damage the landscape of those areas where the deposits occur in large quantities.

The exploitation of the large and newly discovered deposits of base metals (zinc, copper, lead) in the Republic has added a new and dramatic element to the landscape. Mining has commenced at five sites in counties Tipperary, Galway, Longford and Meath, and future prospecting may well lead to further discoveries and new mining enterprises. Unlike the mining activities of the 19th Century, which were mainly in mountainous areas, the modern mines are located in the Central Lowland region and in predominantly rural areas. Here their impact on the landscape is striking; the mining is mainly carried out by open-cast methods and, moreover, it generates local employment and leads to transport developments as well as an increased demand for electricity and power lines. At the Silvermine Hills in Co. Tipperary the lead and zinc is worked by underground methods but the lead, zinc and copper deposits at Tynagh, Co. Galway, which is Europe's largest lead mine, is worked partly by open-cast methods and the ore is crushed and concentrated on the site. The massive deposit of lead-zinc at Navan, Co. Meath, will also involve surface excavations.

Agricultural Modernization and the Farmed Landscape

With modernization of the economy fundamental changes have started to occur within agriculture itself. There has been significant growth in agricultural output but, as industrialization has grown more rapidly, agriculture's share in gross national output has declined. There has also been a rapid decline in the agricultural labour force. In the Republic between 1960 and 1970, although agriculture's output increased by more than 25%, its share of gross national output fell from 24 to 17% and its share of national employment fell from 36 to 27%. The pace of economic change in the agricultural sector has tended to lag behind the industrial, and social changes in the rural areas have also been restrained. Many traditional attitudes and practices have nevertheless declined in the last two decades as farming, even in the remoter areas, came increasingly to be regarded as an economic activity rather than a way of life (Brody, 1973). Agricultural investment in Ireland is still lower than in most developed countries but capital-intensity is increasing, and in the Republic the volume of farm materials (fertilisers, feedstuffs and seeds) purchased increased by over 100% during 1960–70 (Gillmor, 1972). Moreover, the performance of Irish agriculture, particularly in the Republic, can be greatly enhanced, especially through improvement in the general level of farm management—improvement which may now be imminent as the considerable achievements of applied agricultural research in Ireland grow in influence and the educational standards of farmers are raised. The grasslands, which are the basis of Irish farming and generally maintained as permanent pasture, receive scant attention and are often in poor condition. Improved grassland management, and especially an increase in the supply of fertilizers, could transform wide areas in productivity and appearance.

Agricultural modernization will, inescapably, influence the rural landscape and particularly the traditional field patterns. As yet in Ireland there has been no large-scale adjustment of field boundaries, certainly nothing commensurate with the far-reaching changes which have occurred recently in the English landscape where one major trend has been an increase in field size and a gradual loss of hedgerows and trees as farms are mechanized, their management standardized and field shapes and sizes rationalized. Some very specialized farms have removed all internal hedges and in many parts of England the enclosed landscape has gone or is fast disappearing (Hooper, 1968; Countryside Commission, 1974). The effects have been particularly marked in areas of specialized arable farming, where labour reductions and increasing mechanization underlined the need to remove all unnecessary complications in farm operations. Where farming is of a mixed character, however, there has not been a wholesale removal of hedges as the hedges are valued by farmers as stock-proof barriers and as shelter.

English experience may provide a guide to likely patterns of change in Ireland. With the growing modernization of attitudes and methods among Irish farmers, it seems evident that where landscape features are an impediment to higher production and profitability then there will be strong pressure to remove them. There is already a tendency to enlarge fields, for example in the small farm areas of Ulster, in the arable farming areas of Carlow and south Kildare, and in the stony districts of the west of Ireland where dry walling is the chief method of enclosing fields. The removal of field divisions has been aided by land reclamation grants from the State and facilitated by the bulldozer. Enclosure, however, remains integral to the farming. Two or three fields may be converted into one by removing old walls but there has been no attempt to create extensive and open arable areas or livestock ranges. Continued adjustment of the Irish enclosure pattern seems, therefore, to be a very likely development; Irish fields on average are smaller than English fields and the banks which define them and the access roads occupy a significant percentage of the potential farmland, as much as 10% in areas with a close network of fields. Moreover, gradual elimination of unprofitable small farms will permit continued amalgamation of holdings, rationalization of the units involved and thus, probably, further loss of boundary banks and hedges. However, the pastoral emphasis of Irish farming and the heavy dependence on permanent pastures (with almost 90% of the farmed land presently under hay or grass) does distinguish the Irish situation. The continued tendency for the Irish tillage acreage to decline perhaps reflects the increasing world demand for meat products and the resulting tendency to exploit the countryside's grassland resources. More intensive exploitation of the country's grassland resources is a fundamentally sound development, as livestock production based on permanent pasture is the pattern of farming to which the country is environmentally best suited because of its mild and moist climate. Ireland is one of the few countries of Europe where permanent pasture can compete with arable crops, and the number of cattle carried on Irish pasture could be doubled. Specialized livestock farming, as the English experience suggests, does not necessarily lead to radical removal or modification of the existing enclosure pattern. Moreover, the adoption of controlled grazing systems may justify the retention of some enclosures, and providing some arable production is retained, which seems likely, stockproof barriers will continue to be needed.

The basic ecological implications of removing hedgerows and trees from the landscape on a large scale are not yet fully understood, especially the micro-climatic consequences and the effect on wild life. It may well be that improved understanding of the ecology of bocage landscapes (Terrasson and Tendron, 1975) will induce a more cautious policy among farmers towards the removal of field enclosures. Rural land-use planning, which aims to resolve conflicting demands on the landscape and to reconcile, for example, agricultural, recreational and wild-life interests as well as aesthetic and historical considerations, may also be a growing influence in the future. If so, a higher value may be set upon field enclosures and trees, and the hitherto unchallenged tendency of farmers to change the landscape solely in their own economic interests will perhaps be restrained by the requirements of the non-agricultural functions of the landscape. Policies for safeguarding or enhancing the landscape will, however, require considerable change in public attitudes and are only likely to succeed if they have the support of the farming community. It is particularly hard to see how an effective system of overall control of the countryside could be operated with the existing framework of small independent farm proprietors, many of whom are hard pressed to make a decent living on the land. Economic pressures are likely to remain the main determining forces on the landscape, which land-use planning will merely respond to and adjust where possible.

One general trend which does seem likely to continue and intensify is the transfer of poor agricultural land presently utilized by small and increasingly unviable farms to forestry and recreational uses. This transfer has already occurred in many of the poorer hill areas, and, providing that crop yields on the better land can be increased without long-term detriment to the soil resources then the current retreat of farming from poor marginal lands could be continued without an overall loss in food production and low-grade land could be progressively released for forestry in remote areas and for recreational purposes near large towns and cities. It now appears that in many lowland as well as upland areas afforestation offers an economically competitive alternative to the grass production which is currently the main agricultural use. Research in the drumlin belt, for example, (O'Flanagan and Bulfin, 1970) has shown the considerable potential of forestry there, particularly with fast-growing conifers like sitka spruce. At present only a small proportion of the drumlin belt is forested, little more than 5%. Forest productivity on the lowland drumlin soils is particularly high but yields decrease appreciably with elevation and on areas of peaty soils. Moreover, considerable improvement in future forest production is to be expected (Bulfin et al., 1973). Afforestation may well be an economic enterprise in the many moist, ill-drained areas of the north and west. There are possibilities therefore of a large-scale transfer of land from agriculture to forestry, especially in poor western areas where the farming community has long faced acute social and economic problems and the natural environment is certainly suited to forest enterprises.

Ecological and Conservation Problems in the Rural Environment

Owing to the relatively small population and limited industrial development, ecological and conservation problems in Ireland are small in comparison to most other European countries but serious enough in relation to the limited degree of economic development. The absence of a dynamic economy in the 19th Century has spared most of the country from the impact of the industrial revolution and its associated physical clutter. Thus, derelict industrial landscapes and extensive pollution on the scale common in the English Midlands and the Ruhr are absent, but a variety of problems have emerged following the recent quickening of industrial growth, the modernization of agriculture and an upward trend in both the number and the affluence of the population (Lang, 1970). Large-scale mining of base metals and the clear potential for discoveries of off-shore oil resources raise the possibility of massive environmental damage both to inland rivers and to portions of the coastline and off-shore fisheries. However, over most of the country, with its diffuse rural population and scattered industries, environmental problems are not on a dramatic scale and the major risk is of a gradual, almost imperceptible increase of pollution and erosion of environmental quality.

Damage to fragile ecosystems, such as sand dunes, can be caused by over-utilization for recreational purposes; there are instances of this in Ireland, particularly in the Dublin region, but they are relatively rare. In a country with a dispersed rural community and a wet and windy climate, atmospheric pollution is not a general problem either. It exists only in the larger urban centres, and particularly in Dublin and Belfast where domestic fires, increased industrial activity and road traffic have led to pollution of the air. The concentrations of sulphur-dioxide in Dublin City already exceed the levels recommended by the World Health Organization as desirable for human health. Belfast too has long suffered periodic atmospheric pollution mainly caused by coal-burning domestic fires but the recent introduction of clean air zones has considerably improved the situation. Perhaps the most significant environmental problem in the country as a whole is the pollution of water in rivers and lakes by industrial, agricultural and domestic effluent. The National Survey of Irish Rivers (An Foras Forbartha, 1972) indicated that serious degradation of water quality obtained on 7% (200 km) of the Irish rivers surveyed (2900 km), while a further 10% (300 km) was classified in the doubtful category. Most of the serious degradation occurs on short reaches downstream of urban areas and industrial enterprises. Fish life in certain rivers has been seriously affected, for example in the Blackwater in Co. Cork and the Tolka in Co. Dublin. In Northern Ireland the lower reaches of the River Lagan and the River Newry are also polluted and act as a barrier to migratory fish. Pollution of estuaries is not yet a major problem but there is widespread pollution of lakes due to eutrophication. The major source of the pollution appears to be agriculture, and in particular pig slurry and silage effluent falling into the streams leading to the lakes. Lough Neagh in Northern Ireland is a particular problem. With an area of some 400 km^2, it acts as a major source of water for domestic purposes but it also receives the drainage of 40% of the province and it is highly vulnerable to problems of pollution and enrichment from domestic sewage, industrial and agricultural waste. Periodic algal blooms have occurred in the Lough and are likely to grow in frequency. In the Republic many of the lakes in the north-central midlands, such as Ennell, Ramor, Kinale, Sheelin, Sillan, Muckno and Oughter, are now eutrophic and other lakes, even in remote western areas, are at risk.

Litter and the indiscriminate dumping of rubbish and waste materials are a particular problem, common to town and country, and marked enough to merit mention in any survey of the Irish landscape. The problem here is partly owing to the difficulties and cost of collecting waste in areas with a scattered rural population, but fundamental social attitudes are clearly involved, including a weakly developed sense of civic responsibility and a general lack of interest and concern for visual aesthetic matters. These attitudes have received little serious investigation, although the long and demoralizing colonial experience of the country is popularly held to be mainly responsible for them.

The cultural landscape in rural areas has not been extensively modified by modern economic pressures. There have, for example, been no major changes in land use and no large-scale removal of enclosures. However, buildings in the countryside, and especially houses, have undergone substantial change. Much of this, in particular the rehousing of small farmers and agricultural labourers, has been socially desirable but there has also been indiscriminate destruction of valuable heritage. Rising standards of living have led to the large-scale removal of traditional buildings and their replacement by modern structures whose styles are often alien to and incompatible with the rural milieu. Land improvement and road building schemes in rural areas have sometimes involved the destruction of historical monuments, especially prehistoric earthworks. An awareness of the value and significance of the built environment on the basis of its ethnological interest or architectural and visual qualities has been slow to gain ground. There is still no body of informed public opinion sufficient to sustain an effective policy for the conservation of buildings which are valuable for scientific or amenity reasons. Indeed efforts to conserve buildings, including those in the vernacular and the grand styles, have been vitiated by uninformed and sometimes unsympathetic attitudes among the public and at official levels. Sympathy for the rehabilitation and preservation of traditional rural buildings, such as thatched houses and barns, is not strong in a society generally anxious to escape as rapidly as possible from all associations with its peasant past. Grander buildings, on the other hand, and especially the important legacy of substantial town and country houses from the 18th and 19th Centuries, are often dismissed as the products of an alien colonial culture. Northern Ireland, however, has a better record in this respect; the province has a generally more developed tradition of study, care and respect for its ancient monuments, and machinery for physical planning has existed throughout the post-war period. The National Trust (Committee for Northern Ireland) and the Ulster Architectural Heritage Society are bodies which have been particularly active and influential in preserving and increasing public awareness of architectural and landscape features.

In a country where the paramount economic concerns have traditionally been with emigration and a shortage of jobs, environmental protection is always a sensitive issue as there are frequently awkward choices to be made between the provision of more jobs and the preservation of local amenities and environmental quality. However, there is evidence of the beginnings of new and more considered attitudes to the protection of natural and wildlife resources and to the preservation of the cultural heritage, attitudes which may help to reconcile economic and environmental demands and arrest environmental deterioration. In the Republic, for example, An Taisce (the National Trust), a voluntary body concerned with the preservation of the national heritage, has won increased public support and grown in influence. In the early 1960s the Trust, which had in its early stages been most interested in buildings, developed a strong interest in nature conservation and amenity matters. Concern with amenity and environmental issues is also a feature of the many cultural and community associations which have been formed since the early 1960s. In the Republic, local authorities have been given wide powers under the Local Government (Planning and Development) Act of 1963 for the management and conservation of natural resources within the context of physical planning controls. The Act enjoins each local authority to prepare development plans and revise them every 5 years thereafter, and permits the making of special amenity, conservation and tree preservation orders. Moreover, as the tourist trade has expanded and asserted itself as a major element of the economy, especially in the poorer western areas, there has been a growing realization of the need to preserve the natural and man-made amenities which provide the major attractions for tourists, and to upgrade the visual quality and cleanliness of settlements. The Tidy Towns Competition, for example, organized by Bord Failte (Irish Tourist Board), has, since its inception in 1958, stimulated considerable improvement in the appearance of many small rural towns and villages (Shaffrey, 1972). The emphasis in the competition has changed from an early concern with the eradication of litter to cover village and town conservation and renewal on a comprehensive scale. Between 1964 and 1974 the number of town entries to the competition rose from around 400 to over 600. The industrial sector is also showing increased appreciation of the importance of environmental quality, and in the 1970s new industries have had to meet stringent standards of effluent and emission control. Most industrial pollution of water has been caused by factories based on agricultural products, especially meat and vegetable processing factories and creameries, which were usually established long before environmental protection became an important consideration in industrial development. In 1976 much encouragement was given to environmentalists by the decision of the Minister of Local Government and Planning, after a long public controversy, to prevent the establishment of an oil refinery in Dublin Bay. The Local Government (Water Pollution) Act of 1977 is the first major step in the Republic towards control of pollution in lakes and streams.

In Northern Ireland a significant step forward was taken by the Amenity Lands (Northern Ireland) Act of 1965. This provided for two advisory committees—the Nature Reserves Committee and the Ulster Countryside Committee. The first was concerned with wildlife matters and areas of outstanding scientific interest and able to control areas managed for the conservation of their features of interest. The Ulster Countryside Committee was set up to further the conservation of countryside beauty and amenity and has carried out useful work in establishing Amenity Areas, designating Areas of Outstanding Natural Beauty and in planning a series of National Parks. The Forest Service within the Department of Agriculture has provided the notable series of Forest Parks which are extensively used for recreation.

Since the late 1960s there has been significant growth in study and research on natural resources in universities, colleges and research institutes. In the Republic, for example, a wide range of survey, research and advisory work in environmental matters has been undertaken by An Foras Forbartha, the National Institute for Planning and Construction Research, since its foundation in 1964. In Northern Ireland responsibility for environmental problems lies with the Department of the Environment and useful applied research is carried on by institutions of higher education, in particular the School of Biological and Environmental Studies at the New University of Ulster at Coleraine.

Throughout Ireland, a country in which, for the most part, industrialization has had but a marginal impact and whose landscapes are still predominantly rural, it may be possible to avoid many of the environmental problems evident in the older industrial nations. There is need, however, for sustained and judicious planning based on intensive land-use studies and with proper respect for long-term ecological considerations as well as more immediate economic and social objectives.

9
Rural Buildings

Buildings form an important ingredient of the Irish rural landscape. They occupy only a small area but the relatively high proportion of the total national population which still lives in the countryside, combined with the markedly diffuse pattern of rural settlement, make the farmhouses and their associated buildings a pervasive element of the rural landscape. Their visual impact is enhanced by the traditional custom of whitewashing the outer walls so that buildings stand out sharply against the dominant greens and browns of the background vegetation. Buildings are therefore important in the first place simply as visual elements in the landscape. They take on added importance as the focus of human activities: they are of ethnological significance as expressions of local and regional cultural traditions, and their form and the materials and methods used in their construction are illustrative of the ecological adaptation of rural society to contrasting physical environments.

Nature of Vernacular Architecture

Until the present century the form and construction of the buildings used by ordinary people in the rural areas of Ireland and other European countries have been deeply traditional. Buildings exhibited considerable regional variety of style but marked uniformity and continuity of style within particular regions. This generalization applies both to farmhouses and their associated farm buildings, barns, stables, etc. However, attention here will focus on the houses, as these are the most conspicuous category of building in the Irish landscape; traditional farm outbuildings in Ireland are poorly developed, especially in the west where their form is usually an elementary version of the house. A rich diversity of regional building styles flourished in Europe. The majority of people within a region adhered voluntarily to a single model or ideal pattern of house form: the model had no designer, but was part of the anonymous folk tradition. Regional building styles, characterized by conformity, anonymity and continuity, reflected the cultural coherence and conservatism of peasant communities and the deep-rooted traditions of their building crafts.

In many rural areas vernacular or traditional buildings can be distinguished from a growing body of recent buildings whose style is a departure from traditional patterns and reflects national urban tastes. Even in highly industrialized and urbanized nations, however, many traditional buildings still survive in rural areas, but usually the traditions are no longer active and the body of traditional material is a legacy from the past which inevitably is being diminished in absolute and relative importance.

Increasingly the term vernacular architecture is being used to describe the broad mass of traditional buildings (Hall, 1970), but their systematic study is relatively new and the subject therefore requires some general introduction before a detailed description of Irish buildings can be undertaken. The precise significance of regional styles is, in most countries, not fully understood, but it is clear that there is no single cause of regional variations and that the determinants of vernacular forms are multiple. Geographical determinism does not provide a satisfactory explanation of the range and diversity of house forms. The type of local building material and climatic conditions, for example, may influence certain features of the house, particularly the external features, but they do not determine the basic form and plan. In brief, geography may influence the building but it does not determine what is built: it does not determine, for example, whether the local house plans are to be circular, rectangular or square. There is a wide variety of potential forms which could be adopted to meet environmental considerations, and building forms often vary considerably where the geographical environment is little differentiated. In addition, deterministic arguments are vitiated by the tendency for house forms in a region to change considerably through time and to alter fundamentally over the long term. One noteworthy aspect, associated with this tendency to change, is that some features of house plan and construction are cultural relics rather than necessities, features which have survived long after the conditions that brought them into being have disappeared. House forms would appear to be basically determined not by geographical conditions but by socio-cultural factors. (Rapoport, 1969). The historical experience of the society is important as well as its organization at community and family level. In addition, the economic and technological level of the society is a significant variable,

I

particularly the building skills of its members. A wide variety of human factors, their importance varying in different situations, is involved and it is difficult to disentangle these factors and assess their relative importance. One complication here is the paucity of information about the origin and evolution of regional house styles in both historic and prehistoric times. Until historic developments are better known the underlying causes of regional variation in most countries can only be guessed at.

Different types of explanation have been advanced for regional house differences within the British Isles. Some regional differences in building have been attributed to differences in economic and political development; i.e. different traditions may be consecutive stages of the same evolutionary sequence taking place at different rates in different regions (Crawford, 1965; Aalen, 1966). Regional peculiarities of house style have also been viewed as analogous to linguistic and dialectal differences, perhaps originally developed *in situ* by communities whose members lived in close contact with each other and were relatively isolated from neighbouring communities by geographical or social barriers, or, alternatively, introduced into a region centuries earlier by an invading tribe or group. For example, the westerly distribution of cruck constructed houses in the British Isles has been attributed to Celtic origins (Smith, 1964), and in Ireland it is possible that the ''but and ben'' houses of Ulster may reflect the long standing contacts and migrations between that region and Scotland where the ''but and ben'' house is a widespread form (Danaher, 1956). The link between building styles and the type of rural economy has also been emphasized. For example, houses in which family and animals live under one roof tend to be associated with pastoral economies, while cultivating economies are associated with farms in which human beings and animals are housed in separate buildings and the farmyards typically contain a range of specialized buildings. This link can be observed to some extent in Ireland.

Vernacular building was never completely homogeneous within regions. Local geographical variations in house style occurred but many of these seem to be attributable to differing rates and patterns of development from the basic regional models. Moreover, in any one locality there were variations in house style associated with the social and economic status of the residents. In upper-class houses, which are always a minority in a region, vernacular forms and national canons of taste are often fused and the precise boundary of the vernacular is therefore difficult to define. The very largest houses, however, in which figures of national importance usually lived, are rarely tinged with vernacular influences. They have developed in virtual independence of local influences and are often uniform over wide regions and even over national frontiers.

Two broadly simultaneous processes, first the growth of scientific, commercial agriculture and, second, industrialization, have led to the decay of vernacular building traditions. With the growth of commercial agriculture rural society became more stratified and diverse; growing sophistication and prosperity lead to an interest in new building fashions and provide the means to introduce them. There is inevitably more variety in house design and departure from traditional models. Elements of upper-class building fashions, which are national in their distribution, are more readily absorbed into the vernacular zone of building and thereby blurr regional differences. New building fashions spread slowly down the social scale and outwards from the more advanced and innovative areas. However, the decay of the vernacular tradition is difficult to date precisely because it is a protracted process and proceeds at a different pace from region to region. The Industrial Revolution and the Railway Age are normally seen as the terminal stage of the vernacular tradition in Britain. The advent of machinery, the mass production of building materials and their freer movement resulting from railway communications led to standardization in the appearance of houses, local building materials were used less and less and regional distinctiveness accordingly was eroded. Houses were increasingly built to the plans and specifications of specialists who followed national styles; tradition as a regulator of house form was much weakened and regional differences were further blurred.

Vernacular Buildings in the British Isles

It is important to view Irish buildings in the context of vernacular buildings in the British Isles as a whole. Surviving houses as well as documentary sources and archaeological findings show that a striking similarity existed in basic house plan throughout the British Isles during recent historic times, from the end of the medieval period to the 18th Century. Subsequently, with agricultural improvement, industrialization and urbanization, vernacular styles were largely eclipsed and, except in remoter regions, tradition as a regulator almost disappeared. Most vernacular houses possessed simple rectangular plans, characteristically one room in width and divided laterally into two or three internal rooms. The main hearth is usually located in the central room and on the long axis of the house. Opposite doors and a cross-passage are recurrent but not universal features. Regional variations occur in the manner of plan sub-division such as the lay-out of the doors or the cross-passage, and in the building materials and methods of constructing the houses. Most recent research on vernacular architecture has been concerned with the establishment of local and regional variations of internal house plan (Danaher, 1956; Barley, 1961; Eden, 1969). The plan certainly provides a useful focus of study. It is the main element revealed by archaeological investigation; it directly influences other structural features of the house and seems to be the most tenacious element of regional building traditions, often exhibiting basic continuity through a succession of changes in building materials and major economic and social developments.

Until the later Middle Ages in most parts of Britain the houses of ordinary rural folk were often flimsy structures, made with wood and wattles, of which little trace has survived. In southern England and the richer eastern parts of Wales the downward spread of permanent housing was accelerating by the early 16th Century, and during the last quarter of the 16th Century, with the high prosperity of the Tudor period, there is good evidence for a widespread spate of rebuilding and new building among all social classes Hoskins, 1963). In England, for example, it is not until the Late Middle Ages that the surviving structures are plentiful enough to provide evidence of regional types of rural house and even at that stage the evidence is confined to the durable houses of the rising yeoman class. The great bulk of people still lived in hovels built of perishable materials and, not unnaturally, these structures have not survived. In Ireland, Scotland, northern England and the poorer parts of Wales the transition from impermanent hovels to durable houses occurred a good deal later than in England and durable houses were not being constructed for the majority of rural dwellers until the 18th and 19th Centuries. The major rebuilding at this time was often part of a wholesale re-organization of rural society carried out by powerful landowners whose reforms included the remodelling of settlement patterns and field systems as well as houses.

A broad but important distinction can be made between the vernacular buildings of Wales and southern England on the one hand and those of Scotland, northern England (the four northern counties) and Ireland on the other. Contrasts between the two regions reflect deep-rooted differences in social and political history. In southern England and Wales a single effective government was able to ensure internal peace and orderly social development from the end of the 13th Century onwards, long before any central authority could provide this in other regions. A significant result of southern   social   stability   was   the   early   rise   and   continuing importance of a numerous middle-class of substantial farmers whose surviving houses, two-storied, substantial and ornate, are the most impressive component of British vernacular buildings and indicative of a rich and complex rural civilization which is totally unmatched in the remainder of the British Isles. In Ireland and Scotland, for example, vernacular architecture never developed a comparable richness and complexity; society was much more polarized into a few great landowners and a large homogeneous body of peasant farmers, and, taken as a whole, vernacular architecture exhibits only a few simple themes. The predominant element is the single-storey house belonging to a poor peasantry, elementary in plan and construction and conspicuously late in date because the general transition from impermanent hovels to durable houses occurred a good deal later than in the rich lowlands of England and Wales. Throughout Ireland, Scotland and the Anglo-Scottish borders anarchy persisted into the 17th Century and all who could afford it lived in tower houses: the homes of the gentry did not develop as recognizable architecture until much later than in southern England and Wales (Plate 9a). The development of the tower house in Ireland and Wales illustrates the contrasting fortunes of the two countries. In the whole of Wales there are scarcely a dozen tower houses while in Ireland there are several thousand many of which were inhabited until well into the 17th Century (Smith, 1965–6; Leask, 1941).

These broad zonal contrasts in the character of vernacular architecture in the British Isles must not be over-stressed as there are important differences existing within each major zone. Within Ireland, for example, there is an important difference between the richer, accessible lowlands of the east and south and the poorer, moister portions of the island to the north and west where upland areas are more numerous. In the east and south, society has traditionally been more prosperous and socially stratified. Broad contrasts in house styles exist between the north-west and the south-east, as will be shown, and these are matched by a variety of other cultural distributions (Danaher, 1957). Within Ireland, therefore, there is a regional dichotomy reminiscent of the classic division of the British Isles as a whole into highland and lowland culture zones which are located in the north-west and the south-west, respectively.

Irish Vernacular

Rural areas of Ireland have retained a large number of farmhouses and outbuildings built in traditional style and, despite their steady replacement by modern structures in recent decades, these traditional buildings are still a prominent part of the rural scene. The old-style house until recently used by the great bulk of the rural population everywhere in Ireland is a small thatched building, one storey high, with a rectangular plan. The house is rarely more than one room in width; each room opens into the next without any passage or central hall. The entrances to the house as well as the windows are placed on the side, and not the end, walls. Structurally the houses are simple. The roof is supported by the walls and not by internal posts or pillars. Local materials are used to construct the houses, stone or mud for the walls, cereal straw or rushes for the thatch. Irish houses are thus basically similar to the traditional houses elsewhere in the British Isles and particularly the houses of rural folk in Scotland and parts of Wales and western England. It is necessary to remember that the great bulk of the Irish population has always consisted of small farmers who lived at a humble level, close to the soil. Their small, unpretentious houses reflect this simple level of life. They reflect also the geographical environment in which they are set; their steep pitched roofs, for example, are an adaptation to the high rainfall, their thick walls protect the inhabitants against winter cold and wind-driven rain. However, the influence of geographical environment must not be overstressed. Geography does not determine that the basic form of house will be an elongated rectangle with contiguous rooms. It is clear too that other house styles once existed which have now almost totally disappeared. In the Bronze and Iron Ages circular or oval houses were predominant and a tradition of erecting large aisled buildings (houses and barns) seems once to have existed (Richmond, 1932), although it was perhaps confined to the upper levels of society. Such discontinuities are hard to explain by reference solely to geographical conditions. The gradual elimination of forests may have contributed to the demise of the aisled-hall which was almost of necessity made with timber, but the general shift from round to rectangular plans in houses cannot be linked to any change in the availability of particular building materials. The adoption of rectangular plans in place of circular ones seems rather to have been a deep-seated cultural process, one of those slow but decisive shifts in fashion which frequently occur in cultural history and are rarely susceptible to precise analysis and explanation.

In size and external form the traditional thatched houses are similar in all parts of the country and the impression of uniformity is strengthened by the almost universal coat of whitewash, but classification of the houses is possible on the basis of regional variation in the details of structure and style (Fig. 22). Hip-roofed houses with centrally located hearths predominate in the south and east of the country, where they were often made with mud walls. Houses with gable ends, and frequently with their hearths on or near the gables are more typical in the west and also the north (Plate 15). In both these areas stone is the customary building material for walls. The traditional houses of north-eastern Ireland might be considered a separate type as they have certain distinctive characteristics, particularly the two-roomed ground plan and fireplace at

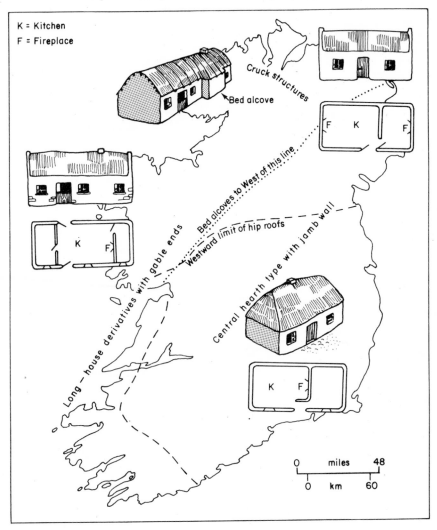

Fig. 22: Regional farmhouse styles.

Plate 15a: Eastern farmhouse, with central hearth, hipped roof and mud walls. The small porch is an addition to the original house (Co. Meath).

Plate 15b: Western farmhouse, with hearth at end of main room and away from door, stone built and gable ended (Co. Kerry).

each gable; this style may have been introduced with the Ulster plantation because it is also found in the peasant houses (called "but and ben" houses) of Scotland. Within Ireland, therefore, there are at least three major regional styles of the traditional house (Danaher, 1956, 1972) but there is, of course, considerable overlapping of types and mixed forms also appear (McCourt, 1968). The reasons for these regional styles, especially the difference between east and west, are not yet fully understood but the differences may derive from cultural forces of considerable antiquity and marked differences between the east and the west of the country can be found in many spheres of folk tradition and custom. However, the contrast in traditional house building materials, stone in the west and mud in the east, seems to be linked to geographical conditions. Timber seems originally to have been an important building material everywhere in Ireland, but it declined in importance as the woodlands were progressively removed and eventually it became a scarce commodity for ordinary people. In the western parts of the country where the soils are shallow and the bedrock near the surface there was probably always a tradition of building in stone as well as in timber and as early as the 18th Century stone had become, and has remained, the main material used by rural folk for building house walls. On the eastern lowlands, where a thick mantle of glacial drift obscures the solid geology, stone houses were less common; here, when timber resources dwindled, mud became the most popular building material and remained so until the present century when industrially produced building materials became generally available. Many thousands of clay-walled houses and barns still survive, especially in the south-east. The mud walls were made with a mixture of wet clay and rushes, built up without any mould or support and trimmed with a spade. Turf was formerly widely used in Ireland as a building material especially for temporary structures on the farm and for peat-cutting shelters. Poor people sometimes built entire houses with turf or used turfs to build the gables of their houses (Evans, 1969).

Western Ireland

In western Ireland (most of Connacht, Donegal and the peninsulas of western Munster) the typical farmhouse possesses a three-roomed ground plan; the kitchen is central with flanking bedrooms (Plates 12b, 15b, 18b). This house form has developed from primitive structures, termed by ethnologists long-houses or byre-dwellings, which were widespread in the west until the 19th Century and incorporated both byre and dwelling in one single compartment (Danaher, 1964). The expulsion of the cattle and the division of the house into different rooms are recent events. In some remote places, such as western Donegal, western Kerry and Connemara, the habit of accommodating livestock within the house (a custom once widespread among peasant communities in many parts of Europe) has only very recently been abandoned and in numerous existing houses oral tradition relates that the former byre-end has simply been divided from the kitchen by an internal wall and converted to a bedroom or storeroom. The customary room beyond the hearth may have originated simply as an extension to the house, or, perhaps more commonly, by a division of the original living area. This division was perhaps associated with the introduction of chimney flues in the 19th Century erected above the open-fire which in the old houses had lain on the floor at some distance from the gable wall. The kitchen in the older houses characteristically possesses two doors immediately opposite each other, a useful arrangement for the regulation of draughts and smoke from the peat fire but probably also linked to the habit of accommodating livestock and human beings together in the same house. It cannot, however, be argued that all old, three-roomed houses are modified long-houses, because the tripartite plan has been perpetuated in many houses not originally built to accommodate livestock; the house style has been conditioned by long-houses antecedents and the structures are best described as derived long-houses.

In some remote parts of the west, particularly in Iar-Connacht and Connemara, there is evidence that the rectangular, undivided long-house with gable ends evolved recently from primitive dome-shaped stone structures (clochans) with oval or circular plans (Plate 9b). This evolution has occurred within the last two centuries or so and extant structures can be observed which represent different stages in the evolutionary development (Aalen, 1966). The possible succession of major forms is shown in Fig. 23. It is not clear, however, that this evolutionary pattern is applicable to all the areas of western Ireland where long-houses were established. Rectangular long-houses may well have been of very long-standing in the richer, more accessible parts of western Ireland, and the development from clochans observable in west Connacht may reflect simply the recent spread into this relatively backward area of a style long established and even indigenous elsewhere in western Ireland.

Eastern Ireland

The basic features of the eastern house, especially the centrally located

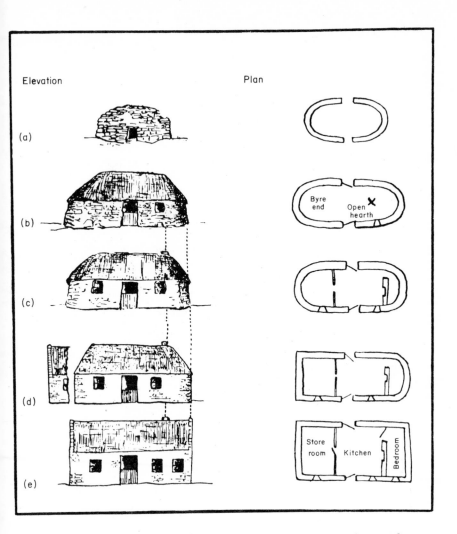

Elevation

Plan

(a)

(b)

Byre end

Open hearth ✗

(c)

(d)

(e)

Store room

Kitchen

Bedroom

Fig. 23: Possible stages in the development of the western house, from **a** primitive clochan to **e** present-day house, where gable ends have replaced hip ends. Sketch **d** is a transitional stage preceding final form where the house might possess one hip end and one gable end or the hip itself might be connected to a straight end wall rather than a curved one. Existing structures can be seen in western Ireland representative of all phases of development. (Aalen, 1966.)

hearth and the hip roof (Plate 15a) are consistent with derivation from a primitive round dwelling such as is known to have been built in Ireland from very early times in both stone (clochans) and with timber and wattles (Campbell, 1938). However, if this is the case, it remains difficult to understand why the most primitive form has survived in the most advanced parts of the country and why most of the surviving clochans are in the west of the country. Alternatively, it is tempting to view the eastern house as an intrusive form, perhaps, in view of its distribution, associated with the Anglo-Norman colonization (Danaher, 1970). A further possible interpretation of this house style is that the aligning and central location of the hearth and door represent a crude post-Renaissance adaptation of an indigenous peasant form to the dictates of polite architecture which placed an emphasis on symmetry of plan and façade. However, the available facts are too few to substantiate fully any of these various interpretations.

It is noteworthy that there is no tradition in eastern houses that animals and people were accommodated together. The greater emphasis on cultivation in the east may be of relevance here, giving rise to the need for a range of functionally specialized outbuildings on the farms. In pastoral economies, such as the west of Ireland has traditionally possessed, the family and their animals commonly lived under one roof. The juxtaposition of hearth and door at the centre of the eastern house seems to be a long-standing feature and it is an arrangement which is clearly ill-suited to the entry and exit of cattle. In long-houses, wherever they occur in the British Isles, there are usually two doors immediately opposite each other and the hearth is located away from the line of the doors at the opposite end of the main room. This separation of doors from hearth tends to persist in regions where the farmhouses are derived from long-house antecedents. It crops up frequently in the hilly areas of England where pastoral traditions are strong and society on the whole has been poorer and more conservative. The style is represented, for example, in the hill areas of Wales while the central-hearth type occurs on the richer lowlands (Smith, 1967). In Ireland the long-house and its derived forms is the dominant traditional type in the west of the country, but the diagnostic separation of hearth and doors re-appears in major hill areas in eastern Ireland such as the Wicklow Mountains (Aalen, 1967).

A number of variations in house construction occur which overlap with the broad classification of central-hearth and gable-hearth types; these include methods of roofing and thatching and the bed-outshot. Roof frameworks are usually simple. Over the greater part of the country the main form of roof support is the couple truss resting on the wall heads. The main exception to this is in east Ulster where the roofs are often framed with purlins which rest upon the gable walls and have no supporting trusses. Cruck constructions have been recorded only in northern Ireland, and mainly in Donegal and Derry. Crucks are pairs of curved timbers rising from the ground level and meeting at the apex of the house. The cruck framework supports the whole weight of the roof and is thus particularly suited for use in conjunction with non load-bearing walls. In Wales, Scotland and western England cruck-truss frameworks were widely used in vernacular buildings but they are rare in the south and east of England where box-framed houses predominated. In view of this distribution the suggestion has been made that crucks may be a Celtic feature. If crucks are a Celtic characteristic their absence over most of Ireland, the bastion of the Celtic peoples, is difficult to explain. It is often alleged that the roots of the Irish vernacular lie in cruck-framed structures but it is only in the north of the country that these structures have been attested (McCourt, 1964–5; Gailey, 1972), and this is an area whose cultural traditions are as closely linked to Scotland as to the remainder of Ireland. Again, if cruck building is a Celtic tradition its absence in south-eastern Ireland is especially difficult to understand; here houses have traditionally been made with mud, and crucks would have been a useful structural adjunct. There is no evidence that timber box-framed houses of the kind which flourished in south-eastern England were ever numerous in the Irish countryside. Timber ''cage-work'' houses were, however built in the Ulster plantation towns and common until the 17th Century in the eastern ports, such as Dublin and Drogheda where their style seems to have closely resembled the houses of Cheshire and Lancashire (Frazer, 1891). The damp Irish climate must have been a deterrent to the use of timber in large structures as the beams suffered severely from the weather. Throughout Ireland timber houses have now completely vanished from town and country.

Thatching techniques and materials vary from one part of the country to another (Buchanan, 1957: Danaher, 1957) and the distribution pattern does not correspond with that of the basic house styles. In most areas of Ireland a thin layer of sods or ''scaws'' was laid upon and tied to the roof timbers to support the thatch and improve heat insulation. Wheaten straw is the most widely used material for thatch. Northern Leinster, however, preferred oaten straw, and reeds were favoured in some localities of Munster and flax in Counties Derry, Donegal and Fermanagh. The most general method of securing the thatch is by pinning the straw to the scraws with scallops—pegs made with thin rods of briar and hazel. Along the northern and western coasts, perhaps mainly in view of the strong winds, it is common for the thatched roof to be held in place by a rope net tied to pegs in the house walls or to a row of stone weights. The gables may project above the level of the thatch to prevent the wind lifting the roof or, alternatively, the thatch is secured to the gable walls by strips of mud or plaster. The distinctive rounded cóntours of the thatched roofs of Co. Donegal appear to be a form of streamlining against Atlantic gales.

Many older houses in north-western Ireland possess a large alcove or recess near the fire. Sometimes this is merely an intra-mural cavity in the thick side walls of the house but frequently it forms part of the external structure of the house and is associated with a box-like projection on one of the side walls of the kitchen. These archaic features were traditionally used to accommodate a bed but have now usually been blocked up or concealed by furniture (McCourt, 1956: Danaher, 1955–6). The bed-alcove, or bed-outshot, has at the present day an interesting and clear-cut distribution, occurring widely in the north-west of the country from Galway Bay to north-east Antrim in association with both gable-hearth and central-hearth house types. There is evidence, however, that the bed-alcove once occurred over a wider area to the east of the present boundary line, suggesting that the feature has died out in other regions and been progressively limited, along with a variety of other ancient cultural traits, to the remote north-western corner of the country (Evans, 1939).

Irish Non-Vernacular Buildings

Until the end of the 19th Century vernacular traditions were still vigorous and hence an important legacy of traditional buildings still survives in the landscape. However, the vernacular tradition is now almost defunct and in the present-day landscape many buildings, probably a majority, are a significant or total departure from the vernacular styles. House forms have diverged from the basic vernacular models in two main ways. First, change has been brought about gradually either by piecemeal alterations and improvements to the older houses by their owners, or through the erection of new houses, by landlords, government agencies or individual farmers, which were improved versions of the old but not dissimilar in general proportions or wholly divorced from traditional styles. Second, quite new house styles have been introduced. For example, in the 18th and 19th Centuries substantial farmhouses were built, mainly in the Georgian style by the minor gentry and the more prosperous farmers, which have gradually influenced vernacular buildings. In recent decades the rural areas, expecially within reach of cities and towns, have been influenced by a widespread building of new houses identical to those in urban areas, and the surviving stock of vernacular houses is beginning to disappear rapidly.

On larger Irish farms there are often substantial two-storied dwellings. Older examples of this style are most numerous in the lowlands of the south and east where the farms are larger, but even here they appear to be of a style which became widespread only in recent centuries. Some of the oldest examples are fine thatched structures exhibiting a symmetry of plan and façade which clearly stems from polite rather than vernacular building styles; local tradition often suggests that these houses were built by immigrant English farmers who were most probably 17th Century planters. However, old and substantial two-storied thatched houses can be found in the Irish countryside which are clearly developments or elaborations of basic vernacular patterns and retain the old ground plans, door and hearth locations. The central-hearth model, in particular, has often been developed into impressive two-storied buildings inhabited by well-to-do farmers and tradesmen. Some of the finest thatched farmhouses in Ireland are in this tradition. County Meath and Co. Limerick possess numerous excellent examples (Plate 16). There has, however, been little systematic investigation of the evolution of the larger houses in Ireland and the relative importance of indigenous and planter influences remains an obscure topic. Interestingly, no extant houses exhibit any clear continuity with the tower houses which were the principal style of large dwelling in Ireland during the Late Medieval period. The tower house tradition seems to have terminated abruptly when the long-standing anarchic condition of Irish society which nurtured this particular form of defensive dwelling was replaced by firm, centralized authority in the later 17th Century.

On larger farms many of the old two-storied thatched farmhouses were replaced in the 18th and early 19th Century by the Georgian style houses which are still characteristic today (Plate 17b). These new houses had two and sometimes three storeys, with slated and usually hip-ended roofs. The door with its Georgian segmented fanlight above is centrally placed in the façade of the house and typically approached by a flight of stone steps, while the windows are also symmetrically arranged in the façade. This is a polite style unrelated to the vernacular forms and used not only by

Plate 16a: Large thatched farmhouse, a developed form of the basic eastern house with central hearth and door and hipped roof (Elton, Co. Limerick).

Plate 16b: Two-storey house with slated roof. Houses of this kind were widely built in the 19th Century, to replace the single-storey thatched houses. This example from West Cork retains the traditional opposite doors.

prosperous farmers but frequently adopted in rectories and in the houses of professional people who chose to live in the countryside but were employed in the town (Breffny and ffolliott, 1975).

In the late 19th and early 20th Century large numbers of two storied stone dwellings with slated roofs were built all over rural Ireland by ordinary farmers (Plate 16b). Usually these houses are extremely elementary in plan, typically with two ground-floor rooms with a fireplace at each gable, and three small bedrooms on the upper storey. Built after the influence of Georgian architecture had waned they do not possess pretentious doors with fanlights; all the windows and doors are rectilinear and plain. The houses do sometimes perpetuate features of the older single-storey houses; they are, for example, very rarely more than one room in width and especially in the more traditional western areas they retain the long-standing arrangement of opposite doors, although the ground floor area is usually divided into two rooms and the doors are connected by a cross-passage or, more commonly, open directly into the kitchen. Expansion of the house has usually been achieved by adding a "lean-to" kitchen at the back of the house, the roof of which is a continuation of the main roof. These newer two-storied houses are thus not a complete break with tradition and as they are so strikingly uniform over wide areas they could perhaps be described as a form of vernacular architecture. In areas such as West Cork, for example, two-storied houses have, since the end of the 19th Century, completely replaced the single-storey house and become the accepted and unquestioned style for a farmhouse. The two-storied houses may have been erected by professional builders but they were made to meet the norms and expectations of country folk (Plate 18a).

Improvements to the houses of ordinary farmers and labourers were encouraged or carried out by numerous landlords in the 18th and, more frequently, the 19th Centuries. Improving landlords sometimes simply provided building materials to their tenants and in these circumstances the new houses, although an improvement on the buildings they replaced, were often built along traditional lines and retained, for example, the thatched roof. In the late 18th Century and during the 19th Century many landowners turned their attention to the erection of model farmhouses and cottages built according to patterns devised by theorists both on practical and aesthetic grounds (Plate 17a). Some of the best illustrations of their work are the numerous gatehouses and terraces of labourers' houses built near the demesnes and designed in a "romantic" style intended to beautify and enrich the rural scene. Concern for the housing of

Plate 17: a Estate cottage, 19th Century, Co. Donegal. **b** Georgian farmhouse, Co. Wicklow, typical of many built on larger farms in the 18th and early 19th Century to replace thatched houses. **c** Co. Council cottage, typical of many built along roadsides by local authorities either at the end of the 19th Century or early in the 20th century (Co. Wicklow).

Plate 18a: West Cork. Two-storey farmhouses with slated roofs and two end chimneys are a widespread style in many areas. They are the dominant form in West Cork where within the last century they have ousted the single-storey thatched houses. Examples of the older houses can be seen abandoned in the foreground.

Plate 18b: The Rosses, Co. Donegal. A cluster of single-storey, three-roomed houses. The thatched structures are abandoned long-houses or byre-dwellings. Uniformity of basic house style is still a striking feature of many rural areas, especially in western Ireland.

the poorer classes was a new phenomenon in this period evident in both urban and rural settings. The amount of building activity in the Irish countryside was sometimes impressive but, despite the major enterprise of noted landlords such as the Dukes of Leinster, the 3rd Earl of Clancarty in Co. Galway and Lord Hill and Alexander Hamilton in Co. Donegal, it did not measure up to the enormous housing problems posed by a rapidly increasing population and the substantial number of people who lived in deep poverty. The 1841 census showed that 40% of the houses in the country, accommodating over 3 million people, were one-roomed mud cabins. In 1861 the census showed that approximately half a million mud cabins remained and nearly a fifth of these contained only one room.

Post-Famine depopulation and the massive reduction in the number of landless labourers was mainly responsible for the decline of the one-roomed cabin. The provision of improved housing by landlords had only a marginal effect on the total problem. To the student of landscape, however, the landlord building programmes are of considerable consequence, as the houses which were erected have survived while the one-roomed cabins have largely disappeared from the landscape (Danaher, 1967). Most of the thatched cabins which survived to the end of the 19th Century were eliminated by the legislation at the end of the century and the beginning of the 20th Century to provide ''labourer's cottages''.

In the western counties of Ireland and especially along the congested western seaboard, housing in the 19th Century was so primitive and the economic conditions so backward that the task of rural regeneration was made the special responsibility of state agencies. The most influential of these was the Congested Districts Board founded in 1891 to encourage economic development and social improvement in the western areas. In 1923 the work of the Congested Districts Board was passed on to the Land Commission whose responsibilities became state-wide. However, the basic tasks of farm consolidation and rural rehousing in the west were continued in much the same way. In the most poverty-striken areas the Congested Districts Board often built new houses for the whole community in a standardized style; indeed where the condition of the houses was particularly bad the Board saw to it that land was not transferred to the tenants until domestic improvements had taken place. Monetary inducements were offered by the Board to encourage tenants to erect outbuildings for livestock and thus terminate the long-standing but unhealthy habit of accommodating animals in the houses. A common house style used by the Congested Districts Board was a small house with a rectangular two-roomed ground plan and a loft bedroom, built with stone or brick and with a slated roof. Some concessions were made to traditional styles and frequently, for example, opposite doors appear in the kitchen. These uniform, box-like houses are still characteristic of numerous western areas especially island communities which were often completely rehoused by the Congested Districts Board. As most islands have in the 20th Century been steadily depopulated, few alterations to the houses have been carried out and few new houses have been built.

The provision of houses by the Land Commission has continued throughout the present century and spread far beyond the western districts. Land Commission houses occur in many areas of the country, including prosperous eastern counties such as Meath and Kildare in which small farmers from the congested western districts have been re-settled on large estates purchased and subdivided by the Commission.

At the end of the 19th Century, county and urban district councils were established and soon interested themselves in the field of housing, especially for the landless and labouring classes. Simple brick or stone cottages with slated roofs were the characteristic products, arranged singly or in small groups along the roadside (Plate 17c). The local authority cottages are a widespread if undistinguished feature of the. landscape, especially in the vicinity of market towns and villages but commonly too in the open countryside. Roinn na Gaeltachta is a state department established in 1928 to promote the cultural and economic welfare of the Gaeltacht and particularly to encourage the use of Irish as a vernacular language. Among its many activities the department operates a variety of schemes, including generous assistance for the improvement of housing, with the object of arresting emigration from the Irish-speaking areas. This assistance has led to considerable recent improvement of the houses within Gaeltacht areas. Grants can, for example, be given for special extensions to dwelling houses in order to accommodate tourists.

Although landlord and government institutions have been influential in the improvement and development of rural housing, the independent activities of individual owners have also been of widespread importance and perhaps over the long term of more consequence than the intervention by authorities. Security of farm ownership, which followed on the Land Acts of the late 19th Century, along with financial support from emigrant members of the family, led to a wave of improvements and extensions to the farmhouses carried out on the initiative of the owners during the first two decades of the present century. A second storey was often added to the whole or part of the house; thatch was replaced by slates, most widely where local slate was available as in West Cork and south-west Clare; small porches were built outside the front doors often in different materials from the main house, and the traditional whitewash on the external walls was increasingly replaced by plaster painted in a variety of colours but with an emphasis on dull greys. Pebble-dash, red bricks and other suburban traits did not become widespread in rural areas until the inter-war period. However, the amount of innovation varies considerably from area to area; some localities have remained conservative in this respect and their houses retain the traditional thatch and whitewashed walls. Conservatism is not always closely correlated with economic backwardness. In Co. Meath, for example, one of the richest farming areas in Ireland, many mud walled and thatched houses are still being lived in while much poorer areas can be found where the traditional buildings have been completely eradicated. Change seems to be infectious, and without an innovator to commence the process of change a local community is often content with the *status quo* or at most a very gradual pace of change; houses therefore undergo piecemeal modification and it is possible in many areas to perceive a slow and interesting transition from vernacular to modern styles.

Since the end of the 19th Century, therefore, the improvement of rural housing has been stimulated by the security of farm ownership and assisted by various government and local-authority building schemes. The standard and style of modern housing have continued to change throughout the present century. Especially since the First World War, suburban house styles, such as the bungalow, built with modern mass-produced materials and lacking any regional distinctiveness have increasingly infiltrated the countryside. In the 1960s and 70s there has been a markedly widespread adoption of urban styles and the abandonment of many old houses in favour of new structures, developments much encouraged by the new affluence of the rural population and by the growing number of urban-employed people living in rural areas and commuting from wide hinterlands into major urban centres. Rural depopulation has meant the abandonment of many old-style farmhouses. Very often the abandoned houses are not demolished but are used for new purposes such as barns and garages, or, more frequently, they are left to decay. New houses exist amidst the copious ruins of an older and much more numerous society. Few landscapes contain so many ruins from all historical periods as the Irish, but the bulk of the dereliction is recent—the houses of small farmers who have left an overcrowded countryside in a massive movement unbroken for over a century. The house is the element of the Irish landscape which has changed most since the 19th Century. The framework of fields and roads and the dispersed pattern of farms have altered little since their formation.

Farm Outbuildings

Barns and other outbuildings on Irish farms are not usually impressive structures; they lack even the most elementary ornamentation and do not, on the whole, appear to exhibit building techniques of any great antiquity. However, in some remote areas the small stone huts (clochans), with circular plans and domed roofs, that are still used occasionally as hen-houses or pig-styes perpetuate an extremely old style of building. Characteristically, the farmer erects only the most functional of outbuildings. Like the farmhouses these are rectangular in plan and built with the same material, either stone or mud. There is nothing aesthetically comparable to the spacious and colourful barns of the American countryside, for example, or the distinctive carved timber storehouses (stabur) of the Norwegian farmstead or the elaborate Bernese "speicher" (grain store), buildings upon which craftsmen lavished considerable skill and which were the pride of their owners.

On the larger farms in south-eastern Ireland where, in view of the traditionally greater emphasis on cereal products, there has always been a need for functionally specialized outbuildings, the farmstead buildings are frequently grouped around a rectangular yard with one side of the rectangle formed by the dwelling house itself, but many of the farms and especially the smaller ones do not exhibit any distinctive lay-out of buildings. In the north and west of the country the older farmsteads commonly constitute a single long range of buildings with house, stable and byre joined together. Sometimes in the poorer areas the farmhouse stands alone in the fields without any paddock or garden and accompanied by only a small crude storehouse. The very poor development of out-buildings on western farms may well be linked to the pastoral traditions and mild climate but it reflects also the long-standing use of the compact long-house which accommodated animals and human beings under one roof. The establishment of detached, functionally specialized buildings has only occurred with the recent breakdown of the long-house tradition. In south-western Ireland on many of the older farmsteads the farmhouse faces the outhouses and is separated from them by a laneway, sometimes known as the "street", which connects to the public road. This "street" arrangement can be found both in farm clusters and on the dispersed holdings.

With the modernization of agriculture in recent decades many new farm buildings have been erected, especially in the richer eastern areas, and these often modify the traditional patterns of farm lay-out. In particular there is a tendency to a looser and generally linear arrangement of farm buildings, consistent with the increased use of tractors and bulky machinery. The erection of large metal barns to provide winter shelter for cattle or storage for crops has been widespread in recent decades. These are structures which dominate the older ranges of buildings and testify to a new and more enterprising attitude to the working of the land.

10
The Towns

Distribution, Size and Functions

Town life came late to Ireland and was mainly owing to foreign influences. Despite the town-building activities of foreign invaders the bulk of Ireland always remained deeply rural. Less than 20% of the population lived in towns in 1841 and only within the past century has the balance between country and town population been materially changed. However, this recent increase of urban population is largely due to growth in the major centres of Dublin and Belfast and the population of many small towns has stagnated or declined since the Famine period. Northern Ireland, through its industrialization, has a higher proportion of sizeable towns than any other part of Ireland. The population of Northern Ireland is little more than half that of the Republic but it contains the same number of towns with populations above 10 000.

The country possesses an unusual urban hierarchy with few medium-sized towns. In the Republic, Dublin, Cork and Limerick are the only centres with populations exceeding 50 000. Dublin (along with Dun Laoghaire and suburbs) contains a population of over three quarters of a million and is over five times the size of its nearest rival, Cork, which along with its suburbs contained around 135 000 people in 1971. Limerick is the third largest centre with a population of 63 000 in 1971. The majority of the larger towns in Ireland, those possessing a population of over 10 000, lie in the richer eastern parts of the country, within a belt stretching from east Ulster, through Leinster, into east Munster. Elsewhere, towns are smaller and more widely dispersed. The poorer western regions have a very weak urban structure—nine counties have no towns of over 7000 population. Indeed, in Co. Leitrim and Co. Sligo, there is only one town in each county with a population exceeding 1000. In the whole province of Connacht only slightly in excess of one fifth of the total population lives in towns with a population of over 1500.

The great majority of the towns function chiefly as service centres for the inhabitants of small surrounding rural hinterlands. This system of service centres has developed on the basis of the distances that could be covered easily from the scattered farms in the course of a day and the centres are thus relatively close together and fairly evenly dispersed over the landscape because the agricultural population was widely distributed. As well as being evenly dispersed the towns are arranged roughly in hierarchical groupings (Buchanan, 1968). At the lowest level there is a large group of small centres, with under 3000 population, spaced at an average distance of 10 miles (16 km) apart and providing only a very limited range of basic services regularly required by the local population. Above these are centres which are distinctly larger in size, ranging from 3000 to 10 000 and providing a greater range of services; they are more widely spaced, normally some 20–30 miles (32–48 km) apart. The top layer of the hierarchy comprises the regional capitals which provide a complex array of commercial, cultural and administrative facilities for wide surrounding areas: usually the regional capitals are over 60 miles (96·5 km) apart. The regional capitals include Dundalk, Athlone, Waterford, Limerick, Tralee, Galway, Sligo and Londonderry, all settlements with populations exceeding 12 000. Some towns, for example Lisburn, Lurgan and Portadown in the North and Drogheda in the Republic, because of their relatively strong industrial employment base, have populations which place them in the same size bracket as the regional capitals, but they do not have service hinterlands of comparable extent. However, the general weakness of industrial growth in Ireland has meant that the fundamental hierarchy of settlement, adjusted to the agricultural background, has not been seriously modified; almost invariably the larger the town is the greater the range of the services it provides and the extent of the service hinterland.

With the exception of Dublin, Cork, Belfast and the regional capitals the majority of the towns are small, stagnant and rarely able to maintain any vigorous social or intellectual life. Expansion of towns has occurred only where they have attracted industry or tourism, or when the towns lie in proximity to major centres. The pattern of service centres will be increasingly modified by declining rural population and the growing use of automobile traffic which enlarges the size of the area that can be served efficiently by a centre. Towns are thus inevitably brought into direct competition with each other and the scale at which shops and services can operate efficiently is changed. The viability of many small centres will inevitably decline as many of the smaller shops and businesses are eliminated—with far-reaching consequences for the economic and social character of the settlements which traditionally have been dominated by a profusion of small family shops. Rationalization and centralization of a number of important public services, particularly education where there is a planned movement towards larger and therefore fewer schools (Hallak and McCabe, 1973), will serve to reinforce the trend towards growth in the larger centres at the expense of the smaller centres.

Historical Growth of Towns

Historical developments much more than current economic and social functions are of importance in understanding the distribution and the morphology of Irish towns. Each major phase of colonization in the historic period has been associated with important steps in town formation and the urban settlements of the different historical periods have, to some extent, complementary geographical distributions and distinctive morphological characteristics (Figs 24, 25). Information on the character of urban settlements in the major historical periods is available in earlier chapters and only a broad summary account of urban development will be provided here with the emphasis on those trends which are of importance in understanding the distribution and appearance of towns in the present-day landscape.

Pre-Medieval Towns

The society of pre-medieval Ireland was almost entirely rural with a strong pastoral emphasis; the establishment of the first towns had to await the advent of the Norsemen in the 9th and 10th Centuries and there was no extensive system of urban settlements until the Middle Ages. The inability of native Irish society to generate urban growth was not the result of destructive invasions or debilitating colonial systems. Indeed, until the arrival of the Norsemen Ireland had experienced considerable periods of relatively peaceful and unbroken development and it seems that the main impediments to urban growth were inherent to Irish society. In most agricultural communities with a tradition of nucleated rural settlement urban life can probably develop spontaneously provided there is a long uninterrupted period of economic and political growth. In Ireland the economic importance of pastoralism and the dispersed pattern of rural settlement associated with it were probably major deterrents to any indigenous growth of towns. The upper strata of society lived in independent family groups in isolated raths, and their traditions of self-

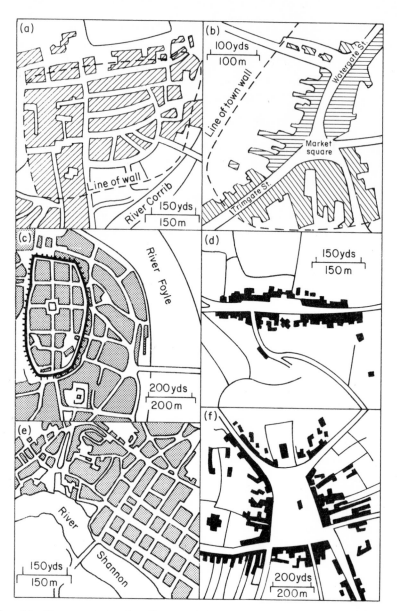

Fig. 24: Characteristic plan forms of Irish towns (note scale variations). **a** Galway. The medieval core of the city. **b** Navan, Co. Meath. Medieval street plan, with narrow burgage plots on Trimgate and Watergate. **c** Londonderry. The fortified plantation town, established in the early 17th Century, is still a clearly discernible element of the city plan with its strong walls surrounding a planned grid of streets converging on a central square or diamond. Around this

sufficiency, their mobility and pride in cattle did not dispose them to urban living. It is also possible that distance from those parts of Europe which possessed an urban civilization from an early date, in particular Greece and Rome, may have contributed to the belated development of an urban tradition in Ireland. Towns in many regions of the world were initiated following the diffusion of the idea of town life from nearby civilizations or through conquest by folk with a tradition of urban life. Foundation of towns and cities was integral to the process of romanization that followed Roman imperial expansion north of the Alps, but a number of the Celtic "oppida", or hill-forts, in western Europe appear to have been quasi-urban institutions well before the Roman conquest and some of their stylistic features may have been copied from Greek polis settlements. Ireland, owing to her remoteness, escaped these early inducements to urban living, both of which seem to have spread no further north and west than southern England; her rural, pastoral mode of life therefore survived unchallenged. The great Irish royal centres and major hill-forts of the Iron Age which seemed the most promising nodes for indigenous urban growth were eclipsed either shortly before or shortly after the advent of Christianity. The major monastic centres tended to replace them in importance but even the most dynamic monastic centres did not grow into true urban communities. Before urban life could take root on Irish soil a radically new cultural and economic milieu was needed and this could only come from outside.

The Viking invaders established themselves in coastal strongholds in Southern Ireland, at Dublin, Wicklow, Arklow, Wexford, Waterford and Limerick. In all these places there appears to have been continuity of settlement down to the modern period. Trading bases may have been established in Cork, Kinsale and Youghal. The strong emphasis on international trade and commerce in the Viking community indicates that their settlements were urban in function. Save for Dublin, however, where recent excavations have revealed timber houses and other artifacts of Viking date, little is known of the morphology of the Norse towns. The

---

original settlement the development is mainly of 18th and 19th Century date. **d** Blessington, Co. Wicklow. A typical one-street estate town, established in the late 17th Century and rebuilt by the Marquis of Downshire mainly in the early 19th Century. **e** Limerick. The formal street plan of the 18th Century suburb, Newtown Perry (now the commercial centre of the city), is in striking contrast to the cramped medieval portion of the city nearby. **f** Castlepollard, Co. Westmeath. An 18th Century estate town consisting of a central square with radiating side streets.

Fig. 25: Origins of towns (of over 1500 inhabitants, 1971). A number of medieval towns which have shrunk to mere villages are not shown on the map. Most of the important medieval foundations are included and there is a noticeable concentration in the south and east. The importance of plantation towns is most apparent in Ulster and, to a lesser extent, in Munster and in Laois/Offaly. A number of plantation and estate towns (e.g. Fermoy, Mallow, Tralee, Ennis, Birr, Larne and Coleraine) may well have had medieval antecedents but the scale

first towns in Ireland, therefore, were peripheral in a geographical and cultural sense, established on the coasts by foreigners to serve as bases for international trading activities.

A major phase of town formation began with the Anglo-Norman conquest in the 12th Century. The Normans occupied the old Norse centres and in the two succeeding centuries built a network of fortified centres over the country, most concentrated in the south-east but with important western outposts in Tralee, Galway and Sligo and to the north in Lecale and at Carrickfergus. Most of Ulster, however, remained conspicuously devoid of towns throughout the Middle Ages. Many of these Anglo-Norman settlements are still important towns and their original lay-out can often be traced in the alignment of the modern streets, properties and buildings. Those modern towns, or portions of them, in which the medieval plan has been preserved usually exhibit a rather irregular plan of winding streets and narrow lanes, sometimes with awkward right-angle bends. This is exemplified in Enniscorthy (Plate 19), Youghal, Kildare, New Ross, Navan, Trim, Carlingford and parts of Dublin, Kilkenny and Galway (Fig. 24). The old market-place is a distinctive feature in most of these towns, forming a broad stretch of street or a triangle or square where streets converge at the centre of the town. Narrow properties lying at right angles to the streets, which may have originated as medieval burgages, are still discernable features of some settlements, such as Navan, Naas and Youghal. The ruins of the substantial medieval stone buildings—the castles, tower houses, churches and monasteries—have sometimes survived, but in very few cases have the medieval walls been preserved in their entirety. Athenry in Co. Galway is the most notable exception; here the town is still contained within its medieval walls.

The 16th and 17th Centuries

Most of the towns in 16th Century Ireland had been established during the Anglo-Norman colonization of the 12th and 13th Centuries. However, the original Anglo-Norman network had declined and decayed during the Late Medieval period when there was a reduction of English interest in Ireland

---

and continuity of this earlier settlement is uncertain. The map does not give an adequate impression of the number and distribution of estate towns many of which are very small and possess less than 1500 inhabitants. Almost all of the modern growths are around Dublin or on the coasts.

Plate 19a: Enniscorthy, Co. Wexford. A town of medieval origin with compact plan and curved streets.

Plate 19b: Strokestown, Co. Roscommon. a good example of an early 19th Century estate town, with a wide, main street leading to the gates of the demesne owned by the landlord who built the town.

and a compensating upsurge of Irish influence. Some towns, especially those in the interior, were much reduced in population and economic strength and a few withered away completely. The most vigorous of the surviving towns were those possessing coastal port facilities and controlling extensive rural hinterlands. Cork and Waterford were conspicuously the most important towns of the south coast, and Galway, Limerick and Sligo on the west coast. Of the inland towns Kilkenny was pre-eminent. All of these towns possessed a notable degree of autonomy; they were veritable city-states and conspicuous for their sustained allegiance to the English crown. Their strong walls and garrisons reflected their independent status and their aloofness from the surrounding countryside. However, as the power of central government grew stronger in the 17th Century the privileges and the independence of the old towns were steadily eroded, and many centres such as Youghal, Kinsale and Athlone were severely damaged by warfare. Their walls and tower houses were destroyed and their commercial life irreparably harmed. In the Medieval period the purely Irish inhabitants had usually lived outside the gates of the walled towns and this seems to have been the origin of the "English" and "Irish" quarters which existed in the 16th Century. Indeed in the 18th Century, although numerous catholic, Gaelic families were represented among the urban merchant classes, ethnic segregation was still a lingering feature in some towns; Limerick and Kilkenny, for example, had English and Irish quarters and so did Athlone where the Irish town lay to the west of the Shannon and the English town to the east.

Plantation Towns

The plantations of the late 16th and the 17th Century began the third and final phase of town formation. Establishing towns was an important part of the policy of anglicizing Ireland and developing the country economically (Butlin, 1968). Between 1604 and 1613 alone, 44 new towns were incorporated as boroughs. Not only were new centres established, but several old, decayed towns such as Armagh, Carrickfergus and Coleraine were rehabilitated. One of the principal results of the plantation was to give Ulster and Connacht a veneer of urban life, but the plantations were also important in introducing a number of towns to central Ireland (Laois and Offaly) and also to south-western Ireland, where Richard Boyle, later Earl of Cork, established a line of fortified centres, including Bandon and Clonakilty, as garrisons against the Irish of Kerry and West Cork.

K

In Ulster, a region largely devoid of towns, the importance of inaugurating towns for strategic and economic purposes was fully recognized in the government's plans for the plantation. It was intended that 25 towns, each with corporate status, should be established in the six confiscated counties, some on completely new sites and others on the sites of Irish settlements or English forts as at Cavan and Derry. Positive action by the state was envisaged to build the towns and to introduce English traders and artificers. The urban policy was not fully prosecuted and the responsibility for town development was eventually left to the private initiative of major landowners. Little more than half of the proposed towns eventually received charters and some of the sites later proved to be unsatisfactory and were either seriously depopulated or abandoned.

Regardless of size, the morphology of the new Ulster towns followed a consistent pattern, geometrical and simple. The essential and often the sole element in the plan is a main street with a market-square or "diamond", a basic lay-out which has been highly resistant to later change. The streets are now lined with solid stone buildings with rather uniform façades of late 18th or 19th Century date, but originally they contained many half-timbered constructions. In larger towns there are frequently two main streets which cross at the diamond and a grid of minor streets lies behind the main axes. Originally many of the towns contained the fortified residence of the grantee with its bawn or defensive enclosure, but these have usually disappeared. Protestant churches were invariably given a prominent position in the towns. The elementary plans of the plantation settlements are still discernible in many Ulster towns and their main features were reproduced in scores of other small centres built by landlords during the 18th and early 19th Century in all the provinces of Ireland. Derry and Coleraine are good examples of the larger variety of plantation town, and Salterstown and Maherafelt of the small settlements. Derry is notable for its massive fortifications; it was the last great bastide town to be established in Western Europe (Fig. 24; Plate 21b).

The great majority of Irish towns were established by the early 17th Century but with the recurrent and widespread warfare of the 17th Century it was difficult for them to prosper. Dublin was exceptional and began to grow in size after the Restoration as the centre of a politically unified country. It was also in a favoured position economically. The English conquest and plantations quickened commercial contacts with England, especially in the east and south of the country where Dublin, along with Cork, became a major claimant for the growing trade. On the west coast, Galway and Limerick experienced slower growth. Limerick was twice devastated by sieges but appears to have recovered quickly. Many of the smaller towns and villages, which were more vulnerable, were severely damaged in the warfare and sometimes completely destroyed. The early history of many of the newly established plantation towns in Ulster was particularly unfortunate. Most of the original timber houses of the English settlers were burnt and destroyed in the Irish rebellion of 1641. No example of the English "cage" house with oak beams and white panels has survived although many of these structures were imported by the London companies into their new settlements at Magherafelt, Moneymore, Bellaghy and elsewhere. Few of the bawns or the early planter churches, which appear to have been built in Late Gothic styles, have survived. Within the strong walls of Derry, however, the cathedral of St. Columb, built in 1633, has survived intact.

Town Formation and Renewal in the 18th and Early 19th Centuries

The 18th Century was a period of relative stability and economic growth in Ireland during which town life was able to progress without serious interruption. Commencing in the latter half of the 18th Century most of the smaller settlements damaged or destroyed in the Cromwellian and Williamite wars of the previous century were rebuilt in a more solid and spacious manner and some completely new settlements were established. The widespread improvement of roads and the building of a new road network, along with the building of the canals, provided attractive opportunities for the siting of new settlements and encouraged the spontaneous development of nucleated settlements at road and canal junctions. Important extensions and renewal schemes also took place in the larger centres. In Dublin, Cork and Limerick new Georgian suburbs with wide streets and squares of large mansions were added to the medieval cores (Fig. 24e) and major buildings, such as the Four Courts and the Customs House in Dublin, were erected. Developments in Dublin and Cork are given fuller consideration later in this chapter. Armagh was converted from a mere village into a handsome town under the primacy of the wealthy Archbishop Robinson. He repaired the cathedral, built the archiepiscopal palace, a diocesan library, the famous observatory, an infirmary and other institutions. Many attractive houses were built in the town, especially on the fine terraces around the Mall. In Belfast the 5th Earl of Donegall carried out important improvements, and planned streets were created around the White Linen Hall, a building which stood on the site of the present city hall.

K*

The bulk of the urban rebuilding and development commenced in the latter half of the 18th Century and continued into the first two or three decades of the 19th Century, and there was a particularly marked spate of civic improvement associated with the economic boom during the Napoleonic wars. However, with the post-war depression and the heavy depopulation which followed the severe famines of the 1830s and 1840s, town development came virtually to a halt. Especially in the Republic the amount of urban rebuilding was minimal from 1840 onwards and most Irish towns, apart from their progressive dilapidation, were to remain relatively unchanged for a long period of time; indeed, it was not until the 1960s that change again became a general characteristic.

The relatively short period during which the physical fabric of the settlements was developed and the assured and uniform architectural tastes of the time help to explain the basic similarity of appearance. Most town buildings are in a demure Georgian style, a style which in Ireland dominated building enterprises into the early decades of the 19th century. Uniformity was further ensured by the way in which many of the towns were planned and built.

The new towns were often the property of improving landlords who saw the new or revived settlements as foci within a completely new framework for life in the countryside, consuming produce from the surrounding farms and, through their factories, mills and stores, providing employment supplementary to farming at a time when the rural population was increasing and agrarian reforms were creating a surplus of tenants on the land. A standard range of models and plans for estate towns and villages were in circulation among improving landlords at the time and these were used widely and imitatively.

The degree of landlord involvement in the creation of townscapes varied from settlement to settlement. In some instances the influence of the landlord was direct and strong and the major buildings and indeed the entire framework of the settlement are the outcome of a coherent design. Elsewhere, the landlords were not intent upon the implementation of an overall plan but frequently sought merely to influence the general character of the towns and, for example, to control the standard of housing by special provisions in leases. Thus, the uniform Georgian character which many towns possess was not always achieved by overall planning; individual buildings were erected at different stages throughout the 18th and early 19th Century and it was mainly the widespread acceptance of stylistic norms at the period which ensured that the settlement as a whole eventually emerged as an architectural unity. The typical arrangement of the main buildings along both sides of a main street also lends a striking coherence to the settlements, but this is a simple linear arrangement, perhaps the simplest and most natural possible, which had been characteristic of many medieval villages and boroughs and widely utilized in the plantation towns in Northern Ireland. There is no reason to suppose that it was in all cases a form imposed by the improving landlords so much as a long-standing feature widely exploited during the spate of 18th Century rebuilding.

In most instances new town building appears to have taken place on the sites of older settlements, such as medieval villages, shrunken medieval boroughs or even large clachans. The transformation of the physical fabric of these older settlements was thorough-going and few buildings which predate the 18th Century have managed to survive. In some cases even the old street plans were decisively changed but this was not, it seems, a general feature of town improvements. In the larger and more flourishing centres of medieval origin, for example, the buildings did not need reconstruction on a new ground plan; an organic evolution occurred and rebuilding tended to take place along the old street lines. In the plantation towns of the north, even where extensive rebuilding was necessary, the original simple plans established at the time of the plantation were generally respected. Examples can be found, however, where a major change of street plan did accompany the rebuilding of the settlement but how frequently this happened is hard to assess owing to the lack of detailed research in Irish urban history. In Co. Kildare, Maynooth was extensively modified in the latter half of the 18th Century by the Earl of Kildare and changed from an irregular medieval settlement with thatched houses into a trim and typical estate town (Fig. 26). The project involved the widening and rebuilding of the main street and the setting out of several side streets on a rectilinear plan. The buildings and basic plan created during this phase of improvement have survived virtually unchanged to the present day. The only subsequent innovation of importance has been the building, at the end of the 18th Century, of the Royal College of St. Patrick, a large Roman Catholic seminary sited near the ruined castle at the western end of the town. Draperstown in the foothills of the Sperrins in Co. Londonderry was another town whose fundamental form was changed. It was built by the Drapers' Company in the early 19th Century on the site of a dilapidated hamlet called Cross of Ballynascreene; the new buildings here were re-arranged around a central "diamond" on the traditional Ulster pattern.

Small towns and villages which were either rebuilt or originated in the

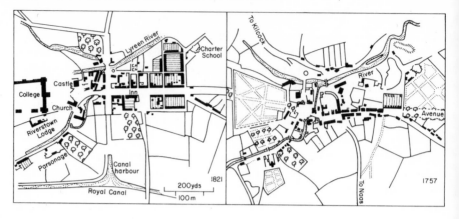

Fig. 26: Maynooth, Co. Kildare, 1821 and 1757. An example of a village redeveloped by a landlord mainly in the second half of the 18th Century. (Based on Horner, 1974.)

18th and early 19th Centuries and have been preserved largely unchanged from that period are the most numerous components of the Irish urban scene. They exist in considerable variety but the majority are very similar; the chief element is a long, wide main street lined for the most part with solid two- or three-storey stone buildings. Most of the buildings serve as shops or offices on the street level with living accommodation overhead. Front gardens were, seemingly, discouraged, and the buildings face right onto the main street. Typically, there is little depth to the towns and open countryside lies behind the long and narrow back gardens. The buildings tend to be of rather uniform height with pitched roofs covered with slates. Thatch, once common in many of the towns, has almost disappeared save on a few of the smaller single-storey houses on the outskirts of the town which usually represent 19th Century additions to the original settlement. As the settlements served mainly as local market and service centres they frequently possess a square and market-place and sometimes a small market-hall or a court-house built in classical style. The old cattle fairs which formerly took place in the main thoroughfare are now commonly held in purpose-built centres on the outskirts of the towns.

There are numerous features which reflect the old association between the towns and the landlords who owned them. Sometimes the landlord's demesne is in close proximity to the town; one of the demesne entrances may even open onto the main street in proximity to the more substantial Georgian-style houses of the town built originally by the landlord for his estate officials. The protestant church, usually built in a simple Gothic style, commonly occupies a prominent place in the town and the catholic churches have a more peripheral position as they have been added only in the 19th Century when the catholic majority won improved status after the sometimes severe protestant domination of the 18th Century. Presbyterian churches, characteristically built in classical idiom with a monumental pilastered façade, are a distinctive feature of the northern towns. Good examples of estate towns can be seen at Blessington and Dunlavin in Co. Wicklow and at Maynooth and Celbridge in Co. Kildare. Celbridge, however, appears to have developed slowly to its present form and was not planned in the same way as Maynooth. Lord Altamont's Westport, in Co. Mayo, is a further fine example; here there is an impressive octagonal square and the local river is channelled down the main tree-lined mall. The old plantation settlement at Cookstown, Co. Tyrone, was extensively developed by William Stewart in the middle of the 18th Century. Here it is the main street, over 1 mile (0·6 km) long and 130 feet wide, which is the most striking element in the town. Strokestown in Co. Roscommon, built by the Mahon family in the early 19th Century, has an imposing main street, 147 feet wide with the demesne entrance at one end and the protestant church at the other (Plate 19). Hillsborough in Co. Down, with its fine market-square, courthouse and protestant church, is another superb example of town planning belonging to the period 1750–80. More ambitious projects can be seen at Birr, Co. Offaly, where the Earl of Rosse carried out extensive improvements in the early 19th Century, including malls lined by elegant terrace houses and opening off a central square. Mitchelstown in Co. Cork was created in its present form by the King family (Earls of Kingstown) between approximately 1770 and 1830 and contains two large squares and a number of connecting streets.

Interesting deviations from the basic linear plan are to be found. For example, Warrenpoint and Castlewellan in Co. Down, both belonging to the latter part of the 18th Century, are good examples of towns dominated by large squares. So too are Castlepollard, Co. Westmeath (Plate 24f) and Rosscarbery in Co. Cork. In Slane, Co. Meath, the central element is four large matching houses facing diagonally on to the cross roads. At Tyrellspass, in Co. Westmeath, an attractive new settlement was built on the site of a medieval village by the Rochfort family in the late 18th Century. The larger houses and the protestant church here are laid out around a semi-circular green.

The formation of the system of towns and the great rebuilding of Irish towns was largely completed by the time of the Great Famine. Some of the final additions to the urban structure of the country were made in the 1820s and 30s with the establishment by enterprising landlords of small towns in the remote western peninsulas where no urban centres had hitherto existed. Cahirciveen in Co. Kerry was begun in 1822; the building of Clifden and Roundstone in Connemara, the latter populated by a colony of Scottish fishermen, began around 1820, and the town of Belmullet in the remote, north-western corner of Co. Mayo dates from 1825. Model industrial villages, intended to provide an improved living environment for working class people, were built by a number of 19th Century philanthropic industrialists in the British Isles, and Ireland had two major examples. The first was Portlaw in Co. Waterford built by the Quaker cotton-spinning firm of Malcomson in the 1820s; the ground plan here was distinctive with a web of streets focusing on a central square. Portlaw may have influenced the second model village built at Bessbrook near Newry in 1846 by the Quaker industrialist Mr. J. G. Richardson. Here, most of the houses were grouped around two large greens. The surrounding farmland was owned by the firm and supplied food to the town. Public houses and betting shops were prohibited.

These initiatives were among the last in the great wave of town creation and renewal supported by 18th and early 19th Century economic expansion and confidence; even while they proceeded there were ominous portents in the country of the major economic reversal which was to terminate further town building enterprise. The abrupt decay of the southern textile industry in the early decades of the 19th Century had the most disastrous results. For example, Prosperous, a small town on the edge of the Bog of Allen in Co. Kildare, was founded about 1780 with a cotton factory, but by 1837 the settlement was little more than a pile of ruins. Stratford-on-Slaney, in Co. Wicklow, was established as a manufacturing town in the 1780s; its textile mills employed 1000 people in the early 19th Century but its industries declined rapidly in the 1830s and the town was soon reduced to the significance of a hamlet. Even the larger and older urban centres which possessed a textile industry, such as Drogheda in Co. Louth and Bandon in Co. Cork, suffered conspicuously in the 1830s. In Drogheda the number of handloom weavers fell to almost a quarter of their strength within a decade and the 1000 remaining of the profession in 1840 were reduced to poverty. Bandon also was crippled by the collapse of its textile industry. At the beginning of the century it was a prosperous place with wool and cotton mills but by 1830 its industries had collapsed, its mills were ruinous and the population in decline.

Towns in the Post-Famine Period

Urban developments in the Post Famine period have been mainly associated with changes in the physical character, areal extent and population of existing settlements rather than with the formation of new settlements. Most towns stagnated economically, especially in southern Ireland where industrialization was weak, and came to rely almost entirely for a livelihood on the provision of services to their rural hinterlands. This, unfortunately, was an insecure basis, as the rural population was usually dwindling away owing to emigration. A limited range of new buildings and institutions were introduced but few towns changed appreciably in general appearance. Large catholic churches were built in most centres, of which the Pugins' great churches at Killarney and Cobh are striking examples; workhouses began to appear on the outskirts of towns in the 1840s and 50s under the Poor Law system, and national schools, hospitals, barracks and railway stations were also characteristic additions. Apart from Dublin and Cork, only the towns of the north-eastern counties, and especially those in the Lagan Valley, experienced marked changes as a result of industrialization. Centres such as Belfast, Lurgan, Lisburn, Ballymena, Newtownards and Portadown, which until the 19th Century had served mainly as market centres and retained the typical characteristics of plantation towns, became predominantly manufacturing centres. The initial impetus to growth came principally from the linen industry but gradually the industrial activity diversified. Large mills and factories were built in the towns and the populations expanded owing to migration from the countryside; the settlements grew in area mainly through the building of rows of new houses for the incoming workers. Most of the new building of the industrial era was in brick, which replaced stone as the most common urban building material. But industrialization was a potent influence on urban form only in Belfast and the towns within a 30 mile (48 km) radius of it. Elsewhere in the north, as throughout the south of the country, most of the towns continued to serve as market centres and their major physical characteristics derive from a pre-industrial era. Even Belfast never experienced the full horrors of squalor and overcrowding which afflicted, for example, Manchester and Leeds in the first half of the 19th Century, and the smaller industrial centres of Belfast's hinterland often retained some of the atmosphere of market towns.

New urban developments in the 19th Century were few and confined mainly to small settlements which grew up on the coasts in response to changes in transport and recreational habits. Steam navigation and the steam packets between Britain and Ireland, in conjunction with the railways, led to the growth of small outports on the eastern and southern coasts, most notably at Cobh in Cork Harbour, Dun Laoghaire on Dublin Bay, Greenore in Co. Louth and Rosslare near Wexford. The introduction in 1872 of regular steamer services to Scotland led to substantial growth at Larne, although a small settlement and port had existed there previously.

Numerous small fishing villages and minor market centres on the coasts developed rapidly in the 19th Century with the growing popularity of seaside holidays, and their tourist trade benefitted greatly from the introduction of the railways. Until the railways came it was difficult for most people to visit the seaside with any frequency. New hotels were built in the holiday centres and lodging houses and local businesses flourished. Nineteenth century coastal resorts include Bray and Greystones near Dublin, Tramore in Co. Waterford, several settlements on Cork Harbour and a few locations on the west coast, such as Kilkee, the Galway suburb of Salthill, Buncrana and Bundoran. In Northern Ireland there was a wide scatter of resorts which included Bangor near Belfast, Newcastle in Co. Down, and Portrush, Portstewart and Castlerock in Co. Derry. Most of these coastal settlements have continued to attract population by broadening into residential suburbs or satellites of nearby cities, and where port facilities existed, as at Larne, Dun Laoghaire and Cork Harbour, a range of new industries has been acquired.

Dublin and Belfast emerged as the major nodes in the national rail network and their economic pre-eminence was thereby reinforced. Inland, the railways had remarkably little influence upon the growth of industry or settlement, save in the north-east where the building of the well developed railway network accompanied the expansion of industry. The railways spread first from Belfast down the prosperous Lagan Valley to central Ulster and helped to promote the rise of the industrial towns.

The great majority of Irish towns altered little in the first half of the present century but in the post-war period, with the expansion of industry and tourism, there have been changes. Fortunes have varied considerably, depending often on the almost capricious distribution of new factories among the many small centres, but a recognizable fringe of new buildings has sprung up, especially since the early 1960s, on the approaches to most towns. This new urban sprawl, which is clearly distinguishable from the old and compact urban cores, typically contains private bungalows, new workers' houses built with governmental assistance, garages and small factories. It has sometimes resulted from population growth but it reflects also a tendency for well-to-do townspeople to move outwards and for countrymen to move towards the towns, their traditional inclination to live in detached houses in the open countryside now married with a new desire to be close to the services of a town or large village. Within the town cores the 18th and 19th Century fabric has changed remarkably little, save for the sometimes garish modernization of the shop fronts.

The continued growth of industry, population and traffic in Dublin and Belfast has led to considerable problems of congestion in these areas and has been accompanied in both parts of the island by growing regional disparities in economic and social development, especially a tendency for trends in population and industrial concentration to favour persistently the already more wealthy and more urbanized eastern areas of the country against the poorer and dominantly rural regions in the west. Regional imbalances, as well as the internal problems of the growing capitals led in the 1960s to renewed interest in spatial planning at both regional and urban level (Forbes, 1970; O'Neill, 1971). In the Republic there has been special concern with the link between urban structure and the problems of economic and social development in the nation and its various regions. National economic growth requires the provision of a large number of urban-based industrial jobs, but the government's regional planning policies require the benefits of such growth to be spread throughout the country. However, the poorer areas are the most difficult ones in which to stimulate planned growth owing to their very weak urban structure. No sizable urban centres exist there to provide a base for new and reasonably large industrial projects which normally need a certain range of tertiary services and infrastructural facilities as well as a large labour pool with diverse skills. In 1968 an important but controversial study, entitled *Regional Studies in Ireland* (Buchanan, 1968), recommended the broad outlines of a national strategy for regional development. It was argued that in order to obtain the stimulus of substantial growth-centres, while at the same time avoiding excessive concentration in Dublin, it was desirable to develop new industrial centres at Cork and Limerick/ Shannon. Dublin should be left to grow but not stimulated to grow, while at Cork and Limerick/Shannon, if modern technologically advanced industry with high growth potential was to be attracted and supported, there should be energetic promotion and efficient physical planning in order to offset any initial deficiencies in size. Buchanan also proposed that minor growth-centres should be selected throughout the country, but essentially the towns of the south and south-west were to be greatly increased in importance while the north-west would be little changed, and this imbalance was in large measure determined by the existing urban structure. These proposals have not been implemented. More recent regional industrial plans place less emphasis on the priority of building up powerful concentrations of industry and population and envisage a more dispersed geographical distribution of industrial activities with a reasonable degree of concentration on the major urban areas in each region. In short, it is maintained that a high degree of industrialization can take place without a radical change in the existing urban structure (I.D.A., 1972). Save at Shannon, where a large housing estate has grown up beside the industrial estate, no new towns have been planned in order to stimulate industrial activities in backward regions.

The Mathew Plan for Belfast (1964) showed that internal migration, focused upon Belfast and the Lagan Valley, was compounding the problems of congestion which the city had inherited from the Victorian era and leading to a disturbing decline in the western parts of Ulster. Physical obsolescence in the capital would necessitate thorough-going urban renewal and this would have to be complemented by "overspilling" of surplus population. If overspill operations were properly planned they could help to restore regional balance and combat the problematic concentration of population and resources in the Belfast area. Policies of containment of large urban areas, which are so deeply rooted in British town planning approaches, have been applied in Belfast and, amid considerable controversy, attempts have been made to contain the physical expansion of the urban area by means of a stop-line. New economic growth has been encouraged in a limited number of selected urban centres in the hinterland of the city, chiefly at Portadown-Lurgan, Antrim and Ballymena.

The New Town idea has also been utilized and linked with the economic growth-centre policy. Following the New Towns Act (Northern Ireland) in 1965 a government-sponsored development corporation commenced the building of a new regional city called Craigavon, with an ultimate population of 100 000 people and incorporating the existing towns of Portadown and Lurgan. Craigavon is intended to serve as an attractive milieu for new industrial and population growth and as a counter-attraction to Belfast. The new town has been planned as an essentially linear growth strung out along the M1 motorway. Although its linear form represents a departure from the main tradition of New Town planning, the predominance of modern housing in distinct neighbourhood groupings, plentiful open spaces and the separation of pedestrian and vehicular traffic are all characteristic features of the New Towns of Britain.

Physical planning in Londonderry (Munce, 1968) is heavily concerned with the related questions of industrial modernization and environmental improvement. In Derry, the basic planning problem, so far as industrial growth is concerned, is different from that faced in Belfast; it is not a question of damping down or diverting growth but of stimulating it in one of the most remote urban centres of its size in the British Isles. However, planning in both cities confronts formidable problems of urban congestion, obsolescent buildings and a generally neglected social environment. Extended programmes of large-scale urban renewal, housing developments and the rationalization of road systems have consequently been commenced. The civil unrest and violence in Ulster since 1968 have resulted in extensive damage and destruction in many urban centres, and the need for immediate restoration and rebuilding when the crisis ends may serve to intensify urban planning endeavour throughout the province.

The Four Major Cities

Dublin

Dublin has developed on a low-lying, level site on either side of the River Liffey where it enters the wide sweep of Dublin Bay (Fig. 27). This site is one of the few sheltered havens on the east coast of Ireland south of Carlingford Lough, and Dublin is therefore the natural approach to, and outlet from, the east Central Lowland of Ireland, which, since prehistoric times, has been one of the most prosperous portions of the country. Maritime trade has been a basic feature of Dublin's commercial life since the foundation of the city by Norse traders in the 9th Century. There may well have been settlement here from an earlier period, associated with a ford across the Liffey at the estuary head, as the Irish name of the city (Baile Atha Cliath, place at the ford of the hurdles) suggests. But there is no firm evidence of a strictly urban community until the Norsemen established their fortified base on a slight ridge above the Liffey in the locality where Christchurch cathedral now stands. Seawards of this ridge there were low, ill-drained areas, raised beaches and the tidal mudflats of the Liffey estuary, and it was not until the 18th Century that they were reclaimed and significant expansion permitted to the east. The quantity and variety of material obtained from recent excavations on the site of Viking Dublin make it abundantly clear that the town was an extremely important

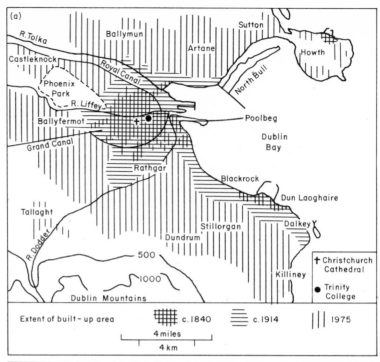

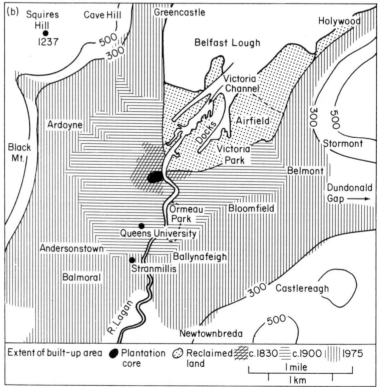

Fig. 27: Site and growth of **a** Dublin and **b** Belfast. (Note difference of scale.)

place in 9th and 10th Century western Europe but little is known about the morphology of the early settlement. In the 12th Century the Anglo-Normans gained control of the town and the Norsemen were re-settled mainly, it seems, to the north of the river. From that time until the 20th Century, Dublin remained the centre of the fluctuating English authority in Ireland. The Anglo-Normans built walls around their town and constructed a castle. Two cathedrals were associated with the city and a number of monastic establishments lay outside the walls.

Between the 13th and 17th Century no significant change took place in the boundaries of the city. Dublin in the early 17th Century was still an essentially medieval city huddled on its low eminence south of the Liffey. The settlement was small and dilapidated; the area within the walls covered only one ninth of a square mile and the castle, walls and Christchurch cathedral were in poor repair. There were small Irish suburbs outside the walls, and to the north of the river lay the old Norse suburb of Oxmanstown. The University of Dublin, Trinity College, had been established in 1591 on the site of the ruined monastery of All Hallows about a quarter of a mile (0·4 km) east of the city wall but there was little else to suggest that the city was on the verge of a remarkable period of growth. Development and expansion in Dublin during the latter half of the 17th Century and especially in the 18th were very marked. The walls were almost entirely removed and little of the medieval fabric has survived, with the major exception of the cathedrals and churches. The basic street plan of the medieval town, however, remains largely intact despite the large amount of post-medieval street widening. High Street, west of Christchurch cathedral, was the main medieval thoroughfare.

As the traditional centre of English authority, Dublin's importance was assured by the emergence of a unified Ireland under powerful English monarchs in the 16th Century. However, growth of the city in the first half of the 17th Century was retarded by the disturbed political conditions in the country and it was not until the 1660s, after the Restoration, that Dublin began to enlarge noticeably in area and population. Her industrial activities, particularly textiles, also grew in importance, encouraged by the immigration of Huguenot and Dutch settlers. During Charles II's reign, numerous extensions to the built-up area were made, for example between the castle and Trinity College and on the north bank of the Liffey behind Ormond and Arran Quays; bridges were built over the river and a number of major institutions, including the Royal Hospital at Kilmainham and the Blue Coat School, were founded. Also important at this time was the reservation of two large open spaces as amenities for the city, spaces which have remained major components of the urban landscape. The first of these was the old commonage to the south of Trinity College which evolved under municipal auspices into St. Stephen's Green, and the second was the vast extent of Phoenix Park to the north-west of the city, an area which originally included the grounds of the Royal Hospital south of the river and comprised over 2000 acres (809 ha). Phoenix Park was provided by the Duke of Ormond, the Lord Lieutenant after the Restoration, as an extensive recreation ground for public usage, and this it has remained even though the Viceregal Lodge and other institutions were later located in it. The first steps in the long and vital process of development in the port area were also undertaken towards the end of the 17th Century when reclamation of the wide tidal estuary of the Liffey commenced and quays were erected along portions of the river banks. This was an early indication that the centre of gravity in the city was to shift coastwards. During the Restoration period most major developments had occurred to the west of the medieval city, the buildings of the Royal Hospital and the Blue Coat school for example, and it had seemed that the city might grow cheifly in that direction.

In the 18th Century, a peaceful era in Ireland, Dublin experienced a period of rapid development which continued into the early part of the 19th Century and left a strong abiding imprint on the city. The latter half of the 18th Century, during which Dublin was the capital of a semi-independent Ireland, was a time of particularly dynamic change. Dublin became a city of style and architectural repute, the expression of the wealth and taste of the Anglo-Irish protestant ascendancy who then dominated most areas of Irish life (Maxwell, 1936; Craig, 1969).

Residential developments for upper-class occupants were the most prominent elements in the new city. These were typically carried out as unified projects on the estates of local landowners such as Luke Gardiner, Lord Fitzwilliam, Joshua Dawson and the Molesworth family, names perpetuated in major streets of the present-day city. Important building enterprises started first on the north side of the river with the erection of Henrietta Street about 1730; later in the century growth occurred mainly to the east in Rutland (now Parnell) Square, Sackville (now O'Connell) Street and Mountjoy Square. South of the river, new development commenced around the middle of the century and continued into the early 19th Century. The dominant features in south Dublin were Merrion Square and Fitzwilliam Square (Plate 20). A few magnificent stone mansions standing in their own grounds, such as Leinster House and Powerscourt House to the south of the river and Tyrone House and

Plate 20a: Aerial view of central Dublin, looking east along the Liffey quays towards the port. Trinity College at the centre right. The level, reclaimed area around the port is clearly visible. Howth island at top left.

Plate 20b: Dublin, south of the Liffey. Georgian squares and terraces with late 19th and 20th Century development to their rear. Merrion Square in the foreground and Fitzwilliam Square at top left.

Belvedere House to the north, were built by major aristocrats but the principal type of housing was the long, uniform terraces of narrow but high, four-storey mansions with plain red-brick façades, highly regular fenestration and ornamental arched doorways. These terraces face directly onto the street, with gardens to the rear of the buildings, and they can give the street, especially if it is narrow, a closed-in, almost canyon-like appearance. However, the new developments were generally well provided with the wide streets and spacious squares typical of the Georgian period and this sets off the terraces to their best advantage.

Major institutions were provided with dignified classical buildings of granite or limestone, many of them erected in prominent places in the city; they close long vistas, for example, or stand at focal points in the street system. Trinity College was substantially rebuilt with its impressive west front facing down the wide expanse of Dame Street, and the old Parliament House nearby, which became the Bank of Ireland after the Union, was enlarged and embellished. The Royal Exchange was built next to the Castle and is fully visible down the length of Parliament Street and Capel Street. The Custom House and the Four Courts, both designed by James Gandon, the most distinguished architect of the time in Dublin, stand in commanding positions along the quays. Other 18th Century buildings of note include the King's Inns, numerous fine hospitals, churches and barracks. But Georgian Dublin, despite its fine institutions, was not an ostentatious city. Residential precincts dominated the town and the foremost consideration was to create a pleasant environment to live in rather than a display of monumental architecture.

The port was also extensively developed in the 18th Century, mainly by the activities of the Ballast Office, and the coastline considerably modified in the process. In 1735 a great wall began to be built seawards to the Poolbeg Lighthouse in order to protect the harbour from drifting sand from the south (Fig. 27). At the rear of the wall, east of Trinity College and Merrion Square, land was reclaimed which later was completely covered by warehouses, factories and housing. During the century, the Liffey, which had formerly been a wide anastomosing stream, was firmly confined between two parallel lines of quays upon which roads were eventually built. These quays, which stretch for almost 3 miles (3·8 km), have remained a major feature of the city centre (Plate 20). In the second half of the century the port became the terminal point for two major canals, the Royal Canal to the north and the Grand Canal to the south, which linked Dublin to the Shannon and ran along the perimeters of the city.

A major contribution was made to the lay-out of Dublin by the bold planning of a traffic circulatory system of wide streets and bridges. This was mainly achieved by the Wide Streets Commissioners founded in 1757, a body given the task of making wide and convenient streets and the authority to demolish buildings in pursuit of that aim. Spacious thoroughfares, such as Dame Street, O'Connell Street, Lower Abbey Street, Westmoreland Street and D'Olier Street are some of the legacies of the Commissioners' enterprise. The older street pattern of the city was extensively rationalized and a network of wide streets created. This rationalized street system assisted the city to develop as a coherent whole even though independent building enterprises were proceeding in its different quarters. There were no major physical obstacles to the expansion of Dublin and the city in the 18th Century consequently grew outwards in a fairly even way forming, by the beginning of the 19th Century, a compact urban area with a circumference of about 9 miles (14·5 km); it was confined within the North and South Circular Roads which lay inside and parallel to the urban sections of the canals.

The expansion of Georgian Dublin had significant consequences in the hinterland of the city. It led to the improvement, and sometimes the re-alignment, of the principal highways from the city. To the south of Dublin the new improved highways utilized the low gaps through the hills, such as the Scalp and the Brittas gap, whereas older routes had often followed the ridges and high ground. Some local villages developed into tourist resorts, Leixlip and Lucan, for example, with their mineral springs, Malahide with its coastal amenities, and Dundrum with its allegedly salubrious climate. The large-scale building enterprises in Dublin led to a boom in granite quarrying on the flanks of the Wicklow Mountains and several small settlements, such as Ballyknockan and Barnaculia, probably originated at this time as groups of quarrymen's cottages. Many substantial residences or villas for city-employed professionals were built along the slopes of the surrounding river valleys, frequently on the sites of old farmsteads. The flanks of the Liffey Valley and the Dodder and its tributaries were popular for the purpose, and the new residences here often lie above older mill sites and their associated cottages on the valley floors.

In the 19th Century Dublin fared much better than most Irish cities. It did not benefit markedly from the Industrial Revolution, certainly not in the profound way that Belfast did, and the old textile industries, which in other cities often pioneered the transition to more productive, mechanized patterns of output, collapsed in the early decades of the century. However, brewing, distilling and biscuit manufacturing flourished, the role of the city as a communication and distribution centre was steadily enhanced, and it remained an important legal, educational, religious and administrative centre. Within Ireland as a whole, the population declined in the latter half of the century, while Dublin experienced a slow but steady increase of numbers, growing from 236 000 in 1841 to 290 000 in 1900. As the century proceeded the preponderance of the city as a centre of population and economic activity was accentuated and the built-up area continued to increase, although rather more slowly than in the previous century.

Building activity in good Georgian style was continued into the early 19th Century but thereafter the character of the city changed considerably and it degenerated architecturally and socially. When, with the Union of 1801, Dublin ceased to be a parliamentary capital, many of the wealthier people moved away. As the century proceeded the prestige of the Georgian centre declined; the upper and middle classes abandoned it and settled in new suburbs to the south of the city, a centrifugal movement accelerated by the introduction of railways in the middle decades of the century, and by other new forms of transport, such as the tramways in the 1880s. A growing proletariat, made up largely of unskilled immigrants from the depressed rural areas, crowded into the vacated Georgian quarters.

A serious slum problem existed in Dublin before the end of the 18th Century but it grew in magnitude during the 19th Century (Craft, 1970). Many of the mansions in the Georgian terraces of central Dublin became dilapidated tenement dwellings subdivided among poor families. The Liberties, for example, a prosperous industrial district around St. Patrick's Cathedral, degenerated completely and so did most of the Georgian developments north of the river, including the once prestigious Mountjoy Square. However, islands of dignity survived amid the extensive squalor, particularly in the south-east of the city. St. Stephen's Green, Merrion Square and Fitzwilliam Street, for example, remained unspoiled. Small amounts of improved working-class housing were provided in the 19th Century by philanthropic bodies and housing associations such as the Dublin Artisans Dwelling Company. Single-storey, brick-built terraces were the usual products but blocks of working-class flats, such as those financed by the Iveagh Trust in the Liberties, were being erected by the end of the century. These schemes, however, made little impact upon basic problems and the grossly overcrowded tenements survived well into the 20th Century as a central concern of Dublin's public housing policies.

Although extensive decay took place during the 19th Century in the Georgian residential areas, important buildings continued to be erected for religious, administrative or commercial purposes, which are now conspicuous parts of the city's landscape. Catholic Emancipation in 1829 brought a spate of catholic church building, especially in the poorer areas. There had of course been catholic churches before this but they had been generally unobtrusive. During the first half of the century huge churches in the classical style were built with awesome porticos and cupolas but in the second half of the century Gothic styles became fashionable. Some imposing public and commercial buildings were also erected, including the major railway stations, numerous large banks and hotels, the Kildare Street Club, the National Library and National Gallery and the industrial architecture of the Guinness brewery. The great quays and docks on the north side of the harbour, including the Alexandra Basin, were built mainly in the last three decades of the century.

Improvements to the port, in order to cater for the new steamship services across the Irish Sea, and the building of a national railway network focused on Dublin served to enhance the status of the city and influenced the pattern of its physical growth. Owing to the shallow waters of its bay, Dublin long had the reputation of the most difficult port to enter in the British Isles, but corrective measures were taken in the 1820s. The building of the Bull Wall from Clontarf protected the harbour to the north and helped to keep the entry channel open by concentrating the scouring effect of the tide. Two outports for Dublin were built, the first on the north side of Howth Head and the second at Kingstown (Dun Laoghaire) which soon became an important packet station for Holyhead. Development along the south coast of the bay was encouraged by the building of the Dublin to Kingstown railway in 1834, the first in Ireland, and between approximately 1850 and 1880 a narrow residential belt grew along the coast, incorporating Sandymount and Blackrock and, in effect, forming an extension of the south-eastern, upper-class sector of the city (Fig. 27).

The development along the south coast of Dublin Bay was one of the most conspicuous additions to the urban area in the 19th Century. In the first half of the century considerable additions were made to the south of the city, especially in Pembroke and Ballsbridge where finely proportioned residential roads in the Georgian tradition were erected, and narrow tentacles of growth spread out along major roads to connect a number of old settlements, such as Donnybrook, Rathmines and Harold's Cross, to the urban area. Spaces between these radial roads were progressively filled up by housing in the second half of the century. The southern suburbs, such as Rathgar, the Mount Pleasant Square area, Ballsbridge and Sandymount, have a distinctive and pleasant character. Housing was provided for a range of income groups and its quality varies. However, classical type terraces remained popular although they were usually lower than the 18th Century terraces in the centre of Dublin. Detached or semi-detached Victorian-style houses became common towards the end of the century but nearly all the domestic building right down to the 1860s and 70s was of a "Georgian" flavour. The suburban streets are generally wide; trees, gardens and open spaces are plentiful and there is a pleasant uniformity of building materials—red brick houses with slate roofs, iron railings, calp or granite boundary walls.

To the north of the city 19th Century growth was restrained and the North Circular Road provided the approximate boundary of the built-up area until the 20th Century. Howth was given a rail connection with Dublin in 1846, which ran through Clontarf, Raheny and Sutton, but suburban development was slight perhaps because the upper and middle-classes were deterred by the belt of slums immediately to the north of the Liffey which effectively isolated them from the prestigious southern parts of the city. Westwards, the expansion of the town was checked to the north of the Liffey by Phoenix Park and a variety of major institutions, including a military barracks and a mental hospital, and to the south of the river by the old and dilapidated area of the medieval town and the poor parts which fringed it.

Dublin has grown rapidly in the present century both in population and area, especially since 1922 due to its emergence as the centre of government and industry in an independent Ireland. The industrial revival encouraged by the government in the Republic has had pronounced benefits for the city. Most new manufacturing in Ireland has depended heavily on imported raw materials and there were clearly advantages in a port location. Dublin, moreover, with its large labour supply and market had exceptional attractions for new industries and hence the concentration of industrial activity and employment in and around the city has steadily grown in importance. Population has increased from 290 000 at the turn of the century to over two thirds of a million. The character and appearance of the city has been profoundly changed not only by the growth of numbers but also by a massive shift of population within the urban area. The old city centre has experienced a sharp diminution of population and the outer areas have been gaining markedly. This shift in population has resulted largely from an extensive publicly-assisted housing programme initiated in the 1920s to provide improved living conditions for the inhabitants of the old slum areas in the central city and to accommodate the flow of newcomers to Dublin from the remainder of Ireland. In the central areas blocks of working-class flats have been built by the Corporation, but most attention has focused on the outskirts of Dublin where large housing estates have been created. The major developments have been to the south-west at Ballyfermot, Drimnagh, Crumlin and Kimmage, where level land was available for large-scale developments, and to the north and north-east at Cabra, Finglas, Killester and Raheny. Municipal estates are now the major residential elements in the city. Most of them are very uniform in design, predominantly two-storey, four-roomed houses with small front and rear gardens. Bricks and pebble-dash are the predominant surface materials with tiled roofs. There are few trees and a relative absence, especially in the earlier estates, of shopping or industrial facilities. A different style of development was initiated in 1965 at Ballymun on the northern edge of the city. The housing scheme here, for around 20 000 people, was built by industrialized methods and sponsored by the government on behalf of the Dublin Corporation. It consists of a variety of houses graded in height from clusters of two-storey houses to several tower blocks and grouped around a central shopping and entertainment area where vehicular and pedestrian traffic are segregated. The Ballymun towers are a striking feature of the generally low and level suburban skyline. As an environment for living they have attracted much criticism, and it is unlikely that similar projects will be repeated in the future.

The quantity of peripheral development has greatly expanded in the 1960s and 1970s, during which time a major contribution has been made, especially to the south of the city, by private developers building for middle and upper-income groups. New housing, mainly built since the 1930s, now forms a ragged belt, on average between one and a half to two miles (2·4 and 3·2 km) in width, around the edge of Dublin and it is greater in total area than the pre-existing city. Within this belt there are numerous open spaces, chiefly convents and colleges which are the properties of the Roman Catholic Church, but also cemeteries, golf courses, schools and public parks. On the outer edge of the belt, agricultural land interdigitates with housing estates, new industry and, occasionally, new shopping centres (Haughton, 1970). To the north of the city and to the south-west, the Corporation has been the main developer, while to the south and south-east, private developments are more conspicuous. Private housing estates of the inter-war period were usually small units set in the open countryside, but in the post-war period the estates have tended to be larger in area and, owing to high land values, the houses have been densely packed, with a level of amenity and open space which is often not an improvement on the municipal estates. The houses are of a uniform pattern, principally semi-detached or in short terraces with gardens to the front and rear, and there is little evidence of imaginative planning or landscaping.

One noticeable feature of the new belt of housing is its rather even width. Marked finger-like extensions of the urban area along major routeways, so characteristic of modern cities, have not developed around Dublin, save on the south coast of the bay. Symmetrical growth has been permitted by the relatively even, well-drained terrain and encouraged by the continuing concentration of much employment in the central parts of the city. Early municipal estates were indeed built around the margins of the city on the assumption that residents would continue to find employment in the centre.

It is striking too that the basic spatial patterns of social segregation established in the city in the 18th and 19th Centuries have been extended outwards into the new suburbs. The high-status south-eastern sector of the Georgian city has been a particularly formative element in the later growth of the city. It was extended outwards in the 19th Century by high quality, terrace housing in Pembroke and Ballsbridge and along the coast to Blackrock and Dun Laoghaire. In the 20th Century private housing estates have proliferated on the outer edge of these areas. The great arc of suburban housing to the north of the city, which includes Finglas, Ballymun, Santry, Coolock and Raheny, is largely a 20th Century extension of the old low-status areas north of the Liffey, from which the population was largely transferred. In the south-west, the large corporation estates are essentially extensions of the low-status areas around the medieval city, such as the Coombe and Dolphin's Barn.

Continued population growth and expansion of the city area and the massive concentration of population in its suburbs have given rise to extended journeys-to-work, and to traffic congestion and land-use pressures in the central business district of the city where employment and shopping facilities are still heavily concentrated. New shopping centres and private industrial estates have grown up on the periphery of the city but not on a scale sufficient to reduce significantly the pressures on the centre. Office employment in the centre of Dublin has grown markedly since the early 1960s. Over half of all the office workers in the Republic are in the Dublin area and the sources of their employment are heavily concentrated in the south-eastern sector of the city. The inner city, that is approximately the area enclosed by the canals, today presents stark contrasts, with some districts of intense activity and others of advanced decay. There are large extents of obsolescent housing and decrepit buildings on the north side of the Liffey which must be replaced, and much of the city area near Christchurch Cathedral lies derelict and in urgent need of comprehensive renewal. The major shopping facilities of Dublin cluster along a busy but narrow north–south axis whose spine is Grafton Street and O'Connell Street. The south-eastern sector of the city is booming, with new office blocks, embassies and luxury hotels. This is an area of high architectural value, the cream of Georgian and early 19th Century Dublin, and conservation problems are consequently acute. The city must therefore, in the near future, undergo considerable changes in its appearance; obsolescent areas require renewal while development pressures in the areas of intense activity will tend to erode their traditional architectural character. A comprehensive regional plan for the Dublin region was prepared in 1966 by Professor Myles Wright. This proposed restrictions on urban growth to the north and south. Dublin airport, it was emphasized, restricts growth possibilities to the north, and if growth continued to the south then the major amenities of the mountains would be encroached upon. The main thrust of Dublin should consequently be to the west and channelled into three new satellites centred on existing small settlements at Blanchardstown, Clondalkin and Tallaght. This broad pattern of future expansion is already emerging on the ground and by the 1990s each of the satellites may have populations comparable to Cork city today. However, there is no clear indication that planned growth to the west will be accompanied by a slowing down of developments elsewhere on the periphery of Dublin. New pressures for further expansion of the port area and its industrial facilities through reclamation of a further 1000 acres (405 ha) in Dublin Bay have also arisen (Kruijtbosch et al., 1971), but there is strong opposition to these proposals, especially from those who see the bay as a major amenity for the city.

Cork

Cork is Ireland's third largest city and second city of the Republic with, if the suburbs are included, a population of around 135 000. The settlement is located in a west to east trending valley and sited near the mouth of the River Lee before it reaches the broad waters of Lough Mahon and eventually turns at a right angle southwards through the hills into the broad branching inlet of Cork Harbour. Cork in the early stages of its history grew up on one of the many small islands among the winding channels of the Lee, and later expansion of the town has entailed reclamation of the surrounding marshes and the erection of numerous quays along the river banks (Plate 21). The name Cork (Corcah, ''marshy place'') suggests the ill-drained environment. Immediately north of the river there is steeply rising ground, breached by the Blackpool Valley, and gentler but often ill-drained terrain stretches to the south. Site difficulties are more than compensated, however, by the advantages of the geographical situation. The harbour facilities at the mouth of the River Lee include the estuarine upper harbour in the city and the extensive, deep-water lower harbour which is the largest and most sheltered haven on the south coast. Access from the port to the interior of the country is provided through a number of low gaps in the east–west trending hill ranges of the immediate hinterland. Cork serves a wide rural hinterland and after Dublin is the most important retail and wholesale distribution centre in the Republic. The agriculture of the surrounding regions is prosperous and the rural population relatively stable.

As at Londonderry, there appears to have been an early ecclesiastical settlement on the site in the form of a monastery located where St. Finbar's Cathedral now stands. However, commercial life originated with Norse traders in the 9th Century and the site was later developed by the Anglo-Normans who built a walled town on a low island among the braided channels of the River Lee. Among the advantages which the insular site provided were protection, a ready water supply and sheltered moorings for ships. Until the 17th Century, Cork remained surrounded by its medieval walls but virtually nothing has survived from the medieval city. Cork has long possessed a strong tradition of successful trading and the commercial growth of the town underlay the considerable physical expansion and renewal of the 18th and early 19th Centuries. In the early 18th Century Cork contained 25 000 people, living in or close to the old city. In the course of the century new bridges were built over the channels of the Lee and more of the swamps were drained. The medieval plan was largely absorbed as wide streets were laid over the earlier waterways and extensive quays constructed for shipping. The cathedral of St. Finbar and other churches were rebuilt and impressive public buildings erected, including the Corn Market, Custom House and Mansion House. A local white limestone was used for the more substantial buildings in the town but many of the houses and more mundane structures are in red brick. By 1841 the population had increased to 80 720.

Plate 21a: Cork city and the quays along the River Lee. Note the dense terrace housing on the side of the valley.

Plate 21b: Aerial view of Londonderry. The original 17th Century walled town (centre left) is still a recognizable element of the city plan. See also Fig. 24.

In the post-Famine period the population of Cork grew relatively slowly until the closing decade of the 19th Century. However, housing spread around the edges of the town and on the steep banks of the Blackrock Valley to the north of the town. As in the 18th Century wealthy merchants continued to build substantial houses on the hills overlooking the Lee and along the banks of the upper harbour. New urban developments also took place in the lower harbour. A number of towns intimately associated with Cork grew up, of which Cobh and Passage West were the principal ones. The use of the harbour as a base for the Royal Navy during the Napoleonic wars first stimulated the rise of Cobh, but it came later to serve as a resort town for the inhabitants of Cork and in the 1860s began to develop as a major emigrant outlet and transatlantic port. In the 20th Century, Cobh has become a residential suburb of Cork and a minor industrial centre with a shipbuilding yard and steel works. Passage West developed as an outport of Cork but the town went into decline with the deepening of the river approaches to Cork in the latter half of the 19th Century.

In the present century, Cork has expanded considerably in area, population and industry. Population in the city and suburbs increased to about 107 000 by 1936 and since the 1950s there has been a particularly rapid growth. The abrupt rise from around 112 000 in 1951 to nearly 135 000 in 1971 is partly owing to outward movements of the city boundary but in the main reflects a real increase of population linked to growing employment opportunities in industry and services. As in Dublin, important extensions to the urban area have resulted from the Corporation's slum-clearance programmes. Many of the families transferred from slum areas in the central city have been rehoused in estates on the city boundaries. New housing estates have now spread widely around the city and although they lack architectural interest they are more spacious in their design and much more liberally provided with parks and open areas than is the cramped city core. Growth to the north and south is hindered by the physical configuration of the site, and the modern city is tending to spread itself from west to east. Future industrial growth in Cork Harbour may well act as a magnet to eastward expansion. Current planning policy aims to induce new developments away from the city environs, in villages and towns in the hinterland, such as Ballincollig, Carrigaline, Glanmire and Blarney.

The industrial life of the modern city of Cork is varied. Heavy industries, including the Haulbowline steel mill and the Rushbrooke shipyard at Cobh, the Whitegate oil refinery and Ringaskiddy chemical works are located in the pleasant rural landscapes of the outer harbour. The large, landscaped Marina industrial estate lies next to the inner port near the city centre, and several smaller industrial estates are located in the suburbs of the city. Manufacturing enterprises include brewing, distilling, food processing, fertilizers, car assembly, textiles, clothing and footwear, machinery and printing. There are numerous educational facilities, including the University which was established in 1849, and a significant tourist trade. The port of Cork remains a vital element in the city's economic life and a major element of the city's landscape. It has grown rapidly in the last two decades and normally handles over 5 million tons of trade per year, an amount roughly equivalent to the port of Dublin. Given careful planning the superb harbour facilities could be the background for substantial industrial growth in the future.

The outstanding characteristics of Cork derive from the relationship of the city to the distinctive topographic features of its site: the dense terrace developments on the steep south facing slope to the north of the city; the churches which overlook the city from rocky outcrops in the Blackpool valley and the wide estuary of the Lee and its channels which wind like canals through the city centre. Although it is not like Dublin and Limerick, a city with a dominant architectural style, Cork has inherited a rich and varied store of individual architecture from the 18th and 19th Centuries and, like many Irish towns, possesses a superb but largely unappreciated stock of urban "furniture" such as decorative iron railings and outstanding traditional shopfronts (Dovell, 1971). However, the built environment is now changing rapidly; many buildings have been allowed to decay probably beyond reclaim and modern office blocks and parking lots have made major inroads on the amenities of the central city. Furthermore, peripheral growth and the presence of the river channels and bridges have led to acute traffic problems in the city to which radical solutions may be necessary, involving further molestation of the urban fabric.

Belfast

Like all the major Irish cities, Belfast was established by foreign invaders, situated on sheltered tidal water and from its inception deeply involved with sea trade. The city is located at the head of a wide, deep and sheltered lough where the River Lagan reaches the shore. An Anglo-Norman castle had been built here, probably to control a strategic ford over the Lagan where a small tributary, the Farset, joins the main stream (Beal Feirste, "the mouth of the Farset"). This castle passed eventually into Irish hands and there does not appear to have been any sizable settlement nearby throughout the medieval period. With the plantation of Ulster, the sheltered lough was selected by the colonists as the site for a harbour to accommodate trade over the Irish Sea; in 1603 a small town, protected by the rebuilt castle, was created by Sir Arthur Chichester and it was made into a corporate borough. The settlement was partially enclosed by ramparts in 1642 and it became a garrison town of some importance. Throughout the 17th Century, however, the town functioned primarily as a market centre for the surrounding farmed areas and carried on a considerable overseas trade, chiefly in cattle. In the 18th Century it broadened its activities and became an important centre for the marketing of linen which was widely produced in the province on a domestic basis.

The Lagan Valley, or "corridor", has been of crucial importance to the growth of the city. With the clearance of the thick woodlands from the valley, Belfast Lough was made readily accessible to the Lough Neagh lowlands and the interior of the country. The role of the corridor was enhanced in the 18th Century by the building of the Lagan navigation (1756–63) and in the 19th Century by the railway, which followed the corridor when it first grew outwards from Belfast. With its nodality established, Belfast was well placed to prosper during the industrial and commercial growth of Ulster in the 19th Century. The town possessed proximity to Britain, port facilities and a nodal position in the province. But there was also a strong tradition of commercial enterprise in the town and, not least, labour was in plentiful supply as famine, poverty and enclosure schemes had forced thousands off the land and into the urban centres to seek employment.

Ulster's 19th Century industrial revolution was largely centred in Belfast and the town became something unique in Ireland, a large dynamic city dependent upon industry for its main livelihood, with its urban landscape similar in many respects to the major industrial conurbations of England and Scotland. Linen and cotton manufacturing organized in factories provided the initial basis of growth but this was supplemented during the 19th Century by engineering, shipbuilding, iron-working and rope-making. Raw materials such as coal and iron, upon which large-scale industrial growth was typically based, are conspicuously absent in Northern Ireland and they had to be imported. Hence, the large-scale improvement and expansion of the port at Belfast which commenced in 1839 was a precondition of sustained industrial growth. Population increase was very rapid. In 1800 there were around 20 000 people in the town and by 1900 Belfast had become a sprawling conurbation with about 350 000 people. The rapidity of the growth in population generated numerous acute problems. Water shortage was one problem, low lying areas were liable to flooding, and insanitary conditions in the rapidly erected and congested areas of working-class housing gave rise to disease and periodic epidemics. It was not until the 1880s that an effective sewerage system served the whole city. Physical expansion, in particular, was beset with many difficulties owing to the nature of the site, and early enlargement of the town was only made possible be extensive reclamation of the mud flats at the mouth of the Lagan. The enlarged port facilities and many of the important industries of 19th Century Belfast were located on this reclaimed land.

The late 18th and particularly the first half of the 19th Century was an important stage in the development of the city, a period of industrial pioneering and growing trade both with the hinterland and overseas, during which firm foundations were laid for future expansion. Increasing prosperity and confidence were reflected in the impressive buildings—mainly schools, colleges and public institutions—erected at this time; they included the Royal Belfast Academical Institution, the Presbyterian Assemblies College, the Queen's College, the Custom House, the Harbour Office, the Deaf and Dumb Institution, the Fever Hospital, the Charitable Institution and the Workhouse. These great institutions lie roughly in a "fringe belt" which marks the approximate boundary of Belfast's growth before the extensive and rapid expansion in the latter half of the 19th Century. Much of the street plan of the central city was delimited in the early 19th Century on the newly reclaimed sloblands; its regularity and spaciousness is clearly reminiscent of Georgian planning approaches and distinct from the cramped gridiron street plans which were built so extensively in the mid century and later to accommodate working-class houses. Unfortunately, the fine Georgian terraces around the White Linen Hall were demolished in the explosive growth of the Victorian city.

The main expansion took place in the second half of the last century and Belfast is thus essentially a Victorian city. This is in contrast to Dublin which grew relatively slowly after the important Georgian developments of the 18th and early 19th Century. The Victorian buildings which form the substance of Belfast fall into a few basic categories. Fine warehouses and ornate banks and office blocks are conspicuous in the central areas, reflecting the great industrial and commercial energies of the city at that time. In the centre and west of the city there are extensive areas of crowded terrace housing built for the most part on a gridiron plan around the factories and ship-building yards (Plate 22). A series of by-laws in 1847 laid down standards for housing, and the Health Acts of 1875 produced

Plate 22: Belfast. Aerial view of south-western portion of city (Donegal Road and Lisburn Road). Belfast City Hospital is in the foreground. The most striking feature is the highly regular pattern of 19th Century, working-class terrace housing. The M1 motorway is visible in the background.

further improvements. The rate of new house building in Belfast accelerated in the latter part of the century and many workers' houses were, because of their later date, of rather better standard than working-class houses in most of the great industrial areas of England. By the middle of the 19th Century the middle class had begun to abandon the congested centre of the city and to colonize the Malone area to the south and the northern shores of the Lough. Their substantial, sometimes palatial, residences and villas, built mostly in the 1870s and 1880s, are an outstanding feature of these areas, even if now generally converted to offices and hotels. Innumerable churches, built mainly in Gothic style, are another characteristic of the middle-class suburbs. Towards the end of the 19th Century Belfast's population temporarily surpassed that of Dublin in size. In 1888 the town was officially made a city and shortly afterwards boundary changes doubled its area. A wave of grandiose building expressed the growing sense of self-importance and prosperity. The new city hall on Donegall Square, built in 1906, is illustrative; so too is St. Anne's Cathedral begun in 1899.

The visual unity of 19th Century Belfast derives not only from the predominance of Victorian architectural and building styles but also from the building materials. Unlike the other Ulster towns Belfast is built largely in red brick, using the local glacial clays and the Triassic Keuper and Bunter marls which form the lower slopes of the Belfast Hills to the north and west of the city. Bunter sandstones, which underlie the greater part of the city, have provided building material for major buildings and city churches.

In the first decade of this century the expansion of Belfast slowed and the city created by explosive 19th Century growth remained relatively unchanged for several decades. It was a city with a high population density by the standards of any comparable English city and notably lacking in amenities such as parks and open spaces. During the 1914–8 war, building virtually ceased and in the depressed inter-war period house building developed slowly. There were no concerted planned efforts to re-house the crowded populations of inner Belfast by building extensive estates on the margins of the city, as was the pattern around many British cities. Most developments were on a small scale, undertaken by private enterprise and largely unplanned.

The greatest expansion of Belfast during the present century has taken place in the post-war period, almost all of it outside the borough where a rapidly advancing mass of houses has encroached on the countryside. Much of this suburban housing has been erected by local authorities or the

Northern Ireland Housing Trust and shows clearly the influence of planning. It is laid out in a much more spacious manner than the Victorian areas, with wider roads and more abundant green spaces, and numerous "neighbourhood units" have been formed by the provision of centralized facilities such as shops, recreational facilities and manufacturing employment. A number of old settlements, such as Glengormley and Dundonald, have been incorporated within the suburban spread. The broad and growing fringe of post-war development now accommodates some 250 000 people, as against 400 000 in the inner city where, moreover, numbers are now declining.

The city's post-war suburban spread has clearly been channelled by the dominant physical features of the region. Major growth has taken place northwards along the shores of the Lough, absorbing Glengormley, and southwards along the shore to Holywood; to the west the city has grown onto the lower slopes of the steep basaltic escarpment and further expansion in this direction is difficult and unlikely. There is a conspicuous tongue of expansion up the Lagan Valley where new development has been strongly encouraged by the railway and the M1 motorway. To the east, Belfast has spread on to the drumlin hills of Co. Down, most markedly in the Dundonald Gap. In this area exciting possibilities exist for the creation of a high-quality living environment which combines urban facilities and pleasant countryside.

Belfast, therefore, is a city which possesses two major zones, of different age and distinctive visual characteristics. There is, first, an older inner area, compact and densely populated with much outdated housing and obsolete infrastructure, which grew rapidly to its present form in the latter half of the 19th Century. Around this stretches a broad outer zone, mainly of post-war origin, which is more open and carefully planned. Throughout the inner and outer zones there is a marked degree of socio-economic segregation, associated with variations of urban landscape. The contrast between the extensive working-class and middle-class suburbs was particularly emphatic in the 19th Century city. Post-war housing on the periphery of the urban area exhibits a more complex mosaic of housing types, with private higher-income developments contiguous to local-authority housing estates for lower-income groups. Boal (1970), however, has identified a clear tendency for socio-economic status to increase and for population density to decline with increasing distance from the city centre; superimposed on these gradients are the socio-economic areas, which display a roughly sectoral arrangement. Within the western low-status sector there is a marked pattern of religious segregation into distinct protestant and catholic districts. The frontiers between catholic and protestant groupings are often sharp and there are few activity linkages between them. Religious differences, however, are not associated with important variations in the visual appearance of the urban landscape.

Industry and manufacturing assume a more prominent place in the urban landscape of Belfast than is the case in Dublin. The port and shipbuilding yards with their great derricks comprise one of the most outstanding elements in the landscape of the city, developed on reclaimed land at the mouth of the Lagan. Associated with the port area is a variety of industrial activity, including engineering and aircraft works, oil refining and chemical plants. Linen and associated manufacturing lies mainly in the west of the city, in the locations where it originally developed alongside the fast flowing streams from the basaltic escarpment, streams such as the Farset, Forth and Blackstaff, which provided power for the mills. In the post-war period, land-use pressures in the city and the government's policy of dispersing industry have encouraged the siting of new industries outside the city, and in the new suburbs a variety of industrial enterprises have been established on compact industrial estates, e.g. at Dunmurry, Castlereagh and Carnmoney.

The centre of the city is concerned largely with retail shopping, commerce and administration. After Belfast became the capital of Northern Ireland in 1920 the growth of government departments and administrative activities added an important new dimension to the life of the city. Since the Second World War the number and scale of government departments and of public and semi-public bodies has notably increased. These have located mainly in the central parts of the city where modern office blocks are now characteristic features. Belfast, however, lacks a distinct governmental and administrative quarter; government offices are widely scattered and Stormont, the seat of the Northern Ireland Parliament, is actually located at Dundonald outside the city boundary.

Londonderry

Londonderry, with a population of over 55 000, is the second city of Northern Ireland and sufficiently far from Belfast to have developed as a regional capital for the north-west, with a cathedral and university college. In 1613 the ancient site, which has a history stretching back to the 6th Century monastery of St. Columba, was granted as part of the Ulster plantation scheme to the livery companies of the city of London who erected a strong fortified town on the commanding hill, 119 ft (36·6 m) in height, which stands to the west of and overlooks a tidal meander of the River Foyle. The great walls of the settlement, with a circumference of over a mile, were completed in 1618 and within them a planned grid of streets was laid out converging on a central square or diamond. This original lay-out remains essentially unchanged (Fig. 24, Plate 21b).

Away from the old nucleus there is a general lack of any planned development and industrial and residential areas intermingle. Growth outside the city walls did not commence on any scale until the 18th Century when a bridge was built over the Foyle and the activities of the port were expanded, mainly through trade with North America. This extra-mural development included long, regular Georgian terraces— Queen Street and Clarendon Street among them—for the towns upper- and middle-class society. At the beginning of the 19th Century some of the finest public buildings were erected, such as the Bishop's Palace, Foyle College and the Deanery. The substantial growth of the town in the 19th Century was based on linen manufacturing and, in the second half of the century, on the successful shirt industry, shipbuilding and distilling. Sprawling working-class suburbs extended along both sides of the Foyle Valley in the Bogside, Waterside and Bishops' Gate areas. Much of the new growth was of a speculative nature and now forms the core of the city's housing problem. Within the newly developed areas the catholic and protestant populations were increasingly segregated.

The traditional clothing industries have experienced some decline in the present century and the commercial functions of the city were curtailed when the trade hinterland was truncated by the establishment of the Border. However, the city has continued to exert a considerable influence in Donegal despite the political frontier, and in the post-war period a new and broader industrial base has been established and the harbour facilities improved. Shirt and pyjama manufacturing is still dominant but other concerns include light engineering, chemicals and food processing. Although new industrial growths have been insufficient to offset the persistently high unemployment levels and high rates of outward migration from the city they have contributed to the considerable post-war expansion of the residential suburbs which has involved both local authority estates and private housing. The original walled settlement, however, has remained the commercial and social focus of the city and population density within the built-up area, which exceeds 25 persons per acre, has remained at a 19th Century level. Population growth is likely to be strong owing to the birth rate in the city which is substantially in excess of the already high Northern Ireland rate.

Consolidated Bibliography

Introduction and Chapter 1

Andrews, J. H., "A Geographer's View of Irish History", in (eds) Moody, T. W. and Martin, F. X., *The Course of Irish History*, (1967), 17–29.

Braudel, F., *La Méditerranée et le monde Méditerranéen à l'Epoque de Philippe II*, 2 vols (Paris, 1966).

Evans, E. E., *Mourne Country: Landscape and Life in South Down*, (1951).

Evans, E. E., *Irish Folk Ways*, (1957).

Evans, E. E., *The Personality of Ireland. Habitat, Heritage and History*, (1973).

Wagner, P. L., *The Human Use of the Earth*, (1961).

Physiography, Glaciation, Climate and Soils

Charlesworth, J. K., *The Geology of Ireland: An Introduction*, (1966).

Cruickshank, J. G., "Soils and Pedogenesis in the North of Ireland", in (eds) Stephens, N. and Glasscock, R. E., *Irish Geographical Studies*, (1970), 89–104.

Gillmor, D., *A Systematic Geography of Ireland*, (1971).

Guerrini, V. H., "Evaporation and Transpiration in the Irish Climate", *Irish Met. Service*, Technical Note 14, (1953).

Haughton, J. P., "Physiography and Climate", in (eds) Meenan, J. and Webb, D. A., *A View of Ireland*, (1957), 1–14.

Mitchell, F., *The Irish Landscape*, (1976).

Rohan, P. K., *The Climate of Ireland*, (Dublin, 1975).

Ryan, P., "The Soils of Ireland", *Irish Forestry*, **20** (1963), 2–16.

Synge, F. M. and Stephens, N., "The Quaternary period in Ireland—an Assessment", *Irish Geography*, 4 (1960), 121–30.

Whittow, J. B., *Geology and Scenery in Ireland*, (1974).

Williams, P. W., "Limestone Morphology in Ireland", in (eds) Stephens, N. and Glasscock, R. E., *Irish Geographical Studies*, (1970), 105–124.

Vegetation

Andrews, J. H., "Notes on the Historical Geography of the Irish Iron Industry", *Irish Geography*, **3**, No. 3 (1956), 139–49.

L

Bower, M. M., "The Cause of Erosion in Blanket Peat Bogs", *Scottish Geographical Magazine*, **78**, No. 1 (April, 1962), 33–43.

Case, H. J., et al., "Land Use in Goodland Townland, Co, Antrim, from Neolithic times until today", *Jnl. Roy. Soc. Antiq. Ireland*, **99**, Pt 1 (1969), 39–53.

Eogan, G., "A Neolithic Habitation-site and Megalithic Tomb in Townleyhall Townland, Co. Louth", *Jnl. Roy. Soc. Antiq. Ireland*, 93, Pt 1 (1963), 37–81.

Jessen, K., "Studies in Late Quaternary Deposits and Flora History of Ireland", *Proc. Roy. Irish Acad.*, **53B** (1951), 111–206.

Leister, I., "Wald und Forst in Irland", *Erdkunde*, **XVII**, Heft 1/2 (Jan. 1963), 58–76.

McCracken, E., "The Woodlands of Ireland", *Irish Hist. Studies*, **XI** (1958–59), 271–296.

McCracken, E., "Irish Nurserymen and Seedsmen, 1740–1800", *Quarterly Jnl. of Forestry*, (April, 1965), 131–9.

Mitchell, G. F., "The Relative Ages of Archaeological Objects recently found in Bogs in Ireland", *Proc. Roy. Irish Acad.*, **50C** (1945), 1–19.

Mitchell, G. F., "The Giant Deer in Ireland", *Proc. Roy. Irish Acad.*, **52B** (1949), 291–314.

Mitchell, G. F., "Post-Boreal Pollen Diagrams from Irish Raised Bogs", *Proc. Roy. Irish Acad.*, **57B** (1956), 185–251.

Mitchell, G. F., "Littleton Bog, Tipperary: an Irish Vegetational Record", *Geol. Soc. Amer., Special paper*, No. 84 (1965), 1–16.

Mitchell, G. F., "Flint Flake, probably of Palaeolithic age, from Mell townland, near Drogheda, Co. Louth, Ireland", *Jnl. Roy. Soc. Antiq. Ireland*, **102**, Pt 2 (1974), 174–177.

Moore, J. J., Dowding, P., and Healy, B., "Glenamoy, Ireland", *Ecol. Bull.* (Stockholm), **20** (1975), 321–343.

Osvald, H., "Notes on the Vegetation of British and Irish mosses", *Acta phytogeogr. Suec.*, **26** (1949).

O'Sullivan, A. M., "A Phyto-sociological Survey of Irish grassland (preliminary results)", *Ber. Internat. Sympos. Stolzenan/Weser* (1963), 223–30.

Smith, A. G., "Late- and Post-Glacial Vegetational and Climatic History of Ireland: A Review", in (eds) Stephens, N. and Glasscock, R. E., *Irish Geographical Studies*, (1970), 65–88.

Smith, A. G. and Pilcher, J. R., "Pollen Analysis and Radiocarbon Dating of Deposits at Slieve Gullion Passage Grave, Co. Armagh", *Ulster Jnl. Archaeol.*, **35** (1972), 17–21.

Walker, D. and West, R. G., (eds) *Studies in the Vegetational History of the British Isles*, (1970).

Watts, W. A., "Post-Atlantic Forests in Ireland", *Procs. Linn. Soc. Lond.*, **172**, 1959–60, Pt 1 (March, 1961), 33–38.

Watts, W. A., "Late-glacial Pollen Zones in Western Ireland", *Irish Geography*, **4** (1963), 367–76.

Webb, D. A., "Vegetation and Flora", in (eds) Meenan, J. and Webb, D. A., *A View of Ireland*, (1957), 40–61.

Webb, D. A., *An Irish Flora*, 5th edition (1967).

Chapters 2, 3 and 4

General References

An Archaeological Survey of County Down, H.M.S.O. (Belfast, 1966).

Ancient Monuments in State Charge, 5th edition, H.M.S.O. (Belfast, 1966).

Evans, E. E., *Irish Folk Ways*, (1957), Chapters 1 and 2.

Evans, E. E., "Ireland and Atlantic Europe", *Geographische Zeitschrift*, **52**, 3 Heft (1964), 224–241.

Evans, E. E., "Prehistoric Geography", Chapter 10 in (eds) Watson J. W. and Sissons, J. B. *The British Isles*, (1964).

Evans, E. E., *Prehistoric and Early Christian Ireland, a Guide*, (1966).

Harbison, P., *The Archaeology of Ireland*, (1976).

Herity, M. and Eogan, G., *Ireland in Prehistory*, (1977).

National Monuments of Ireland, Bord Failte Eireann, (Dublin, 1964).

Norman, E. R. and St. Joseph, J. K. S., *The Early Development of Irish Society*, (1969).

Ó Ríordáin, S. P., "The Prehistoric Period", in (eds) Meenan, J. and Webb, D. A., *A View of Ireland*, (1957), 149–163.

Ó Ríordáin, S. P., *Antiquities of the Irish Countryside*, (1964).

Raftery, J., *Prehistoric Ireland*, (1951).

Raftery, J., "A Matter of Time", *Jnl. Roy. Soc. Antiq. Ireland*, **93** (1963), 101–14.

Renfrew, C., *British Prehistory: A New Outline*, (1974).

Simpson, D. D. A., (ed.) *Economy and Settlement in Neolithic and Early Bronze Age Britain and Europe*, (Leicester U.P., 1971).

Mesolithic

Addyman, P. V. and Vernon, P. D., "A Beach Pebble Industry from Dunaff Bay, Inishowen, Co. Donegal", *Ulster Jnl. Archaeol.*, **29** (1966), 6–15.

Coleman, J. C., "The Kitchen Middens of Cork Harbour", *Jnl. Cork Hist. Archaeol. Soc.*, **43**, 157 (1938), 39–44.

Collins, A. E. P., "Excavations in the Sandhills at Dundrum, 1950–1", *Ulster Jnl. Archaeol.*, **15** (1952), 25.

Herity, M., "The Early Prehistoric Period around the Irish Sea", *Proc. Camb. Archaeol. Assoc.*, (1970), 29–37.

Hewson, L. M., "Notes on Irish Sandhills", *Jnl. Roy. Soc. Antiq. Ireland*, **65** (1935), 231; **66** (1936), 154 and **68** (1938), 69.

Liversage, G. D., "A Note on the Occurrence of Larnian Flints on the Leinster Coast", *Jnl. Roy. Soc. Antiq. Ireland*, **41** (1961), 109–16.

Liversage, G. D., "Excavations at Dalkey Island, Co. Dublin, 1956–59", *Proc. Roy. Irish Acad.*, **66C** (1968), 53–233.

Mitchell, G. F., "An Early Kitchen-midden in County Louth", *Co. Louth Archaeol. Jnl.*, **11** (1947), 169–174.

Mitchell, G. F., "Further Early Kitchen-middens in County Louth", *Co. Louth Archaeol. Jnl.*, **12** (1949), 14–20.

Mitchell, G. F., "Some Chronological Implications of the Irish Mesolithic", *Ulster Jnl. Archaeol.*, **33** (1970), 3–13.

Mitchell, G. F., "The Larnian Culture: A Minimal View", *Proc. Prehist. Soc.*, **37** (1971), 274–283.

Morrison, M. E. S., "The Palynology of Ringneill Quay, a new Mesolithic Site in Co. Down, Northern Ireland", *Proc. Roy. Irish Acad.*, **61C** (1961), 171–182.

Movius, H. L., *The Irish Stone Age: Its Chronology, Development and Relationships*, (Cambridge, 1942).

Movius, H. L., "Curran Point, Larne, Country Antrim: The Type Site of the Irish Mesolithic", *Proc. Roy. Irish Acad.*, **56C** (1953), 1–195.

O'Kelly, M. J., "A Shell-midden at Carrigtohill, Co. Cork", *Jnl. Cork Hist. Archaeol. Soc.*, **60**, 191 (1955), 28–32.

O'Kelly, M. J., "An Island Settlement at Beginish, Co. Kerry", *Proc. Roy. Irish Acad.*, **57C** (1956), 159–194.

Raftery, J., "The Bann Flake outside the Bann Valley", *Jnl. Roy. Soc. Antiq. Ireland*, **74** (1944), 155–159.

Stephens, N. and Collins, A. E. P., "The Quaternary Deposits at Ringneill Quay and Ardmillan, Co. Down", *Proc. Roy. Irish Acad.*, **61C** (1960), 41–72.

Troels-Smith, J., "Ertebølle Culture. Ten Years Excavations in Aamosen Bog", *Arb. Nordiske Old. og Hist.*, (1953).

Walker, D., and West, R. G., (eds) *Studies in the Vegetational History of the British Isles*, (1970), 81–96.

Woodman, P. C., "Mount Sandel: Mesolithic Settlement", *Excavations*, 1973, (ed.) Delaney, T. G. (Ulster Museum, 1974), 9.

Woodman, P. C., "Settlement Patterns of the Irish Mesolithic", *Ulster Jnl. Archaeol.*, **36** and **37** (1973–4), 1–16.

Woodman, P. C., "The Chronological Position of the Latest Phases of the Larnian", *Proc. Roy. Irish Acad.*, **74C** (1974), 237–58.

Neolithic

ApSimon, A. M., "An Early Neolithic House in Co. Tyrone", *Jnl. Roy. Soc. Antiq. Ireland*, **99** (1969), 165–8.

Barber, J., "The Orientation of the Recumbent Stone-circles of the South-West of Ireland", *Jnl. Kerry Archaeol. Hist. Soc.*, **6** (1973), 26–39.

Case, H., "Settlement-patterns in the North Irish Neolithic", *Ulster Jnl. Archaeol.*, **32** (1969), 3–27.

Collins, E. A. P., "A Re-examination of the Clyde-Carlingford Tombs", in *Megalithic Graves and Ritual*, (eds) Daniel, G. and Kjaerum, P., (Jutland Archaeol. Soc., 1973), 93–103.

Davies, O. and Evans, E. E., "Irish Court Cairns", *Ulster Jnl. Archaeol.*, **24/5** (1961/2), 2–7.

De Valera, R., "The Court Cairns of Ireland", *Proc. Roy. Irish Acad.*, **60C** (1960), 9–140.

De Valera, R. and Ó Nualláin, S., *Survey of the Megalithic Tombs of Ireland*, Vols 1–3, (Dublin, 1961, 1964, 1971).

Eogan, G., "A Neolithic Habitation-site and Megalithic Tomb in Townleyhall Townland, Co. Louth", *Jnl. Roy. Soc. Antiq. Ireland*, **93** (1963), 37–81.

Eogan, G., "Excavations at Knowth, Co. Meath, 1962–1965", *Proc. Roy. Irish Acad.*, **67C** (1968), 299–400.

Evans, E. E., *Lyles Hill: A Late Neolithic Site in County Antrim*, (H.M.S.O., 1953).

Herity, M., "Finds from Portal Dolmens", *Jnl. Roy. Soc. Antiq. Ireland*, **94** (1964), 133–43.

Herity, M., *Irish Passage Graves*, (1974).

Liversage, G. D., "Excavations at Dalkey Island, Co. Dublin, 1956–59", *Proc. Roy. Irish Acad.*, **66C** (1968), 52–233.

Lynch, F., "The Megalithic Tombs of North Wales", in (ed.) Powell, T. G. E., *Megalithic Enquiries in the West of Britain* (1969), 107–174.

O'Kelly, C., *Newgrange*, (Wexford, 1967).

O'Kelly, M. J., "Further Radiocarbon Dates from Newgrange, Co. Meath, Ireland", *Antiquity*, **46** (1972), 226–27.

Ó Nualláin, S., "A Neolithic House at Ballyglass near Ballycastle, Co. Mayo", *Jnl. Roy. Soc. Antiq. Ireland*, **102** (1972), 49–57.

Ó Ríordáin, S. P., "Lough Gur Excavations: Neolithic and Bronze Age Houses on Knockadoon", *Proc. Roy. Irish Acad.*, **56C** (1954), 297–459.

Ó Ríordáin, S. P. and Daniel, G., *Newgrange*, (1964).

Patrick, J., "Midwinter Sunrise at Newgrange", *Nature*, 249 (June 7, 1974), 517–19.

Powell, T. G. G., (ed.) *Megalithic Enquiries in the West of Britain*, (1969). Especially article on "The Neolithic in the West of Europe and Megalithic Sepulture: Some Points and Problems".

Smith, A. G. and Pilcher, J. R., "Pollen Analysis and Radio-carbon Dating of Deposits at Slieve-Gullion Passage Grave, Co. Armagh", *Ulster Jnl. Archaeol.*, **35** (1972), 17–21.

Smith, A. G. and Willis, E. H., "Radio-carbon Dating of the Fallahogy Landnam Phase", *Ulster Jnl. Archaeol.*, **5**, 24/5 (1961/62), 16–24.

Watson, E., "Geographical Factors in the Neolithic Colonisation of North-East Ireland", *Trans. Inst. Brit. Geog.*, **22** (1956), 117–138.

Watts, W. A., "C-14 Dating and the Neolithic in Ireland", *Antiquity*, **24** (1960), 111–116.

Watts, W. A., "Late-glacial Pollen Zones in Western Ireland", *Irish Geography*, **4** (1963), 367–76.

Bronze Age

Allan, W., "Ecology, Techniques and Settlement patterns", in ,eds) Ucko, P. J., Iringham, R. and Dimbleby, G. W., *Man, Settlement and Urbanism*, (1972), 211–226.

ApSimon, A. M., "The Earlier Bronze Age in the North of Ireland", *Ulster Jnl. Archaeol.*, **32** (1969), 28–72.

Bourke, A., "Grass and the Irish Climate", *Procs. Grass Conservation Conference*, An Foras Taluntais (Dublin, 1963), 1–22.

Case, H., "Were the Beaker-People the first metallurgists in Ireland?", *Palaeohistoria*, **12** (1966), 141–177.

Case, H., "Settlement-Patterns in the North Irish Neolithic", *Ulster Jnl. Archaeol.*, **32** (1969), 3–27.

Case, H., *et al.*, "Land Use in Goodland Townland, Co. Antrim, from Neolithic times until today", *Jnl. Roy. Soc. Antiq. Ireland*, **99**, Pt 1 (1969), 39–53.

Caulfield, S., "Agriculture and Settlement in ancient Mayo", *Archaeology in Ireland Today*. Supplement to *The Irish Times*, (April 23, 1974).

Dehn, W., " 'Transhumance' in der westlichen Spathallstattkultur?", *Archäologisches Korrespondenzblatt*, **2** (1972), 125–127.

Eogan, G., "The Later Bronze Age in Ireland in the light of recent research", *Proc. Preh. Soc.*, **30** (1964), 268–351.

Eogan, G., "Some Observations on the Middle Bronze Age", *Jnl. Roy. Soc. Antiq. Ireland*, **92**, Pt 1 (1962), 45–60.

Fleming, A., "The Genesis of Pastoralism in European Prehistory", *World Archaeology*, **4** (1972), 179–91.

Harris, D. R., "Swidden Systems and Settlement", in Ucko, P. J. *et al.*, *Man, Settlement and Urbanism*, op. cit. (1972), 245–2.

Harbison, P., "Mining and Metallurgy in Early Bronze Age Ireland", *N. Munster Antiq. Jnl.*, **10** (1966), 3–11.

Harbison, P., "The Daggers and the Halberds of the Early Bronze Age in Ireland", and "The Axes of the Early Bronze Age in Ireland", *Prähistorische Bronzefunde*, Abt. VI, Band 1 and Abt. IX, Band 1 (Munich, 1969).

Harbison, P., "The Relative Chronology of Irish Early Bronze Age Pottery", *Jnl. Roy. Soc. Antiq. Ireland*, **99**, Pt 1 (1969), 63–82.

Harbison, P., "Hartmann's Gold Analyses: A Comment", *Jnl. Roy. Soc. Antiq. Ireland*, **101**, Pt 2, (1971), 159–160.

Harbison, P., "The Earlier Bronze Age in Ireland", *Jnl. Roy. Soc. Antiq. Ireland*, **103** (1973), 93–152.

Hicks, S. P., "The Impact of Man on the East Moor of Derbyshire from Mesolithic times", *Archaeol. Jnl.*, **129** (1972–3), 1–21.

Hencken, H. O., "Ballinderry Crannog, No. 2", *Proc. Roy. Irish Acad.*, **47C** (1942), 1–76.

Herity, M., "Prehistoric Fields in Ireland", *Irish University Review*, (Spring, 1971), 258–265.

Macalister, R. A. S., Armstrong, E. C. R., and Praeger, R. L., "Report on the Excavation of Bronze Age Cairns on Carrowkeel Mountain", *Proc. Roy. Irish Acad.*, **29C** (1912), 311.

Mitchell, G. F., "Post-Boreal Pollen Diagrams for Irish Raised-bogs", *Proc. Roy. Irish Acad.*, **57B** (1954–6), 185–251.

Mitchell, G. F., "A Pollen-diagram from Lough Gur, County Limerick", *Proc. Roy. Irish Acad.*, **56C** (1959), 481–88.

Mitchell, G. F., "Littleton Bog, Tipperary: An Irish Agricultural Record", *Jnl. Roy. Soc. Antiq. Ireland*, **95** (1965), 121–132.

O'Sullivan, A. M., "A Phyto-sociological survey of Irish grassland", *Ber. Internat. Sympos. Stolzenan/Weser*, (1963), 223–30.

Pilcher, J. R., "Archaeology, Palaeocology and C-14 dating of the Beaghmore Stone-Circle site", *Ulster Jnl. Archaeol.*, **32** (1969), 73–91.

Raftery, J., "Irish Prehistoric Gold Objects: New Light on the Source of the Metal", *Jnl. Roy. Soc. Antiq. Ireland*, **101**, Pt 1 (1971), 101–105.

Rynne, E., and O hEailidhe, P., "A Group of Prehistoric Sites at Piperstown, Co. Dublin", *Proc. Roy. Irish Acad.*, **64C** (1965), 61–84.

Waddell, J., "Irish Bronze Age Cists: A Survey", *Jnl. Roy. Soc. Antiq. Ireland*, **100**, Pt 1 (1970), 91–139.

Waddell, J., "On Some Aspects of the Late Neolithic and Early Bronze Age in Ireland", *Irish Arch. Research Forum*, **1**, 1 (1974), 32–38.

Wijngaarden-Bakker, L. H. Van, "The Animal Remains from the Beaker Settlement at Newgrange, Co. Meath: First Report", *Proc. Roy. Irish Acad.*, **74C** (1974), 313–383.

Wolf, E. R., *Peasants*, (1966).

The Iron Age, Early Christian Period, Vikings

Bateson, J. D., "Roman Material from Ireland: a Reconsideration", *Proc. Roy. Irish Acad.*, **73** (1973), 21–97.

Bernard, W., "Exploration and Restoration of the Ruin of the Grianan of Aileach", *Proc. Roy. Irish Acad.*, **1** (1879), 417.

Bersu, G., "The Rath in Townland Lissue, County Antrim", *Ulster Jnl. Archaeol.*, **10** (1947), 30–58.

Bieler, L., *Ireland, Harbinger of the Middle Ages*, (1963).

Binchy, D. A., "The Passing of the Old Order", in *Procs. International Congress of Celtic Studies*, (Dublin, 1962), 119–132.

Bowen, E. G., *Ancient Fields*, (1961).

Bugge, A., *Contributions to the History of the Norsemen in Ireland*, (Christiania, 1900).

Byrne, F. J., *The rise of the Ui Neill and the High-Kingship of Ireland*, O'Donnell Lecture (1970).

Campbell, Å., "Irish Fields and Houses", *Bealoideas*, 5 (1935), 57–74.

Chadwick, N. K., *The Age of the Saints in the Early Celtic Church*, (1961).

Childe, G., "A Promontory Fort on the Antrim Coast", *Antiq. Jnl.*, 16 (1936), 179.

Collins, A. E. P., "Excavations at Dressogagh Rath, Co. Antrim", *Ulster Jnl. Archaeol.*, 19 (1966), 217.

Davies, O., "Ancient Field-systems and the Date of Formation of the Peat", *Ulster Jnl. Archaeol.*, 2 (1939), 61.

Davies, O., "Excavations at Lissachiggel", *Jnl. Co. Louth Archaeol. Soc.*, (1939–40), 209–43.

Davies, O., "Excavations on the Dorsey and the Black Pig's Dykes", *Ulster Jnl. Archaeol.*, 3 (1940), 31.

Davies, O., "The Twomile Stone, a Prehistoric Community in Co. Donegal", *Jnl. Roy. Soc. Antiq. Ireland*, 72 (1942), 98–105.

de Paor, L., "The Age of the Viking Wars", in (eds) Moody, T. W. and Martin, F. X. *The Course of Irish History*, (1967), 91–106.

de Paor, M. and L., *Early Christian Ireland*, (1958; revised, 1964).

Dillon, M., (ed.) *Early Irish Society*, (1954).

Dillon, M. and Chadwick, N., *The Celtic Realms*, (1965).

Dolley, M., *Viking Coins of the Danelaw and of Dublin*, British Museum (1965).

Evans, E. E., "Some Survivals of the Irish Open-Field System", *Geography*, 24 (1939), 24–36.

Evans, E. E., *Irish Folk Ways*, (1957).

Evans, E. E. and Gaffikin, M., "Megaliths and Raths", *Irish Naturalists Journal*, 5 (1935), 250.

Filip, J., *Celtic Civilisation and its Heritage*, (Prague, 1960).

Foote, P. G. and Wilson, D. M., *The Viking Achievement*, (1970).

Hanson, R. P. C., *Saint Patrick: his Origins and Career*, (1968).

Harbison, P., "The Old Irish Chariot", *Antiquity*, 45 (1971), 171–77.

Harper, A. E. T., "The Excavation of a Rath in Mullaghbane Townland, Co. Tyrone", *Ulster Jnl. Archaeol.*, 35 (1973), 37–44.

Hayes-McCoy G. A., *Ulster and other Irish Maps*, (1964).

Hencken, H. O'Neill, *Cathercommaun: A Stone Fort in Co. Clare*, Roy. Soc. Antiq. Ireland, Extra Volume (1938).

Hencken, H. O'Neill, "Ballinderry Crannog, No. 1". *Proc. Roy. Irish Acad.*, 43C (1953–7), 103–239.

Hencken, H. O'Neill, "Ballinderry Crannog, No. 2", *Proc. Roy. Irish Acad.*, 47C (1941–2), 1–76.

Hencken, H. O'Neill, "Lagore Crannog: An Irish Royal Residence of the 7th. to

10th. Centuries, A.D.'', *Proc. Roy. Irish Acad.*, **53C** (1950–1), 1–247.

Henry, F., *Early Christian Irish Art*, (1954).

Hughes, K., *The Church in Early Irish History*, (1966).

Jackson, K. H., "The Celtic Aftermath in the Islands", in (ed.) Raftery, J., *The Celts*, (Cork, 1964), 73–83.

Jackson, K. H., *The Oldest Irish Tradition: A Window on the Iron Age*, Cambridge (1964).

Johnson, J. H., "Studies of Irish Rural Settlement", *Geographical Review*, **48** (1958), 554–66.

Jones, G. R. J., Contribution to "Rural Settlement in Ireland and Western Britain", (ed.) Evans, E. E., *Adv. Science*, **60** (March, 1959), 338–42.

Leask, H. G., *Irish Churches and Monastic Buildings*, 3 vols, (Dundalk, 1955; 1958; 1960).

Lucas, A. T., "Plundering of Churches in Ireland", in (ed.) Rynne, E., *North Munster Studies*, (Limerick, 1967), 172–229.

Lucas, A. T., "Irish Ploughing Practices", *Tools and Tillage*, Pt 1., Vol. 2, 1 (1972), 52–62. and Pt 2., Vol. 2, 2(1973), 67–83.

MacAirt, S., "Co. Armagh, Toponymy and History", *Proc. Irish Catholic Histor. Comm.*, (1955), 1–5.

Macneill, M., *The Festival of Lughnasa*, (1962).

McCourt, D., "The Dynamic Quality of Irish Rural Settlement", in (eds) Buchanan, R., *et al. Man and his Habitat*, (1971), 126–64.

Norman, E. R. and St. Joseph, J. K. S., *The Early Development of Irish Society*, (1969). Especially Chapters 3, 4 and 5.

Ó Fiaich, T., "The Beginnings of Christianity (5th and 6th Centuries)", in (eds) Moody, T. W. and Martin, F. X., *The Course of Irish History*, (1967), 61–75.

O'Kelly, M. J., "An Early Bronze Age Ring-fort at Carrigillihy, Co. Cork", *Jnl. Cork Hist. Archaeol. Soc.*, **56**, 184 (1951), 69–86.

O'Kelly, M. J., "Three Promontory Forts in Co. Cork", *Proc. Roy. Irish Acad.*, **55C** (1952), 25–59.

O'Kelly, M. J., "An Island Settlement at Beginish, Co. Kerry", *Proc. Roy. Irish Acad.*, **57C** (1956), 159–194.

O'Kelly, M. J., "Two Ring-forts at Garryduff, Co. Cork", *Proc. Roy. Irish Acad.*, **63C** (1963), 17–125.

O'Kelly, M. J., "Problems of Irish Ring-forts", in (ed.) Moore, D., *The Irish Sea Province in Archaeology and History*, (1970), 50–4.

Ó Ríordáin, S. P., "Roman Material in Ireland", *Proc. Roy. Irish Acad.*, **51C** (1947), 35–82.

Ó Ríordáin, S. P., "Excavations at Cush, Co. Limerick", *Proc. Roy. Irish Acad.*, **45C** (1940), 83–181.

Ó Ríordáin, S. P. and Hartnett, P. J., "The Excavation of Ballycotton Fort, Co. Cork", *Proc. Roy. Irish Acad.*, **49C** (1943).

Ó Ríordáin, S. P. and MacDermott, A., "The Excavation of a Ring-fort at

Letterkeen, Co. Cork'', *Proc. Roy. Irish Acad.*, **54C** (1952), 89–119.

Palmer, L. R., *Achaeans and Indo-Europeans*, (1953).

Pounds, N., ''The Urbanization of the Classical World'', *Ann. Ass. Amer. Geog.*, **59** (1969), 135–57.

Powell, T. G. E., *The Celts*, (1958).

Price, L., ''A Note on the Use of the word 'Baile' in Place-names'', *Celtica*, **6** (1963), 119–126.

Proudfoot, V. B., Contribution to ''Rural Settlement in Ireland and Western Britain'', (ed.) Evans, E. E., *Adv. Science*, **60** (March, 1959), 336–338.

Proudfoot, V. B., ''Clachans in Ireland'', *Gwerin*, **2** (1959), 110–122.

Proudfoot, V. B., ''The Economy of the Irish Rath'', *Medieval Archaeol.*, **5** (1961), 94–122.

Raftery, B., ''Freestone Hill, Co. Kilkenny: An Iron Age Hill-fort and Bronze Age Cairn'', *Proc. Roy. Irish Acad.*, **68C** (1969), 1–108.

Raftery, B., ''Rathgall, Co. Wicklow: 1970 excavations'', *Antiquity*, **45** (1971), 296–8.

Raftery, B., '' Irish Hill-forts'', in *The Iron Age in the Irish Sea Province*, C. B. A. Research Report, **9** (1972), 37–55.

Raftery, J., (ed.) *The Celts*, (Cork, 1964).

Ross, A., *Everyday Life of the Pagan Celts*, (1970).

Ryan, J., *Irish Monasticism, Origins and Early Development*, (1931).

Rynne, E., ''The Introduction of La Tène into Ireland'', in G. Bersu (ed.) *Bericht über den V. Internationalen Kongress für Vor-und Frühgeschichte, Hamburg 1958*, (Berlin, 1961) 705–9.

Shetelig, H., (ed.), *Viking Antiquities in Great Britain and Ireland*, 6 vols, (Oslo, 1940–54).

Wagner, H., ''The Origin of the Celts'', *Philol. Trans.*, (1969), 206.

Wailes, B., ''Dun Ailinne—a Royal Site of the Iron Age'', in *Archaeology in Ireland Today. Irish Times*, (1974).

Wainwright, F. T., ''The Scandinavians in Lancashire'', *Trans. Lancs. Chesh. Antiq. Soc.*, **LVIII** (1945–6), 71–116.

Walsh, A., *Scandinavian Relations with Ireland during the Viking Period*, (Dublin, 1922).

Waterman, D. M., ''Excavations at Duneight, Co. Down'', *Ulster Jnl. Archaeol.*, **26** (1963), 55–78.

Waterman, D. M., Reported in *Bulletin of the Group for the Study of Irish Historic Settlement*, **1** (1970), 13.

Waterman, D. M., ''A Group of Raths at Ballypalady, Co. Antrim'', *Ulster Jnl. Archaeol.*, **35** (1972), 25–36.

Wood-Martin, W. G., *The Lake-Dwellings of Ireland*, (Dublin, 1886).

Young, J. I., ''A Note on the Norse Occupation of Ireland'', *History*, **35** (1950).

Chapter 5

The Middle Ages

Aalen, F. H. A., "Clochans as Transhumance Dwellings in the Dingle Peninsula, Co. Kerry", *Jnl. Roy. Soc. Antiq. Ireland*, **94** (1964), 39–45.

Beresford, M. and Hurst, J. G., *Deserted Medieval Villages,* (1971).

Brooks, E. St. J., "Fourteenth Century Monastic Estates in Meath", *Jnl. Roy. Soc. Antiq. Ireland*, **83** (1953), 140–149.

Carville, G., *The Heritage of Holy Cross*, (Belfast, 1973).

Curtis, E., "Rental of the Manor of Lisronagh", *Proc. Roy. Irish Acad.*, **43C** (1935–7), 41–76.

Curtis, E., *History of Medieval Ireland from 1086 to 1513*, 2nd edition (London, 1938).

Danaher, K., "Representation of Houses on some Irish Maps of c. 1600", in (ed.) Jenkins, G., *Studies in Folk Life*, (1969), 92–103.

Emery, F., "Moated Settlements in England", *Geography*, **47** (1962), 378–88.

Fitzgerald, W., *The Historical Geography of Early Ireland*, The Geographical Teacher, Supplement No. 1, (1925).

Giraldus Cambrensis, *Topography of Ireland*, Translated by O'Meara, J. J., (Dundalk, 1951).

Glasscock, R. E., "Moated Sites and Deserted Boroughs and Villages; Two Neglected Aspects of Anglo-Norman Settlement in Ireland", in (eds) Glasscock, R. E. and Stephens, N., *Irish Geographical Studies*, (1970), 162–177.

Glasscock, R. E., "Deserted Villages in Ireland", in (eds) Beresford, M. W. and Hurst, J. G., *Deserted Medieval Villages*, (1971).

Glasscock, R. E., "Mottes in Ireland", *Chateau-Gaillard 7*, (Caen, 1975), 95–110.

Gwynn, A., "The Black Death in Ireland", *Studies*, **24** (1935), 25–42.

Gwynn, A., and Gleeson, D. F., *A History of the Diocese of Killaloe*, (Dublin, 1962).

Hadden, G., "Some Earthworks in Co. Wexford", *Jnl. Cork Hist. and Arch. Soc.*, **69** (1964), 118–122.

Henry, F., "Early Monasteries, Beehive Huts and Dry-stone Houses in the Neighbourhood of Cahirciveen and Waterville (Co. Kerry)", *Proc. Roy. Irish Acad.*, **58C** (1957), 45–166.

Lawlor, H. C., "Mote and Mote-and-Bailey Castles in de Courcy's Principality of Ulster", (in 2 parts) *Ulster Jnl. Archaeol.*, **1**, 2 (1938), 155–164 and 2, 1 (1939), 46–54.

Leask, H. G., *Irish Castles and Castellated Houses*, (Dundalk, 1941).

Lydon, J. F., "The Bruce Invasion of Ireland", *Historical Studies*, 4 (1963), 111–25.

Lydon, J. F., *Ireland in the Later Middle Ages*, (1973).

Macalister, R. A. S., "On an Ancient Settlement in the south-west of Corkaguiney, Co. Kerry", *Trans. Roy. Irish Acad.*, **31** (1899).

Mayhew, A., *Rural Settlement and Farming in Germany*, (1973).

Mitchell, G. F., "Littleton Bog, Tipperary: An Irish Agricultural Record", *Jnl. Roy. Soc. Antiq. Ireland*, **95** (1965), 121–132.

Nichols, K., *Gaelic and Gaelicised Ireland in the Middle Ages*, (1972).

O Conbhui, C., "The Lands of St. Mary's Abbey, Dublin", *Proc. Roy. Irish Acad.*, **62C** (1962), 21–86.

O'Loan, J., "The Manor of Cloncurry Co. Kildare, and the Feudal System of Land Tenure in Ireland", *Jnl. Dept. Agric.*, **58** (1961), 14–36.

Orpen, G. H., "Motes and Norman Castles in Ireland", *Jnl. Roy. Soc. Antiq. Ireland*, **37** (1907), 123–152.

Orpen, G. H., *Ireland under the Normans, 1169–1333*, 4 vols, (Oxford, 1911–20).

Ó Ríordáin, S. P., and Hunt, J., "Medieval Dwellings at Caherguillamore, Co. Limerick," *Jnl. Roy. Soc. Antiq. Ireland*, **72** (1942), 37–63.

Otway-Ruthven, J., "The Organisation of Anglo-Irish Agriculture in the Middle Ages", *Jnl. Roy. Soc. Antiq. Ireland*, **81** (1951), 1–13.

Otway-Ruthven, J., "Parochial Development in the Rural Deanery of Skreen", *Jnl. Roy. Soc. Antiq. Ireland*, **44** (1964), 111–122.

Otway-Ruthven, J., "The Character of Norman Settlement in Ireland", *Historical Studies*, **5** (1965), 75–84.

Otway-Ruthven, J., *A History of Medieval Ireland*, (1968).

Russell, J. C., *British Medieval Population* (Albuquerque, 1948).

Russell, J. C., "Late-Thirteenth-Century Ireland as a Region", *Demography*, **3** (1966), 500–12.

Smith, P., and Hayes., "Llyseurgain and Tower", *Jnl. Flints. Hist. Soc.*, **22** (1965–6), 1–8.

Waterman, D. M., "Excavations at Lismahon, Co. Down", *Medieval Archaeol.*, **3** (1959), 139–76.

Chapter 6

The Plantations

Aalen, F. H. A., and Hunter, R. J., "The Estate Maps of Trinity College", *Hermathena*, **48** (1964), 85–96.

Andrews, J. H., *Ireland in Maps*, (Dublin, 1961).

Andrews, J. H., "Geography and Government in Elizabethan Ireland", in (eds) Glasscock, R. E. and Stephens, N., *Irish Geographical Studies*, (1970), 178–191.

Andrews, J. H., "The Maps of the Escheated Counties of Ulster, 1609–10", *Proc. Roy. Irish. Acad.*, **74C** (1974), 133–170.

Barnard, T. C., *Cromwellian Ireland*, (1975).

Boate, G., *Ireland's Natural History*, (1645).

Books of Survey and Distribution, (MSS. 20 vols in P.R.O.I., Dublin). Published for Co. Roscommon, Mayo and Galway by Irish MSS. Comm. (1949, 1956, 1962).

Bush, J., *Hibernia Curiosa*, (1769).

Camblin, G., *The Town in Ulster*, (1951).

Crawford, W. H., "The Woodlands of the Manor of Brownlow's-Derry, North Armagh, in the 17th and 18th Centuries", *Ulster Folklife* (1964), 57–64.

Clarke, A., *The Old English in Ireland, 1625–42*, (1966).

Clarke, A., "The Colonisation of Ulster and the Rebellion of 1641", in (eds) Moody, T. W. and Martin, F. X., *The Course of Irish History*, (1967), 189–203.

Curtis, E., "The Survey of Offaly in 1550", *Hermathena*, **45** (1930), 312–52.

Danaher, K., "Representation of Houses on some Irish Maps of c. 1600", in (ed.) Jenkins, G., *Studies in Folk Life*, (1969), 92–103.

Dunlop, R., "The Plantation of Munster, 1584–1589", *Eng. Hist. Rev.*, **3** (1888), 250–69.

Dunlop, R., "The Plantation of Leix and Offaly", *Eng. Hist. Rev.*, **6** (1891), 61–96.

Emery, F. V., "Irish Geography in the Seventeenth Century", *Irish Geography*, **3**, 5, (1958), 263–276.

Falls, C., *Elizabeth's Irish Wars*, (1950).

ffolliott, R., "Houses in Ireland in the 17th century", *The Irish Ancestor*, **6**, 1 (1974), 16–21.

Goblet, Y. M., *La Transformation de la Geographie politique de l'Irlande au XVIIIe siècle*, (Paris, 1930).

Graham, J. M., "Rural Society in Connacht, 1610–1640", in (eds) Stephens, N. and Glasscock, R. E. *Irish Geographical Studies*, (1970), 192–208.

Hayes-McCoy, G. A., *Ulster and other Irish Maps, c. 1600*, (1964).

Hennessy, J. Pope, *Sir Walter Raleigh in Ireland*, (1883).

Judson, A. C., *Spenser in Southern Ireland*, (1933).

Lucas, A. T., "Wattle and Straw Mat Doors in Ireland", *Studia Ethnographia Upsaliensia*, **2** (1956), 16–35.

Lucas, A. T., "Irish Food before the Potato", *Gwerin*, **3** (1960–2), 8–43.

MacLysaght, E., *Irish Life in the Seventeenth Century*, (Cork, 1950).

Maguire, W. A., *The Downshire Estates in Ireland, 1801–1845*, (1972).

Maxwell, C., *Irish History from Contemporary Sources, 1509–1610*, (1923).

Molyneux, T., "Journey to Connaught, April 1709", *Miscellany of Irish Arch. Soc.*, **1** (1846).

Moody, T. W., *The Londonderry Plantation, 1609–41*, (1939).

O Domhnaill, S., "The Maps of the Down Survey", *Irish Hist. Studies*, **3** (1942), 381–392.

O'Hanlon, J., and O'Leary, E., *History of the Queen's County*, Vol. 1 (1907).

O'Loan, J., "Land Reclamation in Dromiskin, Co. Louth", *Dept. of Agric., Journal*, **4**, 7 (1956).

Perceval-Maxwell, M., *The Scottish Migration to Ulster in the Reign of James I*, (1973).

Petty, Sir W., "The Political Anatomy of Ireland, (1672)", in (ed.) Hull, C. H., *The Economic Writings of Sir William Petty*, (1899).

Prendergast, J. P., *The Cromwellian Settlement of Ireland*, 2nd edition, (London, 1870).

Quinn, D. B., "The Munster Plantation: Problems and Opportunities", *Jnl. Cork Hist. Archaeol. Soc.*, **71** (1966), 19–40.

Quinn, D. B., *The Elizabethans and the Irish*, (New York, 1966).

Renwick, W. L., (ed.) *Complete Works of Edmund Spenser* (which contains "A View of the Present State of Ireland"), **4** (1934).

Salaman, R. N., *The Influence of the Potato on the Course of Irish History*, (Dublin, 1943).

Simms, J. G., "The Civil Survey, 1654–6", *Irish Hist. Studies*, **9** (1954–5), 253–263.

Simms, J. G., *The Williamite Confiscation in Ireland, 1690–1703*, (1958).

Simms, J. G., "The Restoration and the Jacobite War", in (eds) Moody, T. W. and Martin F. X. *The Course of Irish History*, (1967), 204–216.

Simms, J. G., "Donegal in the Ulster Plantation", *Irish Geography*, **6**, 4 (1972), 386–393.

Chapters 7 and 8

The Making of the Modern Landscape and the Contemporary Rural Landscape (A number of sources referred to in Chapters 7 and 8 are listed in the bibliography for Chapter 6.)

Aalen, F. H. A., "Some Historical Aspects of Landscape and Rural Life in Omeath, Co. Louth", *Irish Geography*, **4**, 4 (1962), 256–278.

Aalen, F. H. A., "Transhumance in the Wicklow Mountains", *Ulster Folklife*, **10** (1964), 65–72.

Aalen, F. H. A., "Enclosures in Eastern Ireland. Report of a Symposium", *Irish Geography*, **5**, 2 (1965), 29–39.

Aalen, F. H. A., "The Origin of Enclosures in Eastern Ireland", in (eds) Stephens, N. and Glasscock, R. E., *Irish Geographical Studies*, (1970), 209–223.

Andrews, J. H., "Notes on the Historical Geography of the Irish Iron Industry", *Irish Geography*, **3**, 3 (1956), 139–49.

Andrews, J. H., "Road Planning in Ireland before the Railway Age", *Irish Geography*, **5**, 1 (1964), 17–41.

Andrews, J. H., *A Paper Landscape*, (1975).

Binns, B. O., (ed.) *The Consolidation of Fragmented Agricultural Holdings*, (Washington, 1950), 72–75.

Blume, H., "Some Geographical Aspects of the Palatine Settlement in Ireland", *Irish Geography*, **2**, 4 (1952), 172–179.

Brody, H., *Inishkillane. Change and Decline in the West of Ireland*, (1973).

Brookfield, H. C., "A Microcosm of Pre-Famine Ireland", *Jnl. Cork Hist. Archaeol. Soc.* **57** (1952), 7–10.

Buchanan, R. H., "Common Fields and Enclosure: an Eighteenth Century Example from Lecale, Co. Down", *Ulster Folklife*, 25–26 (1970), 99–118.

Buchanan, R. H., "Rural Settlement in Ireland", in (eds) Stephens, N., and Glasscock, R. E., *Irish Geographical Studies*, (1970), 146–160.

Buchanan, R. H., "Field Systems of Ireland", in (eds) Baker, A. R. H., and Butlin, R. A., *Studies of Field Systems in the British Isles*, (1973).

Bulfin, M., Gallagher, G., and Dillon, J., "Forest Production", in *County Leitrim Resource Survey*, Pt. 1, An Foras Taluntais (Dublin, 1973), 49–56.

Buckley, K., "The Records of the Irish Land Commission as a Source of Historical Reference", *Irish Hist. Studies*, **8** (1952–3), 28–36.

Campbell, Å., "Irish Fields and Houses", *Bealoideas*, **5** (1935), 57–74.

Camblin, G., *The Town in Ulster*, (1951).

Clarke, D., *Dublin Society's Statistical Surveys*, (1957).

Common, R., "Land Drainage and Water Use in Ireland", in (eds) Stephens, N. and Glasscock R. E., *Irish Geographical Studies*, (1970), 342–359.

Connell, K. H., *The Population of Ireland, 1750–1845*, (1950).

Connell, K. H., "The Colonization of Waste Land in Ireland, 1780–1845", *Econ. Hist. Review*, **3** (1950), 44–71.

Connell, K. H., *Irish Peasant Society; Four Historical Essays*, (1968).

Countryside Commission, *New Agricultural Landscapes*, (1974).

Cousens, S. H., "Regional Death-Rates in Ireland during the Great Famine, from 1846 to 1851", *Population Studies*, **14** (1960–1), 55–74.

Cousens, S. H., "Regional Variations in Population Changes in Ireland, 1881–1891", *Trans. Inst. Brit. Geogr.*, **33** (1963), 145–162.

Cousens, S. H., "The Restriction of Population Growth in Pre-Famine Ireland", *Proc. Roy. Irish Acad.*, **64C** (1966), 85–99.

Crawford, W. H., "The Woodlands of the Manor of Brownlow's-Derry, North Armagh, in the Seventeenth and Eighteenth Centuries", *Ulster Folklife*, **10** (1964), 57–64.

Cresswell, R., *Une Communaute Rurale de L'Irlande*, (Paris, 1969).

Cullen, L. M., "Problems in the Interpretation and Revision of Eighteenth Century Irish Economic History", *Trans. Roy. Hist. Soc.*, 5th Series, **17** (1967), 1–22.

Danaher, K., (Ó Danachair, C.), "Traces of 'Buaile' in the Galtee Mountains", *Jnl. Roy. Soc. Antiq. Ireland*, **75** (1945), 248–52.

Danaher, K., "Changes in the Irish Landscape", *Ulster Folklife*, **8** (1962), 65–71.

Danaher, K., "The Use of the Spade in Ireland", in *The Spade in Northern and Atlantic Europe*, (eds) Gailey, A. and Fenton, A., (1970), 49–56.

Davies, O., "Ancient Field Systems and the Date of the Formation of the Peat", *Ulster Jnl. Archaeol.*, **2** (1939), 61–65.

Delaney, V. T. H., and D. R., *The Canals of the South of Ireland*, (1966).

Donnelly, J. S., *The Land and the People of 19th. Century Cork*, (1975).

Drake, M., "Marriage and Population Growth in Ireland, 1750–1845", *Econ. Hist. Review*, 2nd series, **16**, 2 (1963), 301–313.

Edwards, R. D. and Williams, T. D., (eds.) *The Great Famine: Studies in Irish History, 1845–52*, (1956).

Evans, E. E., "Some Survivals of the Irish Openfield System", *Geography*, **24** (1939), 24–36.

Evans, E. E., "Fields, Fences and Gates", *Ulster Folklife*, **2** (1956), 14–18.

Evans, E. E., *Irish Folk Ways*, (1957), Chapters 1–4.

Evans, E. E., "Ireland and Atlantic Europe", *Geographische Zeitschrift* **52**, 3 Heft (1964), 224–241.

Evans, E. E., (ed.) *Facts from Gweedore*, (Belfast, 1971).

Fennell, R., "Structural Change in Irish Agriculture", *Irish Jnl. Agric. Econ. Rural Sociol.*, **1**, 2 (1968), 171–183.

Fitzpatrick, H. M., (ed.) *The Forests of Ireland*, (1966).

Flatrès, P., *Geographie Rurale de Quatre Contrées Celtiques, Irlande, Galles, Cornwall et Man*, (Rennes, 1957).

ffolliott, R., "Houses in Ireland in the Seventeenth Century", *The Irish Ancestor*, **6**, 1 (1974), 16–21.

Foras Forbartha, An, *The National Survey of Irish Rivers. A Report on Water Quality*, (1972).

Forsyth, J., and Boyd, D. E. K., (Compilers) *Conservation in the Development of Northern Ireland*, (Belfast, 1970).

Freeman, T. W., "The Congested Districts of Western Ireland", *Geogr. Rev.*, **33** (1943), 1–14.

Freeman, T. W., *Pre-Famine Ireland*, (1957).

Gailey, A., and Fenton, A., (eds), *The Spade in Northern and Atlantic Europe*, Ulster Folk Museum (1970).

Gillmor, D. A., "The Agricultural Regions of the Republic of Ireland", *Irish Geography*, **5**, 4 (1967), 245–61.

Gillmor, D. A., "Aspects of Agricultural Change in the Republic of Ireland during the 1960's", *Irish Geography*, **6**, 4 (1972), 492–98.

Graham, J. M., "Transhumance in Ireland", *Adv. Sc.*, **10** (1953–4), 74–79.

Green, E. R. R., *The Lagan Valley, 1800–50*, (1949).

Hooper, M. D., "The Rates of Hedge Removal", Monks Wood Experimental Station. Symposium 4, *Nature Conservancy* (1968).

Horner, A., "Land Transactions and the Making of Carton Demesne", *Kildare Archaeol. Soc. Jnl.*, **15**, 4 (1974–5), 387–396.

Johnson, J. H., "Studies of Irish Rural Settlement", *Geographical Review*, **48** (1958), 554–66.

Johnson, J. H., "The Development of the Rural Settlement Pattern of Ireland", *Geografisker Annaler*, **43** (1961), 165–173.

Johnson, J. H., "The Two 'Irelands' at the Beginning of the Nineteenth Century", in *Irish Geographical Studies*, (1970), op. cit., 224–243.

Jones Hughes, T., "East Leinster in the Mid-Nineteenth Century", *Irish Geography*, **3**, 5 (1958), 227–41.

Jones Hughes, T., "Society and Settlement in Nineteenth-Century Ireland", *Irish Geography*, **5**, (1965), 79–96.

Kearns, K. C., "Some Contributions of Irish Base Metal Mining", *Irish Geography*, **8** (1975), 126–131.

Kennedy, R. E., *The Irish. Emigration, Marriage, Fertility*, (Univ. California, 1973).

Lang, J. T. L., "Conservation of the Environment in Ireland", *Studies*, (Autumn, 1970), 279–300.

Leister, I., "Das Werden der Agrarlandschaft in der Grafschaft Tipperary (Irland)", *Marburger Geographische Schriften*, 18 (1963).

Lee, G. L., *The Huguenot Settlements in Ireland*, (1936).

Lee, J., *The Modernization of Irish Society, 1848–1918*, (1973).

Large, D., "The Wealth of the Greater Irish Landowners, 1750–1815", *Irish Hist. Studies*, **15**, 57 (1966).

Loeber, R., "Irish Country Houses and Castles of the Late Caroline Period: An Unremembered Past Recaptured", *Qtly. Bull. Irish Georgian Soc.*, **16**, 1 and 2 (1973), 1–70.

Lucas, A. T., "Paring and Burning in Ireland", in (eds) Gailey, A. and Fenton, A. *The Spade in Northern and Atlantic Europe*, (1970), 99–154.

MacAodha, B. S., "Clachan Settlement in Iar-Connacht", *Irish Geography*, **5**, 2 (1965), 20–28.

McCourt, D., "Infield and Outfield in Ireland", *Econ. Hist. Review*, 2nd series, **7** (1954–5), 369–376.

McCourt, D., "The Rundale System in Donegal, its Distribution and Decline", *Donegal Annual*, **3** (1954–5), 47–60.

McCracken, E., *The Irish Woods since Tudor Times: Their Distribution and Exploitation*, (1971).

McDowell, R. B. (ed.), *Social Life in Ireland, 1800–45*, (1957).

McLysaght, E., *Irish Life in the Seventeenth Century*, (1950).

McParlan, J., *Statistical Survey of the County of Donegal*, (1802).

Maguire, W. A., *The Downshire Estates in Ireland, 1801–1845*, (1972).

Malins, E., and the Knight of Glin, *Lost Demesnes: Irish Landscape Gardening 1660–1845*, (1976).

Maxwell, C., *Country and Town in Ireland Under the Georges*, (1940).

Micks, W. L., *History of the Congested Districts Board*, (1925).

Molyneux, T., "Journey to Connaught, April 1709", *Miscellany of Irish Arch. Soc.*, **1** (1846).

Moody, T. W., and Beckett, J. C., *Ulster since 1800*, 2 vols. (B.B.C., 1955 and 1957).

O'Flanagan, L. P. and Bulfin, M., "Spruce Growth Rates on Drumlin Soils", *Irish Forestry*, **27** (1970), 4–9.

O'Loan, J., "Land Reclamation Down the Years", *Jnl. (Irish) Dept. Agric.*, **55** (1959).

O hUiginn, P., *Regional Development and Industrial Location in Ireland*, An Foras Forbartha, (1972).

O'Neill, T. P., *Sources of Irish Local History*, (1958).

Orme, A. R., *Ireland*, (1970).

Otway-Ruthven, J., "The Organization of Anglo-Irish Agriculture in the Middle Ages", *Jnl. Roy. Soc. Antiq. Ireland*, **81** (1951), 1–13.

Proudfoot, V. B., "Clachans in Ireland", *Gwerin*, **2**, 3 (1959), 110–122.

Salaman, R. N., *The Influence of the Potato on the Course of Irish History*, (1943).

Shaffrey, P., "Community Planning—a Successful Experiment", *Jnl. Roy. Town Planning Inst.*, **58**, 10 (December, 1972), 449–455.

Simms, J. G., "Connacht in the Eighteenth Century", *Irish Hist. Studies*, **9** (1958–9), 116–133.

Simms, J. G., "Co. Sligo in the Eighteenth Century", *Jnl. Roy. Soc. Antiq. Ireland*, **91** (1961), 153–162.

Smyth, W. J., "Estate Records and the Making of the Irish Landscape: and Example from County Tipperary", *Irish Geography*, **9** (1976). 29–49.

Symons, L., (ed.) *Land Use in Northern Ireland*, (1963).

Taaffe, N., *Observations on Affairs of Ireland*, (1766).

Terrasson, F. and Tendron, G., "Evolution and Conservation of Hedgerow Landscapes ('Bocages') in Europe", *Council of Europe*, CE/Nat/VS (75) 1 (Strasbourg, 1975).

Uhlig, H., "Old Hamlets with Infield and Outfield Systems in Western and Central Europe", *Geografisker Annaler*, **43** (1961), 294–6.

Uhlig, H., "Some Remarks on Comparative Research in Settlement Structures", *Scottish Studies*, **6** (1962), 181–183.

Weld, I., *Statistical Survey of the County of Roscommon*, (1832).

Whittow, J. B., *Geology and Scenery in Ireland*, (1974).

Woodham-Smith, C., *The Reason Why* (1953).

Woodham-Smith, C., *The Great Hunger* (1962).

Young, A., *A Tour in Ireland in the Years 1776, 1777 and 1778*. (ed.) Hulton, A. W., 2 vols, (London, 1892).

Chapter 9

Vernacular Architecture

Aalen, F. H. A., "The Evolution of the Traditional House in Western Ireland", *Jnl. Roy. Soc. Antiq. Ireland*, **96** (1966), 47–58.

Aalen, F. H. A., "Furnishings of Traditional Houses in the Wicklow Hills", *Ulster Folklife*, **13** (1967), 61–68.

Aalen, F. H. A., "The House Types of Gola Island, Co. Donegal", *Folk Life*, **8** (1970), 32–44.

Barley, M. W., *The English Farmhouse and Cottage*, (1961).

Breffny, B. de and ffolliott, R., *The Houses of Ireland*, (1975).

Buchanan, R. H., "Thatch and Thatching in North-East Ireland", *Gwerin*, **1** (1957), 123–42.

Campbell, Å., "Notes on the Irish House", *Folk-Liv*, **1** (1937) 207–34, and **2** (1938), 173–96.

Crawford, I. A., "Contributions to a History of Domestic Settlement in North Uist", *Scottish Studies*, **9** (1965), 34–63.

Dunbar, J. C., *Historic Architecture of Scotland*, (1966), Chapter 7.

Danaher, K., (Some articles by this author have appeared under the name O'Danachair, C.), "Hearth and Chimney in the Irish House", *Bealoideas*, **16** (1946), 91–104.

Danaher, K., "The Bed Outshot in Ireland", *Folk-Liv*, (1955–6), 26–31.

Danaher, K., "Irish Farmyard Types", *Studia Ethnographica Upsaliensia*, **11** (1956), 6–15.

Danaher, K., "Some Distribution Patterns in Irish Folklife", *Bealoideas*, **25** (1957), 27–34.

Danaher, K., "Materials and Methods in Irish Traditional Building", *Jnl. Roy. Soc. Antiq. Ireland*, **77** (1957), 61–74.

Danaher, K., "The Combined Byre-and-Dwelling in Ireland", *Folk Life*, **2** (1964), 58–75.

Danaher, K., "The Bothan Scoir", in (ed.) Rynne, E., *North Munster Studies*, (1967), 489–98.

Danaher, K., "Irish Vernacular Architecture in Relation to the Irish Sea", in (ed.) Moore, D., *The Irish Sea Province in Archaeology and History*, (1970), 98–107.

Danaher, K., "Traditional Forms of the Dwelling House in Ireland", *Jnl. Roy. Soc. Antiq. Ireland*, **102** (1972), 77–96.

Danaher, K., *Ireland's Vernacular Architecture*, (Cork, 1975).

Eden, P., *Small Houses in England, 1520–1820*, The Historical Ass., (1969).

Evans, E. E., "Donegal Survivals", *Antiquity*, **13** (1939), 207–22.

Evans, E. E., "The Irish Peasant House", *Ulster Jnl. Archaeol.*, **3** (1940), 165–69.

Evans, E. E., *Irish Folk Ways*, (1957), Especially Chapters 4, 5.

Evans, E. E., "Sod and Turf Houses in Ireland", in (ed.) Jenkins, G., *Studies in Folk Life*, (1969), 80–90.

Frazer, W., "On Irish Half-Timbered Houses", *Jnl. Roy. Soc. Antiq. Ireland*, **21** (1891), 367 et seq.

Gailey, R. A., "The Thatched Houses of Ulster", *Ulster Folklife*, **7** (1961), 9–18.

Gailey, R. A., "The Peasant Houses of the South-west Highlands of Scotland. Distributions, Parallels and Evolution", *Gwerin*, **3**, 5 (1962), 227–42.

Gailey, R. A., "Further Cruck-trusses in East Ulster", *Ulster Folklife*, **18** (1972).

Hall, R. de Z., *A Bibliography on Vernacular Architecture*, (1970).

Hoskins, W. G., "The Rebuilding of Rural England, 1570–1640", *Past and Present*, **4** (1953), 44–89.

Leask, H. G., *Irish Castles*, (1941).

Lucas, A. T., "Wattle and Straw Mat Doors in Ireland", *Studia Ethnographica Upsaliensia*, **11** (1956), 16–35.

Lucas, A. T., "Contribution to the History of the Irish House: A Possible Ancestry of the Bed-outshot (Cuilteach)", *Folk Life*, **8** (1970), 81–98.

McCourt, D., "The Outshot House-type and its Distribution in Co. Londonderry", *Ulster Folklife*, **2** (1956), 27–34.

McCourt, D., "Cruck Trusses in North West Ireland", *Gwerin*, **3** (1961), 1–21.

McCourt, D., "Some Cruck-framed Buildings in Donegal and Derry", *Ulster Folklife*, **11** (1965), 39–50.

McCourt, D., "The Cruck Truss in Ireland and its West European Connections", *Folk-Liv*, (1964–5), 64–78.

McCourt, D., "Hausformen in einem Kulturellen Kontaktgebiet", *Deutsches Jahrbuch für Volkskunde*, (1968), 247–260.

McCourt, D., "Roof -timbering Techniques in Ulster: a Classification", *Folk Life*, **10** (1972), 118–30.

Paterson, T. G. F., "Housing and House Types in Co. Armagh", *Ulster Folklife*, **6** (1960), 8–17 and **7** (1961), 19–22.

Peate, I. C., *The Welsh House*, (1940).

Rapoport, R., *House Form and Culture*, (1969).

Richmond, I. A., "Irish analogues for the Romano-British barn dwelling", *Jnl. Roman Studies*, **22** (1932).

Smith, J. T., "Cruck Construction: A Survey of the Problems", *Medieval Archaeol.*, **8** (1964), 119–51.

Smith J. T., "The Evolution of the English Peasant House to the Late Seventeenth Century: The Evidence of Buildings", *Jnl. British Archaeol. Ass.*, **33** (1970), 122–147.

Smith, P., "Welsh Rural Housing, 1500–1640", in *The Agrarian History of England and Wales*, Vol. 4 (1967), 767–813.

Smith, P., and Hayes, P., "Llyseurgain and Tower", *Jnl. Flints. Hist. Soc.*, **22** (1965–6), 1–8.

Chapter 10

An Taisce, *Amenity Study of Dublin and Dun Laoghaire*, (1967).

Beckett, J. C. and Glasscock, R. E. (eds), *Belfast. The Origin and Growth of an Industrial City*, (BBC, 1967).

Boal, F. W., "Social Space in the Belfast Urban Area", in (eds) Stephens, N. and Glasscock, R. E., *Irish Geographical Studies*, (1970), 373–393.

Buchanan, C., and Partners, *Regional Studies in Ireland*, (1968).

Butlin, R. A., "Urban Genesis is Ireland, 1556–1641", in (eds) Steele, R. W. and Lawton, R., *Liverpool Essays in Geography*, (1968), 211–26.

Butlin, R. A., (ed.) *The Development of the Irish Town*, (1977).

Chart, D. A., *The Story of Dublin*, (1932).

Camblin, G., *The Town in Ulster*, (1951).

Craft, M., "The Development of Dublin: Background to the Housing Problem", *Studies*, (Autumn, 1970), 301–313.

Craig, M., *Dublin, 1660–1860*, (1969).

Dovell, P., *Cork,* An Foras Forbartha, (1971).

Evans, E., (ed.) *Belfast in its Regional Setting*, (1952).

Freeman, T. W., "The Irish Country Town", *Irish Geography*, **3**, 1 (1954), 5–14.

Forbes, J., "Towns and Planning in Ireland", in (eds) Stephens, N. and Glasscock, R. E., *Irish Geographical Studies*, (1970), 291–311.

Hallak, J. and McCabe, J., *Planning the Location of Schools: County Sligo, Ireland*, UNESCO (1973).

Haughton, J. P., "The Site of Dublin", *Irish Geography*, **1**, 3 (1946), 53–6.

Haughton, J. P., "The Social Geography of Dublin", *Geographical Review*, **39** (1949), 257–77.

Haughton, J. P., "The Urban-Rural Fringe of Dublin", in (eds) Stephens, N. and Glasscock, R. E., *Irish Geographical Studies*, (1970), 360–372.

Hunter, R. J., "An Ulster Plantation Town—Virginia", *Breifne*, **4**, 13 (1970), 43–51.

Hughes, T. J., "The Origin and Growth of Towns in Ireland", *University Review* **2**, 7 (1959), 8–15.

Industrial Development Authority, *Regional Industrial Plans, 1973–77*, Pt 1 (1972).

Jones, E., *A Social Geography of Belfast*, (1960).

Kruijtbosch, E. D. J., et al., *Studies in Long Term Development of the Port of Dublin*, (1971).

McParland, E., "The Wide Streets Commissioners: Their Importance for Dublin Architecture in the Late 18th—Early 19th Century", *Qut. Bull. of Irish Georgian Society*, **15**, 1 (Jan–March, 1972), 1–30.

Mathew, R. H., *Belfast Regional Survey and Plan*, H.M.S.O., (1964).

Maxwell, C., *Dublin under the Georges*, (1936).

Maxwell, C., *Country and Town in Ireland under the Georges*, (1940).

Munce, J., Partnership, *Londonderry Area Plan*, (1968).

Newman, J., *New Dimensions in Regional Planning*, (1967).

O'Farrell, P. N., "A Proposed Methodological Basis for the Determination of the Centrality and Rank of Central Places", *Administration*, **16**, 1 (1968), 17–32.

O'Neill, H. B., *Spatial Planning in the Small Economy*, (1971).

O'Sullivan, W., *The Economic History of Cork City from the Earliest Times to the Act of Union*, (1937).

Orme, A. R., "Youghal, County Cork—Growth, Decay, Resurgence", *Irish Geography*, **5** (1966), 121–49.

Shaffrey, P., *The Irish Town—an Approach to Survival*, (1975).

Simms, J. G., "Dublin in 1685", *Irish Historical Studies*, **14**, 55 (March, 1965), 212–226.

Wright, M., *The Dublin Region, Advisory Plan and Final Report*, (1967).

Subject Index

Sites and settlements to which significant reference has been made in the text are included in the index. Numbers in bold type indicate that a relevant figure appears on that page.

A

Act of Union, 156
Aer Lingus, 200
Afforestation, 233, 238–239
Agricultural Improvement, 160–161, 173, 176–177, 191, 212
Agriculture (see Farming)
Allihies (copper mines), 59, 198
Anglo-Irish ascendancy, 147–148, 161–162, 213, 292
Amenity Lands (Northern Ireland) Act, 1965, 243
Anglo-Normans,
    conquest and colonization, 109–117
    decline of colony, 112–115
Antrim plateau, 17, 37, 204–205, **18**
Archbishop of Armagh (estates), 171
Archbishop of Dublin (estates), 171
Ardnacrusha, 199
Arigna coalfield, 198
Armagh city, 121, 131, 279
Armorican folding, 16–17
Athenry, 275
Athlone, 277
Atlantic period, 32, **38**
Augustinians, 122

B

Baile, 95–97
Balliboes, 93

Ballinderry Crannog (Co. Offaly), 73
Ballinderry Lough (Co. Offaly), 88
Ballybetaghs, 138
Ballyglass (Co. Mayo), 51
Ballylynan, (Co. Laios), **161**
Ballymore Eustace (field patterns), 179, **178**
Ballymun (Dublin), 299
Ballynagilly (Co. Tyrone) 48, 51, 66
Bandon (Co. Cork), 277, 284
Bannow (Co. Wexford), 131
Barthelet, R., 84, 126, 139, 150
Battle of the Boyne, 163
Beaghmore (Co. Tyrone), 67
Bed alcove (or outshot), 258, **251**
Beech trees, 30
Beginish (Co. Kerry), 44, 97, **98**
Belfast, 146, 204, 288, **290, 308**
Belmullet, 284
Benedictine monasteries, 105, 122
Bessbrook, 284
Betaghs, 120
Biotic range, 30
Black Death, 114
Black Pig's Dyke (Co. Monaghan), 78
Blarney (Co. Cork), 194
Blessington (Co. Wicklow), 283, **272**
Blessington reservoir, 199
Bingham estates (Co. Mayo), 187
Birr (Co. Offaly), 283

335

Bocage, 215
Bodley's survey, 150
Bogs, 35–39, **21**
  blanket bogs, 35–39
  raised bogs, 36
  growth, 36, 71–72
  clearance, 27, 37–39
  commercial exploitation, 200, 231–232.
Booleying, 75, 138, 183, 233
Bord na Mona, 200
Boreal period, 31–32, **38**
Boullaye-Le-Gouz, 141
Boyne tombs, 56–57
Boyne Valley, 57
Boyle, Richard, 143, 277
Bracken, 34
Braudel, F., 3
Bronze Age, 60–75
  metallurgy, 60
  beaker folk, 61
  burials and settlement, 61–63, **64**
  farming and settlement, 65–71
  pastoralism, 69–75
  cultural decline in Late Bronze Age, 72–73
Bruce invasion, 113
Buchanan Plan, 287
Burghley, Lord, 142
Burncourt (Co. Tipperary), **125**
Burren (Co. Clare), 13, 59, 218–220, **18**
But and ben house, 169, 246, 253

C
Cabins (one-roomed), 264
"Cage-work" houses, 257, 279
Caherguillamore (Co. Limerick), 127
Cahirciveen (Co. Kerry), 284
Cainozoic basalts, 17, **11, 12, 18**
Caledonian highlands, 10, 14–16, **12**
Canals, 155, 195–196
Campbell, Å., 99

Carboniferous rocks, 10–14, **11**
Carrigillihy (Co. Cork), 84, 86
Carrowkeel passage tomb (Co. Sligo), 73
Carton (Co. Kildare), 167
Cashel (Co. Tipperary), 103, 104
Castlecomer plateau, 13, 198
Castlepollard (Co. Westmeath), 283, **272**
Castles (medieval), 117, **118**
Castlewellan (Co. Down), 283
Celbridge (Co. Kildare), 283
Celtic language, 76–77, 227
Censuses, 153
Central-hearth house, 254–255, **252**
Central Lowlands, 10–14, **22**
Ceramic materials, 65
Chevaux-de-frise, 90
Christchurch cathedral, Dublin, 289, 291
Cistercians, 105, 122–123, **118**
Clachans, 93, 95–99, 120, 132, 191, 222–223, **221**
Clare Island (Co. Mayo), 170
Clay (house walls), 253
Clifden (Co. Galway), 284
Climate, 24–26, **25**
Clochans, 124–126, 254, 267, **125, 255**
Clonmines, 131
Clonsast bog (Co. Offaly), **201**
Coalfields, 198–199, 204–205
Cobh, 286, 304
Coill Dubh (Blackwood), 232
Coinage, 107
Collen (Baron Forster's estate), 176–177
Commons, 179, **178**
Communication system, 194–196, 226–228
Cong canal, 195
Congested Districts Board, 154, 188, 190, 217, 264–265

Connemara, 165, 254
Conservation (of cultural landscape), 241–243
Consumption dykes, 35
Continuity of settlement, 92–100, 219–220
Cookstown (Co. Tyrone), 283
Cooley (Co. Louth), 124
Co-operative creameries, 199
Cork city, 202, 301–305, **303**
Corries, 14, 23, **15**
Craigavon, 288
Crannogs, 87–88
Creaghts, 137–138
Cromwellian confiscations, 147, **149**
Cross-passage (in houses), 247–248
Crucks, 257
Cultural landscape, 1–3
Cush (Co. Limerick), 100

D
Demesnes, 120, 166–167, 213, **168**
Deserted settlements, 127, 131–133, 179–181
Determinism (geographical or environmental), 2, 245
De Valera, R., 55, 58
Devon Commission, 187
Dingle peninsula, 126, 174, 222
Diocese, 100–101, 105
Dispersed settlement, 94–100, 181–182, 220–225
Downpatrick (Co. Down), 104
Downshire estates, 148
Down Survey, 150
Drainage projects, 230–231
Draperstown (Co. Londonderry), 281
Drift (glacial), 13, 20–23
Drogheda (field patterns) 179, **178**
Drogheda town, 284
Drumcashel (Co. Louth), 180
Drumlins, 20–23, **21, 22**

Dublin city, 106, 130, 194, 202, 289–301, **290, 293**
Dublin Society, 153
Duffry forest, 122
Duke of Ormond, 292
Dun Ailinne (Co. Kildare), 90
Duneight rath (Co. Down), 96
Dun Laoghaire (Kingstown), 197, 297
Dunlavin (Co. Wicklow), 283

E
Early Christian period, 76–108
  settlements, 81–100
  spread of Christianity, 100–101
  early monasteries, 100–102
East Galway (plains), 63, 163, 183, 220
Ecological problems, 239–243
Einzelhöfe, 92, 99
Electricity Supply Board, 199
Elizabeth, Queen, 142–143
Elizabethan period, 135–136
Elm, 32
Elm decline, post glacial, 32–33
Emigration, 159–160, 184, 228–229
Enclosures, (see also Fields)
  prehistoric, 68–69, 92, 99–100, 219–220, **98**
  spread, 162–163, 165, 171–179, 191–192, **172**
  removal, 237–238
Engrossing (of open fields), 120, 171, 177–179, 180, **172**
Enniscorthy, 257, **276**
Eremiticism, 102
Ertebølle culture, 45
Escheated counties, 144
Estate system, 212–213
Eutrophication, 240
Evans, E. E., 7, 95

F
Fallahogy bog (Co. Londonderry), 48

Farm buildings, 267–268
Farm clusters (see Villages, Clachans and Nucleated settlement)
Farming,
    historical, 1–2, 48–50, 65–75, 85, 109, 133–134, 138–140, 142–143, 154–155, 158–160, 164, 173
    modern, 208–211, 236–239
Farm size, 208, 213–215, **209**
Famines, 159
Fethard (Co. Tipperary), 82
Fews (Co. Armagh), 144
Fields (see also Enclosures),
    field types, 215–218, **216, 174, 175**
    field banks (ditches), 215–218
    field walls, 218–219
Fogous, 85
Foras Forbartha, An, 243
Forest of Trim, 122
Forests (see Woodland)
Fragmentation of farms, 183–184, 188
Freestone Hill (Co. Kilkenny), 90
Friars, 123

G
Gable-hearth house, 251, 252
Gaelic revival (medieval), 113
Galway, 130, **201, 272**
Gandon, James, 294
Gateways, 217
Georgian style,
    in towns, 279–280, 292–298, 307, 312, **293**
    farmhouses, 167, 259–261, **262**
Glaciation, 17–23, **21**
    glacial deposition, 20
    glacial erosion, 23
Glen of Aherlow (Co. Tipperary), **19**
Glens of Antrim, 17
Goodland (Co. Antrim), 72, 134
Gorse, 34
Gowran, 122

Grand Canal, 195
Grand Juries, 152, 227
Granges, 123
Grassland, 34–35, 66, 69–71, 208–210, 236–238
Grianan of Ailech, 89, 90
Guinness brewery, Dublin, 193
Gweedore (Co. Donegal), 188

H
Heather, 34
Hencken, O'Neill, H., 88
Herity, M., 57
Hildebrandine reforms, 104
Hill, Lord George, 187
Hillsborough (Co. Down), 283
Hill-forts, 88–91
    univallate, 89
    multivallate, 89–90
Hither Ulster, 144
House plans, 86, 139, 169, 248, **251**
Houses (see also Vernacular architecture)
    Mesolithic, 41
    Neolithic, 50–51
    Bronze Age, 68, 73
    Iron Age, 85
    Medieval, 124–127
    plantations, 139
    post-plantations, 166–169, 189
Huguenots, 162, 191
Hydro-electric schemes, 199
Hy Kinsella, 122

I
Inchcleraun (Co. Longford), **74**
Industrial archaeology, 193–194
Industrial Development Authority, 203
Industrial distribution,
    Southern Ireland, 202–203, 234, 287–288
    Northern Ireland, 204–206, 234

Industrial Revolution, 196–197, 204

Industry (and the landscape), 192–206, **201**
  18th and Early 19th Centuries, 155, 193–196
  Middle, Late 19th and 20th Centuries, 196–206
  dispersal policies, 203
  industrial estates, 202, **201**
  Northern Ireland, 204–206
  state encouragement, 199–202, 205

Infield-outfield, 71, 183

Irish Sugar Company, 200

Iron Age, 76–100
  and Celtic language, 76–77
  cultural landscape, 92–100
  links with Roman Britain, 78–79
  ploughs, 79
  royal sites, 90–91
  settlements, 81–100

Iron industry, 164

Iron-pan, 27, 72

Island McHugh (Co. Tyrone), 88

J

Jerpoint Abbey, 123, **118**

Jobson, Francis, 150

K

Karst, 13–14, **19**

Kells, (Co. Meath), 104

Kilkenny, 130, 277

Killaloe,
  gap, 14
  slate quarries, 198

Killeens, 103

Kilmacduagh (Co. Galway), **74**

Knockadoon (Co. Limerick) (see Lough Gur)

L

Lagan valley (corridor), 306

Lambay Island, 105

Land Act (1881), 265, 189–190

Landbridges, post glacial, 29–30, 45

Land Commission, 190, 223–224, 265

Land improvement, 231, 237

Landlords, 161–162, 165–167, 213
  and industry, 193
  and town formation, 194, 213, 280–284
  houses and estates, 165–168, 212–213, **168**
  housing improvements, 261–262
  rural reforms (rundale), 185–189, 217, 223–224

Landscape gardening, 167

Larne, 286

Larnian culture, 42

Lazy-beds, 158, **170**

Leaching, 26–27

Leinster mountains, 16

Liffey estuary, 289

Lime kilns, 27

Limerick city, 106, 278–279, **272**

Limits of improved land, 23, 228–229, 232

Linen industry, 155–156, 191, 194

Lissachiggel (Co. Down), 97

Litter, 240–241

Littleton bog (Co. Tipperary), 133

Livestock production, 210–211

Local Government (Planning and Development) Act, 1963, 242

Local Government (Water Pollution) Act, 243

Londonderry city, 146, 289, **272, 303**

Long-houses, 169, 189, 253–254

Lough Foyle, 230

Lough Gur (Co. Limerick), 51, 68

Lough Neagh, 37, 195, 230, 240

M

MacAirt, S., 95–96

MacDonnell, Sir Randal, 144

McCourt, D., 98

Mallow, (Co. Cork), 180

Manorial organization, 117, 120
Mapping of Ireland, 148–151, 153
Mathew Plan (Belfast), 288
Maynooth (Co. Kildare), 281, **282**
Megaliths, 47–48, **52, 54**
  classification, 53
    court tombs, 53–56
    passage tombs, 56–57
    portal tombs, 58
    relation to settlement, 50–51
    stone circles, 53
    wedge tombs, 58–59, 61
Mesolithic settlement, 40–47, **43**
  continuity into Neolithic, 45–46
  distribution, 42–44
  middens, 41
Middle Ages, 109–134
Mining,
  19th Century, 197–199
  20th Century, 203, 235–236
  Northern Ireland, 204–205
Mitchelstown (Co. Cork), 283
Moated sites, 127–128, **110**
Model industrial villages, 284
Molyneux, T., 163
Molyneux, W., 151, 163
Monasteries,
  early christian, 91, 101–102,
    103–105
  medieval, 122–124, **118**
Moorland, 34
Mote-and-bailey, 116–117, **110**
Mountmellick (Co. Laois), 194
Mount Sandel, mesolithic settlement,
  41
Municipal estates, 299–300, 304,
  309–310, 312

N
Napoleonic wars, 155, 157–158
National Trust (Committee for Nor-
  thern Ireland), 241
Navan (Co. Meath), 275, **272**

Navan fort (Emain Macha) Co.
  Armagh, 90
Navan mine, 236
Neolithic period, 47–59
  houses, 50–51
  megaliths, 47–48, 51–59, **52**
  pre-megalithic farmers, 49
  megaliths and settlements, 50
  radiocarbon dating, 48–49
  settlement in Boyne Valley, 57
  settlement in Burren, 59
New English, 136, 213
Newcastle (Co. Dublin), 177, **172,
  175**
Newgrange, 53, 57
Newry Axis, 16
Newry (Co. Down), 196
Nomadism, 73–75, 137–138
Nucleated settlement, 95–100,
  220–225, **221**
Nunataks, 29, **21**

O
Ogham, 103
Oldcastle (Co. Meath), 82
Old English, 115, 136, 180
Open fields, 117, 120, 223–224, **172**
Opposite doors (in houses), 247, 256
Oppida (Celtic), 91, 273
Ordnance Survey, 153
Ó Ríordáin, S. P., 84, 87
Ostmen, 106

P
Paganism, 100
Palaeolithic settlement, 31
Palatine settlement, 162
Pale, 115
Paring and burning, 158
Parishes, 117
Parliamentary Papers, 153
Pastoralism, 8, 69–75, 80, 94–95,
  133–134, 137–138, 157, 208–211

Peripheral position (of Ireland), 7, 80, 95
Petty, William, 150–151
Phoenix Park, Dublin, 292
Physiography, 9–17
Piperstown (Co. Dublin), 73
Place names, 93–94, 121
 baile, 95–97
 diseart, 103
 kil, 102
 pass, 122
 rath, 95
 teampall, 103
 town, 96
Plantations,
 Connacht,147
 Laois and Offaly, 141–142, 164
 motives for, 135–136
 Munster, 142–143
 Ulster, 143–146
Ploughlands, 93
Ploughs, 79
Podsolization, 26, 34
Pollen analysis, 28–29
Polls, 138
Pollution (of air, rivers and lakes), 240, 242–243
Population,
 density and distribution, 207–208, **209**
 growth, 155, 157–160, 182
 recent trends, 234
Portlaw (Co. Waterford), 284
Potato, 139–140, 158
Pottery, 65, 132
Powell, T. G. E., 58
Powerscourt House, Enniskerry, **168**
Promontory forts, 87
Prosperous (Co. Kildare) 284
Pugin, A. W. and E. W., 285

Q
Quarrying, 235–236

R
Radiocarbon dating, 48–49
Railways, 197, 204
Rainfall, 24–25, **25**
Rathcoole (Co. Dublin), 177, 225, **172**
Raths, 81–86, 94, 96–100, **82, 83**
Reclamation, 229–231
Recreational demands, 234
Reformation, 136
Religious segregation (in Ulster) 145, 310–312
Roads, 194–195, 226–228
Robertstown (Co. Kildare), 196
Roinn na Gaeltachta, 265
Roman Britain, 78–79
Rosscarbery, 121, 283
Rosses (Co. Donegal), 188
Round towers, 102, **78**
Roundstone (Co. Galway), 284
Royal Canal, 195
Rundale, 181–182, 183–185, 187, 223–225, **170, 186**

S
Sacred enclosures, 86
St. Mary's Abbey, Dublin, 123
Salaman, R. N., 140
Service centres, 270
Settlement patterns, 98–99, 220–223, **161, 185**
Shannon Free Airport Industrial Estate, 202
Shannon River, 14, 231, **22**
Shell mounds, 44–45
Shifting agriculture, 33, 66
Silvermines (Co. Tipperary), 236
Slane (Co. Meath), 104, 283
Slievethoul ridge (Co. Wicklow), 123–124
Sligo, 121
Sloblands, 229–230

Social segregation (in cities), 300, 310–311
Soils, 26–28, **21**
Speed, John, 129
Sphagnum, 35–37
Squaring, 223–224
Statutes of Kilkenny, 113
Stone walls, 177, 218–220
Strafford Survey, 147
Stratford-on Slaney (Co. Wicklow), 284
Striping, 216, 223–224, **20, 186**
Strokestown (Co. Roscommon), 283, **275**

T
An Taisce, 242
Tara, 90, 107
Tates, 138
Textiles, 155–156, 284, 292
Thatch, 257–258
Tidy Towns Competition, 242
Timber houses, 129, 257, 279
Tower houses, 128, 166, 249, **119, 125**
Townlands, 93
Townley Hall (Co. Louth), 33, 51
Towns (*see also* Urban settlement)
    distribution, size and functions, 269–271
Trim Castle (Co. Meath), 117, **118**
Trinity College, Dublin, 145, 148, 291, 294
Tuaths, 91, 105, 121
Tullychar townland (Co. Tyrone), 188
Turloughs, 13
Twomile Stone (Co. Donegal), 97, **98**
Two-storied houses, 259, 261, **260**
Tynagh mine (Co. Galway), 236
Tyrellspass (Co. Westmeath), 283

U
Ulster,
    industrial growth, 203–206

rural landscapes, 190–192
separateness, 8, 55, 140
towns, 146, 278
Ulster Architectural Heritage Society, 241
Ulster custom, 191, 214
Undertakers, 142, 144
Urban genesis, 91, 271–273
Urban hierarchy, 269
Urban settlement, **272, 274**
    Anglo-Norman, 128–131, 275
    landlords, 194, 280–284
    modern problems and planning, 286–289
    plantation, 146, 277–279
    post-famine, 285–286
    pre-Viking, 91, 271–273
    Viking, 106–108, 273–275

V
Vegetation (on field banks), 217
Vegetation evolution, 28–39
Vernacular architecture,
    Eastern Ireland, 254–256
    in British Isles, 247
    Irish, 249–258, **251, 252**
    nature of, 244–247
    transition from vernacular to modern, 258–267
    Western Ireland, 253–254, **256**
Victorian architecture, 298, 309
Vikings, 105–108
Villages, 117, 120, 211, 213, 224–225, **82**

W
Wagner, P. L., 2
Warrenpoint (Co. Down), 283
Weems, 85
Western Ireland, 8, 182–190
Westport (Co. Mayo), 283

Wexford Slobs, 230
Whitemeats, 139
Wicklow Glens, 16
  mining, 198
Wide Streets Commissioners, Dublin,
  295
Williamite Land Settlement, 147, **149**
Woodlands, 225–226
  afforestation, 233, 238–239
  clearance, 29, 33–34, 66–67,

71–72,   78–79,   84,   122,
  163–165, 226
  natural, 31–33
Woollen manufacturing, 199
Wright, Professor Myles, 301

Y
Youghal, 130
Younger Dryas period, 31, **38**
Young, Arthur, 153, 173, 176–177